THE BIRTH OF PLENTY

THE BIRTH OF PLENTY

How the Prosperity of the
Modern World Was Created

WILLIAM J. BERNSTEIN

McGraw-Hill

New York   Chicago   San Francisco   Lisbon   London
Madrid   Mexico City   Milan   New Delhi   San Juan
Seoul   Singapore   Sydney   Toronto

The McGraw·Hill Companies

1 2 3 4 5 6 7 8 9 0 DOC/DOC 0 9 8 7 6 5 4

ISBN 0-07-142192-0

McGraw-Hill books are available at special quantity discounts to use as premiums and sales promotions, or for use in corporate training programs. For more information, please write to the Director of Special Sales, McGraw-Hill, Professional Publishing, 2 Penn Plaza, New York, NY 10121-2298. Or contact your local bookstore.

Library of Congress Cataloging-in-Publication Data

Bernstein, William J.
  The birth of plenty : how the prosperity of the modern world was
created / by William Bernstein.
    p. cm.
Includes bibliographical references.
  ISBN 0-07-142192-0 (hardcover : alk. paper)
 1. Wealth. 2. Economic history. 3. Quality of life. I. Title.
  HC79.W4B47 2004
  339.2--dc22
                                  2003026155

Contents

SECTION III—CONSEQUENCES

Preface

WHEN MY WIFE BROUGHT P. J. O'Rourke's *Eat the Rich* home from the library several years ago, I wasn't expecting much in the way of historical insight. Mr. O'Rourke aims to amuse, and his lighthearted romp through the world's economic success and sob stories did not disappoint, most memorably his exposition of credit risk: A junk bond is a loan to your little brother; a high-quality bond is a loan to your little brother by the Gambino family.

Mr. O'Rourke's frothy prose hides painstaking legwork. Scattered under the quips were some well-researched passages, including one that briefly mentioned data assembled by an obscure Scottish economist named Angus Maddison, who found a startling discontinuity in world economic growth around 1820: Before that date, growth was essentially nonexistent, and after, sustained and vigorous.

It took me a while to rustle up a copy of Maddison's summary work, *Monitoring the World Economy, 1820–1992.* The bound edition looks as dull and as daunting as the densest legal brief, but inside, Maddison's dry data lay out the greatest story ever told: the economic birth of the modern world. The finest written rendition of Japan's Meiji Restoration and post-World War II prosperity does not do justice to the raw numbers presented in Maddison's book: 6% inflation-adjusted growth in Japanese per capita GDP, a doubling of average life span, a near-quadrupling of educational levels, and the rapid disappearance of illiteracy, all in the four decades before World War I.

I became fascinated with this sudden change in the Western world's fortunes. Maddison himself made a half-hearted stab at explanation, briefly mentioning technologic progress, improvements in trade, finance, and human capital, and exploitation of natural resources, as well as referring to more obscure economic concepts such as "growth accounting." None satisfied me. The commonplace belief that technologic change produces economic improvement explains nothing. Almost by definition, economic growth is the child of technological innovation. Were advances in electronics, transport, and the sciences to suddenly cease, economic growth would almost automatically stop.

The question gnawed at me: Why? Why did world economic growth, and the technologic progress underlying it, suddenly explode *when* it did? Why didn't the Florentines invent the steam engines and flying machines that Da Vinci sketched? Why didn't the Romans, with their metallurgical skills, discover electricity and invent the telegraph? Why didn't the Greeks, with their expertise in mathematics, describe the laws of probability, without which modern capital markets cannot function? For that matter, why did the Athenians remain desperately poor for the two centuries between their defeat of the Persians and their envelopment by Alexander, when they possessed the commonly recognized conditions for economic growth: democracy, property rights, free markets, and a free middle class? Most important of all, why did Hobbes's description of life in a state of nature as "solitary, poor, nasty, brutish, and short"—words that perfectly captured what life was like for the majority of people until the nineteenth century—disappear from Western Europe less than two centuries after it was set down on paper?

Paul Johnson comes as close as anyone to answering these questions in *The Birth of the Modern*. His description of the revolutions in the sciences, politics, literature, and the arts at the beginning of the nineteenth century is nonpareil, a wonderful prose counterpart to Maddison's work—*Early Modern Developmental History for Poets*, if you will. Johnson, however, remained silent on the ultimate question of why this most important of all historical transitions occurred exactly *when* it did. In a different vein, Jared Diamond's *Guns, Germs, and Steel* asks "Yali's

Question"—Why do white men have all the cargo? (Yali is a New Guinea tribesman, and "cargo" is the local term for all technologically advanced inventions—most notably, steel axes, soft drinks, and umbrellas.)[1] Although Diamond's book provides a breathtaking overview of the biological and geographic players in human history, it remained silent on the tribesman's plaintive query.

My task, then, is to uncover the cultural and historical factors that came together during the early nineteenth century and ignited the great economic takeoff of the modern world. Effective nonfiction transcends the mere exposition of facts and narratives, no matter how well told, and provides readers with useful *tools* for understanding the world around them. Any approach to the origins of world prosperity presents two challenges. First, the story—how the world arrived at its present state—is one of the most intrinsically absorbing any author can tackle. If the author cannot command the reader's interest with it, he has no one but himself to blame. The second challenge is to provide the reader with a framework capable of explaining why *any* nation—not just the several covered in this book—is wealthy or poor, democratic or totalitarian, weak or powerful, and perhaps even whether or not its citizens are satisfied with the lives they lead. If the author succeeds, his readers may even be able to catch a glimmer of what the future holds for our planet and its peoples.

This book divides naturally into three parts: why, how, and whither. First, we'll attempt to define economic growth's ultimate sources. Next, we'll describe how these factors played out in various nations. Finally, we'll focus on the remarkable sociological, political, and military consequences of the modern world's explosive economic growth. We will find that an understanding of the sources of that growth provides powerful insights into the other great questions of our time:

- In a world that is becoming not only more wealthy but also more complex, fast-paced, and stressful, what is happening to the overall well-being and satisfaction of the average person?

- What is the relationship between wealth and democratic development? What does economic progress, and the resultant growing inequality of wealth among nations, hold in store for the world's political future? What are the prospects for successfully exporting democracy to countries like Iraq and Afghanistan?

◆ How has the evolution of modern prosperity affected the current balance of power in the world? Is the military ascendancy of the United States a historical accident, and can it be expected to continue? How effectively can non-Westerners, particularly in the Moslem world, wield political and military power?

NO ONE PERSON CAN CLAIM MASTERY of all the fields subsumed in the story of world economic growth—law, history, philosophy, celestial mechanics, theology, public policy, sociology, and, of course, economics. Being an expert in none of these, my list thanking those who pointed me in the right direction, guided my path, edited my output, and provided me with encouragement along the way is a long one.

Ed Tower has been a companion on this journey almost from the beginning, nursing me through the intricacies of trade theory and bringing to bear the wisdom he has gained from initiating decades of undergraduate and graduate students into the mysteries of the dismal science. (Three years ago, Ed suggested to me that I consider writing an economic history title, not knowing that I had actually begun the effort a few months before, giving my spirits the boost they needed to continue the effort.) Robert Ellickson provided unpublished material on property rights in the Fertile Crescent, and Mark Roe, unpublished material on the enforcement costs of property rights. Victor Hanson helped out with the contribution of the Greeks to property law, Richard Easterlin led me through the money-happiness connection, Stephen Dunn refined my understanding of the history of the influence of the Supreme Court, Alex Johnson prodded me to delve more deeply into the history of intellectual property than I otherwise would have, Robert Arnott honed my understanding of the coming generational storm, and Karl Appuhn critiqued my appraisal of the medieval antecedents of the Age of Growth. Robert Barro provided data and graphs for the correlates of growth; Gregory Clark, data for the contours of several centuries of English prosperity; Emmanuel Saez, data for income distribution, and Jim Hirabayashi, data on the activities of the U.S. Patent Office. Waldo Tobler, Jack Goldstone, Jay Pasachoff, Robert Uphaus, Niall Ferguson, Paul Kennedy, Donald Moggridge, Robert Skidelsky, Larry Neal, Jane Alpert, and Richard Sylla gave generous assistance with historical aspects of the story. Ron Inglehart deserves my particular thanks for helping me to sort out the morass of the interaction of economics, culture, and religion, as well as for supplying a number of illustrations.

I've also had help from several past masters of financial and economic journalism. William Schultheis provided critical early advice. Bernard Sherman of Iowa Public Radio was involved in the editing process almost from start to finish and has saved me from embarrassment too many times for me to count, particularly in areas pertaining to public policy. Jonathan Clements of the *Wall Street Journal* generously supplied a wide range of services, ranging from stylistic and structural advice to a fine ear for English intellectual history, central to so many of this book's chapters. Jason Zweig of *Money* magazine lent his stylistic expertise, eye for apocrypha, wicked sense of humor, and encyclopedic grasp of nearly everything to the cause. John D'Antonio, who helped steer the manuscript through the production process, was a stern taskmaster when necessary and a peerless polisher of prose.

Judy Brown endowed the finished product with her expert eye and artistic talents, and Don Goyette also helped produce and refine a large portion of the book's graphics. Catherine Dassopoulos lent both her own impressive talents as well as those of McGraw-Hill to an admittedly ambitious effort to describe the shape of the modern world through the lens of economics.

My friends and family were not absent from the contributors to this book. As usual, Dr. Charles Holloway's facility with dead Europeans and Greeks, as well as syntax, proved highly useful, and my daughter, Katheryn Gigler, provided expert sociologic advice. Kathy and Rick Grossman lent an eagle eye to the final copy. Finally, there would have been no book at all without my wife, Jane Gigler, who molded the unformed lumps of my prose into readable chapters, ruthlessly replaced jargon and shorthand with more understandable wording, and repeatedly challenged muddled logic and flow. She was always there, continuously rearranging, trimming, and grinding through the countless drafts of each chapter. Even this herculean effort pales in comparison with her bemused tolerance and support of an obsessed husband.

William J. Bernstein
North Bend, OR

Introduction

THE CAPTAIN OF HMS *CENTURION* had every reason to thank watchmaker John Harrison, who had accompanied his H-1 marine chronometer—a large and extremely accurate clock used to compute longitude—on its first sea trials in the late spring of 1737. As the faint line of the English coast rose above the horizon, *Centurion*'s navigator, relying on traditional dead reckoning, calculated that the ship was sailing in safe waters south of Dartmouth. Harrison disagreed. His clock placed them about eighty miles from Dartmouth, in hazardous waters just off the Lizard, a peninsula at the far southwestern tip of England. Taking no chances, the captain, a line officer named Proctor, turned east and confirmed a few hours later that Harrison's computation had been dead on.

Proctor's caution would have been readily understandable to any seafaring contemporary. Thirty years earlier, Admiral Sir Clowdisley Shovell, making the same navigational error, drove his fleet onto the Scilly Isles, drowning over two thousand men. That catastrophe riveted British public attention on the need for improved navigational techniques. Seven years later, in 1714, Parliament passed the Longitude Act, establishing a board of longitude and offering a prize of £20,000—roughly $1 million in today's money—to anyone able to provide a method of determining east-west position to within half a degree (about 30 miles) of accuracy.[1]

Aside from possibly owing his life to Harrison, Proctor had also unknowingly witnessed one of history's great turning points, ranking with

1

the invention of the steam engine, the development of representative democracy, or the battle of Waterloo. The advent of a reliable marine chronometer helped transform maritime trade from an uncertain and often
deadly venture into a reliable wealth machine.

Two and a half centuries later, Harrison's clock, on display at the National Maritime Museum in Greenwich and still keeping accurate time
to within a fraction of a second per day, is a marvel. But it was, in fact,
the least conspicuous of the technologic advances of the remarkable era
that ran from 1730 to 1850. Few ordinary citizens ever saw a marine
chronometer, whereas the other great advances of that period—the
modern canal system, the steam engine, and the telegraph—were readily
visible to everyone.

Since the dawn of the modern era, it has been the conceit that the
technologic advances of the day are unique and revolutionary—certainly, the thinking in our time is no exception. This is, however, an il-
lusion. To see the full effect of scientific progress on human affairs, we
have to look to the technologic explosion that occurred in those 120
years and transformed life from the top to the bottom of the social fabric.
At a stroke, the speed of transportation increased tenfold, and communication became almost instantaneous. As recently as the turn of the nineteenth century, it took Thomas Jefferson ten days to travel from
Monticello to Philadelphia, with considerable attendant expense, physical pain, and peril. By 1850, the steam locomotive made the same journey possible in one day, and at a tiny fraction of its former price in
money, discomfort, and risk. Consider this passage from Stephen
Ambrose's *Undaunted Courage:*

> A critical fact in the world of 1801 was that nothing moved faster than
> the speed of a horse. No human being, no manufactured item, no bushel
> of wheat, no side of beef, no letter, no information, no idea, order or in-
> struction of any kind moved faster. Nothing had moved any faster, and, as
> far as Jefferson's contemporaries were able to tell, nothing ever would.[2]

With the invention of the telegraph by William Fothergill Cooke and
Charles Wheatstone in England in 1837, instantaneous communication
abruptly altered the face of economic, military, and political affairs in
ways that dwarf the changes wrought in this century by the airplane and

the computer. Before the telegraph, the primitive state of communication routinely yielded tragedy, both great and small. Andrew Jackson's victory over the British at New Orleans in 1815, for example, occurred *two weeks* after the signing of a peace treaty at Ghent.

Since 1850, the pace of technological progress has been slowing, not accelerating. The average inhabitant of the Western world alive in 1950 would have no trouble grasping the technology of the year 2000. On the other hand, a citizen from 1800 would have been completely disoriented by everyday life fifty years later.

The qualitative examination of history and culture teaches only so much. In the end, the ultimate measure of progress is statistical: What measurable improvements have been made in a nation's literacy, longevity, and wealth? When we look at the numbers, it becomes crystal clear that *something happened* at some point in the early nineteenth century. Before then, the rate of improvement in the lot of mankind was small and stuttering, and after, substantial and steady.

This does not devalue the intellectual and scientific advances during the three centuries after the Renaissance. But the bald fact is, the Renaissance and the early Enlightenment only minimally elevated the lot of the average person. How do we know? From the study of economic history. The best way to measure the impact of intellectual and scientific progress is to examine its footprint at ground level. Just how did the per capita economic output of Italy, France, Holland, and Great Britain grow over the centuries? What happened to life expectancies? Educational levels?

Thanks to the efforts of economic historians over the past several decades, this quantitative portrait of mankind's progress has slowly come into focus. The numbers tell a striking story. Until approximately 1820, per capita world economic growth—the single best way of measuring human material progress—registered near zero. In the centuries after the Fall of Rome, Europe's wealth actually declined, as numerous critical technologies simply disappeared, the most important being cement, which would not be rediscovered for thirteen centuries.

The great tragedy of the premodern era was that large bodies of knowledge would be lost for millennia. Before Gutenberg and Bacon, inventors lacked two critical advantages that we take for granted today: robust information storage and a firm foundation of scientific theory.

The lack of a scientific method meant that technological advances relied purely on trial and error and were thus few and far between. Further, inventors and manufacturers could record their work in only a few places, if at all. Consequently, inventions were frequently "lost," and the technological and economic condition of the ancients retrogressed almost as often as it advanced.

True, beginning about A.D. 1000, there had been improvement in human well-being, but it was of a sort so slow and unreliable that it was not noticeable during the average person's twenty-five-year life span. Then, not long after 1820, prosperity began flowing in an ever-increasing torrent; with each successive generation, the life of the son became observably more comfortable, informed, and predictable than that of the father.

This book will examine the nature, causes, and consequences of this transformation. The first section will unfold the compelling narrative told by these new data. I will identify the points in both time and space where economic growth sprang alive after millennia of slumber. I will also describe and examine the history of the four factors—property rights, scientific rationalism, capital markets, and improvements in transport and communication—that are the essential ingredients for igniting and sustaining economic growth and human progress.

The second section tells the story of when and how these factors came into play: first in Holland, then in England and its cultural offspring, followed in turn by the rest of Europe, Japan, and, finally, the remainder of East Asia. In each case, I will dissect the takeoff in growth and find that not until all four factors mentioned above are in place can a nation prosper.

Although I try to maintain a global perspective throughout this book, many readers will find its focus overly Eurocentric. Were not the Chinese—the inventors of paper, the printing press, and gunpowder—the great innovative engineers of the premodern world? Were not the early Arab empires oases of learning and culture during a time when Europe was mired in the Dark Ages? Did not mathematicians in India devise a numerical system, incorporating the concept of zero, that was far more advanced than the Greco-Roman letter-based system? To all these questions a resounding yes. Yet not one of these societies was able to turn the modern Western trick of continuously and permanently raising its citizens' standard of living. Further, the four factors responsible for modern wealth—property rights borne on the common law, scientific rationalism, advanced capital markets, and the great advances in transport and communication—were largely European in origin. Although prosperity has become a global phenomenon, there is no escaping the fact that the nursery of modern wealth lies in the area between Glasgow and Genoa.

Finally, the book's third section will plumb the sociological, political, economic, and military consequences of the great discrepancies in personal and national wealth that have arisen from this birth of plenty, and what the consequences of growth hold in store for the future.

Recent advances in the social sciences provide us with a fascinating window on the complex interaction of societal values, wealth, and politics. First, the bad news. In a world growing more and more prosperous, people are not necessarily becoming happier, particularly in the West. But the good news is that substantial improvements in individual well-being are occurring in developing nations. As nations pass from the third world to the first, their citizens do indeed become more satisfied. We'll find, moreover, that it is economic development that produces democracy, not the other way around—"too much" democracy may actually be bad for economic growth. The rule of law is the essential bulwark of a robust system of property rights. Property rights, in turn, are essential to prosperity. In turn, prosperity is the essential fertile soil in which democracy flourishes. Thus, optimism about democratic development in a nation whose traditional cultural values are antithetical to the rule of law—such as Iraq or Afghanistan—is likely to prove costly and dangerous.

I will argue that the destinies of nations are determined far more by their economic dynamism than by the vagaries of war, culture, and politics. The current world hegemony underwritten by American military might is no accident. History teaches that the fate of all great world powers is decay and downfall, but this will not occur to the United States until other nations both surpass American economic productivity *and* take an interest in projecting power—something that will not likely come to pass anytime soon.

By examining how our world prospered when and where it did, we just may be able to better divine where it is we are going.

A BRIEF NOTE ON CURRENCIES

This book, as any financial history must, deals in the currencies of the time—English pounds, Spanish pesos, Venetian ducats, Florentine florins, and French livres, to name a few. I've chosen not to sully the text with translations of each and every amount into modern currency—always an inexact exercise.

For readers wishing to have this information, the following rough approximation will serve. Throughout European history, the standard unit of currency of most nations was a small gold coin, such as the guinea (slightly more than a pound), livre, florin, or ducat, weighing about an eighth of an ounce and worth approximately $40 in current value. Between 1500 and 1800, the living expenses of an English gentleman might total £300 per year, while farmers and laborers made do with £15 to £20. However, currency debasement renders even this approximation wildly inaccurate with alarming frequency.

The major European exception is the Dutch guilder, which was worth approximately half as much as the guinea and the livre. Finally, the drachma of ancient Greece was the rough equivalent of a day's wage for a laborer or farmer.

The Sources of Growth

PROSPERITY IS NOT ACHIEVED merely by possessing hydroelectric dams, roads, telephone wires, factories, fertile farmlands, or even great quantities of money. Nor can prosperity be transplanted from one nation to another simply by transferring the key components of an economic infrastructure. In all but the most exceptional cases, national prosperity is not about physical objects or natural resources. Rather, it is about *institutions*—the framework within which human beings think, interact, and carry on business. This section describes those institutions and lays out how they relate to each other.

Four such institutions stand out as prerequisite for economic growth:

- Secure property rights, not only for physical property, but also for intellectual property and one's own person—civil liberties
- A systematic procedure for examining and interpreting the world—the scientific method
- A widely available and open source of funding for the development and production of new inventions—the modern capital marketplace
- The ability to rapidly communicate vital information and transport people and goods

Chapter 1 lays out the logic of the above four-factor model and surveys the sorry state of its affairs at the beginning of the modern era.

Chapters 2 through 5 go on to describe the historical development of each of these four factors. Chapter 6 discusses the interdependency among the four factors. Some of the stories told here will be familiar to most readers, particularly the history of scientific rationalism; others, like the origins of modern property rights in the ancient world, will not. A working knowledge of all four factors will enable us to understand just how, when, and why the world grew rich.

CHAPTER ONE

A Hypothesis of Wealth

The bourgeoisie, during its rule of scarce one hundred years, has created more massive and more colossal productive forces than have all preceding generations together.

—Karl Marx, *Manifesto of the Communist Party*

IT'S ALL TOO TEMPTING TO LAMENT the state of the world, particularly when you focus on the melodramas of mankind—violent conflicts, large-scale malfeasance and failure, and the latest installments in the age-old racial and religious hatreds that permeate the human story.

A paragon of such fashionable pessimism has been journalist Anthony Lewis, who, at the end of a long and distinguished career, was asked whether the world had gotten to be a better place since he had begun covering it a half century earlier:

> I have lost my faith in the ideal of progress. I mean that in the sense that it was used at the beginning of the twentieth century, that mankind is getting wiser and better and all—how, how can you think that after Rwanda and Bosnia and a dozen other places where these horrors have occurred?[1]

Mr. Lewis' problem is that his subjective criterion—that mankind has not achieved moral perfection as defined in Ivy League universities and the editorial suites of the *New York Times*—sets the bar too high. Mr.

Lewis seems unaware that we *can* measure the welfare of mankind; in fact, we can do it superbly. Contrary to his gloomy impressions, the second half of the twentieth century was far less murderous than the first. Further, the proportion of the world's population subjected to totalitarianism, genocide, starvation, war, and pestilence has been steadily decreasing over the past two centuries, with most of the improvement coming in the half century that so depressed Mr. Lewis.

Consider that from 1950 to 1999, average life expectancy in the developed world increased from 66 years to 78 years; in the developing world, it increased from 44 years to 64 years. The nearly universal Western outcome of living to old age, rather than resulting from the rare stroke of luck, may be the greatest accomplishment of the past fifty years. Or consider that over the same period, the world's real per capita gross domestic product (GDP)—the amount of goods and services produced by the average person, adjusted for inflation—nearly tripled. Or that by the year 2000, real per capita GDP in Mexico was significantly greater than that of the world leader in 1900, Great Britain. And if you're not impressed with mankind's material progress in the last fifty years, as measured in dollars and cents, you should at least note that almost any measure of social progress you wish to examine—infant mortality, literacy and mortality rates, or educational levels—has dramatically improved in all but a few still-benighted corners of the planet.[2]

ESCAPING THE TRAP

The modern world seems to stagger under the load of ever-increasing population, with each year adding scores of millions of new mouths to feed. At the birth of Christ, Earth supported slightly more than 250 million people, by 1600, about a half billion. Sometime around 1800, the one billion mark was reached, the second billion was added by 1920, and the third attained in 1960. Presently, there are in excess of six billion souls on our planet.[3] The increasing congestion of urban life, particularly in the third world, gives the impression that the world's population is growing far faster than the 1.85% annual rate of the past half-century.

Overcrowding on our planet is a recent phenomenon, an artifact of the world's newfound prosperity. Before the modern era, famine, disease, and war more often than not overwhelmed the human inclination to procreate. Over the first two million years of human history, population growth did not greatly exceed 0.001% per year. After the advent of agriculture 10,000 years ago, the rate of population growth increased to approximately 0.036% per year, and in the first century A.D., to 0.056% per year. After 1750 the growth rate climbed to 0.5% per year, passing 1% only in the early twentieth century.[4]

In modern times, the dismal economics of increasing population is virtually synonymous with Thomas Malthus. Born of local gentry in 1766, he graduated from Cambridge with honors in 1788. Like many bright young university men of the time in England and Scotland, he fell under the sway of Adam Smith's new science of "political economy" and devoted his life to the quantitative study of humankind.

The England of the aspiring economist's formative years seemed as Hobbesian as Smithian—a time of worsening food shortages and not a little famine, particularly in neighboring Ireland. In 1795–96 and 1799–1801, war and poor harvests combined to cause food riots in England.[5] The root cause of the shortage was obvious to Malthus: "The power of population is infinitely greater than the power of the earth to produce subsistence for men." Humans can reproduce rapidly, whereas agriculture is subject to the law of diminishing returns. The natural tendency, then, is for humanity to outrun its food supply. (The common conception of Malthus's thesis—that population increases geometrically, while the food supply increases arithmetically—is nowhere to be found in his writings.)

Malthus's infamous "positive checks" were not limited to the classic *fama, pestis, et bellum* (famine, plague, and war), but also included a host of lesser evils: unhealthy working conditions, backbreaking labor, overcrowded and unsanitary housing, and poor child rearing. If, for a brief moment, food became plentiful, population would rise rapidly. Soon enough, though, the increased supply of workers would drive down wages. This would make food less affordable and, discouraging marriage, would slow population growth. Low wages would then induce farmers to hire more workers, which would, in turn, bring more land into production, starting the whole process again at a slightly higher level of population and food production—the notorious "Malthusian Cycle."

In Malthus's harsh world, a nation's food supply—and its population—grew slowly, if at all, so the standard of living was inversely proportional to the number of mouths to feed. Were population to increase, there would not be food enough to go around. Prices would rise, while wages, and the standard of living in general, would fall. If, on the other hand, the population were suddenly to plunge, as happened during the Black Death of the mid-fourteenth century, the survivors' food supply, wages, and standard of living would rise dramatically.

Malthus had observed firsthand the late-eighteenth century famines, which burned this sequence of events into his consciousness. Figure 1–1 plots the per capita GDP of England from 1265 to 1595 versus population size. The thin, crescent-shaped distribution of the data

FIGURE 1–1   THE MALTHUSIAN TRAP IN ENGLAND, 1265–1595

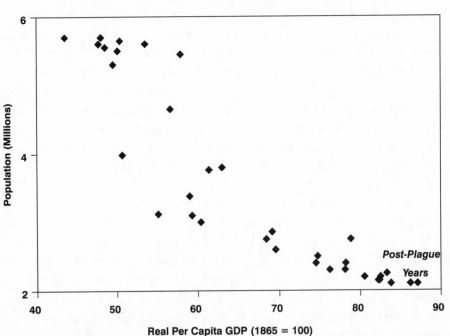

Source: Population data from *British Population History from the Black Death to the Present Day*, Michael Anderson, ed. (Cambridge: Cambridge University Press, 1996), 77; per capita GDP from Gregory Clark, "The Secret History of the Industrial Revolution," Working Paper, 2001.

points depicts the "Malthusian Trap." Historian Phyllis Deane neatly summarizes the concept:

> When population rose in pre-industrial England, product per head fell: and, if for some reason (a new technique of production or the discovery of a new resource, for example, or the opening up of a new market), output rose, population was not slow in following and eventually leveling out the original gain in incomes per head.[6]

In this eternal cycle, agricultural production might rise, but population followed in lockstep, dooming mankind to a near-subsistence-level existence.

Paradoxically, soon after Malthus immortalized this grim state of affairs in 1798 with his *Essay on the Principle of Population*, it abruptly came to an end in Western Europe. Figure 1–2 shows that a bulge developed in the crescent sometime around 1600, and as Figure 1–3 illustrates,

FIGURE 1–2   THE TRAP BREAKS DOWN AFTER 1600

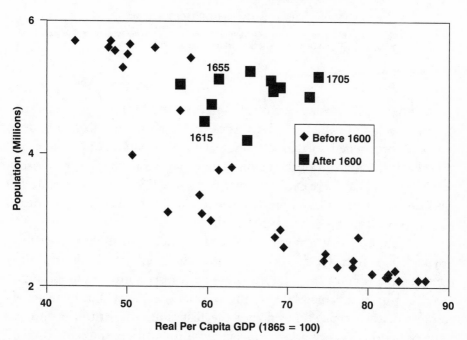

Source: Population data from *British Population History from the Black Death to the Present Day,* Michael Anderson, ed., 77; per capita GDP from Clark, "The Secret History of the Industrial Revolution."

FIGURE 1–3   BREAKING OUT OF THE TRAP AFTER 1800

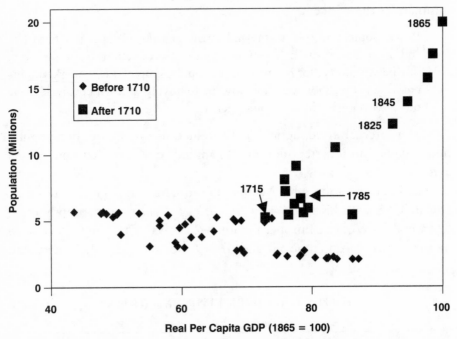

Source: Population data from *British Population History from the Black Death to the Present Day*, Michael Anderson, ed., 77; per capita GDP from Clark, "The Secret History of the Industrial Revolution."

population cleanly broke out of the crescent after 1800, never again to return to starvation's edge. The vertical population scale in Figure 1–3 has been broadened so that the original crescent appears as a flattened pancake at the bottom of the graph. The escape from the trap was made possible not by an increased birth rate but by a 40% decline in the death rate, the result of rapidly improving living standards that were, in turn, born of skyrocketing economic growth.[7]

The nature of that growth changed dramatically in the centuries following 1600. Initially, the growth was "extensive," consisting of a significant expansion of the national economy caused purely by population increase, unaccompanied by real improvement in the wealth or material comfort of the average citizen. For the first time, the British economy mustered enough growth to keep pace with population numbers. By the nineteenth century, however, growth had become "intensive," outpacing even the human urge to reproduce, with advances in per capita income and an increase in material well-being at the individual level.[8]

HOW NATIONS BECOME WEALTHY

Beginning around 1820, the pace of economic advance picked up noticeably, making the world a better place to live in. What happened? An explosion in technological innovation the likes of which had never before been seen. An apocryphal schoolboy, asked to define the Industrial Revolution, is supposed to have replied, "In 1760 a wave of gadgets swept over England."[9] That anonymous boy was on to something. New technology is the powerhouse of per capita economic growth; without it, increases in productivity and consumption do not occur. From first principles, then, the question can be asked, "What is needed to develop gadgets?" Four things:

- Property rights. Innovators and tradesmen must rest secure that the fruits of their labors will not be arbitrarily confiscated, by the state, by criminals, or by monopolists. The assurance that a person can keep *most* of his just reward is the right that guarantees all other rights. Note the emphasis on the word *most*. The right to property is never absolute. Even the most economically libertarian governments, such as Singapore and Hong Kong, levy some taxes, enforce some form of eminent domain, and maintain some restrictions on commercial freedom of action. Similarly, confiscation can be more subtle than that which occurs in feudal or socialist states. A government that fails to control inflation or maintain proper banking controls, such as Brazil's in the 1980s or present-day Zimbabwe's, steals from its citizens as surely as Edward III and Stalin did. In premodern Europe, government-granted monopolies, while highly profitable to those who exercised them, sapped the incentive of the rest of the nation.

- Scientific rationalism. Economic progress depends on the development and commercialization of *ideas*. The inventive process requires a supportive intellectual framework—an infrastructure of rational thought, if you will, with a reliance on empirical observation and on the mathematical tools that support techno-logic advance. The scientific method that we take for granted in the modern West is a relatively new phenomenon. Only in the last four hundred years have Western peoples freed them-selves from the dead hand of the totalitarian, Aristotelian mind-set. Even today, particularly in parts of Africa, Asia, and the Middle East, honest intellectual inquiry places life and prop-erty at grave risk from the forces of state and religious tyranny.

♦ Capital markets. The large-scale production of new goods and services requires vast amounts of money from others—"capi-tal."* Even if property and the ability to innovate are secure, capital is still required to develop schemes and ideas. Since al-most no entrepreneur has enough money to mass-produce his inventions, economic growth is impossible without substantial capital from outside sources. Before the nineteenth century, so-ciety's best, brightest, and most ambitious individuals had scant access to the massive amounts of money necessary to transform their dreams into reality.

♦ Fast and efficient communications and transportation. The final step in the creation of gadgets is their advertisement and distri-bution to buyers hundreds or thousands of miles away. Even if entrepreneurs possess secure property rights, the proper intellec-tual tools, and adequate capital, their innovations will languish unless they can quickly and cheaply put their products into the hands of consumers. Sea transport did not become safe, effi-cient, and cheap until two centuries ago with the development of steam power, and land transport did not follow suit until about fifty years later.

Not until all four of these factors—property rights, scientific rationalism, effective capital markets, and efficient transport and communication—are

---

* The term "capital" is fraught with economic meaning. Economists frequently employ a broad definition of the term, encompassing human capital, knowledge, or "intellectual," capital, as well as physical capital such as plant and equipment. In this book, "capital" is defined in the narrowest possible sense: money available for investment.

in place can a nation prosper. *These four factors first coalesced, briefly, in six-teenth century Holland but were not securely in place in the English-speaking world until about 1820.* Not until much later did the four factors begin to spread over the rest of the globe.

The absence of even one of these factors endangers economic prog-ress and human welfare; kicking out just one of these four legs will top-ple the platform upon which the wealth of a nation rests. This occurred in eighteenth-century Holland with the British naval blockade, in the world's Communist states with the loss of property rights, and in much of the Middle East with the absence of capital markets and Western ra-tionalism. Most tragic of all, in much of Africa, all four factors are still essentially absent.

ECONOMIC HISTORY BY THE NUMBERS

The heroes of this quantitative story are the economic historians who have spent their lives uncovering the outlines and contours of human well-being over the centuries. Chief among them is an obscure Scot-tish economist named Angus Maddison. Born in Depression-era New-castle, his upbringing hints at the source of his fascination with economic development:

> My father had a steady job as a railway fitter but I had two unemployed uncles, and there were many unemployed neighbors. The unemployed were not only poor but depressed. Many loitered aimlessly at street cor-ners, looked haggard, wore mufflers and cloth caps and smoked fag ends. Their children were often sickly and tubercular.[10]

Maddison excelled in school and spent his formative years in the rich intellectual stew that was wartime Cambridge.[11] He fondly quotes one of his instructors, Dharma Kumar: "Time is a device to prevent everything happening at once; space is a device to prevent it all hap-pening in Cambridge." The development of each of the above four critical factors connects strongly to this fabled university. If England was the birthplace of modern prosperity, then Cambridge was its ma-ternity ward, producing many of its principal midwives: Francis Bacon,

FIGURE 1-4   WORLD PER CAPITA GDP (INFLATION-ADJUSTED)

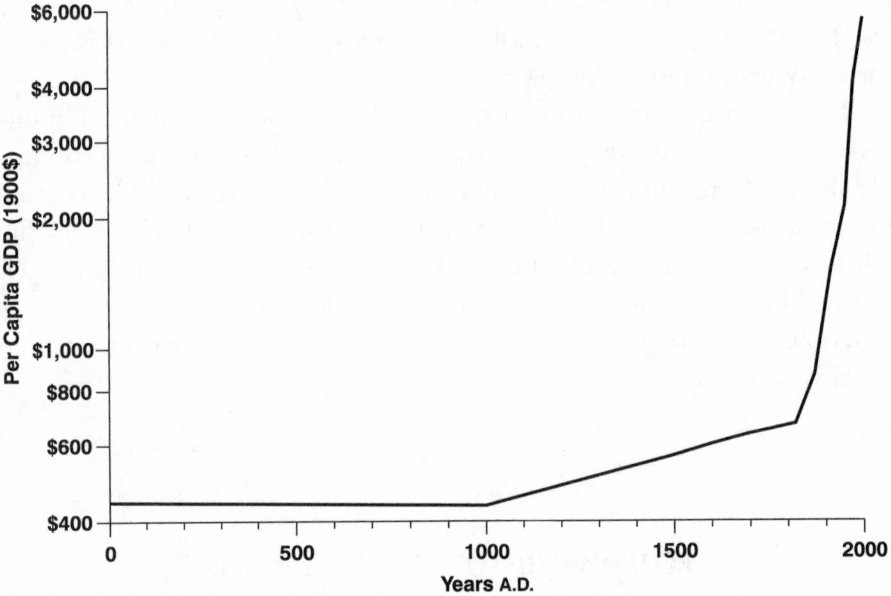

Source: Maddison, *The World Economy: A Millennial Perspective*, 264.

Isaac Newton, and jurist Edward Coke, as well as dozens of others central to the story of this book.[*]

For a quarter-century after his graduation in 1948, Maddison worked for the Organization for European Economic Cooperation (OEEC), which was established to direct Marshall Plan funds after World War II, and its successor, the Organization for Economic Cooperation and Development (OECD).[12] He spent much of his time shuttling to and from third-world nations, particularly Brazil, Guinea, Mongolia, Pakistan, and Ghana. Time and again, he was struck by the enormous differences in wealth and well-being among nations he found on his journeys. In 1978, he accepted a professorship at the University of Groningen in the Netherlands and began to work out a coherent vision of world economic development.

The portrait that Maddison and others painted was as stunning as it was unexpected. The lot of the average individual, measured as real per

---

[*] Ironically, during the twentieth century, Cambridge became a hotbed of anticapitalist rhetoric and, at times, treason born of totalitarian sympathies.

capita GDP, did not change at all during the first millennium after the birth of Christ. Over the next 500 years, between A.D. 1000 and 1500, things did not get much better. Figure 1–4, which plots Maddison's estimates of world per capita GDP since the year A.D. 1, brings the welfare of the average person into sharp focus. Before 1820, there had been only minuscule material progress from decade to decade and century to century. After 1820, the world steadily became a more prosperous place.

The data are "noisy" enough that identifying 1820 as the *annus mirabilis* of world economic growth is more than a little arbitrary. The British data, as we shall see, put the ignition of growth a bit later; the American data, a bit earlier. Whatever date is chosen, however, it is clear that sometime in the first half of the nineteenth century, growth of the global economy took off, bringing prosperity despite the repeated devastation of war, civil strife, and revolution.

Figure 1–5, which summarizes the average annual growth in worldwide real per capita GDP, displays the breakout that occurred about 1820 from a different viewpoint. Once again, prior to 1820, there was little improvement in the material welfare of the average person. This picture is contrary to that commonly taught in the nation's humanities

FIGURE 1–5 ANNUALIZED PER CAPITA WORLD GDP GROWTH (INFLATION ADJUSTED)

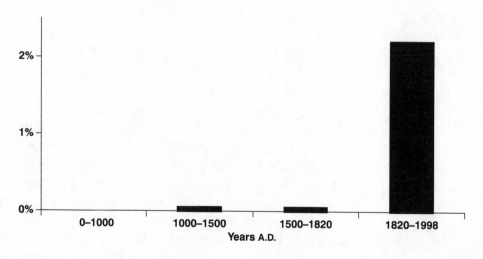

Source: Maddison, *The World Economy: A Millennial Perspective*, 264.

departments. From the perspective of the Romance language expert or the art historian, the Renaissance appears to be the pivotal point of the second millennium. The great writers and artists of that period, however, did little to improve nutrition, to augment transport, or to prevent plague. In an age when the average person never ventured more than a few miles from the place of his birth, the Sistine Chapel frescoes could do little to uplift the collective human spirit.

Economists have found it easy to criticize Maddison's estimates of income and production in centuries long past. After all, how can he be certain that the annual per capita GDP of Japan at the birth of Christ was $400 in current dollars, rather than $200 or $800? Maddison himself concedes the point: "To go back earlier involves use of weaker evidence, greater reliance on clues and conjecture."[13]

The modern era presents a more basic problem. Even the most accurate economic data cannot measure the real value of new inventions. How much would J. P. Morgan have paid for even a cheap seat on a jumbo jet from Kennedy Airport to Heathrow? What value would Shakespeare have placed on the ability to churn out five thousand words a day on a Macintosh and then e-mail them to a few dozen friends? Even the poorest citizens in the developed West have access to goods and services, such as reliable automobiles, television, and the Internet, that were unavailable at any price a century ago. While many modern goods and services are of dubious value, others are not. As late as 1940, pneumonia and meningitis, which today can be prevented with a few dollars' worth of antibiotics, struck down those at the pinnacle of wealth and power almost as frequently as they felled the poor. In a different vein, try to imagine what the great engineers and physicists of the early twentieth century could have managed with a personal computer.

How *do* economic historians measure the GDP of ancient Rome or of the Carolingian Empire? After all, millennia ago there was no Commerce Department and no Bureau of Economic Analysis. Not until the seventeenth century did early demographers like John Graunt and Caspar Naumann begin tabulating actuarial data, and not until two centuries later did economists begin to collect the first accurate aggregate financial data for individual countries.

If you want to measure economic progress over the centuries, you first must ask, How much money is necessary to sustain a subsistence level of existence? Maddison estimated that in an underdeveloped nation in 1990, about $400 per year was required. Next, economic historians use whatever data they can find to determine what percentage of a population existed at this level. A society in which nearly 100% of the population is engaged in farming and that does not export any substantial amount of its agricultural products lives, by definition, very close to the $400 per year subsistence level. It is highly arbitrary to assign the same $400 per capita GDP, as Maddison did, to Europe at the beginning of the first century A.D., to China in 1950, or to modern-day Burkina Faso, but doing so at least provides economic historians with a benchmark against which to measure economic growth.

Another way of viewing this is to look at the "urbanization ratio"— the proportion of the population living in cities larger than, say, 10,000, and, by inference, a measure of the proportion engaged in farming. At the height of the Greek and Roman periods, only a tiny percentage of the populace lived in cities of more than 10,000. By 1500, the largest city in Europe was Naples, with 150,000 inhabitants. Only 865,000 Europeans, or about 1% of the continent's population, lived in cities of more than 50,000. Another 6% lived in towns of more than 10,000. More than 90% of Europeans, then, were engaged in agriculture in the medieval period. In the great civilizations of Asia, which during the medieval era were far more advanced than those in Europe, the percentage of the population engaged in agriculture was even closer to 100%; the vast riches of the tiny ruling elites did little to raise the overall level of prosperity in these domains. So it seems likely that before 1500, the world's overall per capita GDP was close to the $400 subsistence level defined by Maddison.

In the U.S., fully 70% of the working population was employed on the farm as late as 1820. (Since the U.S. exported a large part of its agricultural output, living standards were much higher than suggested by the low urbanization ratio.) By 1998, that figure had fallen to 2%. Those who romanticize farm life should bear in mind that in the modern world, the percentage of population engaged in agriculture is a powerful marker of poverty. (At the dawn of civilization, the situation was reversed; humankind was just making the transition from the even less productive life of the nomadic hunter-gatherer to the relatively more prosperous sedentary existence of the farmer. Perhaps the hunter-gatherers of the period bemoaned the soft, new, soulless ways of the farmer—among many Native American tribes, farming was disdained as women's work.)

In recent years, economic historians have identified periods of sustained economic growth before 1500 in various nations. Economist E. L. Jones points out that vigorous growth took place in Sung China (960–1279) and in Tokugawa Japan (1603–1867).[14] Iron production in the late Sung period reached a level that was not achieved in Europe until the mid-1700s. Jack Goldstone of the University of California at Davis calls such periods "efflorescences," spans of time in which technology and the standard of living, at least among the ruling class, rapidly advanced.[15] Even Jones and Goldstone admit that growth in the premodern world was fragile and ultimately ephemeral. Following the Mongol invasion, the Chinese economy fell into a centuries-long coma from which it is just now emerging.

Europe did produce some economic growth after the fall of Rome. The early medieval period saw the switch from a two-crop to a three-crop rotational system, the invention of the horseshoe and horse collar, the water mill, the windmill, and the replacement of the two-wheeled cart with the four-wheeled variety.[16] Economic historians disagree about just when these changes began to result in growth, with estimates ranging from the eighth century to the fifteenth century.

Although they produced extensive growth, these advances merely resulted in increases in population, leaving the well-being of the average citizen unchanged. The wide range of opinion on dating the renaissance of growth in the post-Roman world is proof enough that per capita growth (the best measure of the improvement in well-being of the individual) could not have been substantial or sustained.

The beauty of examining very long historical sweeps is that this "washes out" even large uncertainties about growth. If, over a period of a thousand years, for example, we overestimated the beginning or ending per capita GDP by a factor of two, this would entail an error of just 0.07% per year in the annual growth rate. Put another way, world per capita GDP growth since the birth of Christ could not possibly have been as high as, say, 0.5%; if it were, per capita GDP would have grown from $400 in current dollars to over $8.6 million by the year 2000! We can be certain, then, that, for most of this period, growth was indeed very close to zero.

Putting it yet a third way, even the most wildly optimistic estimates suggest no more than a doubling or tripling in global per capita GDP between the year A.D. 1 and A.D. 1000, versus the *eightfold* increase in the 172 years following 1820. During this same 172-year period, per capita GDP in the U.K. grew tenfold; in the U.S., twentyfold.

THE TWO PERCENT PRODUCTIVITY CRUISE CONTROL

The vigor of modern economic growth is astonishing. Throughout the 1800s, real per capita GDP growth in what is now called the developed world gradually accelerated to about 2% per year, then maintained that pace throughout the entire turbulent twentieth century. Table 1–1 lists the growth of real per capita GDP in sixteen nations during the twentieth century, dividing them into countries that were physically ravaged by world war or civil war and those that were not.

Notice how tightly around 2% the growth rates cluster—thirteen of the fifteen nations increased their per capita GDP between 1.6% and 2.4% per year. It is as if an irresistible force—a sort of economic cruise control—propelled their productivity upwards at almost exactly 2% per year—not faster, and not slower. Notice also the absence of difference between the average growth rates of the war-torn and non-war-torn nations. The devastation of war, apparently, does no *long-term* damage to the economies of developed nations.

Table 1–1 and Figure 1–6 display another fascinating characteristic of Western economies—those that were the wealthiest in 1900 tended to grow the slowest over the course of the twentieth century, while those that were the least wealthy tended to grow the fastest over the same period. In other words, the per capita wealth of the most advanced nations tends to converge. Japan, which started out the twentieth century as the poorest of the nations listed, saw its productivity grow at 3.0% per year, while the leader in 1900, Great Britain, grew at only 1.4% per year.

The most spectacular example of the resiliency of the Western economies—the tendency to "catch up"—is shown in the recovery of per capita GDP in postwar Germany and Japan. The devastation visited

TABLE 1–1   ANNUALIZED PER CAPITA GDP GROWTH, 1900–2000

War Damaged	Per Capita GDP Growth
Belgium	1.75%
Denmark	1.98%
France	1.84%
Germany	1.61%
Italy	2.18%
Japan	3.13%
Netherlands	1.69%
Spain	1.91%
Average for war-damaged countries	**2.01%**

Not War Damaged	Per Capita GDP Growth
Australia	1.59%
Canada	2.17%
Ireland	2.08%
Sweden	1.96%
Switzerland	1.72%
United Kingdom	1.41%
United States	2.00%
Average for countries not damaged by war	**1.85%**

Source: Data from Maddison, *The World Economy: A Millennial Perspective,* 276–79; Maddison, *Monitoring the World Economy 1820–1992,* 194–97; and Organization for Economic Cooperation and Development.

upon the Axis powers' economic machinery during the war years is clearly visible at the left edge of Figure 1–7. Japan began World War II with a per capita GDP that was 40% of the U.S. value; by war's end that figure had fallen to just 15%. Germany's per capita GDP fell from 80% of U.S. per capita GDP during the same period to 40%. By the 1960s both nations had regained their prewar per capita GDP value relative to the U.S.

In premodern times, such a comeback from disaster would have been impossible: Per capita GDP in China, after flowering under the Sung Dynasty, remained flat for seven centuries after the Mongol invasion. The Western growth machine, in contrast, reduces the catastrophe of conquest to mere historical hiccup. By 1990, Japan's relative per capita GDP had grown to the point where it approached that of the U.S. While the en-

FIGURE 1–6   GROWTH VERSUS BEGINNING WEALTH

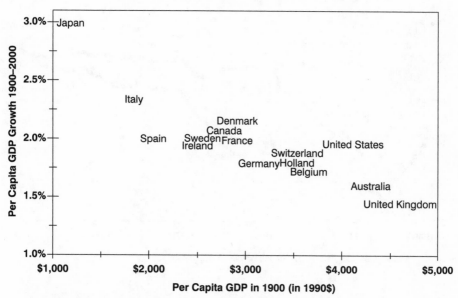

Source: Maddison, *The World Economy: A Millennial Perspective*, 276–79, and *Monitoring the World Economy, 1820–1992*, 194–97; and Organization for Economic Cooperation and Development.

lightened policy of the Second World War's victors was an important factor in Japan and Germany's rapid recovery, such beneficence does not account for Germany's performance after its defeat in the First World War, when, despite the punishment exacted at Versailles, she took just two decades to recover enough to conquer most of Europe.

The beginning of the nineteenth century did not herald the transformation of every corner of the world. At first, only Europe and its New World offshoots prospered. Nonetheless, over the ensuing 200 years, the Western variety of growth spread over the rest of the globe.

Before 1820, there were hints of the coming prosperity. Maddison estimates that in A.D. 1500, European per capita GDP averaged $774, with Renaissance Italy reaching $1,100.[17] But Italy's relative prosperity would not last long. After 1500, it would stagnate, while Holland began to experience persistent, if sluggish, economic growth. About the same time, Britain's growth rate began to increase as well, although more slowly than Holland's.

FIGURE 1–7   PER CAPITA GDP VERSUS U.S. (U.S. = 100%)

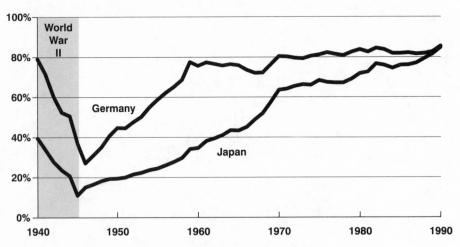

Source: Maddison, *Monitoring the World Economy, 1820–1992*, 194–97.

The Glorious Revolution of 1688 brought a stable constitutional monarchy to England and the importation of a Dutch king, and the cream of Holland's financial institutions and Dutch advances in the capital markets soon followed across the North Sea. Still, it took more than a century for English growth to accelerate rapidly. Not until the middle of the nineteenth century did the average Englishman live better than the average Dutchman—and that came about only because the British enforced a decades-long naval blockade of Holland, which was followed by Napoleon's dismantling and exploitation of the Dutch Republic.

The British seeded its overseas colonies not only with its people but, even more critically, with its legal, intellectual, and financial institutions as well. The great economic transformation did not begin to spread to the rest of Europe and Asia until much later. There, its effects were highly uneven, as shown in Figure 1–8, with the "takeoff" of England, Japan, and China occurring in 1820, 1870, and 1950, respectively.

Why investigate this backwater of early modern history? Because sometime around 1820, the world seemed to turn over on its axis. Because the course of human economic progress before then can best be likened to the stunted growth of underbrush; afterwards it resembled the vigorous and steady growth of an oak. Because the story of how prop-

FIGURE 1-8   PER CAPITA GDP (INFLATION-ADJUSTED)

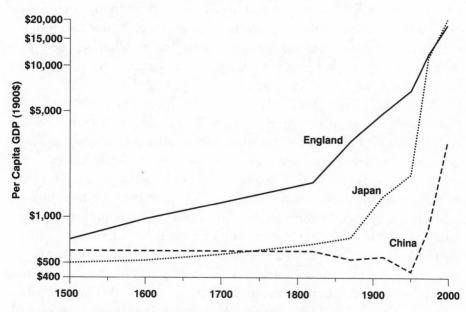

Source: Maddison, *The World Economy: A Millennial Perspective*, 264, 276–79.

erty rights, scientific rationalism, capital markets, and modern transportation and communication finally came decisively together in the
nineteenth century, producing the modern wealth machine, is crucially
relevant to modern life.

To start out, we'll examine the state of everyday life in Western Europe before 1600, keeping in mind the four preconditions for economic
progress. The medieval period can be summed up with some simple vi-
gnettes, loosely organized under the four essential growth factors.

THE PREMODERN ABSENCE OF PROPERTY RIGHTS

Short of outright slavery, no system denied property rights and individual liberty as medieval feudalism did. Today, the very word itself—
"feudalism"—retains only a shadow of its former impact. Imagine, for a

moment, that you are a typical eleventh-century peasant. You kneel before your master, who clasps your hands in his. You then vow to give
him your exclusive, unceasing service. Your pledge is not financial or
commercial; rather, you are pledging your life and honor. You live
without money, exchanging your labor, and not infrequently, your life,
for his protection against the outside world.

The essence of the feudal relationship was that it was *nonfinancial*. The
manor yielded little excess produce for sale, and almost all exchange was
done by barter. Feudal lords rarely thought of their patrimony in monetary terms, and serfs had scant use for coin. Adam Smith noted with
wonder that as late as 1745, a Scottish laird could outfit 800 men for battle with a manorial income of less than £500 per year.[18] Vestiges of feudal rights still existed in several neighborhoods of Paris until they were
finally abolished in the early stages of the French Revolution.[19]

The lords were almost as enslaved as their serfs. As Marx observed, it
was closer to the truth that the land, the preeminent asset of the
premodern world, inherited the lord, rather than the other way around.
As we'll see, land is highly flawed as a society's major storehouse of
wealth, being not easily divided, traded, or improved.

Further, in the moneyless society of the feudal state, goods that could
not be stored had to be consumed before they spoiled. Where modern
society displays wealth through material possessions, feudal society displayed wealth through feasts of consumption.

The very concept of property rights in such a moneyless society was
unthinkable; a peasant's hut and tools were but mere extensions of his
self, a concept that survives to this day in the European tendency to provide dwellings with personal names. The hut, after all, belonged to the
master, and the tools could not be sold at any price, because there were
no buyers, public markets, or money itself. Consider Adam Smith's description of the peasant's lot:

> The occupiers of the land were generally bondmen [serfs], whose per-
> sons and effects were equally his [the lord's] property. Those who were
> not bondmen were tenants at will, and though the rent which they paid
> was often nominally little more than a quit-rent, it really amounted to
> the whole produce of the land. Their lord could at all times command
> their labor in peace, and their service in war. Though they lived at a dis-

tance from his house, they were equally dependent upon him as his retainers who lived in it. But the whole produce of the land undoubtedly
belongs to him, who can dispose of the labor and service of all those
whom it maintains.*

Thus, the medieval serf had little incentive to produce a crop in excess of his manorial obligations or to increase the productivity of the
land he worked. If the lord owned him and the whole of his output,
why should he labor mightily, let alone innovate? Even more critically,
the feudal structure left little room for nationhood. Politics were indeed
strictly local. "Not citizen to state but vassal to lord was the bond that
underlay political structure. The state was still struggling to be born,"
writes Barbara Tuchman.[20]

The feudal system not only failed to protect ownership and recognize equality under the law; it also throttled basic consumer activity.
Sumptuary laws, which specified just what could be worn, according
to rank and income, suffocated an economy whose primary manufactured product was textiles. In Florence, ermine was allowed only to
nobles, physicians, and magistrates, while in France, a lord or lady
could purchase only four costumes per year, one of which had to be
for summer wear, but only if annual income was more than six thousand livres. English law also dictated strict income levels for the wearing of particular garments. Nobility seemed to count double; an
English aristocrat might wear a certain costume if his annual income
was £500 per year, whereas a merchant needed £1,000 of income for
the same privilege.[21]

Early in the second millennium, the spread of the money economy
eroded and eventually destroyed feudalism. The moment that a peasant
could sell his labor to the highest bidder, the ties that bound servant and
master dissolved. Only then could vital *national* legal and capital institutions develop. Not only were individuals able to buy their freedom with
coin of the realm; at times, entire villages did so, as when the northern
French city of Coucy-le-Château bought its charter of liberties from the
penniless widow of the lord for 140 livres in 1197.[22]

---

* Smith, III: 355. A quit-rent was the monetary rent paid by a serf in lieu of services owed
the lord.

THE IMPORTANCE OF TAXING IN EARNEST

All countries require revenue; how governments tax is the stuff of the life and death of nations. In the premodern world, states typically burdened their poorest and most powerless members with taxes. All inevitably failed. Just as successful nations guarantee property rights by demanding impartiality in deciding ownership, so, too, must they demonstrate the same fairness in deciding how they tax wealth and income. Such was decidedly not the case in the medieval world, where the nobles, in exchange for physically "protecting" their serfs, were exempted from land taxes. The priesthood got into the game as well. Since it spiritually "protected" the serfs, the feudal tax structure also spared the clergy, to whom great wealth was often no stranger.

MEAN STREETS

Effective property rights require protection from crime. Medieval towns were unimaginably dangerous places, with a general level of violence so great that homicides were twice as common as accidental deaths. Deadly brawls constituted a routine part of everyday life, and tournaments, which provided surrogate martial activity to knights made redundant by the longbow and siege catapult, were often marred by wholesale slaughter. Only 1% of murderers were brought to justice. Kidnapping was a popular source of livelihood, particularly among unemployed knights.[23]

It could not be any other way. In 1500, the very concept of law enforcement as a governmental charge seemed unimaginable. The London bobby got his name from future prime minister Robert Peel, who gave the world its first metropolitan police force, *in 1829*.[24] Before then, the prudent gentleman did not venture onto London streets without his hangar (sword), dagger, and pistol.

Beyond the city walls, lawlessness reigned absolute. Highwaymen plied their trade, sometimes in roving gangs and sometimes alone, with near impunity. Soldiers, when not engaged in Crusades, dynastic feuds, or papal ambitions, periodically swelled the ranks of highwaymen. Only

walls provided a town with effective protection against its lawless environs. Since walls were expensive, town life crammed itself into as little
space as possible. The streets, nothing more than narrow, open sewers,
teemed with townspeople and disease; the first demographers docu-
mented death rates from infectious diseases that were twice as high inside
the walls as they were outside.

Most people lived in tiny villages and worked small adjacent fields.
Not until 1500 did farmers clear the wolf-infested forests. Everyone,
from toddlers to the aged, performed backbreaking field work, usually
unaided by the plow. Until A.D. 900, it was the rare peasant who could
afford to harness horses and oxen with collars for fieldwork.

The squalor of medieval dwellings was unimaginable. According to
the greatest of all Renaissance humanists, Erasmus of Rotterdam,

> Almost all the floors are of clay and rushes from the marshes, so care-
> lessly renewed that the foundation sometimes remains for twenty years,
> harboring, there below, spittle and vomit and wine of dogs and men,
> beer . . . remnants of fishes, and other filth unnameable. Hence, with
> the change of weather, a vapor exhales which in my judgement is far
> from wholesome.[25]

Families slept together on one foul bed, and chimneys were almost
unknown. Soot covered the walls of all but the newest huts. Lack of
proper exhaust resulted in house fires that brought roaring death to large
numbers of villagers, particularly women, who, clad in highly flammable
dresses, tended wood-fired pits and stoves.

The past few paragraphs describe the circumstances of peasants who
were relatively well-off. The less fortunate had little or no shelter at all. In
the subsistence-level premodern society, famine and pestilence knocked
constantly at the door. During times of extreme famine, cannibalism was
not unknown; travelers were occasionally killed for their flesh, and there
were even reports of gallows being attacked for sustenance.[26]

Pestilence regularly engulfed the Continent. The most famous episode
occurred in 1347, when a Genoese merchant fleet docked at Messina, at
the tip of the Italian boot. Most of the fleet's sailors were dead or dying
from a strange new illness, later recognized as bubonic plague. Within a
few decades, it had killed nearly one in three Europeans.

THE PREMODERN ABSENCE OF SCIENTIFIC RATIONALISM

Today, "separation of church and state" seems a quaint phrase from the era of the Founding Fathers, whose modern relevance is confined to the judicial treatment of fringe issues such as school prayer and public Christmastime displays. In premodern Europe, the Church was a smothering ubiquity, "the matrix and law of medieval life, omnipresent, indeed compulsory. Its insistent principle that the life of the spirit and of the afterworld was superior to the here and now is one that the modern world does not share, no matter how devout some present-day Christians may be."[27]

Jefferson and Madison's obsession with the church/state nexus was grounded in the pervasiveness of organized religion in the premodern world. Paradoxically, the separation of church and state is a notion implicit in Christianity from its earliest days: "Render therefore unto Caesar the things which are Caesar's; and unto God the things that are God's," says Jesus to the Pharisees.[28] Making that separation a reality, however, would take time; from the conversion of Constantine onward, the state showered God's temporal representatives with land and riches. The wealthier the Church grew, the more corrupt and detached it became.

Today, the words heresy, blasphemy, and *auto-da-fé* are most commonly used in a satirical context; in the five hundred years before 1600, they struck terror into every European soul. Hobbes's characterization of life in a state of nature as "solitary, poor, nasty, brutish, and short" aptly described the medieval earthly existence; man's ultimate reward came only in the afterlife. Although incurring the displeasure of the religious authorities could lead to a person's being tied to a furiously burning pile of timber, that punishment paled in comparison to the grisly deaths choreographed by the various Inquisitions. The most infamous instrument of torture was the "old iron maid," a frame contraption that slowly squeezed hundreds of pikes into the victim's body, leaving the person a gory, barely living mass that was then cast into a pit of revolving knives.[29] Yet even the most painful exit from life was preferable to the fear of consignment to the eternal fires of hell.

What sorts of offenses could trigger such awful fates? Almost anything that displeased or challenged the power of the Church, including, but not limited to, questioning its authority, its beliefs, and most important, its wealth. The infractions could be remarkably oblique. For example, early in the sixteenth century the Polish astronomer Mikolaj Kopernik, now better known by his Latinized name, Copernicus, deduced that the earth was, in fact, not the center of the universe, but rather itself revolved around the sun. Heretical views were more or less tolerated as long as they were published in the then-universal language of scholars—Latin. Since this ancient language was understood by almost no one outside the ruling ecclesiastical, royal, and merchant elite, such controversies did not reach the peasantry. Copernicus himself wisely did not cross the Latin/vernacular line, and was thus tolerated by the Vatican. Even the most enlightened scholars of the age, including Erasmus and Thomas More, criticized his new cosmology. Interestingly, he was less well received north of the Alps, with many Reformation leaders, including Martin Luther, calling for his head.

When Italian philosopher Giordano Bruno foolishly circulated pamphlets espousing many heterodox views, including support for the Copernican system that was written *in the vernacular*, a Vatican Inquisition saw him burned at the stake. In the ensuing decades the Church fought a futile rearguard action against heliocentrism, finally bringing its most authoritative supporter, Galileo, before the Inquisition. Shown the instruments of torture, he recanted.

By the late medieval period, the Church held the kind of absolute ideological power that might have been envied by Stalin, Hitler, or Pol Pot. As the saying goes, all power corrupts, and absolute power corrupts absolutely; by 1500, the weakness at the core of the Church was obvious to even the most devout. Bribery, simony (the sale of offices), and extortion became the watchwords of ecclesiastical life. The decay peaked during the Avignon papacy, where "everything the Church had or was, from the cardinal's hat to the pilgrim's relic, was for sale."[30] Bishops and cardinals amassed fabulous fortunes from the sale of tithes and indulgences (forgiveness for sins purchased from the Church). John XXII, who wore the papal tiara from 1316 to 1334, exhibited a legendary appetite for gold cloth and fur. Noble families purchased appointments to the priesthood for small children, and twenty-year-old archbishops were not unknown.[31] Of 624 papal dispensations of legitimacy granted in 1342–43, 484 went to the offspring of clergy. In parts of sixteenth-century England, the clergy

were indicted for almost a quarter of all sex crimes, more than ten times
their proportion of the population.

Opposition to Church corruption, while relatively quiet and scattered, slowly grew, particularly in the postapocalyptic atmosphere that
followed the fourteenth-century plague outbreak. The Beghards, a popular countercultural movement, professed a clergy-free path to salvation,
the right to noble and church property, and free love. Neither the
Church nor the ruling class looked kindly on its members, and many
were burned at the stake. The most popular poem from the period, *Piers
the Plowman,* provides a catalogue of medieval human failing, with pride
of place awarded to the clergy.

A more solid foundation of dissent was laid down by the brilliant
fourteenth-century Oxford don John Wyclif, whose opposition to
Church dominance found shelter in England's long-running feud with
Rome. As Martin Luther's direct intellectual ancestor, he "metaphorically nailed his own thesis to the wall," in the words of Barbara
Tuchman, with his *De Civili Domino* (*On Civil Government*). This tract
proposed the confiscation of Church property and the exclusion of
priests from government. Eventually, Wyclif, like the Beghards, denied
the doctrine of transubstantiation and the very necessity of the priesthood itself. This did not ingratiate him with either the English or the
Roman clergy, who attacked his many heresies.

Wyclif also translated the Scriptures into the vernacular. Fortunately,
he lived in the pre-Gutenberg era, so his crime went unamplified by the
printing press. In 1381, Balliol College, where he had been master, banished him—a relatively mild sanction. In doing so, Oxford harmed itself
more than it did Wyclif. The university went into two centuries of decline, while Wyclif, a highly effective preacher, remained influential until he died of natural causes three years later.[32] After his banishment, his
followers, the so-called Lollards, went underground. Thus began the
long English Puritan/Dissenter tradition.

The Tyndale Affair provided the post-Gutenberg bookend to
Wyclif's English Bible. The 1457 invention of the printing press by
Johannes Gutenberg of Mainz, Germany greatly amplified the heretic's
voice. William Tyndale, a classics scholar at Cambridge and Oxford, had
initially delighted Henry VIII with his opinions on the preeminence of
royal power over that of the Church. In 1525, Tyndale, like Wyclif (and

numerous naughty monks before them), translated the New Testament into English. In the century and a half between the Wyclif and Tyndale episodes, the printing press had changed everything, magnifying Tyndale's heresy a thousand-fold. The very thought that uneducated peasants might now be able to read and discuss Scripture was repellent to the clergy; all that was expected from 90% of the population was illiteracy and blind obedience.

Publishers in Tyndale's native England would not touch the manuscript. He fled to Germany, where his Bible almost made its way into print in Cologne before being discovered by local clerics. Finally successful in the Protestant stronghold of Worms, Tyndale sent six thousand copies of his translation back to Britain, where they were hungrily devoured. At the insistence of then-devout Henry VIII, the Continental clergy imprisoned Tyndale for sixteen months, tried him for heresy, then had him publicly strangled. For publishing the Bible. In English. (This was before Henry VIII broke with the Church over the annulment of his marriage to Catherine of Aragon.)

One hundred and seventy-five Wyclif Bibles survive today, so at least several hundred must have been produced. Possession of one was enough to convict the reader of heresy. Transcribing several condemned the perpetrator to be burned, but since these had to be hand copied, the risk of *auto-da-fé* was relatively small. Tyndale's use of the printing press upped the ante on both sides; heretics who employed the printing press were playing with fire, both figuratively and literally.[33]

When Martin Luther finally used the Gutenberg press as a battering ram to topple Church authority, he replaced it with an equally odious, if less corrupt, tyranny. Typical of this new Protestant zeal was John Calvin's role in Geneva. An itinerant missionary, Guillaume Farel, invited the refugee pastor to the newly Protestant city by the lake. Calvin was not the city's "dictator," as is often represented by modern historians. Instead, he merely served as head of the Consistory, a group made up mostly of ordinary lay people that was charged with guarding the morals of the Republic. (In fact, Geneva did not even grant Calvin citizenship until five years before he died.) Over the sixteen years of Calvin's guidance, the Consistory condemned eighty-nine people to death, mostly for witchcraft. By the standards of the time, this was unexceptional. Neighboring Catholic states executed far larger numbers of heretics, usually after hideously cruel tortures, which the authorities in Geneva generally avoided. Perhaps the most famous judicial episode of the era was Geneva's 1553 trial and execution of the heretic Michael Servetus for denying the Trinity and infant birth. When questioned whether he wished to be tried in Geneva or France, he fell on his knees and begged for Genevan justice.

What Calvin and his Consistory did create was a premodern version of the nanny state. No matter was too small for this merry group, to whom the term "micromanagers" is easily applied. In 1562, they compelled François de Bonivard, an elderly, recently widowed Genevan, to remarry a much younger woman. When the new wife inevitably sought the affections of a younger man, the city beheaded her lover and drowned her. On another occasion, the Consistory discovered five elderly men who could not render an adequate account of the Protestant faith. The Consistory ordered them to hire a tutor and demonstrate the catechism before the next public communion.[34]

Even before the partition of government power among king, parliament, and judiciary guaranteed individual liberties, the rule of law, and property rights, God and Caesar would have to be rent asunder. Fired by ideological fervor, religious wars—Catholic versus Protestant, and Protestant versus Protestant—burned through Europe for almost two hundred years. The conflicts exhausted and weakened the participants. This, in turn, paved the way for both independent secular governments and the more tolerant message of the Enlightenment.

THE PREMODERN ABSENCE OF EFFECTIVE CAPITAL MARKETS

The modern businessperson takes for granted the easy availability of money from others—capital. Today, the most reputable large corporations can obtain long-term loans for improvement and expansion at just over 5% per year from the bond markets, with well-secured small entrepreneurs paying only a few percent more.

Even before money first appeared five thousand years ago, humans lent and borrowed. For thousands of years, loans of grain and cattle were made at interest; a bushel or calf lent in winter would be repaid

twice over at harvest time. Such practices are still widespread in undeveloped societies.

The history of ancient credit markets runs broad and deep. Much of
the earliest historical record from the Fertile Crescent—Sumer, Babylon,
and Assyria—concerns the lending of money. Hammurabi's famous Babylonian Code—the first known comprehensive set of laws—dealt with
commercial transactions. A few small ancient examples will suffice. In
Sumer from 3000 B.C. to 1900 B.C., the usual interest rate for a loan of
barley was 33%, whereas the rate for a loan of silver was 20%. The difference between the two rates reflected the fact that barley loans were
riskier than silver loans, since the latter could not be consumed or spoil;
nor could a "silver crop" fail.[35]

Such high interest rates are prohibitive for long-term projects; at 20%
per annum, the amount owed doubles in less than four years. With such
a crushing future burden, no rational businessman or corporation bor-
rows to fund a project that will not become profitable for five or ten
years, as is the case with most large commercial undertakings.

Interest rates, according to economic historian Richard Sylla, accurately reflect a society's health. In effect, a plot of interest rates over time
is a nation's "fever curve." In uncertain times rates rise because there is
less sense of public security and trust. Over the broad sweep of history,
all of the major ancient civilizations demonstrated a "U-shaped" pattern
of interest rates. There were high rates early in their history, followed by
slowly falling rates as the civilizations matured and stabilized. This led to
low rates at the height of their development, and, finally, as the civilizations decayed, there was a return of rising rates. For example, the apex of
the Roman Empire in the first and second centuries A.D. saw interest
rates as low as 4%. The above sequence holds only on the average and
over the long term, with plenty of shorter-term fluctuations. Even during the height of the Pax Romana in the first and second centuries, rates
briefly spiked as high as 12% during times of crisis.

After the Fall of Rome (traditionally dated A.D. 476), rates in the Empire skyrocketed. Little more than two centuries later, Western commerce received yet another staggering blow—Mohammed's Hejira and
the rise of the Arab empire, which overran most of the Iberian Peninsula. By acquiring control of the Gibraltar Straits, the Arabs effectively
cut off Mediterranean trade.

The historical trace of interest rates simply disappears during the late Roman period and does not reappear until almost a millennium later, in England. There, rates well in excess of 40% were recorded in the twelfth century, and in Italy, rates averaged about 20% later in the same century. The first glimmer of a more reasonable future appears in Holland, where rates fell to as low as 8% as early as 1200.

Such high interest rates suggest a virtual absence of capital markets and constituted a commercial and economic straitjacket from which there would be no escape for centuries. As religious doctrine strangled intellectual progress, so, too, was everyday commerce hamstrung by the absence of capital markets. The Christian prohibitions against moneylending did not help. The ban's origins were scriptural, starting with Exodus 22:25: "If thou lend money to any of my people that is poor by thee, thou shalt not be to him as a usurer." Saint Augustine held that "business is itself an evil," while Saint Jerome opined that "a man who is a merchant can seldom if ever please God."[36]

In A.D. 325 the Council of Nicaea, the first organized Church conclave, forbade lending by clerics, and by 850 the Church began to excommunicate lay moneylenders, not that much demand existed for capital in Europe's stunted commercial markets to begin with.

The strictures against moneylending slowly gained in strength. By 1139, the Second Lateran Council declared even mortgages usurious. The height of ecclesiastical anticapitalist fervor, not to be matched until the era of Lenin and Marx, occurred in the mid-thirteenth century, when Saint Thomas Aquinas revived the Aristotelian notion that *all* large-scale commercial activity was inherently sinful.[*]

Moneylending is as much a part of the human repertoire, and just as difficult to legislate away, as the consumption of drugs and alcohol. Even at the height of antiusury fervor, pawnshops lined medieval streets; Holland actually licensed moneylenders, who regularly supplied capital to the ruling princes. Jews, who could not be excommunicated, lent freely. Not until after 1571, when the Fifth Lateran Council lifted the prohibition against usury, could investors underwrite vigorous commercial activity.[37]

---

[*] While Aristotle considered the farmstead or household small business honorable, he condemned both retail trade and lending. See *Politics*, III, 23.

THE PREMODERN ABSENCE OF EFFECTIVE
TRANSPORT AND COMMUNICATIONS

For a thousand years after the fall of the Empire, the decaying Roman roads were still the best highways in Europe. According to historian Laurence Packard:

> People "stayed put" in the Middle Ages; until the time of the crusades there was very little journeying about. The profound ignorance of geography, of places beyond one's immediate locality, helped to create a fear of strange regions and strangers, which amounted to superstition. Real dangers, such as robber barons, pirates, bad roads—or no roads at all—broken bridges—or no bridges at all—provided very effective obstacles to trade. Each feudal lord, moreover, collected tolls on traffic, and these tolls so increased the cost of goods [that] grain could not be transported from the land of plenty to the land of dearth because costs would eat up the profit, or raise the price so high that the starving people could not pay for it.[38]

As noted by Packard, the mechanical lack of transport was only part of the problem. In the words of economic historian Eli Heckscher, "In the Middle Ages the greatest obstacles to trade were the tolls." In the modern era, the word "toll" conjures up the fee for using an improved road or a border tariff. Before 1800, however, tolls were the unabashedly arbitrary and major source of revenue for many local rulers, who set up toll stations at critical choke points, such as navigable rivers and passes, so that traders could not avoid them.[39]

The absence of roads in northern Europe was a two-edged sword. On the one hand, it protected Scandinavia and most of Germany from permanent Roman conquest. On the other hand, this poor state of transport throttled all commerce north of the Alps, especially in Scandinavia. For a millennium after the Fall of Rome, news and goods traveled only as fast as the cumbersome sailing vessels of the day: five weeks from Venice to Constantinople. To inland destinations, transport was even slower and less efficient—it took four weeks to travel the overland route from Venice to London. Most peasants never left the town of their birth. Only the sturdiest and luckiest could survive long sea voyages, and only the wealthiest could afford the supply of horses necessary for long overland journeys. As late as the turn of the twentieth century, which brought the Ford Model T, the overwhelming majority of Americans lived and died within twenty miles of their birthplace.

Before 1800, lack of adequate transport did not merely threaten commerce; it was deadly in its own right. In the modern world, where food can easily be shipped from areas of surplus to areas of shortage, crop failures rarely cause mass starvation. In the Middle Ages, by contrast, one town could experience catastrophe, while its neighbor in the next valley prospered; this was particularly true of areas not favored with river or sea transport. (In the twentieth century, Communist nations, by interfering with normal market and transport mechanisms, became history's most successful purveyors of mass starvation.)

The cost, danger, discomfort, and above all, the agonizingly slow pace of travel before the advent of steam power stagger modern sensibilities. As late as the mid-nineteenth century, bulk transport on the Continent was lucky to make twenty miles per day. Typically, it took almost six weeks for goods to travel the 290 miles from Paris to Lyon—less than ten miles per day. Coach passengers were fortunate to cover territory at twice that rate.

Traveling expenses were fearsome. In 1820, coach fare from New York to western Ohio—the frontier of civilization at the time—ran $80, or two month's wages. In England, a journey of sixty miles cost a pound sterling, or about a week's wages. (The traveler could save almost half the fare if he were willing to hang off the side of the coach.) Only the wealthiest could afford a coach-and-four.

The main expense of travel involved the repeated change of horses that was necessary over long distances. Finally, the high density of horses, oxen, and mules in the crowded cities created problems of aesthetics and hygiene mercifully long forgotten.

Travel safety in the premodern era proved an even larger consideration. The highwayman did not disappear from England's roads until the mid-eighteenth century, but coach robberies occurred on the Continent with alarming frequency well into the nineteenth. English travelers in Italy reported that as late as 1817, coach passengers were frequently killed, stripped, and then burned in their vehicles. The threat of petty thievery loomed as a constant concern, and coach accidents were remarkably common. In 1829, one coach traveler between New York City and Cincinnati recorded no less than nine overturns on rough corduroy (log-surfaced) roads. Fatalities were an everyday occurrence.

The discomfort of long coach and sailing ship journeys taxed even the hardiest of travelers. The English painter J. M. W. Turner wrote of an Italian journey made in 1829:

> The snow began to fall at Foligno. The coach from its weight slid about in all directions. I soon got wet through and through til at Sarre-Valli the [coach] slid into a ditch and required six oxen, sent three miles back for, to drag it out; this cost four hours, so we were 10 hours beyond our time at Macerta, consequently half-starved and frozen, we at last got to Bologna. But there our troubles began instead of diminishing. We crossed Mont Cenis in a sledge—bivouacked in the snow with fires lighted for three hours on Mont Tarrat while the [coach] was righted and dug out. The same night we were again turned out to walk up to our knees in a new-fallen drift.[40]

From the beginning of recorded history, people, goods, and information moved no faster than the speed of the horse or the sail and continued to do until the dawn of the modern era. The harnessing of the steam engine for use in the ship and the railroad locomotive in the mid-1800s and the elimination of the toll stations by powerful national governments would supply the last of the four factors necessary for economic growth. The development of the railroad, the steamship, and the telegraph ignited prosperity beyond the fevered imaginings of the most optimistic premodern dreamer.

LAND, LABOR, AND CAPITAL

Before 1500, the well-being of the average human being was stagnant. The roots of that stagnation should by now be obvious. First and foremost, there was no incentive to create wealth, since it was not safe from the depredations of the feudal aristocracy, the state, the Church, or common criminals. Second, no European dared to think creatively or scientifically, since original thoughts often condemned their creator to oblivion both in this world and the next. Third, even had wealth-creating inventions and services been conceived, the capital necessary for their development was unavailable. Finally, even had such inventions been produced in large number, their inventors could not have advertised and inexpensively transported their wares to consumers in distant cities.

Traditionally, economists break down the production of wealth into three "inputs": land, labor, and capital. Economists believe that understanding how these classical inputs behave and interact reveals the historical roots of global prosperity. In order to build a farm, a factory, or a satellite network, all three are needed; how productive each factor is separates the rich man from the bankrupt.

If you are an entrepreneur, what matters is not how productive the average tract of land, employee, or loan is, but how productive the *marginal* piece of land, employee, or loan is. The term "marginal" refers to that land, labor, or capital *available to you at the moment*. It does little good to plan to farm in an agricultural district if all of the good land is taken and the only tracts available to you are of poor quality. Or to build a textile factory in an area with a skilled labor pool, but where all of the best workers are already happily employed. Or to plan a tract of apartments in a place where existing mortgages carry low interest rates, but the rates on new loans have risen.

Of the three classical inputs, marginal land—that available to you at the moment—is the least productive. Since at any given time, the most productive land is already under cultivation, only lower-quality land will be easily available for purchase and development. New farms are almost never as productive as existing ones. Therefore, increasing investment in an agricultural economy is a losing game. The law of diminishing returns applies with a vengeance to farming.*

Marginal labor, on the other hand, tends to retain its productivity better than land. As long as a trainable workforce exists, subsequent investment in more factories should be just as productive as the original investment. The hiring of increasing amounts of labor benefits from economies of scale; it is cheaper, on a per-worker basis, to train a hundred than to train ten. Further, marginal labor is blessed with the "learning curve." As creative workers and their supervisors devise ever-better training and work procedures, they become more efficient. Thus, marginal labor often becomes *more* productive with each subsequent hire. In modern terminology, industrial economies, which are labor-intensive, are said to be "scalable" (meaning that their size and output can be rapidly in-

---

* As with all useful generalizations, there are exceptions; the westward expansion of the United States in the eighteenth and nineteenth centuries saw vast quantities of high-quality marginal land brought into production.

creased), while agricultural economies are not. Industrial economies grow easily; agricultural economies, only with great difficulty, if at all.

Finally, capital, along with the communications technology that underlies it, becomes increasingly productive with increasing investment. A point comes when capital markets achieve "critical mass," with dramatic improvements in efficiency.[41] Such was the case with the telephone, the credit card, the Internet, and, most notoriously, the Windows computer operating system—each becoming widespread enough that they became necessities of life.

The capital markets themselves behave in the same way. A nation's savings does little good if it is squirreled away in mattresses or under floorboards or on deposit in an inefficient banking system, as occurred in early industrial France, where distrust of the banking system denied the accumulation of great wealth to worthwhile enterprises. Markets work best when all of the buyers and sellers of a particular item are confined to the same place at the same time. In such a situation, the pricing of that item becomes very "efficient," that is to say, everyone buys and sells at nearly the same price. The most easily understandable example of this is ticket scalping. When the state strictly enforces antiscalping laws, scalpers and their customers will transact surreptitiously and in many places. As a result, ticket prices will vary widely. Further, since the scalpers almost always have better information than the buyers do, prices tend to be high. Such a market is said to be "inefficient." Enlightened communities have discovered that when scalping is allowed at a given place and time, generally just outside the main gate shortly before the event, prices are low and uniform. The reason for this is obvious: Confining the ticket sales to a brief period and small area maximizes the flow of information to both buyers and sellers and thereby eliminates the natural advantage of the scalpers. The Holy Grail of market efficiency is to place all of the world's buyers and sellers of a given item in exactly the same place at exactly the same time—in other words, eBay.

Financial markets work in identical fashion. When large numbers of buyers and sellers of capital can be brought together in one place, such as on the floor of the New York Stock Exchange, capital becomes cheaper and more reliable; the productivity of capital increases.* In other words,

---

* When the New York Stock Exchange recently established after-hours trading, it rapidly became apparent that this was far less efficient than that seen on the floor during regular hours, when trading volume was much higher.

as financial activity increases, interest rates fall and stabilize. Government also plays a central role in the investment process by eliminating uncertainty in the cost and supply of capital. Or, as President Clinton asked of Alan Greenspan in 1993, "You mean to tell me that the success of the program and my reelection hinges on the Federal Reserve and a bunch of fucking bond traders?"[42] *Yes, Mr. President, it did.* William Clinton's overwhelming 1996 reelection victory owed itself in no small part to the success of Greenspan's monetary maneuvering.

The same situation holds with transport: It is more efficient to ship large quantities of goods in large vessels than to ship small quantities in small vessels. Likewise with communication—a messenger or telegraph service that transmits large amounts of traffic will offer its services more cheaply than a less busy one; such businesses are highly scalable. The ultimate high-productivity scalable industry is software. Once you have borne the expense of its development, distribution and sale are practically free, particularly if you are distributing it electronically. The productivity of marginal capital, bolstered by modern telecommunications and benefiting from an increasing number of participants, is thus the highest of the three traditional factors. Marginal labor is less productive; marginal land, least of all.

KNOWLEDGE: THE FOURTH INPUT

Several decades ago, as the rapid, sustained increase in Western wealth and productivity became more and more apparent, economists realized that the classic three-input model, which attempted to explain economic output on the basis of land, labor, and capital productivity, did not adequately explain this happy state of affairs. Economist Paul Romer suggested that at some point, scientific and technological knowledge itself becomes an important factor in growth. He pointed out that society benefited from technology's "externalities"—the rapid adoption by all manufacturers of the best practices of the industry leader—and that the marginal productivity of knowledge grows as more of it is accumulated, similar to the increasing marginal productivity of the capital markets.[43] In Romer's world, economic growth is limited only by the human imagination, and there exists no reason why its rate should be limited to the historical 2% real rate of productivity in the world's industrialized nations.

STAGE ONE: HUNTER-GATHERER

Let's consider how these four inputs (land, labor, capital, and knowledge) have played out in human history. In very broad terms, economic historians separate the human saga into four stages: hunter-gatherer, agricultural, industrial, and postindustrial. This four-stage paradigm is, of course, a gross oversimplification. In present-day Brazil, for example, significant numbers engage in each of the four categories. Even in the world's most advanced nations, the last three stages are all still vitally important.

For more than 99% of our time on earth, however, humans existed exclusively as hunter-gatherers. This extraordinarily land-intense activity supports only about one inhabitant per square mile. Further, nomadic hunter-gatherers quickly exhaust edible fauna and flora in a given locale and are constantly on the move. Hunter-gatherers retain only minimal physical possessions and forgo fixed housing.[44]

In terms of the four economic inputs, hunter-gatherers are most dependent on land and labor, and the productivity of both remains constant. It is impossible for the tribe to increase the number of animals or berries over the thousands of square miles of its range. Labor is similarly limited, with improvements in hunting-gathering productivity few and far between. While increasing the amount of labor (the number of hunters and gatherers) on a given piece of land may temporarily increase the production of the land (measured in berries and buffalo), output will quickly fall as they pick the territory clean.

Hunter-gatherer societies do not need capital. In economic terms, then, such societies are economically crippled, since they depend on the least productive of the four inputs—land—and the productivity of their labor forces improves slowly, if at all. Finally, the stock of knowledge in a hunter-gatherer society also improves only glacially. Since advances in "hunter-gatherer technology" were made over such long time frames, measuring in the thousands of years, the calculation of growth rates becomes meaningless.

STAGE TWO: FARMING

About 12,000 years ago, humans first began to settle the Fertile Crescent and farm. Agriculture is vastly more productive than hunting and gathering, allowing for population densities of up to a few hundred inhabitants per square mile. When farming communities came into contact with hunter-gatherers, the latter had small chance of survival, for four reasons. Foremost was simple population density—hunter-gatherer societies with one person per square mile could not compete militarily with farming societies having scores, and in exceptional cases such as the islands of Java and Honshu, hundreds, per square mile. Second, farming societies evolved a relatively small elite of soldiers who specialized in the annihilation of their nomadic neighbors. An even smaller elite of rulers planned and directed these efforts. (The specialization in societal roles made possible by farming, when well-enough developed, became known as "civilization.") Third, the close proximity of humans and domesticated animals in agricultural communities gave rise to pathogenic microorganisms such as smallpox and measles. While the agriculturists developed immunity to these microbes, the microorganisms proved lethal to their hunter-gatherer neighbors. Smallpox killed far more Aztecs than the arms of Cortez, and in the seventeenth century, this pathogen may have killed as many as twenty million Native Americans in North America before substantive contact with the white man even occurred.[45]

Last, and most important, many farming communities embraced the institution of individual property rights. It is nigh on impossible for hunter-gatherers to establish discrete ownership of vast tracts of wild habitat. While many, if not most, early farming ventures were communal, we shall find that soon after the dawn of recorded history, farmers began to individually own and run their plots. Such farms became far more efficient than their communal competitors, and societies that favored property rights quickly found themselves at an enormous advantage not only over their hunter-gatherer neighbors but also over communal farming societies as well.

Nobel Prize-winning economist Douglass North, who has called the agricultural transition "the first economic revolution" (the second being the Industrial Revolution), says that

The first economic revolution was not a revolution because it shifted man's major activity from hunting and gathering to settled agriculture. It was a revolution because the transition created an incentive change for mankind of fundamental proportions. The incentive change stems from the different property rights of the two systems. *When common property rights over resources exist, there is little incentive for the acquisition of superior technology and learning.*"[46] (Italics added)

Farming's main economic handicap lies in the fact that, as in hunting and gathering, land is the most critical input. If the population grows, for example, by 10%, then farmers must bring more land into cultivation in order to maintain the same per-person food consumption. This marginal farmland will not be of the same quality as existing farmland and will consequently be less productive. Farmers will thus have to cultivate *more than* 10% additional land in order to feed the increased population. This does not mean that progress in agricultural productivity is impossible—advanced irrigation and fertilization techniques, crop rotation, and the tandem-hitched plow dramatically increased per-acre yields. But many centuries separated these advances. If, as historians have suggested, crop yields quadrupled in the years between A.D. 1000 and 1500, that represented a growth rate of just 0.28% per year over the period. Between these two dates, population increases forced poor-quality marginal land into cultivation, canceling out most, if not all, of the increase in agricultural productivity that occurred in that half-millennium. *Thus, the standard of living of purely agricultural societies remained relatively static.*

Yes, the shift to an agricultural economy around 12,000 years ago produced a vast increase in world population. And, yes, modest subsequent improvements in agricultural technology resulted in further population increase. However, these advances did not produce a sustained improvement in living standards. As recently as the mid-eighteenth century, famine was a regular occurrence in Europe; in the nineteenth century, the Great Hunger killed over a million Irish citizens.

Some "knowledge gains" were made in the medieval era, but these were sporadic. Eighteenth-century England's "improving farmer," who constantly sought to apply the latest agricultural methods, was still a long way away.

Such was the sad state of affairs so compellingly described by Malthus: a world where population growth overwhelms the glacial improvement in agricultural output.[47] The classic Malthusian "positive checks"—*fama, pestis, et bellum*—supplied the inevitable solution to the imbalance between need and nourishment.

STAGE THREE: INDUSTRIALIZATION

By about 1500 the modest improvements in agricultural techniques, coupled with the first stirrings of property rights, capital markets, and transportation technology, allowed substantial numbers of workers to leave the farm and engage in manufacturing. In both northern and southern Europe, manufacturing meant one thing: textiles. In Italy, skilled weavers processed silk and other exotic fabrics into luxury items. The English shipped raw wool to Burgundy (roughly, modern Holland, Belgium, and northern France), where highly skilled artisans spun and wove it into fine cloth. Shipbuilding and machinery gradually developed as well. Although the Chinese had long exported textiles and porcelain, these industries were not proportionately large enough to allow a significant percentage of the Chinese population to escape agriculture, as occurred in Europe.

Manufacturing requires little land; its limiting factors are labor and capital. Although the law of diminishing returns occasionally governs labor, labor is not as sensitive to increasing scale as land is: The productivity of workers generally does not suffer greatly as more are hired. In the modern era, labor productivity may actually increase with growth, since the increasing density of workers and work places facilitates communication among producers—witness Detroit's automobile assembly lines and Silicon Valley's chip factories.

Better yet, manufacturing is capital-intensive. As old plants become obsolete, new ones must be built at great expense. Increasing population density begets more efficient capital markets; with growth, the financing of manufacturing capacity becomes progressively easier. Last, in an industrial society, knowledge becomes increasingly recognized as the road to wealth, with "best practices" quickly evolving and spreading, raising the output of all.

At some point in the nineteenth century in Europe and in the U.S., a "virtuous circle" came into being: Advances in technology begat improvements in productivity, which, in turn, begat increasing wealth, which then begat yet more capital to fuel still more technological progress. As the industrial economies increasingly employed highly productive capital and knowledge inputs, growth became self-sustaining and unstoppable.

"BUILD IT AND THEY WILL COME"

The rapid economic growth of industrial societies bewitched entire generations of economists. Surely, they argued, the key to economic development was industrialization itself. The mere construction of factories and modern infrastructure and the training of workers should automatically result in the vaunted "economic takeoff."[48] Alas, as the sorry modern history of Soviet industrialization and gargantuan third-world infrastructure projects built with foreign aid have demonstrated, there is more to prosperity than factories, dams, and railroads. (*Plus ça change*: In Chapter 9 we'll explore the failure of industrialization-from-above in the eighteenth-century Ottoman Empire.)

A nation reaches the industrial stage of development not merely as the result of industrialization per se but because of the existence of the vital underlying institutions of property rights, scientific inquiry, and capital markets. Once a nation has reached that stage, it has broken the chains of poverty. Economic growth, if you will, becomes encoded into its very culture. Even when such nations suffer massive destruction of the outward physical manifestations of their economies, as occurred to the Axis Powers during World War II, they rapidly regain and surpass their former prosperity.

Far worse than war is the corrosion of property rights. Twice in the twentieth century, eastern Germany recovered within a few decades from the physical effects of devastating world war. It will take her generations to recover from communism.

STAGE FOUR: POSTINDUSTRIAL SOCIETY

The outline of yet another stage in human economic development—so-called postindustrial society—slowly emerged in the last part of the twentieth century. In a postindustrial society, manufacturing gives way to the provision of services. The postindustrial economy requires even less labor and land than its industrial predecessor. While this new regime requires at least as much capital as the old industrial system, its appetite for the knowledge input, mainly in the form of technological innovation, is ravenous. Where a telephone company might have hired armies of operators forty years ago, it now makes do with far fewer technicians, servicing the public with massively expensive satellite, cellular, and fiber-optic networks. Since the capital markets and knowledge base are the most "scalable" of the four input factors, capital- and knowledge-intensive postindustrial societies should sustain the highest growth.

The Western world did not arrive at such an agreeable state overnight. It took most of the second millennium to correct feudalism's suppression of property rights, throw off the intellectual stranglehold of the Church, overcome the lack of capital markets, and rectify the absence of effective transport and communication. Only with the completion of these four tasks could citizens of the new industrial and postindustrial societies enjoy the fruits of their labors.

CHAPTER TWO

Property

You cannot have a free society without private property.

—Milton Friedman

Müezzinzade Ali Pasha, commander of the Ottoman Turks, had a terrible day at Lepanto, off the western coast of Greece, in the sunny fall of 1571. In a sea battle lasting several hours, his fleet was engulfed by the combined naval forces of Spain, Venice, and the Vatican—the Holy League—under the leadership of Don Juan of Austria. It was one of the bloodiest battles in history, with 40,000 lives lost on both sides—about 150 souls per minute. Sailors from a number of Holy League vessels, including Don Juan's *La Reale*, boarded Ali Pasha's flagship, *Sultana*, and both commanders were intimately involved in the fighting. Ali Pasha wielded a small bow, and Don Juan brandished a battle-axe and broadsword. The Turkish commander was felled by a bullet to the brain, and his fleet scattered in panic. In one of the great turning points of world history, the forces of Western Europe stemmed the rising tide of Turkish influence in the eastern Mediterranean and almost certainly prevented the Ottoman conquest of Italy.

At Lepanto, Ali Pasha lost more than the battle and his life; he lost his entire family fortune as well. Like all wealthy Turks, he kept his liquid assets physically close to his person. Holy League sailors who boarded

Sultana found 150,000 gold pieces in Ali Pasha's treasure chest. Why would a naval commander store his entire wealth in his personal quarters? As good an explanation as any was provided by Adam Smith, in *The Wealth of Nations:* "In those unfortunate countries, indeed, where men are continually afraid of the violence of their superiors, they frequently bury and conceal a great part of their common stock, a common practice in Turkey, in Indostan, and I believe, in most other governments of Asia."*

Except for the sultan, no Turkish citizen—not even Ali Pasha, an imperial brother-in-law—was a free man. A citizen's life, his freedom, and his fortune could be confiscated in a moment and on a whim. Therein lies the reason for the ultimate demise of all totalitarian societies and for the strength of the free market system: Without property rights and civil rights, little motivates the inventor or businessman to create and produce beyond his immediate needs.

THE FIRST BUILDING BLOCK

Of the four foundations of modern prosperity—property rights, scientific rationalism, ready access to capital, and efficient transportation and communications—property rights arose earliest, their most important elements first seeing the light of day in the ancient world. In the modern world, property is also the most critical of these four factors; as put by that great economist, P. J. O'Rourke: "North Korea has a 99% literacy rate, a disciplined, hardworking society, and a $900 per capita GDP. Morocco has a 43.7% literacy rate, a society that spends all day drinking coffee and pestering tourists to buy rugs, and a $3,260 per capita GDP."[1]

At the same time, property rights alone do not suffice to encourage economic growth, as is demonstrated by the stagnation and decline of Greece and Rome, neither of which possessed the other three elements.

The relationship between property rights and civil rights is complex. Socialists tend to deny any connection between the two. Consider nineteenth-century French socialist Pierre-Joseph Proudhon, a staunch

* Smith, II: 301. In Smith's usage "common stock" means all wealth, not company shares.

believer in civil liberties who nonetheless equated property with theft. Although the traditional view asserts that property rights flow from civil rights, the opposite view stands just as well. No less a socialist luminary than Leon Trotsky, arguing otherwise, observed that civil liberty flowed *from* property rights.[2] The right to property is the right that guarantees all other rights. Individuals without property are susceptible to starvation, and it is much easier to bend the fearful and hungry to the will of the state. If a person's property can be arbitrarily threatened by the state, that power will inevitably be employed to intimidate those with divergent political and religious opinions.

Friedrich Hayek realized over a half century ago that civil rights and property rights are cut from the same cloth and cannot exist in isolation. Those who surrender their property rights soon find themselves, to borrow the title of his signature volume, on "the road to serfdom."

The standard humanist interpretation credits John Locke with inventing the concept of the sanctity of private property rights. But Locke, while a key player in the story, was a latecomer to the property game. Though the publication of his *Two Treatises of Government* in 1690 enshrined the protection of life, liberty, and property as the primary function of enlightened government, basic civil and property rights had by that time been embedded for centuries in English common law. Further, the origins of these rights were solidly rooted in the ancient Greek city-states.

OUT OF HISTORY'S MISTS

Since the origins of property rights are lost to time, when and how to begin the story is an arbitrary matter. Certainly, many, if not most, primitive societies must have contained elements of property rights, particularly involving land ownership. Hunter-gatherer societies, nonetheless, have trouble maintaining property rights because there is a cost. A single tribal group cannot patrol the thousands of square miles of range needed for its survival.

Tribes that succeeded in protecting property rights were probably more efficient than those that did not. A plausible scenario might have resembled the following: As large mammals, the preferred food source,

grew scarce in late prehistoric times, any group of hunters that monopolized and carefully managed the dwindling local herd of mammoths must
have had a competitive advantage over its neighbors. This is highly speculative, however, and since we are dealing with prehistory, we cannot
know with any certainty.

In contrast to the speculative nature of dealing with prehistoric
hunter gatherers, we can feel more certain about preliterate farming
communities. In the earliest recorded land sales, historians have found
details of how prehistoric societies transferred property. In the Old
Testament, for example, Abraham purchased a burial plot for his recently deceased wife, Sarah, from his Hittite neighbor Ephron. At first,
Ephron offered the property to Abraham as an outright gift, but Abraham insisted on paying for it. He weighed out the silver and had the
sale proclaimed *in the presence* of the other Hittite villagers.[3] Both parties seemed to display neighborly generosity, but Abraham had powerful motives for insisting on a witnessed payment. First, he established
his right to the property in perpetuity; Ephron could not rescind the
transfer. Second, the presence of the other neighbors assured Abraham
that no competing claims to the land existed. Third, payment released
Abraham from having to return the favor in the future. Similar descriptions of communally witnessed property transactions were commonplace in the ancient world.

At a very early stage in recorded history, we have encountered the essence of effective property rights. First, those rights were clearly defined—
there was no question that Abraham and his descendants now owned the
property. Second, those rights were *alienable*—that is, they could be freely
bought and sold. Over the ensuing millennia, the fates of nations would
hinge on just how well they respected those two conditions.

The earliest civilizations in the Fertile Crescent and Egypt were hierarchical, totalitarian societies. An uncritical reading of ancient history
suggests that the pharaoh owned all Egyptian land; this was almost certainly not true. Some land was privately held, and modern historians actively debate the extent of the property rights of ordinary farmers and
citizens in ancient Egypt.

The site of the earliest human civilizations in Mesopotamia, "the land
between the rivers," corresponds roughly to modern Iraq, a flat and arid
territory lying between the Tigris and Euphrates. Intensive agriculture

on such terrain requires sophisticated irrigation technology. This can only be created by a strong central government, hence the historian's observation that the successive Mesopotamian civilizations were "hydraulic societies." Over the centuries, these societies built massive earthen conduits, likely with slave labor. These vast engineering projects made possible highly productive farming and high population densities.

In early Mesopotamia, the witnessed, face-to-face land sale of Abraham and Ephron gave way to permanently recorded sales, stored in public repositories. Archaeologists have uncovered government archives of land sales dating back to 2500 B.C., roughly five hundred years after the earliest evidence of writing.

Large-scale agriculture developed somewhat later in the Nile valley, and records of land sales also began to appear around 2500 B.C. Because Egyptian hieroglyphics were less compact than Mesopotamian cuneiform, the history of property transactions in Egypt is less detailed than that in Sumer and Babylon, where stone pillars (*stelae*) described land transactions and the laws governing them as far back as 2100 B.C., culminating in the Code of Hammurabi in 1750 B.C. Finally, the Israelites left a detailed description of their property transactions in the first five books of the Old Testament (the Torah), whose first chapters were written about 1150 B.C.

All three historical sources—Sumerian, Egyptian, and Israelite—provide a detailed record of property transactions in the ancient world, but not, unfortunately, about the overall structure of landholdings. For example, both Sumerian and Egyptian temples owned vast tracts of land, but private landholding was also common. Unknown is the relative importance and productivity of temple and private land or the degree of protection available to private holdings from the greed of the religious and temporal authorities.

The Tenth Commandment makes a tantalizing comment on this issue, saying, "Thou shalt not covet thy neighbor's house. . . ." Even the most rigidly totalitarian regimes of southern Mesopotamia, in the Ur III period of Sumer, around 2050 B.C., recorded sales of private houses and lands, as well as leases and royal grants to individuals.

The "lawsuit of Mose" (not to be confused with the Hebrew Moses) provides a fascinating glimpse into Egyptian property procedures. Around 1600 B.C., the pharaoh granted land to a sea captain ancestor of Mose. About three centuries later, a dishonest official named Khay bribed officials in the royal departments of justice, granaries, and treasury in order to embezzle the ancient land grant from Mose to himself. Mose was able to reverse this perfidy in court by producing old tax records from the local government office. The lawsuit of Mose supplies a startling instance of ancient private property protection from government treachery, demonstrating the existence of legal and recording systems that were robust enough to keep a family's land intact over the centuries.

Over time, restrictions on land sales in Mesopotamia and Israel were gradually relaxed. At first, in both places, clan members could prevent sales by others in the clan. But as time passed, there was an acceleration of the trend away from communal holdings of land toward private, individual ownership, and at some point between 700 B.C. to 500 B.C., land was freely bought and sold.

Property ownership was influenced by the physical nature of the landscape. At one extreme lay southern Mesopotamia's dry, flat terrain, which necessitated large-scale irrigation; that tended to concentrate ownership into a relatively few hands. At the other extreme spread Israel's hilly terrain. There, almost no mention of large landed estates was made; small landholdings were the norm.

A populist element occasionally disrupted ancient land law. To curry support among their subjects, Mesopotamian kings, usually at the beginning of their reigns, declared *misharum*, which canceled debts and tax claims. This, in turn, was one cause of high Mesopotamian interest rates, as lenders, fearful that a misharum might be declared, thereby wiping out an investment, demanded 33% for loans of grain and 20% for loans of silver.

The Deuteronomic Code called for the cancellation of debts every seven years.* Most radical of all, the Jubilee provisions of Leviticus returned property to its ancestral owners every fifty years. Despite their mention in the Bible, however, these provisions were probably fictional; had they been carried out, they would have crippled ancient Israel's market for land.[4]

---

* Thus the origins of the term sabbatical.

THE FORGOTTEN FIRST DEMOCRACY

In his influential *The Other Greeks*, classicist Victor Davis Hanson suggested that the origins of Western democracy lay in the agrarian societies
that preceded Periclean Athens by several centuries.[5] Hanson theorized
that these ancient Greek democratic roots developed because of the
strength of individual property rights in the hill country of Attica (Athens and its environs). Hanson's theory, although controversial, provides
the vital link between property rights and individual liberties. This link,
seen by thinkers as disparate as Trotsky and Hayek, thus seems to be as
old as antiquity itself.

The Hanson hypothesis begins during the Mycenaean period
(roughly 1600 B.C. to 1200 B.C.). The collapse of this civilization
brought about a revolution in the relationship between farmers, rulers,
and property that echoes down to the present day. Mycenaean society
was in many respects similar to Mesopotamia and feudal Europe, with
large collectivized landholdings that were farmed by slaves and serfs and
managed by an aristocratic minority. When this culture mysteriously im-
ploded around 1200 B.C., control of the estates fell to a few landed elites.
The chaos following the Mycenaean collapse allowed adventurous farmers to begin colonizing the marginal hilly land overlooking the prime
bottomland of the large estates. (This recalls the differences between
Mesopotamian and Israelite farming.) These "new men" overcame the
poor quality of their plots with the ambition and innovation that is characteristic of free men working private land. They soon outproduced the
old estates and, in many cases, took them over. All other things being
equal, the free farmer has an economic advantage over the owner of the
feudal estate. Hanson writes:

> No ingredient, I believe, is so dramatically successful in agricul-
> ture as free will, the ability to implement the new idea, to de-
> velop a proven routine, to learn once, not twice, from the hard
> taskmaster of error, to be left alone from government planning
> to grope for a plan of survival. . . . Renters, serfs, indentured ser-
> vants, or lessees cannot invest in capital crops such as trees or
> vines in any efficient manner. Nor will they take the consider-
> able risks entailed in viticulture and arboculture without clear ti-
> tle to the land they farm.[6]

This is not a new concept, of course. Consider Aristotle's assertion that "the best material of democracy is an agricultural population; there is no difficulty in forming a democracy where the mass of the people live by agriculture or tending of cattle."[7]

These early post-Mycenaean farmers could be said to be the first "middle class"—neither rich nor poor. The great paradox was that the availability of this marginal farmland—*eschatia*—dictated that democracy and its attendant respect for property rights would develop where this kind of land was most abundant, namely, in the hilly terrain of Attica. The wealthy had no need to make the eschatia bloom, and the poor could not afford to. The parts of Greece that were rich in bottomland, like Macedonia and Sparta, would not develop democracy, private property rights, and individual freedoms. It was not by chance that Alexander the Great, the very antithesis and destroyer of Greek democratic values, hailed from the flat, fertile north.

We can also credit the early Greek small farmer—the *geôrgos*—with pioneering the ancient equivalent of the Protestant work ethic that is so familiar in American farm culture. He invested backbreaking work on the soil with nobility and honor, an unusual concept in any age. In his *Works and Days*, the Boeotian farmer Hesiod makes clear the value of this dedication to the land: "Both the gods and men are angry at those who are idle."[8]

The typical geôrgos did his best to diversify his produce, growing a complex mix of grapes, cereals, legumes, and fruits, as well as raising livestock. In the long run, however, the elements or the Fates ruined even the most skillful yeoman on the most diversified farm. Fortunately for Western civilization, the smallholders' competition—the large Greek landowners—did not have the corporate risk-management techniques of modern agribusiness, and farm ownership did not concentrate excessively until Alexander's conquest swept away the autonomy of the ancient city-states.

In an era when inherited wealth and power almost always trumped intelligence and drive, the post-Mycenaean period was a brief moment when the opposite occurred. The era beginning around 1100 B.C. presented a protocapitalist opportunity to Greek peasants, and they exploited it in great numbers. By 700 B.C., as many as 100,000 small farms, averaging ten acres in size, flourished in Greece. Fiercely individualistic and antiauthoritarian, *geôrgoi* manifested their independence in ways that are deeply embedded in modern Western life, and they changed the course of civilization itself. They did so in three ways:

- They valued private property—most important, the farm, its tools, and its produce. And lest we idealize them too much, they valued their slaves as well. The typical geôrgos owned one or two. Plentiful in the ancient world, particularly in the aftermath of military victory, slaves were typically acquired by the Greeks following the conquest of neighboring city-states, when the resultant "glut" would drive the average sale price to as low as a few dozen drachmas—about $100 in current value. (In "normal" times, slaves usually sold for 100 to 150 drachmas.)

- They treasured their egalitarianism. The roots of Western democracy lie largely with these illiterate, sunburned, raggedly dressed rustics, not with the famous urban politicians—Solon, Cleisthenes, and Pericles (and even less with the great Greek philosophers, most of whom were profoundly antidemocratic). The operative concept in the Greek world of the sixth and seventh centuries B.C. was *timocracy*, a system that based voting rights on landholding. Greece's great good fortune was that the holdings were small and widespread. Not until the late sixth century did the most radical of the Greek city-states, Athens, extend full voting citizenship to the landless urban poor.

- They were militarily self-sufficient. Neighboring farmers would typically band into the hoplite phalanx: fifty to sixty soldiers, each outfitted with his "panoply" (spear, shield, helmet, and body armor), marching in dense formation and cutting to pieces everything in their path.

The powerful interaction of these three factors—property rights, timocracy, and military self-sufficiency—was transformative. The geôrgos placed himself in three analogous grids alongside his neighbors: the farmland, the legislative assembly, and the phalanx. Because he and his neighbors formed their own military units, they were able to protect their property rights against invaders from neighboring states and would-be tyrants. Their military self-sufficiency had another, more subtle, benefit. Most battles were afternoon affairs, and in the sleepy seventh and sixth centuries they occurred only every decade or two. Accordingly, warfare was cheap. The major expense was the panoply, costing perhaps a hundred drachmas (about $500 in current value) and handed down from generation to generation. The early Greeks thus avoided the economic scourge of succeeding nation-states—high taxes to pay for military expenditures.

With their newly granted voting rights, they established a solid legal framework. This legal structure defended life, liberty, and property millennia before English legal scholars conceived of these basic rights. Finally, their productivity allowed, possibly for the first time in history, a significant percentage of ordinary people—not just the ruling, priestly, and military elites—to escape farming altogether. This sophisticated, urban, nonfarming aspect of Greek society is the face so dearly treasured by the later Western world. Make no mistake: The cosmopolitan world of the later Greeks would not have been possible without its timocratic agricultural foundation. The very basis of Western civilization—that of the free citizen possessing the right to own and dispose of property—owes its origin to the early city-states that flourished several centuries before the height of Periclean Athens.

The decentralized Greek city-state could not conscript the militarily self-sufficient geôrgos for extended foreign campaigns, it could not subject him to crippling taxes, and, most important, even tyrants could not bully him, because the city-states could not assemble large-scale forces without common consent. Hoplite armies were self-led, and the commanding "general" typically occupied an unobtrusive position in the phalanx and wielded his spear and shield with his compatriots.

SOLON'S PRESCIENCE

As we've seen, Attic farms averaged only about ten acres in size. Why were they so uniformly small? This may have been intentional. Around 592 B.C., Solon, scion of a wealthy merchant family, was elected *archon*, or chief magistrate. In order to prevent massive land foreclosures and civil strife, he canceled the oppressive debts borne by many farmers, as had previously been done in Mesopotamia and Israel.

Solon may also have been at least partially responsible for the absence of large farms, although the details are not well established. By the eighth century B.C., Athens, along with most of the other city-states, had divided most of the arable land into very small plots tilled by tens of thousands of individual farmer-hoplite-citizens. Socrates ascribed the invention of geometry to the need for accurate calculation of farm size and yield. Small plots became a hallowed institution, revered even by the conservative philosophic elite of later centuries, including Plato and Aristotle, the latter of whom wrote more than 100 political commentaries on the various Greek states.

The critical moment in the birth of Athenian democracy came when Solon organized the judicial system around assemblies of ordinary Athenians, even landless free noncitizens, who at that time were barred from the ruling legislative Assembly. Although Solon did not "invent" democracy, he discovered the secret to its survival—a judiciary that was *independent* of the state's power. Such a judicial apparatus could be counted on to protect the life, liberty, and property of ordinary people. The history of Athens amply demonstrates that such protection, while often far from perfect, was a vast improvement over what had preceded it and what would follow. We cannot pinpoint the origin of these bulwarks of modern property rights—rule of law and equality under the law—with accuracy, but Solon's judicial reforms are as good a candidate as any.

The hugely expensive Peloponnesian War (431–404 B.C.) destroyed the pattern of widespread small Greek landholdings. High wartime taxes gradually forced an overwhelming majority of geôrgoi off their land, and the archaic pattern of large aristocratic estates returned. By the second century B.C., farms ran to thousands of acres. These huge farms, worked by noncitizens and slaves, supported only a fraction of the former Greek population. Since these large "corporate" farms were less efficient than the small farms of the hoplites, total tax revenues fell. The authorities had no choice but to raise taxes still higher, forcing yet more farmers off the land and triggering a societal death spiral.

A nation's long-term success depends on the extension of economic opportunity to a majority, or at least a substantial minority, of its citizens. In an agricultural society, this means only one thing: land ownership. Unfortunately, there is only so much land. In the ancient world, the tendency for it to accumulate into large tracts as it fell into fewer hands eventually proved fatal to the Greek city-state, as it did later in Rome. Democracy in a predominantly agricultural nation is a fragile bloom. Once property holdings concentrate excessively, as inevitably occurs, political and economic stability vanish.

Why should we care about the brief flowering of property rights in a small, if culturally influential, region of the ancient world? Because the story informs us of three things:

- Vigorous property rights require an independent judiciary.

- An economically enfranchised citizenship is crucial to a society's productivity.

- Property rights alone are not sufficient to produce vigorous and sustained economic growth.

Advanced as the ancient Greeks were, they did not possess the other three conditions necessary for economic growth: an adequate scientific framework, sophisticated capital markets, or efficient transport and communication. It would be another two thousand years before the convergence of all four of these factors blessed mankind with sustained prosperity.

PROPERTY RIGHTS IN ROME

From its founding in around 500 B.C. until the Triumvirate of Caesar, Pompey, and Crassus in 60 B.C., Rome was theoretically a republic, ruled by two consuls elected to one-year terms by popular assemblies. The judges, or *praetors*, ranked next in the hierarchy. The supreme legal authority was the urban praetor, first appointed in 367 B.C.

Ostensibly, the praetor did not create the law. Roman law initially consisted of the so-called Twelve Tablets, supposedly promulgated around 450 B.C., and a thin trickle of statutes passed by popular assemblies. In practice, however, the praetor both interpreted and created the law by suppressing old causes of action or creating new ones with judicial statutes known as *ius honorarium*.

The first praetors were priests, but by the third century B.C. a secular legal tradition had evolved. This new system established a complex scheme of property rules, much of which seems remarkably enlightened to the modern reader. For example, a woman's property remained under her control during marriage and reverted fully to her in the event of divorce. Although a dowry became the husband's property during marriage, it, too, reverted to the wife with divorce. A peculiarity of female property rights was that women required an administrator, or *tutor*, for formal property transactions, such as the sale of land or slaves.[9]

Other parts of Roman law strike the modern eye as bizarre. The senior male family member—the paterfamilias—held the power of life and death over every other family member. While he was alive, his children and grandchildren could not own property. Theoretically, even a fifty-year-old consul remained beholden to his father. In practice, however, this was rarely a serious problem because of the short life expectancies of the time. Historians estimate that only 10% of forty-year-olds had living fathers. Further, with the passage of time, Roman law gradually relaxed these strictures, first for the war earnings and plunder of soldiers and later in much wider circumstances.

Strangest of all to the modern observer is the notion that even highly respected professionals such as doctors, teachers, and businessmen could be *slaves*. In the Roman world, property rights over one's mere self could not be taken for granted, even by society's most accomplished members.

The Romans enforced strict, detailed, and highly sophisticated laws on commercial transactions and property rights. They well understood the subtleties of stolen property, for example. Since lax enforcement encouraged thievery and overly strict enforcement made good-faith purchases difficult and hindered commerce, Roman law carefully distinguished *ownership* from *possession*, which could be adjudicated separately, if need be.

For the first time in history, the law distinguished between ordinary small transactions, for which simple physical conveyance (*traditio*) sufficed, and valuable transfers, particularly of land, for which the law required formal written conveyance (*mancipatio*).

The Romans greatly advanced the law concerning capital markets. The law carefully differentiated among different classes of lenders.

Typically, a bank deposit that produced interest was known as a *mutuum*. Since the deposit yielded interest, the depositor necessarily bore the risk associated with bank failure and had a relatively low claim on the bank's assets in that event. On the other hand, a deposit that was not lent out, but remained in the bank's coffers and did not yield interest (*depositum*), could be recovered by its owner more easily if a bank failed.

Complex laws governed loan security arrangements. In modern society, large loans are secured with real property, that is, collateral. When a homeowner defaults on a mortgage, the lender may repossess his house. In Rome, all security was by personal guarantee. Further, it was almost always backed by a friend, associate, or family member. In the event of default, guarantors became personally liable. Curiously, creditors had only a single opportunity for recovery from guarantors. They could sue only one; if unsuccessful, they could not proceed down the list. It was thus in a creditor's interest to possess detailed information about each guarantor. In today's world, a request for such a loan guarantee would strain most relationships and would likely be refused. In Rome, its provision was part of the code of every day social responsibility.

The ancient world, as might be expected, dealt harshly with default. In Rome, failure to repay even the smallest debt could result in the seizure of a debtor's whole estate, which would then be sold off at auction. In extreme cases, the debtor was jailed until he discharged his debt, a practice that persisted into the nineteenth century in the Western world as the debtor's prison. Thus, default was not solely a legal remedy; it was also a mode of punishment whose severity far exceeded the demands of simple justice. Harsh as it was, it greatly improved upon Greek practice, which punished default with slavery.

Requiring such drastic forms of personal surety greatly hobbled and stifled innovation. All new ventures carry with them a significant probability of failure, and the effective entrepreneur willingly embraces the high risk implicit in such enterprises. Losing your wealth in a failed business is bad enough, but it's quite another thing to lose your freedom in the bargain. When the English abolished the debtor's prison and invented the limited liability company fifteen hundred years later, they vastly improved the state of the capital markets and helped ignite world economic growth.

ROME'S FATAL FLAW

Still, by laying out the rules of the commercial game in plain sight, Roman law did make it easier to conduct business. In the social and political spheres, however, Roman law failed. We have seen that over time, the Greek representational system progressively broadened. The opposite happened in Rome. By 200 B.C., foreign conquest had become the driving economic force of the Republic, as slaves and booty poured into Italy. This rush of liquidity created huge plantations assembled from land bought from small farmers.

Rome heavily "taxed" poor farmers by prolonged conscription into its legions. The rich avoided the conscription problem by working their land with slaves, who could not serve in the army lest they rise up against their masters. The Republic's popular assembly, the *Concilium Plebis*, did attempt reform in 133 B.C., when two of its leaders, the brothers Tiberius and Gaius Gracchus, proposed the distribution of state land to the poor. Almost immediately agents of the patrician Senate assassinated Tiberius; Gaius's turn came twelve years later. The overthrow of the Republic and the dictatorship of Julius Caesar in 45 B.C. destroyed the last shred of public accountability. It also spelled the end of Roman judicial independence.

After the fall of the Republic, the emperor made the law. Although he usually had help from legal professionals, some emperors, notably Claudius and Septimius Severus, delighted in handling court cases themselves. Most legal issues, of course, did not involve the emperor; separate offices, each staffed with a large retinue of civil servants, dealt with petitions. No matter how sophisticated the statutes and no matter how complex the apparatus, the emperor, an absolute ruler, corrupted Roman law. In this regard, Roman law was little different than that of a primitive tribe, in which the chief also acts as judge and jury.

Even during the Republic, jurists worked under intense political pressure. The position of praetor was in reality a stepping-stone to a consulship, which was itself the gateway to membership in the all-powerful Senate. In the last years of the Republic, eight praetors vied for only two positions as consul. Praetors could not afford to make powerful enemies, and most historians doubt that they had any real judicial independence. Accordingly, the civil and property rights of ordinary Romans without connections or influence were precarious.

During the Empire, all semblance of judicial independence disappeared. The emperor, if he so desired, both made and enforced the law.
Such an environment imperiled the life and property of the ordinary citizen, who thus had little incentive to innovate and invest.

The Roman system had yet another major flaw: Political and civil
rights were subordinated to property rights, an arrangement that
destabilized the societal structure. In all societies, slavery and conscription corrode the spread of property rights. Cheap and available slaves
make it easy to work large estates. Worse, the Roman system exempted
most large landowners from taxation and conscription. If the state can
punish free citizens with decades of conscription and crushing taxes, why
bother to work a family plot when it is far easier to sell it to a wealthy
neighbor who is exempt from both?

Both slavery and prolonged conscription were too deeply ingrained
into the Roman system to be seriously questioned. While the Greeks
also sanctioned slavery, they also gradually lowered the property bar for
the full enjoyment of civil and political rights. By the time of the
Peloponnesian War, most city-states had bestowed full citizenship, with
all its privileges, upon the majority of native-born males.

A nation that subsists on conquest lives on the sword's edge. When
the spoils of empire-building ceased to flow into Rome in the third century A.D., the deficiencies could not be made up by taxes on its atrophied agricultural and commercial sectors. As a consequence the
Western Empire collapsed in the fifth century A.D.[10]

THE RISE OF THE COMMON LAW IN ENGLAND

The concept of property rights is as old as civilization itself, and probably
older. This is not the case with the rights of individuals, which in the ancient world were protected only by a few Greek city-states. In the ancient world, individual rights, supported by an independent judiciary,
was a fragile concept, briefly flowering in Greece and republican Rome
before disappearing completely under the Empire and the dark centuries
that followed its collapse.

By 1600, the powerful combination of individual rights and property rights was in full bloom in England, well before John Locke described his system of natural law. Americans, in their turn, give far too much credit to Thomas Jefferson's proclamation of the self-evident rights of "life, liberty, and the pursuit of happiness."

In fact, in the Constitutional debates of 1787, opponents of the document fretted that it did not sufficiently protect their liberties, typically referred to as the "rights of Englishmen."[11] As a concession to the Anti-Federalists, the Bill of Rights—the first ten amendments—were appended to the Constitution. The Fifth Amendment specifically guaranteed due process and protection from unjust confiscation. Further due-process protection was later added by the Fourteenth Amendment.

The origins of modern economic prosperity are inextricably intertwined with the development of property rights and individual rights in England, beginning shortly after the start of the second millennium. This does not mean that property rights did not evolve independently in other locations, most notably in Renaissance Italy and, later, in Holland. But it was in the Sceptered Isle that these rights attained a vigor, momentum, and importance that forever altered the course of world history.

We can trace the lineage of the relevant clauses in the Fifth and Fourteenth amendments, and perhaps the very origins of Western prosperity itself, back to the beginning of the second millennium, to the seeming inability of King John of England to get along with both his subjects and Pope Innocent III. During the medieval period, most Western rulers were theoretically vassals of the pope. In effect, the ruler transferred ownership of his kingdom to Rome, which then leased it back as a feudatory of the Church for tribute—in John's case, one thousand marks of silver per year. The system was, in a manner of speaking, a holy shakedown racket. In return for this kickback, the king could count on the pope, for example, to threaten rebellious barons with excommunication. As a bonus, the Holy Father also shielded the king from the fires of eternal damnation.

But John balked at this arrangement, and in 1209, Innocent III excommunicated him. Three years later, the Vatican officially dispossessed him of his kingdom. The next year, John capitulated to the pope's demands.

After being roundly beaten by Philip Augustus in a campaign to re-cover Normandy in the summer of 1214, John desperately needed funds for further military action. He pressured his barons, encroached on their lands, raised rents on royal tenants, and confiscated their property. John's mistake was that he took from the barons arbitrarily, without the re-quired proceedings—what we now call due process. Worse, he promul-gated and applied laws and penalties *retroactively* and without warning. He also seized Church land, hanged prisoners of war, and took baronial offspring hostage in order to secure their fathers' loyalty.

John had already acquired a reputation among the barons and their subjects for outrageous behavior, and late in 1214 they finally rose up against him. Under the leadership of Robert Fitzwalter, they occupied London and forced the king into a negotiation at Runnymede. On June 15, 1215, the combatants ended the hostilities by signing a lengthy agreement, sixty-three chapters in all, that was initially called the Articles of the Barons, then the Great Charter, and, in modern times, the Magna Carta. The barons forced John to execute the agreement because, in seizing their property, he had flagrantly violated the nation's implicit code of conduct—the common law.

ENGLAND'S HAPPY ACCIDENT

By the time John and his barons met at Runnymede, English jurists had laid down a solid foundation of case law governing the rights, duties, and punishment of all Englishmen—commoners, aristocrats, and, theoreti-cally, even the monarch himself. The term "common law" refers to this accumulated case law. The primacy of this accretion of judicial decisions makes common law unique—until 1600, Parliament rarely legislated in the absence of common law precedent. Even then, parliamentary statute almost always served to summarize and streamline preexisting case law. Parliament rarely acted upon areas in which common law was silent and never passed legislation that contradicted common law.

The renowned seventeenth-century jurist Edward Coke was fond of saying that common law was superior to statute law.[12] In modern times, the English origins of common law serve to contrast it with the "civil law," which derived from Roman statute and predominates throughout the rest of Europe and in much of the world. The differences between common law and civil law are well beyond the scope of this book. As a broad generalization, however, common law emphasizes the primacy of legal precedent and the division of power between the judiciary and other branches of government, while the institutions of civil law are more centralized, with legislative action having primacy. The key difference between the two systems is this: Those wishing to influence the institutions of a civil law nation need only capture the legislator, whereas in a common law nation, one must influence all three major branches of government, a difficult task indeed.[13]

Previous Plantagenet and Norman rulers had granted less extensive charters to commoners and nobility. The Magna Carta acquired its pride of place in the minds of Englishmen over the succeeding centuries from the dramatic circumstances of its birth.

The Magna Carta applied four remedies to the conflicts between King John and the baronial nobility. First, it forced the king to disgorge all of his ill-gotten gains. Second, it required that he not repeat his thefts, kidnappings, and murders. Third, it codified the "rights of Englishmen" and explicitly extended them to all freemen. Finally, and most important, it described in detail the procedures required to secure those rights.[14]

Many chapters of the Great Charter seem arbitrary or obscure to the modern ear. The first and last chapters promised the Church freedom from royal interference. Chapters 10 and 11 detailed how interest was to be paid to Jewish moneylenders. Chapter 54 stated that no one could be arrested on the testimony of a woman, except when the case involved the death of her husband.

Particularly resonant to the American reader, however, is Chapter 12, which linked taxation and parliamentary participation—i.e., no taxation without representation. Magna Carta made explicit that new taxes could not be levied without the consent of "the general council of the nation."

Not surprisingly, the bulk of the Charter—Chapters 17 through 61—dealt with the area most abused by John—the administration of justice.

Chapter 20, for example, forbade unjust fines, as well as the confiscation of tools necessary for a man's livelihood. What determined whether a fine was unjust? "The law of the land"—that is, English common law. Chapters 28 through 31 forbade various arbitrary takings of specific kinds of property by the king.

For the first time in history, the king was held not to be above the law. The most momentous promise was contained in Chapter 39, which stipulated that no freeman could be "arrested, or detained in prison, or deprived of his freehold, or outlawed, or banished, or in any way molested; and we will not set forth against him nor send against him, unless by the lawful judgment of his peers or by the law of the land."

Moreover, these protections were granted to *all* free men, not merely to clergy, earls, and barons. In other words, the king could not arbitrarily deprive any man of his life, liberty, or property. *Due process* was required, predating Coke, Locke, and Jefferson by six centuries.

Additional bad news awaited the king. Chapters 52 and 53 compelled him to restore property that had been unjustly taken in the years before the signing of the Magna Carta. Perhaps most galling of all to King John was the provision in Chapter 61 that set up a committee of twenty-five barons that was empowered to review and, if necessary, reverse royal injustices.

The Great Charter even struck a small blow for free trade. Chapters 41 and 42 forbade the king from impeding the travel and trade of merchants, both English and foreign, except during time of war.[15]

Not since the halcyon days of Greek democracy had so much freedom been granted to so many. With that freedom came the opportunity to prosper. It is not too great a leap to see King John's capitulation on June 15, 1215 as the fuse that would detonate the later explosion of world economic growth.

By contrast, the flowering of individual rights in Greece was confined to a four-century period and was limited to a small group of valleys that were within a few days' walk of the Athenian agora. The laws of the Roman Empire had offered no such protections. Attempting to limit the emperor's power did not promote one's longevity, and in any case, it was not likely to succeed. Attempting to place limits on the rulers of Europe's medieval successor states was an equally futile exercise. For all practical purposes, Magna Carta marked ground zero for the explosion of individual personal and property rights whose shock waves reverberate around the globe to this day.

Eight centuries later, there still remain vast swaths of territory untouched by this revolution. We cannot, however, mistake its relentless progress. Princeton University political scientist Michael Doyle has traced the history of "liberal democracy," by which he means the presence of representative democracy, judicial rights, and property rights (i.e., a market economy). Below are tabulated the number of nations so blessed. As late as 1790, there were only three—Britain, the U.S., and Switzerland. As can be seen, their number has increased dramatically in the past two centuries, with only a brief interruption that coincided with the interwar rise of fascism.*

Year	Liberal Democracies
1790	3
1848	5
1900	13
1919	25
1940	13
1960	36
1975	30
1990	61

Needless to say, liberal democracy in England did not burst into full blossom on that spring day at Runnymede, but its seed had been planted in fertile soil. Of the lasting importance of Magna Carta, David Hume said, "The barbarous license of the kings, and perhaps for the nobles, was thenceforth somewhat more restrained: Men acquired

---

* An even better definition of "liberal democracy" is provided by Francis Fukuyama: "Liberal" means that individual rights, particularly property rights, are protected by the state. "Democracy" means that a nation's leaders are chosen from a universal electorate voting by secret ballot in multiparty elections. According to this paradigm, nineteenth-century Britain was liberal, but not a democracy, and the Islamic Republic of Iran is a democracy, but not liberal. See Francis Fukuyama, *The End of History and the Last Man*, (New York: Avon Books, 1992), 42–44.

some more security for their properties and their liberties: And government approached a little nearer to that end. . . ."[16]

The treacherous John, of course, had no intention of honoring the
agreement, and the royalist counterattack began within months. On August 24, 1215, he received a dividend on his belated investment in the
Vatican: a papal bull that nullified the charter. Fortunately for England,
the old scoundrel was dead within a year. His son and successor, Henry
III, required a regent. The weak boy king and his regent compromised
with the barons; under some duress the regent twice confirmed the
charter. When Henry III formally ascended the throne, he reissued the
charter in a special ceremony. In 1225, he streamlined the document to
thirty-nine chapters.

Henry's 1225 charter is considered by most scholars to be the defini-
tive version. Henry III and his successor, Edward I, confirmed the document about a half-dozen times, with Parliament doing so dozens of times
more over the ensuing centuries.

Chapter 29 of the 1225 document replaced Chapter 39 of the 1215
charter. It is worth repeating its most commonly accepted translation
from the Latin:

> No freeman shall be taken, or imprisoned, or be disseised* of his free-
> hold, or liberties, or free customs, or be outlawed, or exiled, or any
> otherwise destroyed; nor will we not pass upon him, nor condemn
> him, but by lawful judgment of his peers, or by the law of the land.
> We will sell to no man, we will not deny or defer to any man ei-
> ther justice or right.[17]

This is a much more sweeping and powerful declaration of rights
than that found in Chapter 39 of the original charter. The new version
replaced the narrow protections of the older document with a general
guarantee of the "liberties" and "customs." No man was to be denied
"justice or right." Very little in the U.S. Constitution's Bill of Rights, in
fact, cannot be inferred from this remarkable paragraph. The new charter
forbade the king from arbitrarily depriving any free citizen of his rights.
Thenceforth, the abridgement of anyone's freedom or property rights
required due process.

---

* To be disseised is to be wrongfully dispossessed.

Both the 1215 and 1225 charters ensured the protection of property from the Crown's greed. Numerous chapters in both versions detailed precise procedures and payments required of the king before he could requisition private property such as corn and carriages, forming the basis for the takings clause of the Fifth Amendment to the U.S. Constitution.

Early on, Henry Bracton, a thirteenth-century jurist and compiler of the first known British legal compendium, *The Statute and Common Law of England* (in Latin, of course), recognized the revolutionary implications of the Magna Carta. For the first time, the king was explicitly subject to the common law: "The king must not be subject to any man, but to God and the law; *for the law makes him king.*" (Italics added) Thus did equality under the law, applying to both the free peasant and to the king, make its first appearance in human history. Since it applied to the king, then it certainly applied to judges and members of Parliament. Thus was established one more constituency for property rights: If the law applies to the lawgiver, then he can hardly be expected to sanction a capricious taking of another's life, liberty, and possessions, lest the same fate befall him—the golden rule writ large.[18]

For the first time since ancient Greece, the law treated all free men equally, from the humblest farmer to the king. This was very different from the state of affairs in ancient Rome and in the medieval world, where the law recognized several different classes of people. Only in England and in parts of ancient Greece did the leveling of social class allow the emergence of the rule of law, and with it, property rights. To paraphrase Churchill, it was not the end of tyranny. It was not even the beginning of its end. In 1215, the beginning of despotism's decay was, however, first glimpsed in the English-speaking world, a process that continues to this day in slow, stuttering fashion around the globe.

For the next five hundred years, successive English monarchs attacked property rights and the rule of law with varying degrees of vigor and cunning. But for the nurturing and protection of generations of jurists, philosophers, and parliamentarians, property rights and individual liberties might have been snuffed out by the Plantagenets, Lancasters, Yorks, Tudors, or Stuarts, and Western prosperity might never have been born. Among this story's heroes, two stand out—Edward Coke and John Locke.

PROPERTY'S STONEMASON

In the centuries following Runnymede, the British began to regard the Magna Carta, together with subsequent royal and parliamentary charters, as the bulwark of their individual freedoms—the rights of Englishmen. Sir Edward Coke was born into this tradition in 1552 at Mileham, in Norfolk. Upon graduating Cambridge he entered Lincoln's Inn in London to study law. His rise was meteoric, and his judicial skills and encyclopedic knowledge of jurisprudence propelled him at an early age into the thick of the high-profile cases of the era. He rapidly became the greatest legal practitioner of his time and occupied the highest judicial and legislative offices, including Speaker of the House of Commons. Although brilliant and scrupulously honest, his courtroom behavior was outrageous. When, as attorney general, he prosecuted Sir Walter Raleigh for treason, he treated the great man with contempt, famously remarking, "Thou hast an English face, but a Spanish heart!"

In 1606, he was appointed to head the court of common pleas and was later made justice of the King's Bench. His terrifying performances in these offices served to enhance his judicial independence and buttressed the power of the courts against both the king and Parliament. His decisions and opinions in large part formed the foundation of the modern tripartite separation of powers among executive, legislature, and judiciary.

The Tudor prosecutorial instrument of choice was the Privy Council, which favored Roman (civil) law, as opposed to the common law observed in the kingdom's ordinary courts. Roman law provided the Privy Council and the Crown's other agents with the flexibility to pursue the monarch's divine rights, and the seventeenth century saw the climax of the great battle between the courts, Parliament, and the Crown, that is, between the common and Roman-style Crown courts.[19]

Coke's judicial archrival was none other than Sir Francis Bacon, who served as the attorney general for James I. In that rivalry lies Coke's best-known judicial defiance of royal authority. In 1606, the Bishop of Litchfield brought suit claiming that James had granted him a benefice (the salary and expenses of a bishop). The king denied having made the grant and, through Bacon, requested that a verdict be delayed until he (the king) could personally discuss the case with the judges. Though such a request would shock a modern court, there was nothing particularly unusual about it in the seventeenth century. Coke denied the request and convinced his fellow judges to declare, in writing, that the king's demand was illegal.

A highly displeased James summoned the judges to his chambers, where he demanded that they reverse their ruling. Coke's colleagues fell upon trembling knee and begged royal forgiveness. But Coke did not cower. He calmly informed His Majesty that he could not comply. When further pressed by the king, Coke insisted that he would fulfill his charge as a judge.

James exacted retribution by having Coke removed from office; Coke's neck was saved only because of the immense popularity he had earned as protector of the common man. He returned to Parliament, where, true to character, he continued to defend parliamentary rights against royal prerogative. Years later, under Charles I, Coke suffered the indignity of seeing many of his opinions edited out of a book of his reports.*

This episode, while not unique for the era, was emblematic. The ancient Greeks had been the first to realize that the protection of property rights was the duty of an *independent* judiciary. Now, for the first time in European history, a judge had faced down royal power. Coke probably had this very thought in mind when he refused to prostrate himself before James. In an earlier era, such *lese-majesté* would have proved fatal. But Coke had correctly calculated that by the seventeenth century, such absolute power had long slipped from the royal chamber.

Coke's most enduring accomplishment, his four-part *Institutes of the Laws of England,* was written between 1600 and 1615, spanning both his government and judicial careers. His influence was particularly strong in the American colonies. The *Institutes* formed the core of colonial legal training, and Coke's ideas permeated the thinking of the Founding Fathers. One commentator noted in wonderment that even Coke's mistakes were the common law.[20]

---

* In 1631, fifteen years after the confrontation with the Crown, Charles sought to prevent Coke from publishing, as "he is held as too great an oracle amongst the people, and they are mislead by anything that carries such an authority as all things do that he speaks or writes." See William Holdsworth, *Some Makers of English Law* (Cambridge: Cambridge University Press, 1966), 116–118.

The *Institutes* enshrined the Magna Carta as the foundation of common law. Coke, who favored the 1225 version, wrote that the document was known as the "great charter, or Magna Carta, not for the length or largeness of it . . . but . . . in respect of the great weightiness and weighty greatness of the matter contained in it; in a few words, being the foundation of all the fundamental laws of the realm."[21]

Coke's special insight lay in discerning that the common man needed protection not just from the king but also from Parliament. The bulwark of that protection was, of course, the common law, "the best and most common birthright that the subject hath for the safeguard and defense, not only of his goods, lands, and revenues, both of his wife and children, his body, fame, and life also."[22]

While the various versions of Magna Carta were sometimes ambiguous about the rights of ordinary men, Coke steadfastly maintained that the charters guaranteed the rights of all free men, not merely those of barons, other nobles, and clerics. He considered Chapter 29 of the 1225 charter the centerpiece of common law and described it as containing no less than nine "branches." These guaranteed that due process had to be observed in any case involving the following five actions: imprisonment, taking of property, denial of legal counsel, exile, and execution. Further, he believed that Chapter 29 forbade the king, *under any circumstances*, from doing four things: passing sentence or direct punishment, selling any man's rights, denying justice, or conferring special rights upon any man.

It is noteworthy that although the original 1215 charter signed at Runnymede contained a clause—Chapter 61—providing for a committee of barons to oversee the king. Henry III's 1225 charter did not. By the time that Coke wrote the *Institutes*, the judiciary had long been overseeing the king. In 1628, Coke told Parliament, "Magna Carta is such a fellow that he will have no sovereign."[23]

Coke's rulings and opinions permeate English and American law. They do not make for easy reading, but a number of his opinions speak directly to the modern world.[24]

Dr. Bonham's Case was typical of Coke's legal craftsmanship. Thomas Bonham, a physician, practiced in London. Henry VIII had authorized, and Parliament had confirmed, the right of the London-based College of Physicians to license doctors in the city. Although Bonham was clearly competent to practice, it was his misfortune to have trained at Cambridge. The College exercised its monopoly power and excluded Bonham. The College then fined and imprisoned him.

In 1610 Bonham brought a charge of wrongful imprisonment against the College. Coke presided and ruled in favor of the doctor. Although Coke agreed that the College had a duty to license physicians in order to protect the public from incompetent practitioners, he ruled that the College had unjustly deprived Bonham, who was clearly well trained, of an essential liberty—the ability to make a living. By so ruling, Coke asserted almost two hundred years before Adam Smith and three hundred years before the Sherman Antitrust Act, that free markets, unencumbered by monopoly power, were also an essential right. Ruled Coke, "Generally all monopolies are against this great charter, because they are against the liberty and freedom of the subject, and against the law of the land."[25]

The College of Physicians had attempted to cloak its monopolistic behavior behind its status as a guild. The public face of the medieval guild was that of guarantor of high professional standards. In reality, guilds were cartels that restricted entry into a trade or profession and kept prices high. Common law generally held that while *one* seller constituted a monopoly, the guilds constituted *many* sellers, and exempted the guilds from the common law's prohibition of monopolies. The Crown often exploited the guild loophole in the common law (and the 1624 parliamentary statute that codified it) to grant monopolies, and this convenient fiction served to stifle competition and economic development in England as late as the nineteenth century.[26] Coke observed that the College had also violated the common law's principle of disinterested judgment when it levied a fine of ten pounds payable to itself. No judicial body, he ruled, should be allowed to preside in a matter involving its own interests.

As a modern jurist might say, "It's the process, not the outcome, that matters." In much of case law, the most important consequence was procedural, as opposed to substantive. In his decision Coke fired a legal shot that still reverberates. He held that in granting the College the right to imprison and fine physicians, *Parliament* had violated common law right of due process. Coke thus asserted judicial supremacy over the king *and* Parliament. This challenge stood for some time, but the House of Commons eventually overcame judicial supremacy after the parliamentary victory in the Glorious Revolution of 1688. Having bested the Stuarts, Parliament was not about to hand over its newfound power to the courts. To this day, Parliament retains the upper hand over British courts. It was in England's American colonies, which revered Coke, that judicial supremacy took its deepest root.

It is said that judicial supremacy works well only when supported by an explicit and vigorous written constitution, which England does not have, but the U.S. does. (It is also true that judicial supremacy is not spelled out in the U.S. Constitution, but rather was the product of "the accident of John Marshall," the first chief justice of the U.S. Supreme Court.) Whatever its ultimate origin, it was Coke who bequeathed to America the philosophic underpinnings of this essential element in the constitutional separation of powers.

By the early seventeenth century, the connection between individual rights and property rights that we so revere today had been established in England. From our modern perspective, Coke's insistence on these rights, backed up by the force of common law, strikes us as profoundly progressive. Yet many seventeenth-century observers came to the opposite conclusion. At that time, the newly centralized large, absolutist national states, buttressed by the recently rediscovered and reinterpreted Roman law, seemed to be the face of a modernizing Europe. England, by contrast, was considered a backwater, and Coke's musty common law, the accretion of centuries of case law from a jumble of medieval jurisdictions, must have appeared hopelessly outdated.*

The seventeenth century began with Coke's emasculation of royal prerogative at the hands of the common law and ended, in the wake of a disastrous civil war, with the ascendancy of the English Parliament. Although Coke's judicial supremacy fell victim to the parliamentary victories in the Civil War and in 1688, this took nothing away from the benefits that resulted from the Crown's downfall.

---

* In Coke's time, the common law courts battled for preeminence with the courts of the King's Council, Chancery, and Admiralty. The King's Council was run by and answered directly to the Crown; the other two courts were concerned mainly with commercial disputes. The most infamous organ of the King's Council was the Star Chamber, which shared with the Inquisition the use of torture. After emerging victorious over their three rivals, the common law courts adopted much of their case law as precedent. See Holdsworth, 111–13, 131–32.

The next century would see John Locke and the American colonials spread word of the blessings of judicial and parliamentary power throughout the rest of the Western world. This nearly continuous process of dividing and limiting the power of the state among its three branches—the executive, legislative, and judiciary—in turn enhanced the rights of individuals to liberty and property.

By the time of the English Civil War in the mid-seventeenth century, the Englishman's property was more secure than at any previous time in human history. Yet because the other three factors were not well developed, England did not prosper. Over the next 200 years, England would acquire these other three factors, culminating with the invention of steam propulsion and the telegraph in the nineteenth century. At that point, the advantages of England and her daughter nations in the arena of property rights would propel them to a level of prosperity unimaginable to previous generations.

JOHN LOCKE—"THE FUNDAMENTAL LAW OF PROPERTY"

If Edward Coke was the master mason who laid the foundation blocks of civil liberty and property rights, then John Locke was an ornamental sculptor, who eloquently declaimed their rationale and beauty to the wide world beyond the law's cloistered halls.

Born in 1632, shortly after the death of Coke, Locke came of age in the vortex of the English Civil War, which pitted Parliament in a life-and-death struggle against the Stuart Dynasty. His Puritan father saw to it that his son was educated at home and trained in the military service of the parliamentary party. As a young man, Locke wrote, "From the time that I knew anything, I found myself in the storm, which has continued to this time."[27] His career was inextricably bound up with that of Anthony Ashley Cooper, a close friend from Oxford who later became the Earl of Shaftesbury. The wealthy earl became Locke's patron; Locke became his trusted advisor.

Shaftesbury later found himself in the thick of the Civil War on the parliamentary side. Both fled abroad at various stages of the conflict. After Shaftesbury fell from influence in 1675, Locke spent time in France

before returning to London and Oxford. It was in Oxford that he probably wrote most of his seminal *Two Treatises of Government*, which spelled
out his theory of natural law and property rights. In 1681 Shaftesbury
was imprisoned for participating in the "cabal" against Charles II.
Fearing for his safety and in ill health after his release, Shaftesbury fled in
early 1682 to Holland, where he died the next year.

After Shaftesbury's death, Locke remained at Oxford, where he greatly
feared that the eyes of the king were upon him. In fact, lip readers did
routinely monitor his private conversations in the halls of the university.
Like Shaftesbury, Locke eventually escaped to Holland. With the final
victory of the parliamentarians in the Glorious Revolution of 1688, Locke
returned to England a hero, although his continuing fear of the king's
power led him to deny authorship of *Two Treatises* to his dying day.[28]

Writing in reply to Sir Robert Filmer's *Patriarcha*, Locke began *Two
Treatises* around 1680; it was finally published in 1690. Filmer's tract was a
fawning essay on the legitimacy of absolute monarchy, based on the idea
that both common law and the right to property emanated from divinely
derived royal power. In *Two Treatises*, Locke agreed with Hobbes that in a
state of nature, life was "solitary, poor, nasty, brutish, and short." Of necessity, men formed governments to protect themselves. But where Hobbes's
solution was an all-powerful totalitarian state, the "Leviathan," Locke proposed a benign state, whose primary purpose was *the preservation of property*.
(In fairness, Hobbes disputed the divine right of kings and derived governmental legitimacy from the rights of common people.) Further, according
to Locke's natural law, the state's legitimacy derived solely from its ability to
discharge this responsibility. If the state failed, it could be replaced "when-
ever the Legislators endeavour to take away, and destroy the Property of the
People . . . they put themselves into a state of War with the People, who
are thereupon absolved from any further Obedience."[29]

If Locke's *Two Treatises* mirrored sentiments in post–1688 England,
they were music to the ears of the American colonials, who hungrily
seized upon them as justification for insurrection. Indeed, much of the
Second Treatise was lifted nearly intact into the Declaration of Independence, including the following:

> Man being born, as has been proved, with a title to perfect freedom and
> an uncontrolled enjoyment of all the rights and privileges of the law of
> Nature, equally with any other man, or number of men in the world,

hath by nature a power not only to preserve his property—*that is, his life, liberty, and estate. . . .*[30] (Italics added)

Compare the famous third paragraph of the Declaration: "We hold these truths to be self-evident, that all men are created equal, that they are endowed with their Creator with certain unalienable Rights, that among these are Life, Liberty, and the pursuit of Happiness."

Changes in English usage render Jefferson's wording more agreeable to our ears, but given the close similarity, it is perhaps fortunate that to-day's plagiarism police weren't around in 1776.

Notice also how Jefferson changed Locke's "estate" to the more vague "pursuit of happiness."* Columbia University historian Charles Beard created a sensation in 1913 with his *Economic Interpretation of the Constitution,* which emphasized the economic interests of the document's authors. Locke was fixated on property rights, and he exerted such an influence on the Founding Fathers that one might see the origins of the American Revolution itself in a concern for property. For example, in the second treatise, he lays out the right of a legitimate state to tax its citizens but warns that anyone who levies taxes "without such consent by the People, he therefore invades the Fundamental Law of Property."[31]

Locke couched his discussion of individual liberty and property rights in terms of natural law. In doing so, he may have come as close as anyone to identifying the awesome economic potential of common law. Human societies, even the smallest and most primitive, naturally evolve rules governing acceptable customs, behavior, and, eventually, property. Such ancient codes are the ultimate source, and strength, of English common law. Legal scholar Bruno Leoni writes, "The Romans and the English shared the idea that the law is something to be *discovered* more than *enacted* and that nobody is so powerful in his society as to be in a position to identify his own will with the law of the land."[32] In the same vein, Peruvian economist Hernando de Soto points out in his masterful *The Mystery of Capital* that people will not obey laws that are declared by fiat—a successful legal structure must root itself in a society's culture and

---

* Even "pursuit of happiness" was not original to Jefferson. In an early draft of Virginia's Declaration of Human Rights, George Mason, clearly in need of an editor, wrote of "the enjoyment of life and liberty, with the means of acquiring and possessing property, and pursuing and obtaining happiness and safety." See David Greenberg, "Debunking America's Enduring Myths," *New York Times,* 29 June 2003.

history. In other words, property laws must be easily recognizable and acceptable to the populace.[33]

No system of law so incorporates the historical wisdom of its people, and at the same time protects individual liberty and property, as well as does English common law. Today, wherever it flourishes, so, too, does the wealth of nations.

PROPERTY OF THE MIND

Property cannot only be tangible; it can be intellectual as well. Beginning about 1730, the world saw an unprecedented burst of technological innovation. It has continued to the present day and owes itself in no small measure to the birth of patent law. Economist Douglass North points out that inventions produce both private and social benefit—they profit society as well as the inventor.[34] If the law does not reserve a high enough share of that bounty for the inventor, he will not invent. By generously rewarding the inventor, society rewards itself. No sane person expends the enormous amount of capital, time, and effort involved in the creation and mass production of an invention if others can knock it off without penalty. In Imperial China, the situation was even worse. There, the emperor might quickly appropriate a new invention, a fate that befell the creators of printing, paper, and the bill of exchange.[35]

When we talk about "intellectual property," we mean three things: inventions, that is, patents; written material, that is, copyrights; and trademarks. In this section we will concentrate mainly on patent law, the most important economically.

All three types of intellectual property give their owners a *monopoly* on the use of their inventions, writings, and trademarks. Like any other property, this monopoly use is alienable—it can be sold at will to others. Unfortunately, monopolies carry with them a long and sordid history. Rulers frequently granted them to cronies, guilds, and individual tradesmen, usually in exchange for revenues.

We will see in Chapter 8 that during the medieval and early modern periods, the granting of monopolies was a mainstay of state revenue, particularly in Spain and France, where the practice served to stunt innovation and inhibit competition. Moreover, such government-granted monopolies were expensive to police and required huge bureaucracies to enforce.

We'll also discover—in Chapter 7—that a major reason why economic growth took hold first in Holland and England was that government there abandoned its monopolistic practices and instead developed excise taxes as a major source of state revenue.

This brings us to the central paradox of patent law: Too little protection for the inventor saps the incentive to create and produce, while too much protection stifles competition and strangles commerce. This fact was first appreciated in Renaissance Italy, as the critical importance of patent protection to trade and commerce became apparent. Florence granted the first recorded patent in 1421 to Filippo Brunelleschi, famed designer of the Florentine cathedral dome, for the design and use of a large boat that was intended to carry marble and other goods up the Arno to the city.* Little advance in patent protection was made until 1474, when the Venetian Senate passed the first patent law, which stated:

> We have among us men of great genius, apt to invent and discover ingenious devices; and in view of the grandeur and virtue of our City, more such men come to us every day from diverse parts. Now, if provision were made for the works and devices discovered by such persons, so that others, who may see them could not build them and take the inventor's honor away, more men would then apply their genius, would discover, and would build devices of great utility and benefit to our commonwealth.[36]

The law commanded inventors to apply for patents from the Republic's General Welfare Board. If the inventor satisfied the board that the device was original and functioned properly, the board granted patent protection for ten years. Imitators had their devices destroyed and were fined one hundred ducats (about $4,000 in current value). This law, a marvel of legislation for its time, recognized the societal value of a patent system, its incentive to create wealth, and most critically, the importance of granting monopoly only to *original* devices and for a limited time.

---

* The ship, the *Badalone* ("seagoing monster") was not a great success. It sank in the Arno while carrying a load of white marble for the construction of the dome. See Bruce W. Bugbee, *Genesis of American Patent and Copyright Law* (Washington, D.C.: Public Affairs Press, 1967), 17–19.

The early English experience with monopolies and patents was not as salutary as that in Italy. The Crown occasionally granted monopolies for worthwhile endeavors, such as the one granted to Flemish wool and cloth artisans in the fourteenth and fifteenth centuries in order to attract them to Britain. More often than not, however, monopolies were bestowed upon court favorites in exchange for a share of the profits. These royal edicts became known as "letters patent," the word "patent" signifying that the letters were not sealed—that is, public. These early English procedures were distinctly inferior to the Venetian ones. Venice relied on a public body and a well-defined application procedure, while the English Crown granted patents on a whim. Elizabeth I particularly abused letters patent for her own gain; Sir Walter Raleigh, long one of her favorites, was granted a monopoly on wine bars.

In 1571, early in Elizabeth's reign, the first parliamentary opposition to this practice appeared.[37] Undeterred, Elizabeth continued issuing letters patent for many long-established processes, including the production of salt, saltpeter, and lubricating oil. The economic depression of 1597, which forced the public to pay the high costs of monopoly products with falling incomes, reinforced outrage at these practices, and in that year the Queen's Bench ruled that monopolies violated common law. In 1601, Elizabeth backpedaled, reversing many of her earlier grants. Not coincidentally, Coke's defiance of her successor, James I—discussed earlier in this chapter—occurred only five years later. The end of the sixteenth century marks the point at which the rule of law completely eclipsed royal divine rule in England, setting the nation on the path to civil war.

Further legal challenges ensued. The most notorious was Darcy v. Allin, in which the courts found that Elizabeth's grant of a monopoly on the sale of playing cards to Darcy, her groom, was a violation of common law.[38]

The courts did uphold monopolies for "projects of new invention, so they be not contrary to the Law, nor mischievous to the State, by raising prices of commodities at home, or hurt of trade, or otherwise inconvenient."[39] In 1615, in the Cloth Workers of Ipswich Case, the court held that this particular monopoly, granted by James I, was legal, since it was valid for a limited time and it applied to a new invention.

These two requirements for patent protection—novelty and limited duration—have remained with us to the present day and form the philosophic basis for patent law in all Western nations. In 1624, Parliament rolled up the accumulated case law into the Statute of Monopolies, which outlawed all monopolies except those that met the above two criteria.

The case law and statute did not solve the fundamental problem with English patent procedure: The Crown still granted them, and monarchs still abused the process. Patents even became a minor issue in the English Civil War, with the parliamentarians demanding curtailment of the royal patent prerogative. Further, the process itself was extremely cumbersome. Inventors had to visit ten different offices and incurred fees totaling nearly £100, then a small fortune. Not until 1852 would royal involvement in the English patent system cease.

From the outset, American patent procedures bested those in the mother country. Prior to the American Revolution, most of the American colonies had sophisticated patent procedures, in many cases more streamlined and more efficient than in England. After the defeat of the British in 1781, the fledgling United States stole the lead in patent law from the mother country.

The Articles of Confederation limited the U.S. government to the conduct of war and foreign affairs, leaving taxation and the regulation of commercial activities, including patents, to the individual states. But the inefficiencies of this decentralized system soon manifested themselves—an inventor might patent a device in Pennsylvania, which could then be copied in New York, where the imitator himself would then apply for patent rights. Thus would begin a costly daisy chain of imitation and litigation that would spiral out of control throughout many states.

The Founding Fathers keenly understood the importance of intellectual property, none more so than the U.S. Constitution's chief architect, James Madison. He had extensive experience with patent matters in the Virginia Assembly and was well aware of the weaknesses of a patent system that was fractured across thirteen jurisdictions. With the strong backing of northern industrialists, Madison inserted this clause into Article 1 of the Constitution: "The Congress shall have the power . . . to promote the Progress of Science and useful Arts, by securing for limited Times to Authors and Inventors the exclusive Right to their respective Writings and Discoveries. . . ."

Jefferson, unhappy with the Constitution and with a strong federal government in general, opposed the clause. In a reply to Jefferson in October 1788, Madison reasoned,

With regard to Monopolies, they are justly classed among the greatest nuisances in Government. But is it clear that as encouragements to literary works and ingenious discoveries, they are not too valuable to be wholly renounced? Would it not suffice to reserve in all cases a right to the public to abolish the privilege at a price to be specified in the grant of it? Is there not also infinitely less danger of this abuse in our Governments than in most others? Monopolies are sacrifices of the many to the few. Where the power is in the few it is natural for them to sacrifice the many to their own partialities and corruptions. *Where the power as with us is in the many not in the few, the danger cannot be very great that the few will thus be favored. It is much more to be dreaded that the few will be unnecessarily sacrificed to the many.*[40] (Italics added)

When the first Congress mandated by the new Constitution convened on March 4, 1789, the life-and-death legislative and fiscal issues of the new republic occupied its time, and comprehensive intellectual property legislation took a back seat. But soon enough, writers and inventors began to seek the passage of "private legislation" that would grant protection to their books and devices. A scant five weeks after Congress first met, Thomas Tucker of South Carolina presented the first of these bills for his constituent, a physician named David Ramsay, for a history of the Revolution. Thus began an avalanche of such private requests to the House and Senate for copyright and patent protection. Congress soon recognized the need for patent and copyright legislation, and set about creating it.

After considerable wrangling in the House and Senate, George Washington signed the first American patent act into law on April 10, 1790. Its provisions seem fantastic to the modern reader—entry into the system began at the secretary of state, who acted in conjunction with the secretary of war and the attorney general. The key point about the act was that it created a *system*, an impartial mechanism manned by disinterested, if high-ranking, officials, who evaluated each proposal solely on its merits. It was light years ahead of the cumbersome, royalty-based procedures in England.

It is a sublime irony indeed that administration of the patent act fell to Thomas Jefferson, the first secretary of state. Although an opponent of an intrusive central government and of centralized patent procedures in particular, Jefferson was an avid inventor and thus was uniquely qualified to be the first patent examiner. He applied himself to the task with relish and skill.

The new system was efficient and inexpensive. On a single day in 1791, Jefferson issued fourteen patents, costing between four and five dollars each, in sharp contrast to the king's ransom required by the English process.

In 1802, Jefferson, as president, oversaw the establishment of a separate Patent Office in the Department of State, now headed by Madison. In the ensuing decades, the system became a little *too* efficient—by 1835, the Patent Office granted in excess of 9,000 patents. Fraud and duplication were widespread. In 1836, Congress created the Commissioner of Patents and added a staff of professional assistants—a revolutionary concept for the time. A more rigorous examination procedure was instituted, and the new system soon aided in the birth of many of America's best-known industrial firms, including those producing Colt's revolvers, Otis's elevators, and Eastman's cameras.

The British soon realized that they were losing the Patent Race to the U.S. and finally reformed their three-hundred-year-old system in 1852. The explosion in the number of patents granted in the U.S. and the U.K. in the nineteenth century, plotted in Figure 2–1, mirrors the rapidly

FIGURE 2–1   PATENTS GRANTED (BY YEAR) 1800–70

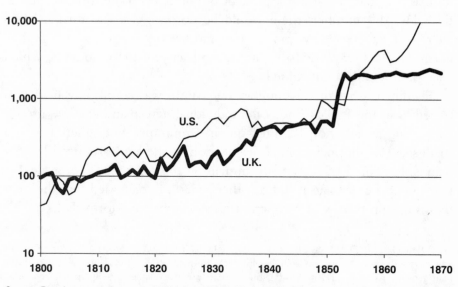

Source: Data by personal communication from James Hirabayashi, U.S. Patent and Trademark Office, and from Allan Gomme, *Patents of Invention* (London: Longmans Green, 1946).

increasing prosperity of the two nations. In retrospect, the eclipse of the mother country by its revolutionary offspring was foreshadowed by the slight American edge in creative energy that is evident in the graph.

The protections provided by the patent apparatuses of England and the U.S. dramatically advanced the concept of private property ownership, and with it, the incentive of individuals to create wealth. It would be no accident that the material manifestations of the nineteenth century's new prosperity—factories, steamships, railroads, and telegraphs— were created by men hypnotized by the prospect of the great profits made possible by the new legal system.

THE TRAGEDY OF THE COMMONS

In 1968, a human ecologist at the University of California named Garrett Hardin published an article in the magazine *Science* carrying this section's title. In the article Hardin spelled out the advantages of property rights as he thought they existed among primitive herdsmen.[*] He asked the reader to imagine a common pasture on which the herdsmen grazed their cattle. The land supported a certain number of cattle; as long as war, famine, and disease kept the numbers of herdsmen and cattle below this number, there would be no problem. Eventually, however, as the society grew more stable and healthy, increased numbers of grazing animals exceeded the carrying capacity of the commons, which was soon befouled and ruined.

Hardin realized that as long as the pasture was commonly held, this tragedy was inevitable. Since each individual herdsman benefited greatly by placing an additional animal on the commons, but suffered only a small share of the incremental degradation of the land produced by that animal, he would graze as many animals on the commons as possible, regardless of the damage it did to others. Hardin concluded that the only fix for this problem was "property rights or something formally like it."[41]

---

* Garrett Hardin, "The Tragedy of the Commons," *Science* 162 (1968): 1243–1248. Hardin's article was intended as an environmentalist plea for population control and global resource management; paradoxically, its most lasting influence may well be as a libertarian economic manifesto.

The relevance of Hardin's conclusion to both ancient and modern agriculture is obvious. In the years following the article, "the tragedy of the commons" found application in many other fields. It has particular relevance to the crisis in health care, for example, where the "overgrazing" of the medical commons by patients insensitive to cost leads to a decline in the availability and quality of medical care for all.

Both common sense and the logic of the commons dictate that the individual herdsman or farmer on a privately owned plot will be far more productive than he would be on communally owned land or on land owned by others. It is not necessary for societies to *consciously* strive, as modern nations did, toward policies, laws, and customs regarding property rights. The normal random variation in customs and rules among communities ensures that some will place a greater or lesser emphasis on individual ownership.

Throughout history, then, and all other things being equal, agricultural societies that placed special emphasis on property rights gained a competitive advantage over their neighbors. Since their crop yields were higher, their populations grew more rapidly and they developed more effective armies. More subtly, when these better-off societies went to war, it was to defend their own land and crops; consequently, their citizen-soldiers had higher fighting morale.

This is precisely what happened in ancient Greece and, in our own time, during the Cold War, the outcome of the latter being decided on the economic, not the military, battlefield. Even the most casual examination of national prosperity in the twentieth century and of the history of the Communist experiment, in particular, cleanly decides the issue: Property matters.

Today, in fact, property rights matter more than ever. In most of the modern world, secure property rights are all that separates the rich from the poor, and the winners from the losers in the race for national prosperity. In the Communist world, for example, the other three foundations of prosperity—scientific rationalism, abundant capital, and modern transport and communication—were solidly in place. In a cruel economic experiment of nature, the postwar governments of Eastern Europe stripped their citizens of property rights and individual liberties with devastating results.

Bear in mind, too, that the meaning of property rights has dramatically changed in the past few centuries. Before about 1800, property was synonymous with land. As we have seen, there is only so much land available. That was how ancient agricultural societies, such as the Greek city-states and the Roman Empire, became unstable. As land grew scarce and expensive, an ever-smaller proportion of the populace could own it. This narrowed the base of landowning citizens who had a stake in that society's welfare. For a nation to thrive, a significant proportion of its citizens need to be property owners so they will have a personal interest in its political process: the "stakeholder effect." In the premodern world, when the land ran out, stakeholders became thinner on the ground, and that nation's days were numbered.

Agricultural concentration, on the other hand, does not destabilize industrial and postindustrial societies. There can be no question, for example, that individual farms in the United States have become far fewer in number—and bigger in size—since the Great Depression. From 1870, when the U.S. Census Bureau began collecting data, until 1935, the average farm size was 155 acres. By 1987, it had tripled to 462 acres. In 1900, 9% of Americans owned farms; today that number is below 1%. Yet few would argue that democratic institutions in the U.S. are less stable now than they were a century ago. The reason is simple: Postindustrial economies no longer need to provide land to citizens in order to turn them into stakeholders. Ownership of nonreal property and capital, both of which are unlimited, serves that purpose nicely. Modern capital ownership can satisfy a much wider proportion of the population than could ever have been achieved even in ancient Attica, where only 200,000 acres of arable land were available to a population of 250,000. Land ownership is finite; capital ownership is limitless.

Our modern Western system was derived largely from English common law, was assembled slowly and painfully over the past thousand years, and was spread worldwide by the sword-point of British colonization and on the wings of American revolutionary idealism. With the fall of Communism, few today question the primacy of property and individual rights as the modern world's fount of prosperity.

CHAPTER THREE

Reason

*Wisdom, which we have derived principally from the Greeks,
is but like the boyhood of knowledge, and has the characteristic
property of boys: It can talk, but it cannot generate.*

—Francis Bacon, *The New Organon*

EVERY DAY, THOUSANDS OF PEOPLE around the world log onto NASA's Website and download a small software program to calculate the local viewings of the International Space Station for the coming week. A few times every month, in almost any location on earth between 60° north latitude and 60° south latitude, spectacular overhead passes grace the skies just after sunset or before dawn as sunlight reflected from the station's massive panels races through the stars.

A small number of the Website's users are aware that three hundred years ago, any celestial calculation, now performed so easily on an ordinary personal computer, required hundreds of hours of mind-numbing labor by the world's greatest mathematicians. In the late seventeenth century, this science of astronomical computation, then in its infancy, hypnotized the public.

The development of celestial mechanics (the study of celestial motion), which culminated in the publication of Newton's *Principia Mathematica* in 1687 and the stunning confirmation of its predictions,

91

heralded a momentous shift in Western thought. The new science was also one of the seminal events in the genesis of modern prosperity.

If one constant defines the modern West, it is the relentless march of scientific progress. It is hard to fathom that there was ever a time during which the observational, experimental, and theoretical study of the natural world was not welcomed. Yet, such was the state of intellectual affairs before the seventeenth century.

Until four hundred years ago, the natural world was a terrifying master and humanity the helpless victim of forces it could not comprehend: disease, drought, flood, earthquake, and fire. Even benign astronomical events, such as comets and eclipses, were frightening occurrences, fraught with superstitious and religious import. Indeed, many of the pioneers of modern astronomy, including Copernicus and Kepler, earned their keep by making astrological predictions that were used by ruler and peasant alike to make everyday decisions.

Mankind combats ignorance and fear by devising belief systems, and civilizations amplify these belief systems into organized religions. Judaism, Christianity, and Islam succeeded not only because they offered a satisfying monotheistic explanation for the calamities that befell mankind, but also because they consoled those suffering the misery of earthly existence with the promise of a more agreeable hereafter. Unfortunately, until very recently organized religions—particularly those with a highly hierarchical priesthood—rarely tolerated alternative worldviews.

In economic terms, until a few hundred years ago, most religions functioned as monopolies and engaged in classic monopolistic behavior—extracting gold, property, and status from their adherents in exchange for approbation in this world and salvation in the next. Modern economists call this "rent-seeking behavior."* In the ancient and medieval West and Middle East, organized religions ossified into static belief systems that stifled inquiry and dissent. Howsoever these belief systems benefited spiritual life on this earth, they simultaneously beggared the material side of existence.

This chapter is concerned with the breaking of the Roman Church's intellectual monopoly, which could not be accomplished without dis-

---

* For a fascinating discussion on the inverse correlation of the intensity of societal spiritual faith and degree of monopolistic behavior on the part of organized religion, see Gary S. Becker and G. N. Becker, *The Economics of Life* (New York: McGraw-Hill, 1997), 15–17.

crediting its methodologies—methodologies that dated from Aristotle. In the two centuries following 1550, this monopoly was finally broken by a courageous group of natural philosophers on the unlikely battleground of celestial mechanics.

Many readers will find this a curious emphasis in a book devoted to economic history. At base, however, the history of economics is the history of technology—after all, modern prosperity rides in the cockpit of invention. Economic growth is virtually synonymous with increased productivity, which in turn is almost entirely the result of technologic advance. The worker who has the command of thousands of horsepower at his fingertips or communicates across the globe in a fraction of a second with the click of a computer mouse is vastly more productive—and prosperous—than the worker who can do neither.

About three centuries ago, the pace of technologic innovation dramatically accelerated. The list of significant mechanical inventions prior to 1700 is a short one: The windmill, the waterwheel, and the printing press pretty well exhaust the roll call. After 1700, in contrast, inventions flowed in an ever-increasing torrent, and with them poured forth the wealth of mankind.

Spurring this burst of innovation was a revolution in the very way Western man observed the natural world and endeavored to understand it. That Western man and Western culture itself are *defined* by this birth of scientific rationalism is not an overstatement. This revolution required that science, or as it was known then, natural philosophy, be severed from its ecclesiastical roots. Mankind could not prosper until it cleaved the spiritual from the temporal and adopted Galileo's credo that "the intention of the Holy Ghost is to teach us how one goes to heaven, not how the heavens go."[1]

THE STARS OVERHEAD

The advent of artificial illumination in the last century divorced mankind from the nighttime sky. In a society without appreciable outside lighting, there is little else to look at during the night *but* the heavens, and the nightly motion of the stars dominated life after sunset in the premodern world. While a very few early modern intellectuals studied the scientific aspects of physics, chemistry, and medicine, a large portion of the populace did have a palpable interest in the prediction of celestial events.

This premodern concern with the skies meant that confirmation of many of the predictions of the new astronomical theories was instantly, publicly, and almost universally demonstrable. This was most spectacularly the case with the predictions of comets and eclipses by Halley and Newton that occurred around 1700. In a flash, mankind had seized the mysteries of the heavens from God and nature. Man was no longer wholly captive to forces beyond his comprehension. The new science freed the European intellect from Western Christianity's stranglehold, itself already weakened by the Reformation and the nonscientific aspects of the Enlightenment.

THE ANCIEN RÉGIME

In the modern world we often refer to the medieval intellectual framework as "Aristotelian," in honor of its deviser, who was also Plato's most famous student and the tutor of Alexander the Great. Aristotle's output was staggering—a system of rhetoric and syllogistic reasoning that forms one of the foundations of Western thought as well as numerous essays on the political structure of the Greek city-states.

Since the dawn of history, man has wondered about the structure of the heavens. Looking up at the night sky, he saw that the stars moved through the firmament around the polestar. Yet their positions relative to one another seemed to be fixed, producing the constellations familiar to humankind. Even the earliest civilizations were aware of this phenomenon. To the ancients, the individual stars and their constellations seemed to be attached to the inside of a perfect sphere that had Earth as its center. Once a day this sphere revolved around the fixed earth. The universe, in this early view, was geocentric. Roughly contemporaneously with Aristotle, other philosophers of the Greek world, including Apollonios and Aristarchus, entertained the idea of a heliocentric system, in which the Sun is the center of the celestial system.

One problem with the geocentric universe was that seven heavenly bodies seemed to meander through this fixed system. The Moon moved against the fixed background of stars and constellations once per day, and the Sun had a similar motion. That much was clear. What was complex and mysterious beyond comprehension was the motion of the other five bodies: Mercury, Venus, Mars, Jupiter, and Saturn. All five followed the same path as the Sun and Moon—the ecliptic—but their motion along the ecliptic through the stars was irregular. This was particularly true of Mars, which in the course of its motion through the constellations made frequent backward loops, as shown in Figure 3–1, a plot of the red planet's course through the heavens for the year 1982. Greek astronomers rejected the heliocentric system of Apollonios and Aristarchus, quite correctly, because its predictions of planetary motion were off by more than ten degrees from what was actually observed.[2] The reason for the inaccuracy was simple—the heliocentric model assumed that the planets moved in perfect circles, when in fact they follow elliptical paths.

In the second century A.D., an astronomer in Alexandria named Claudius Ptolemaeus, later known as Ptolemy, came up with an ingenious system that corrected most of this inaccuracy, which is diagrammed in Figure 3–2. Each of the seven bodies rotated around Earth with two circular motions, not one: a larger primary cycle (called the deferent) around Earth and a smaller epicycle rotating around a focal point on the deferent.[3]

FIGURE 3–1 THE PATH OF MARS ALONG THE ECLIPTIC IN 1982

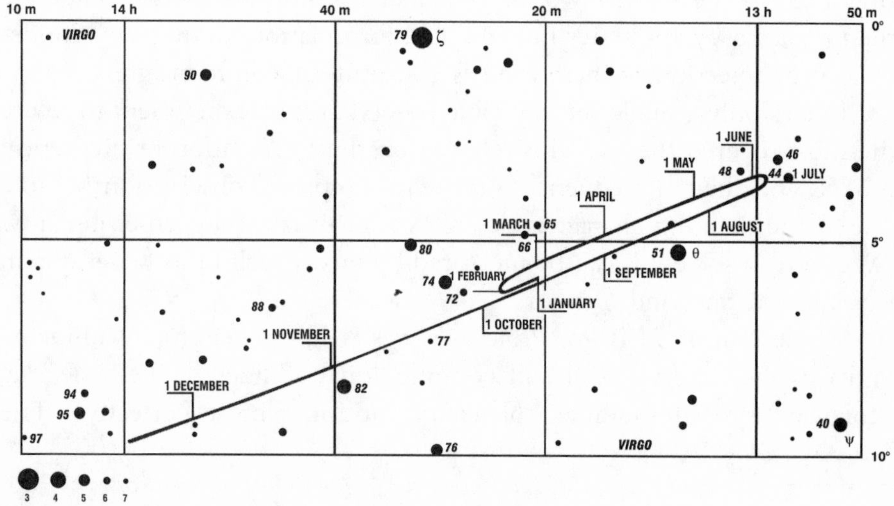

Source: Reproduced and modified with permission of publisher, Ivar Ekeland, *Mathematics and the Unexpected* (Chicago: University of Chicago Press, 1990), 5.

FIGURE 3–2   SIMPLIFIED DIAGRAM OF THE PTOLEMAIC MODEL

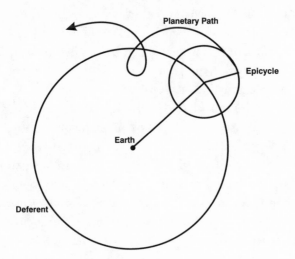

The systems of Ptolemy, Apollonios, and Aristarchus were what scientists would now call "models," that is, simplified, abstract ways of explaining natural phenomena. In this case the models explained how the seven heavenly bodies moved through the constellations. The history of science teaches us that most, if not all, models, no matter how successful they explain the natural world, eventually demonstrate flaws. They are then replaced by yet better models. The formulation, testing, and confirmation or rejection of these models constitute scientific progress.

It takes only a single reproducible observation or experiment to refute the most revered theory. This reliance on the formulation of theoretical models and their subsequent testing with empirical observation became one of the defining characteristics of Western man. In a sense, just how "Western" a society is can be measured by how much of its belief system is subject to this kind of rigor.

As scientific models go, Ptolemy's was wildly successful. Within the limits of the observational and computational abilities of the time, the Ptolemaic system predicted planetary motion almost perfectly.[*] The

---

[*] To the naked eye, the Sun and the Moon appear to have no epicycles. However, very small epicycles were required to explain the seasonal accelerations and decelerations in their orbits. The epicycles were so tiny that they did not produce the backwards motion seen in the planets.

Ptolemaic model's indisputable "advantage" was that astronomers could endlessly fudge the size and timing of the cycles and epicycles to fit new observations. The key point, however, is that to naked-eye observation the Ptolemaic system worked better than a heliocentric system with *circular* orbits. Almost all informed observers of the time found the Ptolemaic model far more appealing intuitively than its alternatives.

The real problem with the Ptolemaic model was not that it was imperfect—all models are—but that over the millennium following its invention, the Church eventually adopted it and invested it with divine authority. Proposing a competing model was not conducive to one's health, either in this world or the next.

As astronomers accumulated more data over the centuries, they called upon the Aristotelian/Ptolemaic system to account for an increasingly complex mass of observations. These demands finally overwhelmed the model. By 1650, the findings spewing from Tyco Brahe's Danish observatory and Galileo's telescopes mandated no less than fifty-five concentric Ptolemaic spheres, Earth being the innermost. (The outermost sphere was called the *primum mobile*, loosely, "prime mover." Its motion was transmitted sequentially to the inner spheres, and finally to Earth.*) The increasing absurdity of this venerated system became obvious, and it finally collapsed of its own weight.[4]

THE TRAJECTORY OF SCIENTIFIC RATIONALISM

Beginning about 1600, the Ptolemaic model served as a warning to astute observers that all was not well scientifically. Natural philosophers in Western Europe were forced to dramatically and irrevocably change the way they thought about the world around them. Figure 3–3 shows the life spans of the principal actors in this story and places them in historical context.

Copernicus, with his heliocentric theory that Earth revolved around the Sun, is credited with breaking the logjam and beginning the revolution.[5] It was continued by three brilliant men of the next generation—

---

* During the Middle Ages, most educated people knew that the world was not flat; the Aristotelian system made sense only with a spherical earth.

FIGURE 3–3

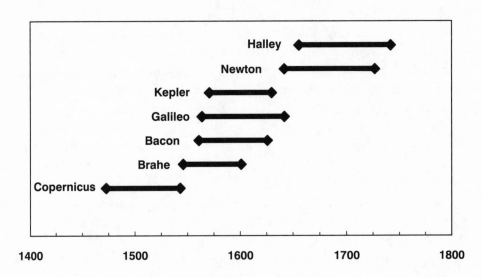

Brahe, Kepler, and Galileo—who produced astounding observational and theoretical scientific advances. Their contemporary, Sir Francis Bacon, although a mediocre experimental scientist, lawyer, and economist, brilliantly diagnosed the flaws in the existing Western intellectual framework and articulated the new scientific method.

A century after this remarkable quintet did their seminal work, Isaac Newton and Edmond Halley stunned the Western world by unlocking the secrets of the cosmos. At a stroke, the Church's role as the guardian of all temporal knowledge was rudely and publicly wrested away from it. Thereafter, the Western citizen might still look to religion to unlock the secrets of the next world, but he would no longer trust it to explain the mechanics of this one.

A NEWER, BUT NOT BETTER, MODEL

Mikolaj Kopernik, or Copernicus, as he is known today, was born in 1473 in Prussian-controlled Poland. The child of wealthy parents, he was educated both north and south of the Alps—in Cracow, Poland and in Rome and Padua. We have already discussed how he did not, as is commonly supposed, invent the heliocentric system, which had been suggested by Aristarchus almost two thousand years earlier in Greece. Similarly, the Greeks had also postulated that Earth was round. Not only did the ancients arrive at this remarkable conclusion seventeen hundred years before Columbus, but their estimate of Earth's diameter was vastly more accurate than that made by the Genoan sea captain.

By A.D. 1500 many intelligent observers began to doubt the Ptolemaic system. In Padua, Copernicus encountered one of them, Domenico Novara, who had exposed several serious flaws in the Ptolemaic model. Copernicus returned to Poland, practiced medicine for many years, and finally settled down at Frauenburg, in Poland, to observe the heavens with the primitive tools of his time. Increasingly convinced of the strength of the heliocentric model, he laid out the arguments in favor of a heliocentric cosmology in *De Revolutionibus Orbium Coelestium*, which was finished in 1530 but not published until just before Copernicus died in 1547.

Contrary to modern belief, the Copernican model was not only highly flawed but it also failed to draw much attention. First, it was not published until the year of its author's death, and, of course, it appeared in Latin. Since Latin was understood only by the ecclesiastical and commercial elite, his model did not greatly threaten the Church. Further, the mortal coil soon placed Copernicus beyond the reach of the Inquisition. Andreas Osiander, an associate of Copernicus who feared for his own safety, wrote an anonymous preface proclaiming that the book's precepts were purely hypothetical. Earth did not *really* move around the Sun, he wrote, but supposing that it did made possible more accurate astronomical calculations.

The Copernican model explained the motions of the planets better than the Ptolemaic one, particularly the fact that Mercury and Venus never strayed more than 28° and 48°, respectively, from the Sun, since they were both inside Earth's orbit.

In the end, Copernicus's universe was as inelegant as Ptolemy's. The rub, as Kepler later discovered, was that the planetary orbits were actually elliptical, while the Ptolemaic and Copernican models posited that the orbits were perfectly circular and thus required epicycles. In fact, the Copernican system required *three* sets of orbits and epicycles.[6,7] Worse yet, Copernicus accepted the Ptolemaic concept that each sphere nestled into intimate contact with its inner and outer neighbors and that the entire universe consisted entirely of their aggregate thickness. He failed to grasp that there might be a vast emptiness to space, a concept not suggested until more than a century later by Englishman Thomas Digges.[8]

Today, we revere the Copernican system for its break with the Earth-centered Aristotelian universe, yet it was more complex and clumsier than the Ptolemaic system. The Copernican system was, in fact, so complex that most histories of astronomy do not describe it in great detail. Ultimately, both models suffered from the same flaw. Their flexibility could accommodate almost any data, making it virtually impossible to disprove them.

To be worthwhile, a scientific model must be "falsifiable." That is, it should be possible to easily imagine evidence that is inconsistent with it. This was not true of either model, since their cycles and epicycles could always be adjusted to fit new data.

Comfort with falsification lies at the heart of the modern West. What separates Western societies from traditional non-Western societies is not merely the love and appreciation of Greek and Renaissance culture that is touted by modern academic scolds like Allan Bloom, but rather the amount of knowledge subjected to challenge. True, in most advanced Western societies, many religious beliefs are still held to be untouchable, even among some scientists. But for the most part, the modern West can analyze and change its mind about almost anything; premodern societies can do this about almost nothing. This peculiarly Western perspective is best illustrated by an apocryphal rejoinder usually attributed to John Maynard Keynes. When a colleague of his pointed out that Lord Keynes had just contradicted an earlier opinion, the great economist supposedly replied, "When somebody persuades me that I am wrong, I change my mind. What do *you* do?"* That outlook was inconceivable to most medieval Europeans and remains so in many traditional societies today.

Before the seventeenth century, neither the Copernican nor the Ptolemaic system was falsifiable. Nearly a full century would pass before a revolutionary tool, the telescope, would be used to finally discredit

---

* Although these words sound like Keynes, he in fact never uttered them. Personal communication from Donald Moggridge (Toronto University) and Lord Robert Skidelsky (University of Warwick, U.K.).

both systems. Just as complex as the Ptolemaic system and intuitively less appealing, the Copernican system did not pose a great challenge to Church dominance of intellectual inquiry. Pope Leo X admired and supported Copernicus and sought his counsel on the most pressing astronomical issue of the day, the increasingly obvious problems with the old Julian calendar.*

Martin Luther did not share the pope's admiration of the Polish astronomer. Luther tried to suppress publication of Copernicus's work and called for his head. South of the Alps, Italian astronomer Giordano Bruno ignored the fiction in the preface of *De Revolutionibus* that the heliocentric universe was merely a hypothesis and presented it as fact, in Italian. Bruno, as we saw in Chapter 1, was burned at the stake for this heresy, and his association with the work of Copernicus finally brought with it the disapproval of the Catholic Church. (Bruno was likely also the first astronomer to suggest that the fixed stars were suns just like ours, faintly visible only because of their great distance from Earth.)[9]

At the time, *De Revolutionibus* was not terribly influential. It was, however, the first real crack in the Church's monopoly on scientific inquiry and would bear the most fruit in England, whose embrace of Protestantism freed it from the religious strictures forbidding acceptance of the heliocentric theory.

THE FIRST WESTERN MAN

Even in the remarkable history of English prodigies, Francis Bacon stands apart. Born to the purple, he was the son of Sir Nicholas Bacon, lord keeper of the great seal (the Queen's legal officer) and the nephew of Lord Burghley, Elizabeth's treasurer and most trusted advisor. In 1573 he entered Cambridge. He was twelve years old.

---

* The Julian calendar, with its origins in the reign of Julius Caesar, assumed an annual length of 365¼ days—i.e., the familiar system of 365 days plus a leap year. Unfortunately, the true solar year is ten minutes shorter. By 1500, the calendar was a full ten days out of synch with the seasons, a discrepancy that was obvious even to medieval observers. Copernicus tactfully suggested to the pope that the cosmological issues had to be sorted out before the calendar could be fixed. James E. McClellan III, and Harold Dorn, *Science and Technology in World History* (Baltimore: Johns Hopkins University Press, 1999), 208.

Tutors recognized Bacon's talents early on, but he rapidly tired of the university's sterile intellectual atmosphere. Like much of the late medieval world, little had changed at Cambridge for centuries. The mainstay of Elizabethan higher education was still Aristotle. Imagine, if you can, our entire education system consisting of either religious instruction or rhetorical logic, dominated by such ancient scholars as Pliny and Cicero. Before the eighteenth century this was what confronted the best young minds. (Conceptually it was not much different from the curriculum that is offered in the less advanced parts of the Muslim world today).

Bacon spent most of his time preparing for "disputations," which were competitions with other students over three-part syllogisms. His spare moments he devoted to studying the intricacies of the Aristotelian universe, soon to be demolished by Copernicus, Galileo, and Newton.[10]

In Bacon's time, young scholars could apply themselves to only one field of study—theology. Even a century later, when John Locke attended Oxford, there were sixty senior student berths: one in moral philosophy, two each in law and medicine, and fifty-five in theology.[11]

Bacon recoiled at such meager intellectual fare. Three years later, in 1576, he followed in his father's footsteps by entering Gray's Inn to study law. Shortly afterward, Bacon's father died, leaving the young man impoverished, a supplicant to wealthier relatives (particularly his famous uncle) and royalty.

In order to understand the curriculum that greeted Bacon at Cambridge, we must consider the ancient Greek intellectual framework. The invention of geometry over two thousand years ago was a dazzling achievement. The computation of the shape and near-exact diameter of Earth before the birth of Christ ranks among mankind's greatest tours de force. The backwardness of the era that followed—the Dark Ages—is defined by its loss of this knowledge for more than fifteen hundred years.

In many ways, however, the ancients were gravely disadvantaged. The concept of zero had not yet been invented—the Greeks depended on a clumsy alphabetic numbering system that was later inherited by the Romans. But the real flaw of Greek and Roman intellectual life was that neither possessed any hint of what we now call the scientific method.

The Greeks and Romans did not learn how the world worked from what is now known as *inductive reasoning*—the collection and synthesis of observations into models and theories. Rather, the ancients described the workings of the natural world using *deductive* techniques, which determined natural law and the shape of the universe from so-called first principles—facts that were assumed to be true, never questioned, and used as the basis of all further reasoning. These artificial precepts were then followed logically to the desired conclusion, in much the same way that mathematical formulas are derived from assumed facts, or axioms.[12]

What were these axioms? The same Ptolemaic/Aristotelian system that greeted Copernicus a century before. In short, they constituted a belief system so flawed that it precluded the possibility of scientific progress. Worse, this system assumed that everything that could be known about the universe was already known, at least in theory. For over a thousand years, Western man's approach to understanding the natural world could be summed up in two words: Don't try. This faulty, self-contained, self-satisfied system brooked no serious dissent, as Bruno and Galileo discovered. The Aristotelian cosmos certainly did not stimulate inquiry. Nor did it allow creative thought or real advance in our knowledge of the world, nor, ultimately, real improvement in the lot of the average human being. The great medieval historian Johan Huizinga wrote, "The idea of a purposed and continual reform and improvement of society did not exist. Institutions in general are considered as good or as bad as they can be; having been ordained by God, they are intrinsically good, only the sins of men pervert them. . . ."[13]

It did not much bother the average sixteenth-century European that no real social, intellectual, or scientific advance had occurred for a thousand years; the human condition was universally assumed to be static. Bacon's staggering genius lay in realizing three things: (1) that there actually *was* a problem, that the state of medieval man was in no way "natural"; (2) that the deductive system was at fault; and (3) that knowledge of the natural world could be continuously improved, and with it the welfare of mankind. *Improving the lot of mankind would necessitate replacing the old Aristotelian framework with an "inductive" system in which facts would first be gathered without preconception, then analyzed.*

Bacon showed that there was another way to improve the human condition—through the acquisition of useful knowledge. Knowledge, indeed, was power. Between 1603 and 1620 he completed successive drafts of what became his great intellectual call to arms, *The New Organon*.

Book One of *The New Organon* is a somewhat longwinded *j'accuse* that lashes out at those who had "done the sciences great injury. For as they have been successful in inducing belief, so they have been effective in quenching and stopping inquiry. . . ." The problem, according to Bacon, was simple: Sterile theorizing, detached from experimental data, did not rise to the task of describing the real world, because "the subtlety of nature is greater many times over than the subtlety of argument."

Further, man's very observational tools were deeply flawed and subject to several different kinds of errors, or "idols":

- *Idols of the Tribe*. Bacon defined the tribe as mankind itself; this idol is its way of looking at the world, common to all men—a "false mirror" that distorted our perceptions of the world. In a word, human nature.

- *Idols of the Cave*. These are the differing ways in which individual men and women perceive the material world. Here, he is hearkening back to Plato's Cave, some distance from which there is a campfire. Things pass between cave and campfire, and man knows their nature only by the shadow they cast on a wall of the cave. An American Indian seeing a large shadow might assume that it is a buffalo; an Australian aborigine, a kangaroo. This is the seventeenth-century version of "one man's sacred cow is another man's Big Mac."

- *Idols of the Market*. These are ideas "formed by the intercourse and association with each other."[14] Here, Bacon was referring to the changes in a word's meaning over time. The impact of the word witch was different in seventeenth-century Massachusetts than it is today. In short: fashion.

- *Idols of the Theater*. This most fascinating of the Idols is the result of "received systems" that are "but so many stage plays representing worlds of their own creation after an unreal and scenic fashion."[15] The Aristotelian system was probably his prime target, but it is tempting to suggest that Bacon is also dancing around the word religion.

◆ Finally, although he did not elevate this flaw of human nature to the status of Idol, Bacon brilliantly prefigured, by more than three centuries, modern behavioral psychology's notion that humans have a proclivity to "suppose the existence of more order and regularity in the world than it finds."[16] Man is little more than a pattern-seeking primate, with an unerring ability to see connections and suspect conspiracies where none exist.

In Book Two of the *Organon* Bacon laid out his new method of inductive reasoning. Foremost, he wrote, it was necessary to observe and measure nature by the most objective means possible—preferably avoiding the direct use of the human senses, which he saw as being prone to individual misinterpretation. Rather, scientists needed to use methods and machinery that yielded identical data in the hands of different observers.

Bacon was also certain that no one man could know the whole truth—*that* was reserved for the Almighty. Even Newton, as we shall see, needed a little help in making his brilliant discoveries. The remainder of Book Two consists of a mind-numbing list of possible areas of investigation and an equally tedious description of how scientific progress should progress from direct observation of unadorned facts to lesser axioms, to middling axioms, and finally to major, all-encompassing axioms.

Of course, this is not how the scientific method actually works. The scientific community, unable to decipher the exact methods described by Bacon in Book Two, quickly concluded that it was more economical to formulate hypotheses first, be they "minor" or "major" axioms, and proceed directly to empirical testing.

Late in life Bacon acquired riches by marrying wealth. His lord chancellorship was also not without its pecuniary rewards. He was eventually charged with bribery, an accusation that did not greatly set him apart from his peers, and was forced to resign the position. Soon after his death in 1626, Bacon's disciples institutionalized his ideas with the founding of the Royal Society of London for the Promotion of Natural Knowledge (now known simply as the Royal Society), which received its charter in 1662 from Charles II. Devoted to furthering the new science, or, as it was known then, "philosophy," the Royal Society included men of all backgrounds and creeds. In the words of one of its earliest historians, it was to be concerned only with "the New Philosophy . . . precluding matters of Theology & State Affairs."[17] Isaac Newton later remarked that "religion & Philosophy are to be preserved distinct. We are not to introduce divine revelations into Philosophy, nor philosophical opinions into religion."[18] Although these strictures might seem high-minded to the modern reader, their origins were more likely practical: The society's fellows had no desire to suffer the echoes of the religious conflicts of the time, particularly the raptures of Quakers and the tirades of Dissenters.

It would be a mistake, however, to assume that Bacon and the fellows of the Royal Society were antireligious. To a man, they were devout, finding the hand of God in all of nature. The Society's fellows correctly saw that Newton and Halley's discovery of the physical laws of the heavens was a solitary island of knowledge in a vast sea of ignorance about nearly every other natural phenomenon, in particular, the inner workings of the human body. Certainly, man himself could not have designed and constructed so marvelous a machine; only the Almighty was capable of such handicraft. Even the compound eye of the lowly housefly, when viewed under the microscope, was a marvel. Consisting of approximately 14,000 separate units, or "pearls," it moved Robert Hooke to declare that "there may be as much curiosity of contrivance and structure in every one of these pearls as in the eye of a whale or elephant, and that the Almighty's fiat could just as easily cause the existence of the one as the other. . . ."[19]

The microscope made visible to humankind a previously unimagined universe of life forms—protozoa and small multicellular creatures—that only added to the awe of the Creator. The experimentalist Robert Boyle, discoverer of the laws governing the behavior of gases, viewed himself and his fellow natural philosophers as "priests of nature." Accordingly, Boyle confined his holy experiments to the Sabbath.

Still, the process of separating science and religion had begun, to the everlasting benefit of both. Science concerned itself solely with the *what* and the *how*. Religion confined itself to the *who* and the *why*. Much later, so, too, would government and religion be rent asunder, helping to clear the path for an explosion of economic prosperity.

THE MASTER OBSERVER

Bacon's emphasis on methodically painstaking observation and measurement was, in fact, anticipated a generation earlier by Tyco Brahe, the eminent Danish astronomer. Born in 1546 into very wealthy nobility in southwestern Sweden (which was then ruled by the Danes), he observed the solar eclipse of 1560 as a young man and immediately decided to devote his life to plumbing the mysteries of the heavens. While at university in Rostock, Germany, he lost his nose in a duel; for the rest of his life he wore an artificial one made of metal. He was educated in law and chemistry but secretly studied astronomy, and when he returned home in 1571, his uncle set up a small observatory for him in the family castle.

Brahe was also born lucky. On November 11, 1572, he observed a "new star" (what is now called a supernova) in the constellation Cassiopeia. He published his observations the next year in his pamphlet *De Nova Stella,* and by 1574 was delivering royal lectures in Copenhagen. He began to travel, widely publicizing his desire to settle in Basel, Switzerland. Whether or not this was a ploy to extract concessions from the Danish king is unknown, but in 1576, Frederick II, not willing to lose this national treasure, gave Brahe the island of Hvem in the straits between Copenhagen and Sweden and had the observatory of Uraniborg constructed for him there. To cement Brahe's loyalty, Frederick also provided him with other property in the kingdom, as well as a healthy stipend.

Brahe's genius lay in his observational skills. While most astronomers of his time observed the planets only intermittently, he noted their positions *continuously,* unless daylight or clouds obscured them. His instruments at Uraniborg, huge quadrants and sextants, sighted with finely measured crosshairs, were of the highest quality.

Ironically, Brahe's great theoretical accomplishment was realizing that measurements are never exact, no matter how carefully made, no matter how fine the equipment. All experiments entail error, and the error itself must be quantified. Brahe meticulously measured his errors and, by incorporating them into his observations, made the observations still more accurate.[20]

Brahe attempted to formulate a theory of planetary motion, but failed miserably and took a step backward by suggesting that while Mercury and Venus revolved around the Sun, the other planets still moved around Earth. Brahe was perhaps the last of the great Renaissance scientists to be shackled by religious superstition. Interpreting the Bible literally, Brahe took as truth its assertion that Earth stands still.* When Frederick II died, Brahe found his successor to be less accommodating and spent his last years in Prague, where fortune again smiled by providing him with an able young assistant named Kepler.

Brahe bequeathed to succeeding generations of astronomers a vast treasure of celestial observations of the highest order. Without them the workings of the heavens might have remained hidden from mankind for centuries.

MODELS DISCARDED, MODELS KEPT

Unlike his mentor Brahe, fate did not favor the young Johannes Kepler. He was born prematurely in 1571, and both of his parents may have suffered from severe personality disorders. His mother was poorly educated and undisciplined, and his father considered home life so disagreeable that he volunteered to serve in the Spanish Duke of Alba's murderous campaign against the Dutch not long after he fathered Johannes. At age four Kepler contracted smallpox, which harmed his eyesight and left him with crippled hands. Given these disabilities, his parents enrolled him in a seminary, destining him for a clerical career.[21]

Fortunately for Kepler and Western civilization, his seminary teachers recognized his mathematical talents. He eventually secured a position producing popular astrological almanacs. Kepler found the Ptolemaic system deeply unsatisfying for his computations and concluded that there must be a force unifying the universe. Aware of the Copernican heliocentric hypothesis, he set about to unravel the complexities of planetary motion. His early academic career was centered around the southern German university town of Tübingen and was buffeted by the religious conflicts that were endemic to that region. Eventually, he took shelter in

---

* "Thou didst cause judgment to be heard from heaven; the earth feared, and was still," Psalms 76:8.

Prague in 1600 as Brahe's assistant. His master's unexpected death a few years later made him head of one of Europe's greatest observatories, providing Kepler not only with the means to pursue his research, but also with Brahe's unique store of observations.

Recall that early Greek astronomers rejected the circular orbits of the heliocentric systems of Apollonios and Aristarchus, whose predictions were off by more than ten degrees—obvious even to the naked-eye measurements of the ancients. The Ptolemaic system later gained acceptance because it produced inaccuracies of only a few degrees. While this sufficed for more than a thousand years, Brahe's measurements were accurate to about *one-tenth* of a degree. His data shone a harsh, unyielding light on the flaws of the Ptolemaic model, which could not accommodate such precise observations.[22] Kepler's special genius lay in realizing that if he wanted a better explanation of how the heavens worked, he would have to reject the circular orbits used by all previous astronomical models.

Kepler was particularly fascinated by the orbit of Mars. Its orbit is the most eccentric of the observable planets, and this departure from perfect circularity was clearly apparent in Brahe's data.[*] Kepler discarded the epicycles that were superimposed upon the circular orbits of both earlier systems and replaced them with *elliptical* orbits. The challenge then presented him was to determine the orbital periods of such an arrangement. Kepler suspected that the velocity of a planet in an elliptical orbit would vary according to its distance from the Sun, and he set about methodically examining different mathematical models of planetary motion.

Although the mystery of the Martian orbit was not easily solved, the combination of Kepler's mathematical talents and Brahe's observations won the day. Kepler had a further advantage over Brahe: his belief in Bacon's observation-based system. Though the most skilled observer of his time, Brahe, like nearly all of his contemporaries, continue to accept the moral authority of the Aristotelian/Ptolemaic system. Kepler did not. For almost a decade, he wrestled with Brahe's numbers on Mars. They did not fit the Copernican model, nor did they fit Brahe's best efforts to

---

[*] Although the orbit of Mars is the most irregular of the five planets that were known to the ancients, it is only slightly elliptical. Its long axis is less than 1% longer than the short axis. However, since the Sun sits at one of the ellipse's foci, it is about nine degrees "off center," making the irregularity of Mars' motion readily apparent.

modify it. Therefore, he reasoned, both models had to be discarded.[23] Kepler, unlike his late mentor, held no theory to be inviolate. In the modern West, we take for granted that no scientific model or belief system is so sacred that it should survive contradictory data. This is, at base, what separates Western societies from non-Western ones. Kepler was one of the first natural philosophers to adopt this empirical framework, so fundamental to the modern way of life. When theory collides with reliable data, theory must go.

Being a skilled mathematician, Kepler had no trouble imagining alternative models. He tried dozens of them before settling on three laws of planetary motion that fit Brahe's data perfectly. These laws described the relationship of the shape, distance, and speed of the planets' orbits around the Sun.* Kepler probably had preconceived notions about which models would work better, but his prejudices on these matters were irrelevant. In the end he simply settled on those models that fit the data best.

Kepler discovered the *how* of planetary motion, but he could not explain the *why*. For example, his third law describes how planets closer to the Sun move faster and have shorter periods than those that are farther away. He did not know why this was so, and he was unable to explain why the Moon's revolution around Earth did not follow the same laws as that of the planets around the Sun.

Like Copernicus, Kepler's work was not influential during his lifetime. Today, it is simple to point to his three laws as his crowning achievement, but his contemporaries had greater difficulty in discerning his genius. The three laws were hidden in a morass of often-mystical speculation about the music of the spheres and alternating magnetic attraction and repulsion between the Sun and the planets. It fell to Galileo to further advance observational astronomy with the aid of the telescope

---

* The three laws are (1) All planets move in ellipses. An ellipse has two foci: The Sun occupies one of them; (2) The relationship between the distance of a planet from the Sun and its orbital period is of the second to the third power. For example, Pluto is roughly one hundred times further from the Sun than Mercury is. Therefore, Pluto's year is a thousand times longer; (3) A planet speeds up as it approaches closer to the Sun; the area swept out by a planet is the same for a given time period. This is most easily visualized with comets. At a great distance, the "pie slice" bounded by the comet during this time is long and skinny, whereas when it passes close to the Sun, it is shorter but wider. Over any given month, the "pie slice" has the same area.

and to Newton and Halley to round out man's understanding of the motions of the heavenly bodies. Their towering contributions freed scientific inquiry from the smothering grasp of Church dogma, and in the process they removed yet another roadblock on the road to prosperity.

THE ECLIPSE OF THE CHURCH

It was no accident that the Renaissance began in Italy. The fall of Constantinople to the Turks under Muhammad II in 1453 brought a westward flood of Byzantine treasure and artifacts. Prime among them were entire libraries of ancient Greek manuscripts. Simple geography dictated that Italian scholars were the first in Western Europe to examine this trove, which rekindled a long dormant interest in Hellenic art, literature, and architecture. But Italy's proximity to the disintegrating Byzantine Empire was both a blessing and a curse. Greatest progress was made in the arts, particularly sculpture and painting, where the Church gave creative genius a wide berth. In the sciences, unfortunately, the heavy hand of dogma blocked serious inquiry. Of all the great personages whose names grace this chapter, only one spent most of his life south of the Alps—Galileo Galilei, born in 1564 at Florence, epicenter of the conflict between Church and science.

Galileo's father, Vincenzio Galilei, was the impoverished scion of a noble Tuscan house. As many parents are still wont to do, Vincenzio saw that the family's path back up the social ladder lay in a medical career for the son. Vincenzio Galilei, himself a competent mathematician, observed his son's aptitude with numbers and concluded that if the boy were exposed to the beauty of mathematics, he would spurn medicine. Vicenzio was right. In the court of a local grand duke, young Galileo overheard a mathematics lesson intended for another student and was seduced by its intellectual beauty.

He eventually settled into a poorly paid mathematics post in Pisa, where he began attracting attention by dropping objects from the Leaning Tower. There, he demonstrated the falseness of the Aristotelian law that the speed of a falling object was proportional to its weight. Galileo, who did not suffer fools easily, offended the grand duke by criticizing a harbor-clearing machine designed by an illegitimate son of Cosimo de Medici and quickly found himself back home in Florence.

Soon after, he was appointed to a university chair in mathematics in Padua, which was then under Venetian rule. He prospered there, lecturing to huge audiences and inventing, among other things, the first sealed-bulb thermometer.

In 1608, a Dutch optician named Johannes Lippershey invented a crude telescope and applied for a patent in Holland. Word of this invention reached Italy the next year. Meditating on the principles of optics for a few hours, Galileo produced his own design and improved upon it until he had reached a magnifying power of thirty-two, far stronger than that of the Dutch device. Galileo produced hundreds of these telescopes and sold them all over Europe. What he saw through their lenses nearly cost him his life.

The effect of the telescope was electric. Astronomers resolved the Milky Way into individual stars, found mountains on the Moon, and observed that its phosphorescence was a result of sunlight reflected from Earth. The telescope showed the planets to be spheres, but the stars still appeared as twinkling points of light, no matter the magnification. The telescope revealed a multitude of "new" stars, more than forty in the star cluster Pleiades alone, compared with the seven that were previously known. The Sun was observed to have spots, and Saturn had a "triple form," later realized by the brilliant Dutch astronomer and mathematician Christian Huygens to be rings.

The significance of these observations paled in comparison with Galileo's discovery that Jupiter had moons of its own. Anyone peering through Galileo's lenses could see that these new celestial objects *revolved around another heavenly body*, a direct contradiction of the Ptolemaic universe. Adding further insult, Galileo saw that Venus had phases that were completely different from those predicted by Ptolemy's model. One hope arising from the discovery that the planets had regular motions was that they might somehow be used as an extremely accurate "astronomical clock" and solve the great navigational problem of the era—the computation of longitude.

Although the University of Padua offered Galileo a handsome sum to remain there, the great patrons of Florence lured him back to his home city, and Jupiter's newly discovered satellites were renamed the Medicean Stars.[24] But Galileo's return to Florence was a horrible mistake.

In 1605, during Galileo's tenure at Padua, a momentous religious conflict pitted Pope Paul V and Venice, long independent of Church authority, against one another. The cause of the conflict was minor. Two Venetian clerics were accused of attempted seduction and mayhem. Venice wanted them tried in a civil court, but the pope insisted that only the Church could pass judgment on clergymen. When the men were not handed over to Rome, the pope issued an "interdict," which effectively excommunicated the entire Republic. Venice refused to comply with the demands of Rome, and in direct violation of the interdict its priests continued to celebrate Mass.

The Republic had called the pope's bluff. The hand of God did not strike down the Most Serene Republic, and its audacity revealed Rome's theological impotence to the world. Ultimately, it was the pope who backed down.[25] Since Padua was under Venice's protection, her university offered one of the world's freest intellectual environments. In contrast, Florence's ruling Medicis were conscious of the extent to which their wealth and power depended on papal favor. They would provide Galileo with far less protection than Padua could.

Copernicus might disguise his conflict with Scripture as a hypothetical construct, but Gallileo's discoveries baldly challenged Church doctrine. Conflict was inevitable; a fuse had been lit, and Galileo's impetuous nature only made it burn more surely.

Though he took the fight to the Church, the dispute proceeded innocently enough. In his Letter to the Grand Duchess Christina (the mother of his patron, Cosimo II de' Medici), Galileo argued, with characteristic intellectual brio, that the Copernican system was actually consistent with Scripture. The church hierarchy had not taken kindly to Galileo's support of the heliocentric system. Being told by the brash upstart how to interpret Scripture was even more galling. By early 1615 the Vatican summoned Galileo to Rome and laid the matter before the Inquisition.

Initially, things did not go badly for Galileo. The prosecutor was Cardinal Robert Bellarmine, the most influential member of the College of Cardinals and Galileo's personal friend. The inquisitors did not directly punish Galileo; they simply suspended teaching of Copernicus's *De Revolutionibus*, since its matter was merely "theoretical." The inquisitors ordered Galileo not to "hold, teach, or defend" the forbidden doctrine. He gladly submitted to their wishes; in return, Bellarmine furnished him with a certificate stating that the Inquisition had not censured or punished him in any way.

Believing that he had escaped severe retribution, Galileo returned to Florence, where he remained silent for seven years. When Maffeo Barberini, Galileo's strongest supporter in the College of Cardinals, was elected pope in 1624, Galileo returned to Rome in triumph. He was feted by the greatest of the Church's princes and had no fewer than six private audiences with the new pope, now known as Urban VIII. On each occasion Galileo sought revocation of the 1615 prohibitions. On each occasion, Urban rebuffed him.

Inexplicably, Galileo did not take the hint. He convinced himself in the years following his 1624 visit to Rome that the pope, in reality, favored the lifting of the injunction. The delusion was fed by well-meaning friends. In 1630, a monk named Tommaso Campanella wrote to Galileo that the Holy Father had expressed dissatisfaction with the injunctions. This was more than enough to convince Galileo that he had been right. He began work on his *Dialogo dei due massimi sistemi del mondo*—Dialogue of Two Great Systems of the World—the two systems being the Aristotelian and Copernican universes.

The dialogue involved three characters. The first, a patient and methodical teacher named Salviati, represented Galileo himself; the second, an intelligent, sympathetic friend and sounding board, was named Sagredo; and the third was a cretinous Scholastic named Simplicio. Ostensibly, Galileo named Simplicio after one of Aristotle's later interpreters, but the play on words was clear enough. To maximize its impact, *Dialogo* was written in Italian, not Latin, and flaunted the evidence that by itself disproved the Ptolemaic model of the universe: the phases of Venus, now visible to all with the new telescope.[26] Worse, widespread rumor had it that Galileo's contemporary model for Simplicio was none other than the pope.

Published in January 1632, *Dialogo* created an immediate furor. The Church prohibited its sale that August, and in October Galileo was once again summoned before the Inquisition. Pleading old age and illness, he finally arrived in Rome in February 1633 and was shuttled between the residential "apartments" of the Inquisition and the houses of friends. During that time, the aging astronomer was shown the instruments of torture. When he finally appeared before the tribunal in June, he maintained that he had never really believed in heliocentricity. He publicly recanted, was subsequently condemned as "vehemently suspected of heresy" (one step below heresy itself, which mandated burning at the stake), and was assigned an innocuous penance. Legend has Galileo stepping out of his coach for confinement in Siena, exclaiming *"Eppur si muove!"* ("And yet it moves!" That is, Earth moves around the Sun.) But since the first assertion that he did so appears 130 years later, the anecdote is likely apocryphal.[27]

The Church's victory was Pyrrhic. Although Galileo had lost the battle, he won the war. Just as Venice had earlier exposed the Church's lack of theological clout, Galileo's trial exposed the lack of intellectual honesty at the core of its teachings. In the drawn-out conflict, the Church lost enormous credibility. Never again would it obstruct meaningful scientific advance. The trial of Galileo cleared an enormous roadblock from the path of mankind's progress.

Although blind in his last years, Galileo continued working until his death in 1642—the year of Newton's birth. His output was staggering, but it was not without flaw. He dismissed Kepler's theory of elliptical orbits in favor of the Copernican notion of perfectly circular orbits with superimposed epicycles. He could not make the intellectual leap necessary to imagine the nature of gravitational force, only dimly perceiving that the great force holding Earth in its orbit around the Sun might be the same one that binds the Moon to Earth and Jupiter's moons to it. Like Brahe, Galileo's signal strength was his skill in observation and mechanics. It would take Isaac Newton's unparalleled genius, building upon Galileo's prodigious practical and observational talent, to unlock the final secrets of heavenly motion.

THE CLOCKWORK REVEALED

The lives and careers of Isaac Newton and Edmond Halley are best considered together. Although Newton, born in 1642, was older by sixteen years, the two came of scientific age in the same intellectual milieu, and together they cracked the most important of the era's natural mysteries—the laws that govern the motions of *all* the heavenly bodies, not merely the planets. Of the two men, Newton possessed the most recognizable genius, a mathematical ability so devastatingly great that even modern scholars gasp at how he accomplished so much so quickly. He also had a personality to match: hypochondriacal, humorless, dogmatic, and at once shy and prickly. Halley, on the other hand, was described by men of all classes as charming, generous, and open. While his genius was not as deep as Newton's, it was broader, extending to areas far beyond the basic sciences.

Newton's childhood circumstances were humble. His mother was widowed three months before he was born, sickly and premature, in Woolsthorpe, Lincolnshire. Forced to remarry an older man for financial security, she left young Isaac to the care of his maternal grandmother. Who first recognized his genius—perhaps an uncle or the headmaster of the school he attended in the nearby village of Grantham—is unknown, but miraculously, Isaac Newton entered Trinity College at Cambridge in 1661 as a "subsizar"—a scholarship boy who paid his way through menial labor.

If we know little of Newton's grammar school days, we know even less of his early years at Cambridge. Sometime around 1664, it became clear to him that he knew as much about mathematics and the natural world as could be learned from other people. From that point forward, he would have to break new ground alone.

To Newton's great good fortune, the first cracks had appeared by that time in England's Aristotelian educational system. Trinity was the first college to discard the stifling, ancient pedagogy.[28] A generation earlier, René Descartes had invented analytic geometry, the essential tool needed to solve the problem of orbital mechanics. When Newton entered Trinity, it was the only institution in England that freely taught the new Cartesian mathematics.

In June 1665, an outbreak of the plague closed down Cambridge, and Newton went home to Woolsthorpe, remaining there, except for a brief return to Cambridge the following year, until April 1667. During his eighteen months of rural solitude, he completely transformed mathematics, physics, and astronomy.

He first addressed a problem that had long perplexed him: Was it possible that the force that kept the Moon in its orbit also caused an apple to fall from a tree? Indeed it was, he concluded, and that force was gravity. (And, yes, this inquiry really *was* stimulated by Newton's watching apples fall in his mother's garden. No authoritative account of this episode, however, involves head injury.)

He soon discovered that analytic geometry was insufficient to deal with this computation, so he invented the calculus. Unfortunately, Newton, as he often did, made an absentminded error. Not having his library with him, he used the wrong value for the radius of Earth (the distance from the center of the earth to the apple in the tree) and so came up with an incorrect estimate of gravity's force, based on his observations of the Moon's motion. Hamstrung by this mistake, he could make no sense of heavenly motion, placed his erroneous computations into the bottom of a drawer, and moved on to other areas: the three laws of motion and, while he was at it, groundbreaking work on numerical series. As if that were not accomplishment enough, he invented modern optics by using prisms to deduce the chromatic composition of light.

EDMOND HALLEY: GENIUS LENDS A HAND

Born the son of a wealthy tradesman in 1658, Edmond Halley was provided by his father with a first-rate education at Saint Paul's School in northeast London. The young Halley excelled at astronomy, and by the time he arrived at Oxford in 1673 he had acquired enough astronomical equipment to outfit a respectable observatory on his own account.[29]

For nearly twenty years after Newton's sojourn at Woolsthorpe, the problems of planetary motion and gravity continued to confound scientists, including two of Newton and Halley's most brilliant contemporaries—Robert Hooke (inventor of the microscope and, later, Newton's most bitter enemy) and famed architect Christopher Wren. Halley, Hooke, and Wren had all intuited the nature of the gravitational force, but the mathematics involved in proving its existence was much too daunting for even these great men.

By the 1680s, Newton's mathematical genius was well known, but unfortunately, the antagonism between Hooke and Newton was already well advanced. Hooke claimed to have a mathematical solution to the problem, but would not show it to Halley or Newton. Halley, disbelieving Hooke, went to Cambridge to seek Newton's advice.

Halley knew of Newton's theory of gravitation—a planet should be attracted to the Sun with a force proportional to its mass and inversely proportional to the square of the distance between them. Halley asked Newton what the orbit a planet subjected to such a force might look like. Newton responded without hesitation that the planet's orbit would be elliptical. This dumbfounded Halley. Like all scientists of his time, he subscribed to the Aristotelian notion that all orbits should be circular. How did Newton know this? Halley asked. Newton replied that he had nearly worked it out twenty years earlier while at Woolsthorpe. Legend has it that Newton then rooted through his desk drawer and retrieved his erroneous old calculation, whereupon Halley quickly spotted the error in Earth's radius and arrived at the correct equation. At the time, scholars joked that all of Europe had been looking for the solution to the problem of heavenly motion, and that Newton had lost it.

In an instant, the true nature of heavenly motion was revealed to man. Halley prodded Newton to publish his work, the justly famed *Philosophiae Naturalis Principia Mathematica,* and even paid for its printing.[30] (This heightened the ill will between Newton and Hooke, who accused Newton of plagiarism. The diplomatic Halley sought to reconcile the two, but failed. The poisoned relationship ended only when Hooke died in 1703, whereupon Newton assumed the presidency of the Royal Society from him.)

Spellbound, Europe watched as the previously unimaginable happened. One after the other, precise astronomical predictions came true. Even the heavens seemed to cooperate. If you were trying to demonstrate the power of the new science, you couldn't do any better than the total solar eclipse that swept right across London on April 22, 1715. Halley published "before" and "after" maps of the eclipse's path. His first map, printed about two weeks before the eclipse and reproduced in Figure 3–4, displayed the expected path of the eclipse. This map had a twofold purpose. First and foremost, Halley wanted to forestall alarm among the populace and reassure them that the coming total eclipse, the first in England for centuries, was not a sign of God's displeasure. The aim of the published prediction was that

> the suddain darkness, wherin the Starrs will be visible about the Sun, may give no surprize to the People, who would, if unadvertized, be

apt to look upon it as Ominous, and to Interpret it as portending evill
to our Sovereign Lord King George and his Government, which God
preserve. Hereby they will see that there is nothing in it more than
Natural, and no more than the necessary result of the Motions of the
Sun and Moon. . . .[31]

Second, Halley used the eclipse to solicit observers from southern
England to time its course and observe its duration of totality—the period during which the Sun was entirely hidden by the Moon. Halley obtained dozens of such reports, from which he was able to determine how
accurate his prediction had been.

These observations yielded a second map, shown in Figure 3–5, that
was nearly identical to the first. Halley's prediction was nearly perfect,
with only slight inaccuracies in both the direction and width of the actual
path.[32] As a bonus, the second map displayed the path of the next eclipse,
expected in 1724; it is the path sweeping from northwest to southeast.

Halley's exact prediction of the eclipse's path electrified the public. It
was the coup de grace that signaled the triumph of Bacon's inductive
scientific method: observe, hypothesize, and test. By the mid-eighteenth
century, the new science had vanquished the Aristotelian system of de-
duction and diminished along with it the influence of the Church in scientific affairs.

At least another century would pass before religion and science were
entirely separated. Like all men of their time, Halley and Newton were
devout, believing the Almighty to have preordained the laws of heavenly
motion. Further, they both believed in the literal truth of the Scriptures.
Halley, for example, thought that the Deluge might have been caused by
a close encounter between Earth and a comet. Newton disagreed, believing that some other sort of planetary collision was responsible. In the
1700s, William Whiston, who had succeeded Newton as the Lucasian
Professor of Mathematics, lectured to large audiences in London on the
connections between astronomical occurrences and scriptural events.
Even Newton could not totally escape the clutches of medieval superstition. Most of his professional life and writings concerned alchemy, and
he shared a lively correspondence on alchemical secrets with other luminaries of the scientific enlightenment, including John Locke and, before
the rupture with him, Robert Boyle.[33]

FIGURE 3–4   HALLEY'S PREDICTION OF THE PATH OF THE 1715 ECLIPSE

Source: Reprinted with permission of the Houghton Library, Harvard University.

FIGURE 3–5   THE 1715 ECLIPSE'S ACTUAL PATH

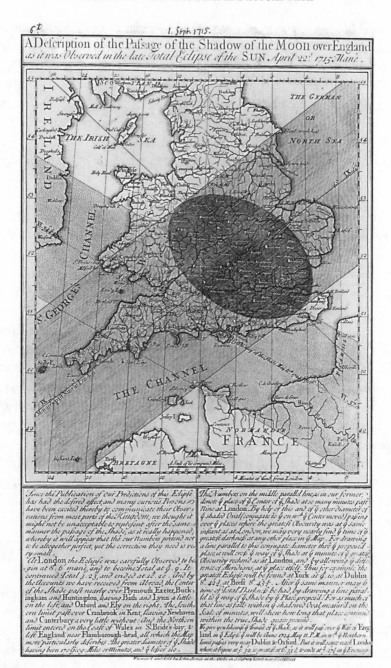

EDMOND HALLEY: PROSPERITY'S GREAT FACILITATOR

Edmond Halley's accomplishments and associations, independent of his work with Newton, are astonishing in their own right. In 1682 he discovered the comet that bears his name and calculated that its elliptical orbit had a period of seventy-six years. It was thus the same comet that had been seen in Europe and Asia in 1531 and in 1607. He predicted that it would return at Christmastime in 1758, even factoring in a slight delay caused by the gravitational pull of Jupiter and Saturn. Since he would be long dead by that date, he appealed to later astronomers that they not forget his prediction.

He needn't have worried. Since time immemorial, comets have been charged with religious and historical import. For example, Halley's comet also appeared seven months before the Battle of Hastings in 1066. Later, it was stitched into the Bayeux Tapestry, the glorious embroidered depiction of the Norman Conquest of England. The comet's punctual return in 1758 added one more brick to the edifice of popular faith in the new scientific method.[34]

In a spare moment, Halley assembled death records from the German city of Breslau into the first actuarial tables, an essential element of the new insurance industry that was then coming into being. As astronomer royal he was an *ex officio* member of the Board of Longitude. In that role, he provided sorely needed encouragement, advice, and monetary support to John Harrison in his quest for a reliable and accurate marine chronometer.

And if all that were not achievement enough for one lifetime, he helped set in motion the European discovery of a continent. He suggested that an expedition be sent to the Pacific Ocean to observe the transits of Venus between 1761 and 1769 (two decades after his death) in order to more precisely measure the distance between Earth and the Sun. Captain James Cook undertook these voyages and in the process became the first European to visit many Pacific Ocean locations, including Australia and the Hawaiian Islands. Because Edmond Halley played key roles in the development of three of modern prosperity's four foundations—scientific rationalism, the capital markets, and modern transportation—it is not too great an exaggeration to identify him as the central character in our story.

THE SPREAD OF RATIONALISM: BEYOND CELESTIAL MECHANICS

In spite of the brilliant advances made with the new scientific method, more than two centuries would pass before this revolution would begin to greatly enhance the world's wealth. Before 1850, few scientists worked in industry; most inventions were created by talented craftsmen and inventors like Thomas Edison and John Smeaton, the rediscoverer of concrete, which was forgotten with the Fall of Rome. The nineteenth-century steel industry was the first to make routine use of a modern industrial scientific laboratory that was staffed by full-time researchers who continuously monitored the relationship between ore quality and the final product. Steel baron Andrew Carnegie exulted in the advantage his lab gave him over the competition. "Years after we had taken chemistry to guide us [competitors] said they could not afford to employ a chemist. Had they known the truth then, they would have known that they could not afford to be without one," he said.[35] It would not be until well into the twentieth century that a well-staffed and well-funded research facility would become a constant feature of the large manufacturing firm.

Just how much things have changed since Copernicus is best summed up by Martin Luther's condemnation of the great Polish astronomer: "The fool would overturn the whole science of astronomy."[36] In Luther's world, subverting received wisdom was a capital crime; within three centuries, doing so was likely to bring the perpetrator honors and wealth. In a possibly apocryphal story, Napoleon asked his astronomer, Joseph Lagrange, if there would ever be another Newton. Lagrange's supposed reply sums up the era: "No, sire, for there was only one universe to be discovered."

Thus did mankind's obsession with the stars lead in fits and starts to our ability to calculate, with a few strokes on a computer keyboard, the paths of orbiting artificial satellites. The lion's share of the progress occurred during the seventeenth century and did no less than revolutionize the relationship of man to his surroundings. English scientists and craftsmen, their intellectual and property rights protected by the common law, now also possessed the proper intellectual tools with which to innovate.

Over the next two centuries, the developing capital markets would fund their efforts, and the coming of modern power, transport, and communication would spread their wares across the nation and the globe and so yield the first wave of modern wealth.

CHAPTER FOUR

Capital

SIMPLY PUT, MARKET CAPITALISM REQUIRES *CAPITAL*—the financial wherewithal to carry on a business enterprise. Businesses large and small must purchase equipment and supplies before they can produce goods and services, just as farmers have, since time immemorial, borrowed to purchase seed and implements before harvesting and selling their crops. Frequently, there is a long delay between expenditure of capital by a business and the flow of revenue into it. Even in purely agricultural societies, the delay between planting and harvest can stretch for decades, as it does in the case of viniculture.

In industrial societies, a long delay between capital outlay and revenue is typical, and the amounts of money required are enormously greater. In the modern Western economy, a large portion of income comes from inventions that did not exist in the previous generation, and almost all revenue comes from inventions that did not exist a century earlier. Capital, great gobs of it, is needed to bring these products to market. Consider the period between 1900 and 1950. The automobile, aircraft, and household appliance industries that dominated the economy in 1950 did not exist in 1900. What *did* exist in 1900 were inventors and entrepreneurs who dreamed of bringing these creations to ordinary citizens.

It is a humbling truth that at any given moment, the lion's share of Western society's prosperity originates in the minds of a few geniuses, people who truly are one in a million. Translating their ideas into economic reality requires the staggering amounts of capital that can be supplied only by a robust financial system that is trusted by investors.

125

Thomas Alva Edison's invention of the incandescent light bulb in 1879 is a case in point that vividly illustrates how the modern capitalist process works. (Edison did not, as is commonly supposed, invent the electric light itself. Two years earlier, a Russian electrical engineer named Paul Jablochkov had illuminated a Paris boulevard with arc lights.) Although a wealthy man, Edison could only afford to turn out a small number of bulbs. Producing them for the mass market required building large factories, hiring thousands of trained workers, and purchasing large amounts of raw materials, tasks that not even the nation's wealthiest individuals could manage alone. Worse, light bulbs were worthless without a reliable supply of electricity. Anyone wishing to sell the first light bulbs would have to build power generating stations and a transmission grid to move the electricity. Suddenly, investors willing to risk their capital on bringing Edison's vision to fruition became a premium commodity.

In the U.S. in the late 1800s, the most obvious source for the necessary investment capital for any large-scale enterprise was J. P. Morgan. Even Morgan's personal fortune, however, was not large enough to underwrite the Edison Electric Light Company, the firm established to commercialize Edison's invention. (John D. Rockefeller, upon hearing that Morgan left an estate worth $80 million upon his death in 1913, remarked, "And to think, he wasn't even a rich man."[1])

The House of Morgan was, however, able to supply much more than its immediate assets. By the turn of the twentieth century, Morgan's leadership of the American banking industry was such that he could muster armies of banks into syndicates that could furnish huge amounts of capital. Economic historians frequently point out that the U.S. had no central bank between the expiration of the charter of the Second Bank of the United States in 1837 and the creation of the Federal Reserve System in 1913—coincidentally, the years of Morgan's birth and death. For much of that time, Morgan functioned as the nation's *de facto* central bank, on one occasion even bailing out the U.S. Treasury.

Morgan was the one man who could easily arrange the movement of the hundreds of millions of dollars necessary to create the railroads, utilities, and steel companies that propelled the U.S. to the forefront of the industrializing nations. He was also aware that financing new technologies was most often a losing proposition, as an entire generation of Internet and technology investors has recently rediscovered. This was old news, even in Morgan's time. The history of technology investing in England was one of fraud, woe, and loss, starting with the diving companies* of the 1600s, through the canal companies of the 1700s, and culminating in the spectacular railway bubble of the 1840s. Consequently, Morgan financed only well-established technologies.

In Edison's case he made an exception. An electricity enthusiast, Morgan outfitted his mansion at 219 Madison Avenue in New York City with some of the first incandescent bulbs. This required having a noisy and odiferous generator installed behind his house, and the house's wiring not infrequently caught fire; on one occasion his desk was destroyed. He funded the building of Manhattan's first large-scale power plant, which supplied electricity to the offices of the Morgan Bank at 23 Wall Street. When proudly showing the facilities off to the press, Morgan carefully hid the fact that the generators came in 200% over budget.

The Morgan/Edison saga also highlights the constructive role played by the capital markets. Morgan and investment banker Henry Villard helped capitalize Edison's early ventures in the 1880s and subsequently consolidated the original Edison Electric Light Company into Edison General Electric. By the early 1890s, it became apparent to Morgan and his colleagues that while Edison might be a brilliant inventor, he was a poor businessman. At the time, both direct current (DC) and alternating current (AC) generators and appliances were competing for acceptance in the electrical marketplace. Because DC operated at lower voltage, Edison favored it over the AC system. Unfortunately, DC power was poorly suited to long-distance transmission, limiting its market potential. A rival company, Thomson-Houston, operated plants that produced both kinds of electricity. In 1883 a transformer that "stepped down" long-distance high-voltage AC electricity for local use was patented in England. Within a few years, George Westinghouse licensed the system in the U.S., and Thomson-Houston used it to cut into Edison's market share.

Morgan and his colleagues quickly realized that the only way to stave off the failure of Edison General Electric would be to merge it with Thomson-Houston, and the new company took the name General

* The English stock market of the 1690s saw the enthusiastic sale of shares of companies formed to recover sunken treasure; this was the first recorded stock mania. See Edward Chancellor, *Devil Take the Hindmost* (New York: Penguin, 1999), 36–38.

Electric. GE continued to require capital throughout the recession years of the 1890s until it finally became the behemoth that dominated the American electrical market for more than a century. Ever in character, Edison sold his shares in the combined company in a fit of pique soon after the merger and plowed the proceeds into future inventions. When he was later informed how much his GE shares would have been worth had he held on, he is reported to have replied, "Well, it's all gone, but we had a hell of a good time spending it."[2] The story points out that not only did Edison Electric's bankers, like generations of venture capitalists before and since, supply funding, they also provided the enterprise with vital guidance at a key juncture in its development.

As J. P. Morgan's role in this episode demonstrates, investors do not just provide capital. They also *risk* it. In fact, in most cases they are pouring it down the drain. As the recent dot-com fiasco has so painfully illustrated, the overwhelming majority of new companies and business ventures fail. Only in hindsight, as we focus on success stories like Edison Electric/General Electric, General Motors, and Microsoft, does investing in new enterprises seem profitable. In this sense, the capital market for new enterprises behaves much like a public lottery. Millions buy tickets, but only a lucky few win. In our capital-oriented society, the ready availability of public and private capital may itself provide a powerful incentive to innovate and invent.

The financial dance performed by Edison, Morgan, and Villard marked the pinnacle of the late-nineteenth-century capital markets. This chapter, then, will lay out the narrative of that system's birth in ancient times and its development in the late medieval and early modern periods. At its most basic, this is a story about three factors: *cost, risk, and information*.

THE COST OF CAPITAL

All business ventures consume money. Like any other commodity, money has a cost—the rate of interest. The farmer who requires seed and plow in spring must repay his loan with interest. When interest rates are high, money is said to be *expensive*; when interest rates are low, it is said to be *cheap*. Cheap money encourages business investment and expensive money discourages it. When interest rates go high enough, the farmer forgoes planting and the businessman defers commercial activity.

Many factors help determine the cost of money, the most fundamental being the balance between supply and demand. When there are many lenders and few borrowers, money is cheap, and when there are few lenders and many borrowers, it is expensive. Figure 4–1 tracks the fall of interest rates in England, the Netherlands, Italy, and France between 1200 and 1800. The gradual decline in rates happened for many reasons; the most important was the increase in the supply of investment capital, that is, money available for lending. This fall in the cost of capital could not help but lead to increased business activity and growth.

The first economists well understood the importance of interest rates. One of the earliest English economic observers, Sir Josiah Child, noted in 1668 that "all countries are at this day richer or poorer in exact proportion

FIGURE 4–1   EUROPEAN INTEREST RATES, 1200–1800

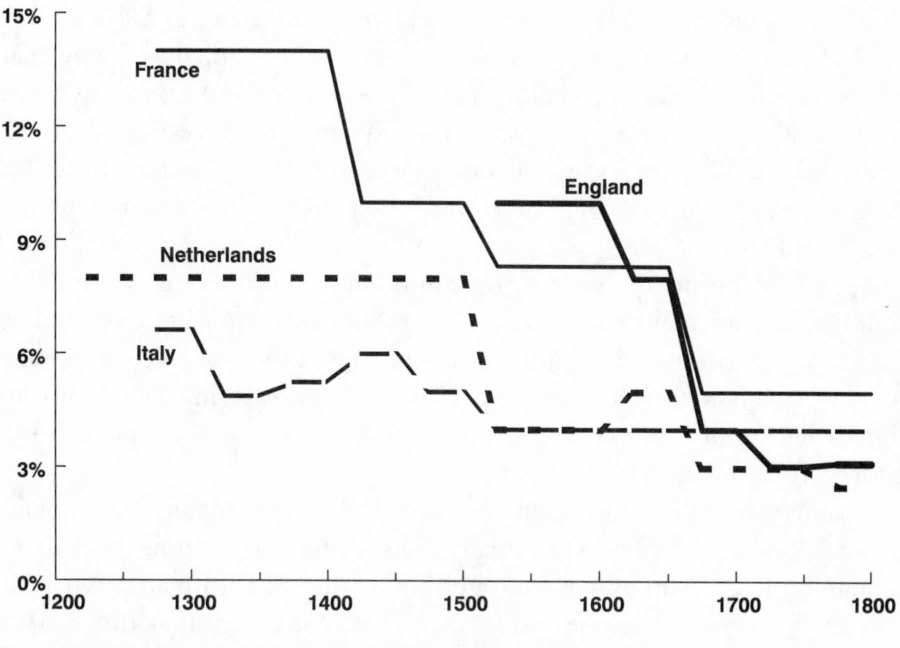

Source: Data from Homer and Sylla, *A History of Interest Rates*, 137–38.

to what they pay, and have usually paid, for the Interest of Money."[3] For Child, the relationship was mathematical; if a businessman could afford a given amount of interest payment, twice as much capital was available to him at a rate of 3% as was at 6%. Said historian T. S. Ashton,

> If we seek—it would be wrong to do so—for a single reason why the pace of economic development quickened about the middle of the eighteenth century, it is to low interest rates we must look. The deep mines, solidly built factories, well-constructed canals, and the houses of the Industrial Revolution were the products of relatively cheap capital.[4]

The concept of the cost of capital for loans to individuals and for bonds issued by governments and corporations is easy to understand. This cost is simply the rate of interest on the loans or bonds involved. Many investors have more trouble understanding how the cost of capital applies to ownership shares (company stock), but apply it does. Start with the notion that the price of one share of stock, that is, the rights to a share of a company's earnings, is expressed in "dollars per share." Next, simply reverse this expression, and think of "shares per dollar"—the amount of ownership that the company must pay investors for a dollar of investment capital needed to purchase plant, equipment, and labor.

When share prices are high, the cost of equity capital—money that the company obtains by selling its shares—is low, and companies will happily issue new shares to investors in exchange for investment capital. This is exactly what happened during the recent Internet/tech boom, when new companies sold ridiculously expensive shares to the public with wild abandon.

When share prices are low, on the other hand, the cost of capital is high. Companies must surrender a larger slice of ownership to outsiders in exchange for financing, and investment lags. This occurred during the 1980s, when stock prices were so low that company managers actually borrowed money in the form of junk bonds to buy back their existing shares from the public.

Sometimes, as occurred in the late 1990s, a company can obtain capital more cheaply by selling stocks instead of selling bonds or obtaining loans. Sometimes the opposite is true. But no matter where it comes from, capital always has a cost. That cost determines how much business gets done and how rapidly wealth grows.

THE RISK OF CAPITAL

Simple supply and demand is not the whole story—the *risk* of a business venture also plays a critical role in the price of its capital. A loan to a trusted and reliable borrower carries a much lower interest rate than a loan to an unreliable borrower does. The bonds of the U.S. Treasury carry a far lower interest yield than those issued, for example, by Trump Casinos. During a period of civil unrest or external military threat, all bonds, including the government's, become riskier, and rates rise. As was mentioned in Chapter 1, a nation's interest rate plot can be thought of as its "fever chart," an indicator of its economic, social, and military health.[5]

Risk can be concentrated or diluted. Suppose that you are considering a business opportunity that carries a one in five chance of success. It requires that you invest or borrow $100,000. If you succeed, you wind up with $1,000,000 (that is, you make a profit of $900,000). This is tempting, but you also realize that there is an 80% chance of failure, a scenario that will cause you to lose the entire $100,000. Since there is a 20% chance of making a profit of $900,000 and an 80% chance of losing $100,000, the expected payoff of this investment is $100,000—that is, "on average," you will double your money.* Except, of course, you cannot obtain the average return—you either lose big or win even bigger.

Even with such a favorable expected payoff, you might be hesitant to pursue the opportunity. If you cannot easily spare or borrow the $100,000, the pain of losing or owing it may be greater than the pleasure of earning a $900,000 windfall. Now imagine that you live in premodern Europe, where default means debtor's prison, or in ancient Greece, where it means enslavement to your creditor.

Such risk is highly concentrated, and before the modern era, few braved it. In the nineteenth century English financiers became acutely aware of the impediment to investing caused by harsh default consequences, and the House of Commons enacted bankruptcy laws. Easing of the menace of debtor's prison produced an explosion of investment activity.

Premodern entrepreneurs were not the only ones liable to experience personal ruin for default. Until relatively recently company shareholders also were. Obviously, if mere ownership of company shares exposes you

---

* The calculation is $900,000 × 0.2 + (−)$100,000 × 0.8 = $100,000.

to the possibility of draconian punishment for the failure of a firm to meet all of its obligations, you will be far less inclined to supply the company with capital by buying its shares. The solution was the modern limited liability corporation, a related nineteenth-century legislative advance that shields shareholders from a company's creditors. We'll explore its development later in this chapter.

Returning to our example, suppose that instead of bearing the entire risk of losing $100,000 yourself, you are able to *syndicate* your risk. That is, you share it with many other investors. If there are one hundred shares, each carries only a $1,000 loss in the event of failure and a $9,000 gain in the event of success. By spreading out the risk, many more investors will be willing to invest.

Consider, finally, that as an individual investor, you can diversify your risk among a large number of such syndicated deals. Your chances of overall failure are much reduced, since 90% of the above investments would have to fail for you to lose money. The greater the number of ventures, the lower the chance that you will lose money. Figure 4–2 shows how the probability of success in this example, defined as making money or breaking even, rises with the number of ventures available. By investing

FIGURE 4–2   PROBABILITY OF SUCCESS WITH INCREASING DIVERSIFICATION

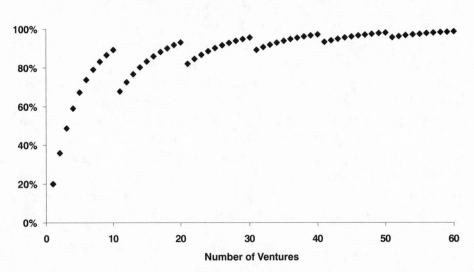

in just four, your chances of success are more than 50%; by investing in eighteen, you have a 90% chance of success.*

Where you can purchase shares in many different syndicated ventures, your chances of success are much greater, and you will be so much more likely to provide capital to needy businesses. The advent of the joint-stock company in the seventeenth century was the answer to both of these needs—the syndication and diversification of risk, thus increasing the amount of investment capital to new ventures.

INFORMATION AND CAPITAL

Even if capital is cheap and plentiful, the markets must still match up borrowers and lenders, just as they must also connect companies that are selling stocks and bonds with investors willing to buy them. This is no trivial task. The capital markets behave just like those for groceries, used cars, or diamonds. Markets establish appropriate prices as buyers and sellers negotiate and exchange information.

Markets are said to accomplish these goals—matching up buyers and sellers and establishing prices—with varying degrees of *efficiency*. An efficient market is one where buyers and sellers freely and openly transact business in high volume at nearly identical prices. Gasoline stations provide a superb example of an efficient market. Merely by driving to work every day, the average commuter gets an excellent idea of the fair market value of a gallon of regular unleaded. An inefficient market is one in which transactions in nonidentical goods are made infrequently and largely out of public view—the sale of houses, for example.

In most of Europe before the seventeenth century, the capital markets were extraordinarily inefficient. They matched borrowers and lenders only by word of mouth or dumb luck—even though the two parties most often lived in the same city. As a result, both the users and suppliers of capital could not easily ascertain the true cost of capital, and because

---

* The curious stepwise nature of this plot is an artifact peculiar to the example—with ten ventures, you need only one success to avoid losing money, but with eleven, you need two successes, for which the odds are lower.

of this uncertainty, both sides were reluctant to transact. The outcome
was that only a trickle of capital flowed to new business enterprises.

One can say, with not a little justification, that in medieval Europe the
markets for almost all commodities, not merely capital, were beyond inefficient—they were virtually nonexistent. Today, the proper price is one
that has "cleared the market," that is, has induced the greatest number of
buyers and sellers to do business together. Before about 1400, the market
did not determine "proper" prices. Instead, an arbitrary moral system prevailed. Economic historians Nathan Rosenberg and L. E. Birdzell observed, "The ideology of the system was epitomized in the phrases 'just
price' and 'just wage.' Prices and wages expressed a moral judgment of
worth. Supply and demand were morally irrelevant."[6]

Rosenberg and Birdzell went on to note that only in times of famine,
when the supply of food fell precipitously, did prices rise. This served
mainly to direct public outrage at the concept of what we now term the
"free market economy."

Economists have long known that markets operate most efficiently
where they can bring together as many buyers and sellers as possible at
the same time and in the same place. The famous medieval trade fairs,
some of which survive to the present day, served this function. You may
have noticed that in many foreign countries (and even in some U.S.
cities, such as in the warrens of tiny shops in New York's Diamond
District on West 47th Street) all of the butcher or jewelry shops cluster
tightly on the same street. In a world without telephones and
newspapers, clustering maximizes the flow of pricing information to
both buyers and sellers and increases the overall volume of commerce. In
the seventeenth century the Dutch made spectacular use of this
phenomenon by locating multiple financial exchanges within a few
blocks of each other in Amsterdam.

Sadly for the Dutch, geographic proximity only goes so far. It is
highly inefficient to force buyers and sellers to travel to different streets
or cities to buy and sell the multitude of goods and financial items
exchanged in a complex modern economy. The invention of the
telegraph and the laying of the transatlantic cable in the mid-nineteenth
century solved this problem and utterly transformed the capital markets.
Consumers and suppliers of capital, as well as other goods, no longer
needed to meet face-to-face or even reside on the same continent.

Participants increasingly perceived prices as fair, and capital flows rose exponentially, and transactions were completed almost instantaneously.

THE ANCIENT ROOTS OF THE CAPITAL MARKETS

Capital markets have been an intrinsic part of the human repertoire since the beginning of history in the Fertile Crescent and very likely for millennia before that. The Code of Hammurabi weighed in on capital market transactions, setting, as we saw in Chapter 2, interest-rate ceilings at 20% for loans of silver and at 33% for loans of grain, the primary medium of exchange. Here, for the first time, we encounter the nexus between risk and return. Loans of grain, since they were forfeit if the crop failed, were riskier for the lender than loans of silver. This added risk is what demanded a higher interest rate.

Before the Lydians of Asia Minor invented stamped coins in the seventh century B.C., the ancients used weighed-out pellets and bars of silver for symbolic deposits in their temples, which functioned as the central banks of their day.[7] The modern investor is used to capital markets that involve both debt—that is, loans and bonds, which pay off fixed interest and principal—and equity, or a shared partnership, which pays out a portion of a business's profits. In the modern world, equity most often means shares of common stock. This kind of arrangement—the joint-stock company—first saw the light of day in Rome and in medieval France, but did not become widespread until popularized in seventeenth-century Holland. In ancient times a simple partnership, where one side provided capital to the enterprise's operator in exchange for a share of the profits, served much the same purpose.[8]

From earliest recorded history until very recently, equity financing of any type was in fact seldom used. Debt, not equity, was the preferred method of financing. The problem with equity financing is simple to understand—what economists call "information asymmetry." The person running the business—the operating partner—finds it easy to conceal profits (and losses) from the investor, who in turn finds it time-consuming and expensive to monitor the arrangement to ensure that he is not cheated of his due portion. As the recent corporate accounting scandals show, the same problem, though on a much larger scale, remains a real concern to the modern investor as well.

Debt financing, that is, a simple loan repaid with interest and secured by the borrower's possessions and person, is far less complex, more direct, and easier for an investor to monitor. Both the borrower and lender expect fixed payments to occur on fixed dates. Mortgage lending is particularly attractive because the lender can seize the borrower's real property as compensation in the event of default.

In the ancient world, the informational and enforcement costs associated with equity financing were insurmountable. For this reason debt—loans and bonds—was used far more commonly than equity to finance entrepreneurial activity before the twentieth century.[*]

The Code of Hammurabi made debt financing the preferred method of supplying capital, at least from the investor's point of view, because it allowed the borrower to present to the lender his land, houses, slaves, concubines, and even children as collateral. However, the provision of such highly effective collateral also had its drawbacks. The prospect of losing the most precious things in life does not encourage risk taking, which is the lifeblood of a vibrant economy.

THE RISE OF MONEY

Reliable money is a modern commonplace, and it is difficult to conceive how the world got along without it before the Lydians stamped the first pellets of electrum (an alloy of gold and silver) into coins.

Imagine a primitive economy in which only ten different commodities are traded. Without coinage, traders must barter these commodities in pairs: six bales of cotton in exchange for a cow, two bushels of grain for a cartload of firewood, and so forth—forty-five possible different pairs in all, each pair with its own price.[†8] Worse, a person wishing, for example, to

---

[*] There are other explanations for the premodern preference for debt over equity. The premodern uncertainty of life expectancy likely worked against the more distant payoff of stock ownership, as did stock ownership's much higher risks.

[†] The formula for the number of possible pairs of N different commodities is N(N−1)/2.

purchase cotton from someone else would have to possess something needed by the other person. Coined money simplifies the exchange process. With coinage, there are only ten prices, and the purchaser no longer has to worry about matching his desires with those of someone else. In the unlovely vocabulary of economics, gold and silver coinage become the "medium of exchange." It is remarkable that humankind got along without money for so long.[9]

Insurance, another technique for managing risk, was invented by the Greeks in the form of the "bottomry loan," which was used to finance trading voyages. Such loans were canceled if the ship sank; they can be thought of as an insurance policy that was packaged along with a loan. Because of the implicit insurance feature, this capital did not come cheap. In peacetime, interest was 22.5%; in wartime, 30%. The peculiar structure of these loans was dictated by the scarcity of information in the premodern world. Absent this insurance feature, the lender had to collect against the borrower's other assets in the event the ship was lost. This in turn required the impossible task of determining the financial strength of each and every shipper. It was far easier to simply include a uniform "insurance surcharge" as an intrinsic part of the bottomry loan, and be done with it.

At a very early stage in human history, then, we have encountered the fundamental currency of the capital markets: *information*. When knowledge of a borrower's financial strength, a partner's honesty, crop yields, prevailing interest rates, and a myriad of other things is readily available, lenders are willing to lend and borrowers are eager to borrow. All other things being equal, the economy hums. In the premodern world, however, information was either very expensive or completely unavailable. That dictated debt financing at high interest rates, which in turn stunted economic growth.

ROME'S CAPITAL MARKETS

All other things were not equal in Rome. Her relative social stability allowed interest rates to fall to approximately 4% in the first century A.D. Unfortunately, the empire's major source of revenue was war booty. After the conquests tapered off in the second century, Rome endured almost constant fiscal crisis. The Romans then resorted to taxes on farms and the contracting out of tax collection to private parties. Ironically, Roman businessmen formed the first recorded joint-stock companies for this purpose, trading their shares in the Temple of Castor.

Exploitative tax rates relentlessly pressured Roman farmers. Crop failures and economic depressions that would have been easily weathered in earlier times squeezed farmers off their land. This depopulated the countryside and devastated agricultural activity, the primary source of income in all premodern societies. The Fall of Rome was largely a fiscal affair. The low interest rates of the *Pax Romana* were not sufficient to offset the unhealthy effects of an economy based on conquest, rather than commerce.[10]

RENAISSANCE ITALY

The early medieval economies and their capital markets, which were hobbled by ecclesiastical prohibitions against usury, were even more dysfunctional than those in Rome. Capital flows all but ceased, but there were some bright spots. The most dramatic early advance was the trade fair, which quickly became the high point of the annual commercial calendar. Local rulers granted protection to foreign merchants who attended the fairs, no small privilege in an age when lawlessness in the countryside was nearly absolute.

The fairs also solved one of the great problems of medieval commerce—the scarcity of gold and silver coins—by evolving clearance methods. Each merchant kept a book of purchases and sales that he then submitted to an official who would annul counterbalancing exchanges. If, for example, a merchant purchased goods worth fifteen hundred florins and sold goods worth fourteen hundred florins, his debts were settled by paying only the hundred-florin difference.[11]

Credit lubricates the wheels of commerce. Where there is none, the machinery barely turns; where it is plentiful, the wheels hum. The trade fair clearance mechanism created a form of credit that stimulated trade. Later Europeans would develop the credit mechanisms of these early trade fairs into far more powerful financial tools.

Gradually, as commercial activity resumed across Europe, the Church made exceptions to the prohibition against the payment of interest. If the money lent could otherwise have been used profitably, Church law allowed payment of interest on the loan. If, for example, the lender had to sell property to raise the loan amount, the lender could charge the borrower interest, since the land sold would otherwise have yielded income to the lender. Loans forced by the state could also pay interest. As the practice of state loans spread, the Church found it increasingly difficult to maintain its prohibitions on usury.

In the fifth century A.D., as Germanic tribes rampaged up and down the length of the Italian peninsula, increasing numbers of refugees found safety on a small group of islands hidden in the isolated lagoons at the northwestern edge of the Adriatic Sea. Attila the Hun's conquest of the nearby ancient Roman fortress of Aquileia, at the head of the Adriatic, in A.D. 452 turned this stream of refugees to the islands into a torrent. In the chaos of the century that followed the Fall of Rome, control of this area seesawed between the Goths and the Eastern Roman Empire, which was led from Constantinople.

Left to fend for themselves in the maelstrom going on about them, the lagoon communities became fiercely independent. Initially, the largest settlement was located at Grado, just south of Aquileia, where the refugees founded a loose confederation of communities. Gradually, leadership shifted southwest to the islands of the Rialto, on which the city of Venice was founded. Initially under the dominion of Constantinople, Venice rebelled in 726, after Byzantine Emperor Leo III ordered the destruction of all icons and religious images. The young city chose as her commander and leader one Orso, who was crowned *dux*. This title later became doge—the first in an unbroken line of 117 rulers of a city-state that was to become Europe's most prolific source of financial innovation and, at times, its strongest bastion of ideological resistance to the Church.[12]

State loans to support the almost constant warfare that characterized Venice's turbulent history were an important feature of Venetian capital markets. By the thirteenth century, the Republic was raising large amounts of money by demanding loans from its wealthiest citizens. These loans, called *prestiti*, never matured and yielded permanent interest payments. *Prestiti* could subsequently be sold by their owners (usually at a much lower price than was originally paid to the Venetian treasury) on the domestic and foreign capital markets. The records of these sales span three centuries and provide economic historians with a nearly uninterrupted picture of interest rates in one of Europe's most important capital markets.

Venice rapidly grew into a military power and maritime commercial giant that would dominate the eastern Mediterranean for five hundred years. In time, other Italian cities such as Florence, Milan, Pisa, and Genoa would follow suit. All inherited the flawed Roman system of commercial law, which discouraged large-scale commercial enterprise. Roman law mandated that all partners in a company, or *societas*, be personally liable for its debts. Since default resulted in the confiscation of all of one's property, and in extreme cases, enslavement of the partner and his family, the societas usually confined its membership to family groups, where kinship ties provided some measure of trust.

But even when commerce was restricted to the bosom of honest family members, the extreme penalties for failure discouraged prudent risk taking, the very basis of commerce and economic progress. It is no accident, then, that the first great commercial enterprises arose in the form of family-run merchant banks, epitomized by those of the Medicis of Florence. The family structure lessened the probability of ruin for all by a single bad apple, and banking was a business that was blessed by the availability of easy capital from depositors.

THE BILL OF EXCHANGE

In the early sixteenth century, bills of exchange became the lifeblood of European commerce. These were simply promissory notes given by a debtor in one location to a creditor in another, usually a foreign country. Although their origin is lost to time, by the beginning of recorded history, bills of exchange were already in common usage in the Fertile Crescent. Babylonian merchants, who used silver and barley as currency, acquired bills denominated in the currency of Assyria—lead—before departing for business there.[13]

The Greeks also extensively employed bills, but it was the great pre-Renaissance Italian banks that brought their use to its fullest flower. In order to understand how a bill worked, let's start with a Florentine silk merchant who wishes to pay for a shipment of material costing five hundred ducats that has just arrived at the docks of a silk importer in Venice. Not having the five hundred ducats immediately on hand, the Florentine must borrow the money, so he writes a bill—effectively, an IOU—to the Venetian importer.

But why would the Venetian be willing to accept an IOU from an unknown Florentine? Sometime around 1500, merchants in Antwerp introduced a dazzling innovation into the concept—they made these bills negotiable. That is, they were transferable to someone other than the original creditor.[14] This advance found great favor in Italy. This negotiable bill of exchange written by the Florentine now functioned as *cash* in the hands of our Venetian silk wholesaler.

The Venetian importer, in reality a wholesaler, might then take this bill to a local bank and exchange it for cash. Of course, he would not get the full five hundred ducats for it—the bank would give him somewhat less. Just how much less than five hundred ducats he received depended on three things: the creditworthiness of the Florentine silk merchant, the due date of the bill, and the location of the transaction. The sooner the bill was due, the more solid the creditor, and the closer the redemption location to the bank, the more the bill was worth.

In settling the transaction with the importer, the Venetian bank was thus said to "discount" the bill. Our example here represents a relatively simple case. More often, a bill of exchange transacted in two different currencies over a period of up to several months. In this case, the bill involved the exchange rate between the two currencies, as well as the interest-rate component that took into account the time between issuance and final payment.[15] During the seventeenth century, one of the world's busiest commercial routes lay between Amsterdam and London. Figure 4–3 illustrates how the flow of the bills correlated with the flow of goods, debt, and cash between the two cities.

THE RISE OF DUTCH FINANCE

During the late fifteenth century, capital flows gradually shifted to the north, first to the Hansa cities—the area around Bremen and Hamburg, Germany. There, the Fugger family made huge fortunes from mining, then even bigger ones from moneylending. They financed innumerable

FIGURE 4–3

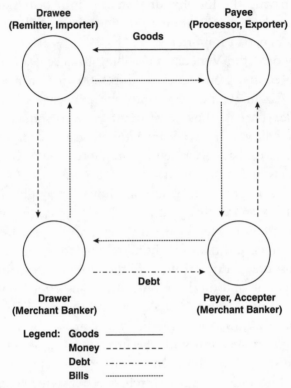

Source: From Larry Neal, *The Rise of Financial Capitalism,* 6, with permission from Professor Neal and Cambridge University Press.

wars and overseas expeditions, most notably Magellan's circumnavigation of the globe. The list of regents who did *not* owe the Fuggers money in the fifteenth and sixteenth centuries was a short one. The Vatican was one of the most militarily aggressive states in Europe. Naturally, the Fuggers became its biggest creditor. At that point, the Church could no longer maintain its prohibitions against usury; in 1517, the Fifth Lateran Council abolished most strictures against lending at interest.

During the fifteenth and sixteenth centuries, the financial center of northern Europe gradually shifted from the Hanseatic states to Antwerp. When Spanish forces sacked Antwerp in 1576, Amsterdam, the center of the new Dutch confederation, assumed the leading financial role. The most voracious consumer of Dutch capital was Holland's military, which for much of the sixteenth and seventeenth centuries fought a brutal war of independence against Spain.

The special genius of Dutch finance was getting everybody into the act. Anyone with a few extra guilders was as liable to purchase government securities as someone today would be to plow savings into a money-market or stock mutual fund. The Dutch provinces and cities issued three kinds of securities. *Obligatien*—short-term notes—were "bearer bonds" that their owners could readily sell for cash at any time to a bank or broker. *Losrenten* were perpetual annuities, very similar to Venetian *prestiti*. Unlike bearer bonds, the holder of these securities recorded his name in a public ledger and received regular interest. They could be sold in the secondary market, and upon the death of the holder they passed to his heirs. Last were *lijfrenten*, similar to *losrenten,* except that payments ended with the death of the holder.

The Dutch do not take the word *perpetuity* lightly: In 1624 a woman named Elsken Jorisdochter invested twelve hundred florins in a bond paying 6.25% that was issued to finance dike repair. Free of all taxes (similar to a modern municipal bond), she handed it down to her descendants. About a century later, as interest rates fell, the Dutch government negotiated the rate down to 2.5%. In 1938, the bond came into the hands of the New York Stock Exchange, and as late as 1957, the exchange presented it for payment of interest at Utrecht.[16]

Lijfrenten required a higher yield—initially 16.67%—because their interest payments ceased with the death of the holder. The difference between the 16.67% *lijfrenten* rate and the 8.33% that *losrenten* paid speaks volumes about European life expectancies at the time. Although the Dutch financial markets were advanced, they were not sophisticated enough to vary the interest of *lijfrenten* according to the age of the purchaser! By 1609, these rates had fallen to 12.5% and 6.25%, respectively. The cessation of hostilities with Spain in 1647 and the Spanish recognition of Dutch independence the following year had a salutary effect on interest rates. Not only was the survival of the Republic assured, but its demand for capital was also greatly diminished. By 1655, the government could borrow at 4%, a rate of interest not seen in Europe since the height of the Roman Empire. The final great advance of Dutch finance occurred in 1671, as Johan de Witt, who was both Holland's grand pensionary (chief magistrate) and a crack mathematician in his own right, applied Pascal's new theories of probability to finance. De Witt arrived at a formula that used the age of a purchaser to determine the interest paid on *lijfrenten*.[17] De Witt's rise to power itself illustrates that the Dutch understood the importance of promoting their best and brightest to high government office.*

The low interest rates energized an already vigorous Dutch commerce, and that of northern Europe along with it. Contemporary accounts suggest that reputable Dutch citizens could borrow at rates as low as those available to the provincial and city governments. The cutting-edge technologies of the day—drainage and reclamation projects, construction of canals, peat mining, and shipbuilding—benefited greatly from cheap capital. So, too, did ordinary citizens who wished to purchase houses, property, and farms. More important, the easy availability of credit at low rates meant that merchants could maintain large inventories of goods. Amsterdam and the other Dutch trading cities became known as the place in Europe where anything could be obtained, at any time.

The efficiency with which the Dutch handled monetary transactions made Amsterdam Europe's financial center. By 1613, the *Price Courant*—the seventeenth-century version of the *Wall Street Journal*—published exchange rates on a twice-per-week basis. By 1700, regular quotes were available for ten currencies, and on a fairly regular basis for fifteen more. For example, when England financed the participation of the German states in the Seven Years War in the mid-eighteenth century, its bills were cleared through Amsterdam. Across the North Sea, Englishman John Castaing began publishing the *Course of the Exchange* in 1697, which listed, also twice weekly, prices for fifty-two different stocks and government annuities and bills, as well as foreign exchange rates.[18]

The *Price Courant* and Castaing's broadsheet supplied that most effective of financial lubricants—information. Without that vital ingredient investors will not offer capital and capitalism itself grinds to a halt. Never before had the world seen such a concentration of financial services as there were in Amsterdam. Within a few blocks of the city hall could be found the *Wisselbank, Beurs* (stock exchange), and *Korenbeurs*

---

* Unfortunately, de Witt's rise to power did not have a happy ending. In retribution for his perceived failings during France's invasion of Holland in 1672, he was shot and hanged, and his body was mutilated by an angry mob. See Poitras, 190.

(commodities exchange), as well as the offices of the major insurance, brokerage, and trading companies. In the slow-moving world that existed before the telegraph era, the physical proximity of the major Dutch financial institutions to one another gave them a nearly insurmountable advantage over their foreign competitors.* Even in the modern era such geographic dominance becomes self-sustaining at a certain point, as more and more specialists in a given field gravitate to the same place. It will be a long time before Hollywood, Silicon Valley, and Manhattan lose their grip on the modern movie, electronics, and financial scenes.

It is thus no accident that several financial innovations saw their genesis in seventeenth- and eighteenth-century Holland, including maritime insurance, retirement pensions and annuities, futures and options, transnational security listing, and the mutual fund. The most important advance was the birth of modern investment banking. For the first time in history the risk of loans could be parceled out among thousands of investors, who could reduce their own investment risk by diversifying their holdings among the many different bonds sold by the investment bankers. Reduced investment risk led to an increased willingness to invest, which, in its turn, brought interest rates down still further.

The Dutch appetite for foreign investments was voracious. Economic historian Jan de Vries estimates that Dutch foreign investment in 1800 reached approximately 1.5 billion guilders, or twice Holland's annual GDP. By comparison, U.S. investment abroad today is less than half of American GDP. In every age, capital flows from nations with mature economies and excess wealth to nations that require it for development. As England transformed itself from a political and economic backwater into a world power in the seventeenth century, the major river of capital flowed from Amsterdam to London. In the nineteenth century, the highly developed English economy provided capital for the developing United States. The U.S., in its turn, became the major source of capital for developing nations in the twentieth century. And so it goes.

---

* In both London and Amsterdam, coffeehouses, which were located near the wharves, served as informal stock exchanges at which caffeinated brokers could act on information as soon as it hit the docks. For an entertaining semifictional account of the interaction between coffee and the early capital markets, see David Liss's delightful *The Coffee Trader* (New York: Random House, 2003).

THE FALL OF DUTCH FINANCE

The experience of Dutch finance after 1770 was not at all an agreeable one. The reasons for the decline of Dutch financial dominance after that date are complex, but two stand out. For starters, Amsterdam never employed the kinds of vigorous central bank and regulatory bodies charged with protecting the investing public that later were developed in Britain and the U.S. Second, and more ominous, the Dutch found themselves overwhelmed by the financial and military colossus that slowly rose on the opposite side of the North Sea—a giant that they had helped create with their own capital.[19]

The Dutch, unfortunately, marched in the vanguard of another trend in modern finance: the shearing of small investors by investment banks. The late-eighteenth-century war bonds of foreign nations, many of which would default no matter which side won the conflict, were priced to yield slightly more than the secure 4% domestic issues—profitable for the underwriters but a rotten deal for credulous small investors because of the risk of default that was involved. The touting of hyped-up Internet stocks in the late 1990s to a gullible public by mendacious investment bankers would not have surprised the average Dutch investor of 1800.

DEBT IN ENGLAND AND AMERICA

While the seventeenth century had built Holland into the world's colossus of trade and finance, it was less kind to England. For the first half of the century, Parliament and the courts skirmished with the Stuarts—James I and Charles I. This conflict culminated in the defeat of the Royalist army by the parliamentary forces at Naseby in 1645 and the beheading of Charles in 1649. It also devastated England's economy.

Even before the conflict broke out, British state finances were shaky. Incredible as it seems to the modern reader, the English crown, like almost every other European monarchy, possessed no reliable source of financing. As we have seen, a prime source of the Crown's revenue was the sale of monopolies, as well as the sale or rental of state lands and tariffs on imports and exports—all actions that served to stifle enterprise and trade.[20] English monarchs, like royalty everywhere, borrowed to pay for their expensive military adventurism. They frequently defaulted on loans, and because it is very difficult to dun a sitting sovereign, interest rates remained high. After the restoration of the Stuart monarchy in 1660, England's debt grew so large that it became increasingly difficult to service. This resulted in the most infamous loan default in all English history: the Stop of the Exchequer in 1672, through which Charles II bankrupted most of the banks that had extended credit to him.[21]

The Glorious Revolution of 1688 brought an end to nearly a century of civil strife, and the English "invited" stadholder Willem III to assume the British throne as William of Orange. (The stadholder was a peculiarly Dutch institution—the appointed, and at times hereditary, ruler of Holland.) Willem/William did not come to England alone. Sensing that Amsterdam's days as the world's financial capital were numbered, Holland's financial elite, including the Barings and Hope families, followed him across the North Sea. The Portuguese Jews of Amsterdam, having been driven by the Inquisition from Spain to Portugal to Holland, arrived in London en masse. Abraham Ricardo, father of the economist David Ricardo, was perhaps the best-known Portuguese Jewish immigrant.

Dutch ideas came with them. The English enthusiastically copied "Dutch finance," and within a few short decades following the devastating civil strife of the seventeenth century, their capital markets eclipsed those of the Dutch. Naturally, frictions arose between established English financiers and the newcomers. English author Daniel Defoe grumbled in verse:

> We blame the King that he relies too much
> On Strangers, Germans, Huguenots, and Dutch
> And seldom does his just affairs of State
> To English Councillors communicate.[22]

After the Glorious Revolution, the financial situation rapidly improved in England. First, the former royal reliance on short-term loans was replaced with Dutch-style long-term government debt whose interest and principal payments were backed by excise taxes. Next, the English Treasury began cooperating with the banking community, experimenting with different kinds of debt to gauge which were best received by the investing public (that is, attracted the lowest interest rates). Parliamentary supremacy restored trust. Successful businessmen packed the House of Commons; a parliament whose members could be gored by government default is not likely to let that occur. Finally, in 1749, Henry Pelham, the chancellor of the exchequer, consolidated the confusing array of government loans into a single series of bonds, the famous "consols," which, like Venetian *prestiti* and Dutch *losrenten*, never matured and provided perpetual interest. Consols trade in London to this day.[23]

Although state borrowing may at first blush seem irrelevant to commercial lending, a healthy market for government debt is, in fact, essential for funding business. The reasons for this are twofold:

- Because the creditworthiness of the government is widely known and the trading volume in its debt is so high, this debt is the simplest to price and sell. Since the mechanisms for the pricing and sale of commercial capital are the same as for government bonds and bills, a successful market for government debt must exist before a commercial debt market can function smoothly. In the developing premodern economy, government debt acted as the "training wheels" for the supplying of capital to entrepreneurs.

- Government debt provides an essential benchmark, that of the "risk-free" investment. Government bonds and bills, which trade actively, provide businessmen and entrepreneurs with an ongoing measure of the rate of return demanded by perfectly safe enterprises. This forms a "baseline" to which can be added a "risk premium": the amount of extra interest demanded because of a loan's risk. For example, at the time of Pelham's debt consolidation, consols yielded 3%. This represented the lowest possible rate available to that most reliable of borrowers, the post–1688 English Crown. Thus, a moderately risky commercial venture might require a 6% rate, and a speculative one, in excess of 10%. The presence of an easily observable risk-free rate (that on government bonds) makes it easier to price loans to entrepreneurs.

The importance of first establishing a healthy market in government debt was vividly demonstrated in the U.S. during the Civil War. In 1862, when Lincoln's treasury secretary, Salmon P. Chase, failed to float a $500 million war issue, he called on financier Jay Cooke for help. The well-known Philadelphia investment banker used the telegraph to deploy an army of twenty-five hundred agents to sell those bonds directly to the public. Cooke floated an even larger issue in 1865, and beginning in 1870, he used the same techniques to raise capital for the Pennsylvania Railroad. His method split the task between two groups. The first constituted the underwriters, who purchased a company's debt at a discount, bearing the risk of being left with a large amount of unmarketable securities in the event that sales should fail. The second group was the large number of distributors who sold the issue directly to the public. In this manner were the vast capital needs of the new nation met.[24]

THE RISE OF THE JOINT-STOCK COMPANY

Of all the financial devices exported across the North Sea to London in the seventeenth century, the joint-stock company had the greatest long-term impact on subsequent economic development. The pervasive influence of giant, publicly held multinational corporations virtually defines our modern way of life. In fact, one feature that distinguishes life in the developed world from that in the undeveloped world is the amount of day-to-day interaction between ordinary citizens and these behemoths. Leaving aside the powerful political emotions evoked by large multinational corporations, it is beyond dispute that economies dominated by them are more stable and prosperous than those that are not. (We shall later address the question of whether people are happier in the modern corporate state.)

Why do these huge organizations so permeate modern commerce? The reasons have to do with the syndication and diversification of risk discussed earlier in this chapter. Breaking up business risk into thousands of small pieces increases the willingness of investors to shoulder that risk; lowering the individual ante broadens the spectrum of potential investors. In addition, being able to purchase shares of many different enterprises further lowers the risk level for individual investors, making them yet more willing to supply capital.

Moreover, the modern public company is a *limited liability corporation*; that is, the shareholder is not personally responsible for the venture's obligations. He can only lose his investment; the corporation's creditors cannot come after his personal possessions. In a world without limited liability—where all business partners and ordinary shareholders are fully liable for each other's actions, and where business failure can result in imprisonment or even slavery—large impersonal corporations are not possible. In this situation, the only viable structure for businesses of even modest size is the trustworthiness of the family group.

Beyond the perspective of trust, the family is not particularly well suited for the long-term development of very large businesses. Success in commerce demands intelligence, leadership, and vision. Executives possessed of all three qualities are hard enough to find in the general population; ensuring a steady supply of such talent over the generations from within one family is virtually impossible.

The ability to manage any large enterprise is a valued skill, but the rise of the factory in the eighteenth and nineteenth century required an even rarer commodity: the ability to mold a workforce of hundreds or thousands of employees—each performing a highly specialized task— into an efficiently functioning organism. Before the advent of the factory, this ability was reliably found only in the best high-ranking military officers.[25] The challenge of supplying the large numbers of such talented individuals needed at the middle levels of a giant company from within a single family is insurmountable, the reason being that financial success tends to corrode ambition and thrift in succeeding generations of family members—"from shirtsleeves to shirtsleeves in three generations," as the saying goes.

Limited liability is a near-absolute requirement for healthy public participation in company ownership; without it, the public will not supply equity capital to growing companies. The Bubble Act of 1720 stipulated that any business without a parliamentary charter could have no more than six partners, each of whom was liable "to his last shilling and acre" for the obligations of the entire enterprise.[26] Large and vigorous businesses do not thrive in such an environment.

The joint-stock company is not an unvarnished blessing. The interests of the company's management, who might own little or no stock, may be very different from those of the shareholders, who wish only to see their share prices and dividends rise. Modern economists call such inefficiency "agency cost." In its most extreme form, management can brazenly loot a company, as happened recently with WorldCom, Enron, and Adelphia. More subtly, managers can pad expenses or invest company capital more in the interest of empire building than profit. The merger of Time Warner and AOL is a prime example of this phenomenon. In response to such flagrant acts of corporate misbehavior, shareholders can theoretically limit these agency costs by voting their shares to toss out incompetent or self-interested management. However, this does not happen nearly as often as it should.

Thus, the modern joint-stock, limited liability corporation does more than dramatically lower the risk of investing via the mechanisms detailed above. The above considerations aside, it also increases productivity by favoring lean and hungry "new men" for leadership roles over the often increasingly jaded and indolent heirs of the founding family, who may possess stock, but no substantial control.

Such a system did not arise fully formed after the Glorious Revolution of 1688. Contrary to the orthodoxy of today's mullahs of market fundamentalism, a vigorous culture of stock investing requires strong government-run institutions to ensure that shareholders are not damaged by "information asymmetry"—that is, they are not cheated by the company's managers. The recent accounting scandals vividly demonstrate that even after four centuries of active joint-stock operations, perfection has not yet been attained. Both shareholders and government must vigorously police businesses.

The origins of the joint-stock company are lost to history. Roman companies that were organized to collect taxes and provide provisions to the empire traded shares at least intermittently. Around A.D. 1150, a three-hundred-year-old water mill in Bazacle, in southern France, divided its ownership into shares. Nearly continuous records of the company's share price are available from about 1400. The company traded on the Paris Bourse until 1946, when the French government, lacking an appreciation of the capital markets as well as a sense of history, nationalized the mill.[27]

The first joint-stock companies were timid affairs, protected by monopoly power. The English Crown established one early example, Staple of London, in 1248 to control the nation's wool trade. In 1357, Edward III granted Staple the right to collect export duties from other wool producers in exchange for financing from Staple for his French military adventures; Staple then agreed to grant Edward further loans. The company's operations were based in Calais, and the exchange of wool monopoly rights for royal loans continued for two centuries—until Calais fell to the French in 1558.[28]

Arguably, the first modern joint-stock companies were the Dutch East India Company and the English East India Company. In 1609, the Dutch company, or the VOC (*Vereenigte Ost-Indische Compagnie*), as Low Country natives and economic historians know it, was the first to raise large amounts of capital by issuing permanent dividend-paying shares. In the early eighteenth century, scholars estimated the company's value at about 6.5 million florins, consisting of about two thousand shares valued at three thousand florins each.* The returns to shareholders were prodigious—for over a century, the shares paid a dividend of about 22%.[29] The outsized rewards of VOC shares reflected two different risks: first, the intrinsic dangers of conducting a new and extremely hazardous long-distance trading operation, and second, the uncertainties surrounding the new joint-stock institution itself. As always, high returns have their disadvantages. They may be a boon to investors, but such a high cost of capital is a disaster to companies needing it. A venture must be very successful indeed to support a 22% annual payment to shareholders!

The capital markets in seventeenth-century England were much less developed than those on the other side of the North Sea, and the history of the British East India Company (EIC) best illustrates the problems encountered by the first joint-stock companies. The EIC conducted an extremely risky business operation—the triangular trade in spice and cloth involving England, India, and the Indonesian archipelago. Typically, Spanish silver was used to purchase Indian cotton, which was then exchanged in Indonesia for pepper, nutmeg, and cloves. These were then shipped back to England and sold for silver coin. Trade in

---

* Roughly $140 million in today's money. See Neal, 17.

sugar, coffee, tea, indigo, and silk with China and other Southeast Asian ports supplemented the basic triangular trade route.[30]

The enormous profitability of the trade was offset by the enormous risks that were faced. Aside from the normal vicissitudes of commerce—a fall in the price of cotton in Java coupled with a spice shortage could be disastrous—the journey itself was fraught with danger. Horrific mortality rates among crews from disease and shipwreck were a given, to say nothing of marauding local pirates and very unfriendly Dutch, Portuguese, and Indian forces. It was not unusual for ships to disappear without a trace.

Each voyage was a sixteen-month operation that was choreographed around seasonal winds. The associated capital operation was relatively simple. The outfitting of about a dozen ships and the initial outlay of silver for each voyage required large amounts of money. If all went well, sixteen months later, these same ships, laden with spices and other goods from the East, would sail back up the Thames. High demand and low supply ensured that these goods would fetch high prices and return huge profits.

The VOC and EIC quickly discovered that this trade was so risky that it was better to confine as much of it as possible within Asia and ship only the final product—gold and silver specie—back to Europe. This had two advantages. First, limiting most of the trading to the Indian Ocean cut the murderous costs, both in treasure and human lives, of frequent round-trips via the Cape of Good Hope route. Second, trading locally in Asia did not require the shipment of specie from Europe to pay for spices and textiles. This kept with the era's mercantilist spirit, which equated a nation's health with the size of its silver and gold stock.

The company's initial voyages took place in 1601. Although capital was freely available to Dutch companies from their sophisticated capital markets, the English markets of the period were rudimentary. In 1601, the English had little access to Dutch capital, and the Dutch were unlikely, in any case, to finance a competitor to the VOC. Finding that long-term capital was unavailable, the EIC was reduced to selling shares in its individual voyages. Typically, each voyage required about £50,000 of capital, divided into five hundred shares that sold for £100 each. When the goods arrived in London sixteen months later, the company stored them in warehouses and gradually auctioned them off in order to avoid flooding the market and depressing prices. In this manner, the proceeds were distributed among shareholders over the following year or so. These periodic auctions became a regular part of the London commercial calendar. Later, the auctions served another, and perhaps more important, purpose. Since they attracted large numbers of shareholders, they evolved into a reasonably efficient market for trading the company's shares.

Almost all of these individually capitalized voyages earned high returns for shareholders. In fact, only one lost money. For example, the tenth voyage in 1611 returned £248 for each £100 share purchased. This high-lights the central feature of the capital markets of the time: *High investor returns mean a high cost of capital to the company.* The EIC would have much preferred to finance its voyages with cheap loans at low rates and keep the enormous profits for itself. Unfortunately, cheap capital was not available in the London of the early seventeenth century, particularly not for highly speculative ventures. As the EIC began to demonstrate an ability to reli-ably "deliver the goods," its cost of capital fell, and it began to successfully float short-term bonds at reasonable rates.

The original joint-stock companies, besides being monopolies, were bound to the government in yet another way—via the debt market. The Bank of England provided an excellent example of this. Contrary to the implication of its name, the bank was a private joint-stock company until a Labor government nationalized it in 1946 (the same year, you will recall, that the French nationalized the Bazacle mill).

In the years following the Glorious Revolution, the Bank of England was a fragile, young organization. In 1697, it pioneered a technique known as engraftment. The bank began to purchase government debt; in practice, this meant that private holders of government bills and bonds exchanged them for Bank of England shares. This government debt provided a steady stream of income to shareholders, supplied collateral for further borrowings, and also kept the bank informed about the future borrowing needs of the government—valuable information indeed.

The EIC carried out a similar engraftment operation. The South Sea Company, which was granted a monopoly in 1711 for trade with South America in return for assuming substantial government debt, also employed engraftment. This monopoly ultimately proved worthless in the face of Spanish and Portuguese ownership of the continent.[31] In

1719, a much larger South Sea engraftment operation led to the infamous South Sea Bubble. Naïve investors, impressed with the South Sea Company's South American trade monopoly, exchanged their government bonds for the company's skyrocketing shares. When the bubble inevitably burst, thousands of shareholders were sheared. One of the shorn was none other than Master of the Mint Sir Isaac Newton, who declared, "I can calculate the motions of the heavenly bodies, but not the madness of people."*

The English government also protected the shareholders of the overseas trading companies, including the South Sea and the EIC. For the first time, in 1662 limited liability status was conferred upon the companies, a move that favored shareholders at the expense of creditors. While sensitive to the rights of both shareholders and creditors, Parliament reasoned that the engrafted government debt held by these trading companies afforded creditors more than enough protection in the event of bankruptcy. Because most businesses did not possess engrafted government debt, Parliament did not grant limited liability status beyond the trading companies until 1856, when the Companies Act finally extended limited liability to the shareholders of most companies. Limited liability protection came earlier in the U.S.; it was granted to many companies soon after independence. By the 1830s, limited liability sheltered virtually all U.S. public corporations.[32]

In his remarkable contemplation on the nature of money, *Frozen Desire,* English writer James Buchan movingly documents the devastation that could be wrought on shareholders unprotected by limited liability status. Buchan comes from a long line of authors, one of whom was his great-great-grandfather, John Buchan, whose misfortune it was to own shares in the City of Glasgow Bank. When the bank failed in 1878 in a hail of managerial fraud, it owed depositors more than £6 million. John Buchan was responsible, under the law, for £2,700 of this—an amount approximately equal to his net worth and far in excess of the value of his shares. The court ruled that the Companies Act did not apply in his case; he died broken, embittered, and impoverished a few years later.[33]

---

* Each South Sea share yielded about £5 in interest from the government bonds it held. At the prevailing 3% interest rate, this implied a stock value of about £150, almost exactly the price that share prices fell to from their bubble high of about £1,000. See Chancellor, 69, 93.

This short history of joint-stock companies once again vividly demonstrates the importance of government in establishing and maintaining efficient capital markets. In seventeenth-century England, few investors would have provided capital to the risky ventures of the time without monopoly protection, engraftment of government debt, and in the case of the trading companies, limited liability shareholding. The first two institutions passed into extinction, but the third remains. Recent market history reinforces two notions: (1) in an economic state of nature, company managers will cheat shareholders, and (2) without vigorous regulatory oversight of the securities industry by the government, investors are loath to extend equity capital.

The development of the English capital markets, which began in the seventeenth century and continued in earnest in the eighteenth, came to full fruition in the nineteenth, when British capital was called upon to finance the great industrial expansion that occurred after the Congress of Vienna. The steam engines of Watt and Boulton would power the transformation of manufacturing and transport, and the miracles of the era—canals, railroads, and steam-driven factories—gobbled huge amounts of capital. The number of power looms in English textile mills increased 100-fold between 1813 and 1850, and iron production rose over thirtyfold between 1806 and 1873.[34] English capital paid not only for English railroads, factories, and canals, but also for those in the rest of Europe and in the even more rapidly developing but cash-poor former colonies.

THE ENGLISH CAPITAL MARKETS IN FULL FLOWER

After the abuses of the South Sea episode (1719–21), only Parliament could charter a company with more than six owners. It also forbade short selling and options trading, operations that enhanced market liquidity and efficiency. In a series of acts beginning in 1820, Parliament gradually eliminated the restrictions of the Bubble Act of 1720, simplified the formation of joint-stock companies, and broadened the umbrella of limited liability protection. Other legislation also aided trade and commerce. In 1846, Parliament finally repealed the Corn Laws, which for four centuries had protected domestic producers and gouged consumers by regulating and taxing grain imports and exports.

Finally, the nineteenth century also saw the elimination of debtor's prison, a point that is almost universally ignored by economic historians. In England, the Debtors Act of 1869 largely accomplished this end. (The act still permitted imprisonment if it could be proven in court that the debtor clearly had the wherewithal to pay.) Almost simultaneously, all of the individual U.S. states and many Western European nations passed similar statutes. The abolition of imprisonment for default could not help but encourage entrepreneurial risk taking.

By the late nineteenth century, England had become the planet's preeminent source of investment capital. The world's most talented businessmen and inventors flocked to London for financing, and the English economy became the globe's powerhouse. The most engaging description of the English money markets of the period is found in journalist and economist Walter Bagehot's *Lombard Street* (the very name deriving from the early Italian bankers of Lombardy), which was published in 1873:

> The briefest and truest way of describing Lombard Street is to say that it is by far the greatest combination of economical power and economic delicacy that the world has ever seen. . . . Everyone admits that it has much more immediately disposable and ready cash than any other country. But very few persons are aware how much *greater* the ready balance—the floating loan-fund which can be lent to anyone for any purpose—is in England than it is anywhere else in the world.[35]

Bagehot listed the amounts of known deposits available in the major financial centers in early 1873:[36]

London	£120,000,000
Paris	£13,000,000
New York	£40,000,000
German Empire	£8,000,000

Anyone seeking the reason for British economic and military dominance in the nineteenth century need not look further. The English entrepreneur freely pursued any commercial idea he chose. If he had satisfactory credit, the markets would shower him with capital sufficient to bring his plans to fruition. In Bagehot's inimitable prose, it was capital *"which can be lent to anyone for any purpose."*

The most striking feature of the above numbers is the ninefold difference in size between the London and Paris money markets, given that the English economy was only 28% bigger than France's at the time. In fact, these figures understate the difference. The English had active money markets outside of London, while capital activity in the French countryside was negligible. Why did the French (and Germans as well) have such small capital markets? The reasons, according to Bagehot, were cultural and historical:

> Of course the deposits of bankers are not a strictly accurate measure of the resources of a Money Market. On the contrary, much more cash exists out of banks in France and Germany, and in all non-banking countries, than could be found in England or Scotland, where banking is developed. But that cash is not, so to speak, "moneymarket money:" it is not attainable. *Nothing but their immense misfortunes, nothing but a vast loan in their own securities, could have extracted the hoards of France from the custody of the French people.* (Italics added)[37]

In other words, the French and Germans did not trust their financial institutions; the surplus franc and mark went under the mattress, not into enterprise. The French or German entrepreneur was no less clever and hard-working than his English counterpart was, he merely had less access to capital. Driving the point home, Bagehot points out that this concentration of capital in the nation's great banks was a unique English advantage, for

> a million in the hands of a single banker is a great power; he can at once lend it where he will, and borrowers can come to him, because they know or believe that he has it. But the same sum scattered in tens and fifties through a whole nation is no power at all: no one knows where to find it or whom to ask for it.[38]

Bagehot positively exulted in this state of affairs, "a luxury which no country has ever enjoyed with even comparable equality before." He went on to point out that the easy availability of capital provided opportunity to the "dirty crowd of little men," who during the nineteenth century pushed out the comfortable aristocracy (many of whom had been dirty little men just a generation or two before). "The rough and vulgar structure of English commerce is the secret of its life, for it contains 'the propensity to variation,' which, in the social as in the animal kingdom, is the principle of progress."[39] Not only did the dirty little "new man" innovate, but he also undersold established merchants and brought the fruits of innovation to the masses. In short, the bounty of available capital fed a constant stream of technological and commercial innovation, that is, economic growth itself. Capital had, in effect, become "blind." Prior to the nineteenth century, the borrower and lender knew each other personally. Bagehot's new system was anonymous. For the first time, an increasingly complex and efficient system of intermediaries separated the consumer of capital from its provider, just as industrialization increasingly divorced the producers of goods from consumers.

Why, then, did the Dutchman, the Englishman, and the American bring his savings to the bank to earn interest in the money markets, while the Frenchman, the German, the Indian, and the Turk did not? Bagehot is silent on the topic. To answer this question, we must examine the premodern history of national governance.

Recall how the lack of capital markets and property rights in Turkey forced Müezzinzade Ali Pasha to keep his wealth near his person. The rot in the Ottoman Empire, in the pre-Renaissance period in general, nay, in many nonwestern nations today, now comes into sharper focus. Where there was or is no protection of personal property, there is no incentive to innovate. And even if somewhere in such a benighted land there did beat the heart of an inventor, *there would be no capital to develop and bring his creations to market.* All of a country's capital would be frozen under mattresses, worn in ornament and jewelry, and most important, secured in private vaults—especially the emperor's.

The Islamic prohibition of interest saddled the Turks with yet a further disadvantage. Without interest, there are no loans, and without loans, there is no investment. By the time of the Battle of Lepanto, in which Ali Pasha met his end, these strictures had largely fallen away in the West. Not so in the Muslim world, whose poor economic showing compared with the West has been in large part a consequence of the resulting rudimentary state of its property rights and capital markets. Private property, financial markets, and banking, as we know them, did not exist in the Ottoman Empire before 1856, when the first banks were established in Turkey—by Europeans.

History's judgment of the Turks is perhaps best summed up by Lepanto's most famous (if only a minor) participant, Cervantes: "All the world learned how mistaken it had been in believing the Turks were invincible."[40] The Turks were neither the first nor the last nation to suffer such a fate. Cervantes' observation would echo through the ages as other seemingly indomitable states—seventeenth-century Spain and the Soviet Union come quickly to mind—ultimately withered because of the absence of free citizenry and functioning markets.

CHAPTER FIVE

Power, Speed, and Light

THE DAUGHTER-IN-LAW WHO DOESN'T SPEAK

Several years ago, an ungainly contraption known as the multifunctional platform began popping up in villages in West Africa. Invented by a Swiss aid worker, this device married a ten-horsepower gasoline engine to a variety of tools—funnels, grinders, blenders, and pistons. Local women's associations usually owned and operated these machines, and they revolutionized life wherever they appeared. For example, a village woman might rent the machine for ten minutes, at a cost of about twenty-five cents in local currency, in order to grind and blend fifteen pounds of peanuts into peanut butter—a task that previously would have taken a day of backbreaking toil. Since such menial work had traditionally been the province of the family's lowest-ranking females, villagers nicknamed the device "the daughter-in-law who doesn't speak."

The benefits of the machines have been proven beyond calculation. Families with productive peanut farms were able to vastly increase the amount of peanut butter they sold on the open market. Younger women, freed from an unending stream of drudgery, were able to afford the time and money to attend school. Older women gained the time to expand their businesses and plant new crops.

The machines turned generators that supplied electricity to lights, allowing stores to do business and babies to be born more safely after sunset. Even the men, who usually had little to do with these machines, were pleased. Said one husband, "Our wives aren't so tired anymore, and their hands are smoother. We like that."[1]

These devices make understandable to the modern reader the thoroughgoing changes that swept everyday life in the nineteenth-century West. They also help make clear the essential reason why world economic growth skyrocketed in the nineteenth century, but not before. The other three foundations of modern prosperity—property rights, scientific rationalism, and efficient capital markets—had already been secured in the English-speaking world and on much of the European continent. All that entrepreneurs lacked was transport, efficient communication, and reliable power for manufacturing. The coming of the steam engine and the telegraph supplied the final ingredient for modern Western economic growth and instantaneously and irreversibly altered the way people had lived for thousands of years.

POWER

Whether you're growing soybeans, pouring steel, or assembling sophisticated electronic circuitry, you need *power* to enable you to produce. The more, the better. The farmer who does not have an ox falls behind his neighbor who does; the farmer with a tractor buries his ox-driven competitors with his machine-powered output.

Until about A.D. 1000, human muscle performed almost all agricultural, industrial, engineering, and military work. How much power can we humans produce? Pitifully little. The bicycle ergometer, usually feeding a dim light bulb, is a staple of science museums. If you are in excellent physical condition, you can comfortably generate about one-tenth of a horsepower for long periods. For a very short while, you might make it up to one-half of a horsepower, but after a few seconds your legs will ache mightily and your lungs will feel as if they are about to burst.

The ancients, especially the Greeks, did invent a multitude of clever devices based on screws, pulleys, and levers to employ our puny human output to fullest advantage. However, the primary method of completing tasks involving large size and great weight in the premodern era was by using what historians euphemistically call "the social device": conscripting and harnessing together large numbers of workers to construct temples, pyramids, canals, and aqueducts.

Clever devices and massed human labor only went so far. As long as the only source of power was human muscle, any sustained growth in agriculture and manufacturing was not possible. European governments did not phase out the infamous *corvée*—involuntary labor used for road construction—until the mid-nineteenth century.[2]

To supplement brute human strength the ancients did use draft animals. The table summarizes the amounts of continuous power available from humans and various beasts of burden today, as measured by a dynamometer:[3]

	Sustained Horsepower
Man and mechanical pump	0.06
Man and winch	0.08
Ass	0.20
Mule	0.39
Ox	0.52
Draft horse	0.79

Although the ancient world did see the use of animal power, it was expensive and inefficient. In the classical and medieval worlds, humans and domesticated animals were both smaller than they are today. Thousands of years ago, draft animals probably produced only one-third of the power that they do today. The Greeks and Romans reserved horses, which were costly, for lighter tasks that required speed. Further, the poor quality of harnesses and lack of hoof protection denied the ancients the full use of horse power, and the traditional ox-yoke choked the fleet animals.[4] It would not be until the twelfth century that farmers employed an effective horse harness.

THE WHEEL OF FORTUNE

Even humans deployed their power inefficiently. Not only were people smaller and less healthy in the ancient world, they were also poorly motivated. Slaves or peasants without property rights performed most work;

economic historians estimate slave productivity at half of that of free men performing the same work.[5]

The waterwheel provided the first real advance in power production. The earliest and most inefficient type—the so-called noria—appeared in late Hellenic Greece, around 150 B.C. (Figure 5–1) Throughout history, the mills' major task was to grind grain. Echoes of the modern West African "daughter-in-law who doesn't speak" are obvious from one upbeat ancient description of the waterwheel: "Cease from grinding, ye women who toil at the mill; sleep late, even if the crowing cocks announce the dawn."[6] In spite of this anonymous chronicler's enthusiasm, the new devices found relatively little use in Greece and Rome because their design was primitive and their power output low.

In Western Europe, over the ensuing two thousand years, the waterwheel's design went through several incarnations, finally emerging around A.D. 1500 as the familiar geared overshot wheel that is depicted in Figure 5–2. Only the most rapidly moving streams could power the earlier ungeared mills, but the introduction of gearing made mills on slow-moving rivers and creeks practicable. A builder dammed the stream

FIGURE 5–1   NORIA

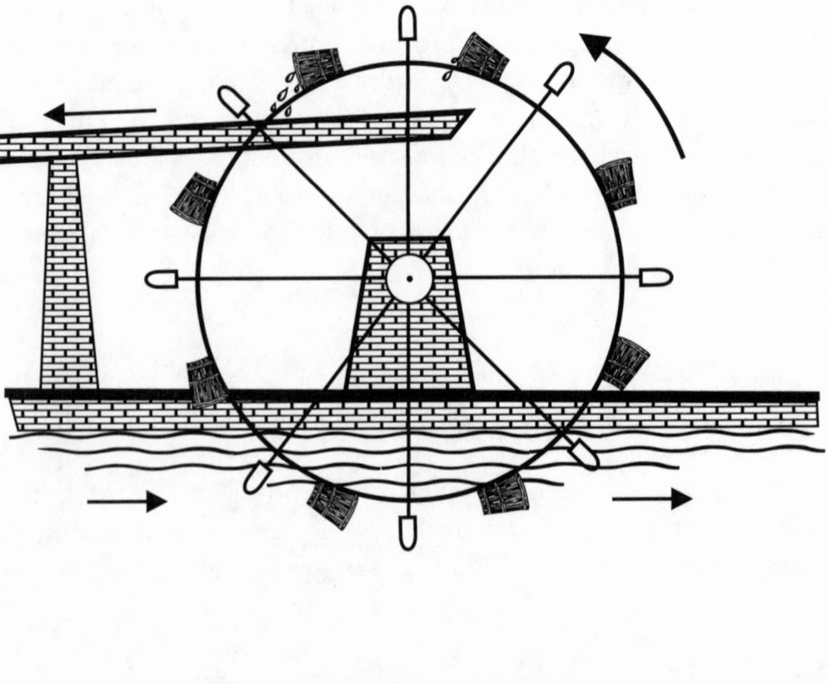

FIGURE 5–2   OVERSHOT WHEEL

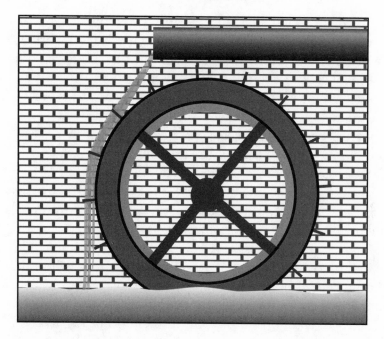

and captured its flow at the top of the device, providing the most efficient use of the stream's power.

Even a small mill that generated only a few horsepower could do the
work of scores of men. An early primitive mill of the "undershot" design
(in which the water passed under the mill's blades or buckets) could grind
four hundred pounds of corn per hour—the equivalent of three horsepower, versus ten pounds per hour for a "donkey mill" that was manned
by two laborers.[7] By the medieval era, mills not only ground corn and
wheat, they also ran foundries, powered sawmills, and crushed iron ore.

In A.D. 1086 the Domesday Book recorded 5,624 mills in southern
England, serving a population of about 1.5 million. Each mill produced
five horsepower, just 0.02 horsepower per inhabitant. Mankind's escape from physical limitation was now within reach. The waterwheel
remained a fixture of Western life well into the nineteenth century. An
overshot device at London Bridge pumped London's water supply until 1822.[8]

REAPING THE WIND

Although man has harnessed the wind to power sailing ships since time immemorial, wind energy was not used to do mechanical work until relatively recently, when tenth-century Persians first used it for industrial purposes. Windmills have two inherent disadvantages. First and most obvious, they cannot provide reliable power on a day-to-day basis. Second, they must be continuously aligned with the wind. The earliest "post" windmills utilized a cumbersome single-piece design; the operators had to turn the entire heavy device en bloc. Later, the turret mill, which was turned only at the top, came into wide use in Holland. Finally, in 1745 Edmund Lee invented the fantail, a large vertical fin that automatically aligned the blades of the windmill, a familiar fixture on American farms even today.

Although the windmill improved productivity, it did not supplant human power for most tasks. It could average only about ten horsepower and so was no great improvement over the waterwheel. In seventeenth century Holland, approximately 8,000 such devices, used mainly for pumping seawater, served a population of well over one million—about a tenth of a horsepower per inhabitant, five times the amount of power per person as in the England of the Domesday period.

The whims of nature limited where and when the windmill and the waterwheel could be used. The most powerful waterwheel of the premodern era was Louis XIV's Machine of Marly, which was used to run the fountains at Versailles and was said to generate as much as seventy-five horsepower.[9] The economic takeoff of the West awaited the development of a technology that was capable of supplying greater power, without regard to location or weather.

STEAM HEATING THE MODERN ECONOMY

The ancients knew that boiling water could do physical work. Around 100 B.C., Hero of Alexandria described two steam-powered devices. The first, depicted in Figure 5–3, was a round vessel, mounted on a horizontal axle, the familiar Hero's Engine. When heated, tangentially oriented vents directed the exhaust steam so that the vessel spun.

FIGURE 5–3   HERO'S ENGINE

The second ancient steam engine was a Rube Goldberg device that was used to open and close temple doors in Alexandria. Steam drove water from a large vessel into a smaller bucket, which in turn fell by force of gravity, which in turn powered the movement of the doors via a complicated system of pulleys and posts.

The two devices, described in Hero's *Pneumatica*, may or may not have existed. If they did, they were demonstration pieces—mere toys, at best, that did no useful work. Mankind made little practical use of steam until late in the seventeenth century. The most pressing engineering problem of that era was the removal of water from coal mines. For centuries, miners knew that they could not pump water from depths of greater than thirty feet. This limitation made it impossible to exploit deep coal seams efficiently. When Cosimo de Medici's engineers failed in their attempts at deep drainage, they asked Galileo for help. He turned the problem over to his brilliant assistant, Evangelista Torricelli. Although Torricelli could not create an effective pump, he discovered something even more valuable in the process of trying: The thirty-foot limit was the result of atmospheric pressure. That pressure, exerting an immense opposing force of more than fourteen pounds per square inch, was equivalent to the pressure exerted by a column of water *precisely thirty feet high*.

In 1654, German scientist Otto von Guericke demonstrated the potential of atmospheric power by an ingenious experiment. He placed together two metal hemispheres twenty inches in diameter and then evacuated the air between them. The resulting vacuum was so strong that two opposing teams of large horses could not separate the hemispheres.

Scientists quickly realized that harnessing the force of the vacuum would generate huge amounts of power. Christian Huygens made the first attempts, creating a partial vacuum by igniting gunpowder in a cylinder. The hot gas expelled itself and the surrounding air through a valve. With cooling, the valve closed, resulting in a partial vacuum. While useful for demonstration purposes, this method was not much more efficient than producing a vacuum through mechanical pumping. (This device can also be said to be the first internal combustion engine.)

Huygens' assistant, Denis Papin, theorized that steam would provide a much more efficient way of producing a vacuum:

> Since it is a property of water that a small quantity of it turned into vapor by heat has an elastic force like that of air, but upon cold supervening is again resolved into water, so that no trace of the said elastic force remains, I concluded that machines could be constructed wherein water, by the help of no very intense heat, and at little cost, could produce that perfect vacuum which could by no means be obtained by gunpowder.[10]

Soon after penning those fateful words, Papin created a working model of the first piston steam engine. A small amount of water in the cylinder was boiled, driving up the piston. At the top of the stroke, the fire was removed and a catch held the piston in position. The device was then cooled. The steam condensed, thus creating a vacuum. When fully cooled, the catch was released, driving the piston forcefully down. Strictly speaking, this device was not a steam engine, but rather a *vacuum* engine. Papin's steam piston was not driven by the force of steam under pressure, but by the near-perfect vacuum created when the steam condensed into water, the ratio of water to steam density being about 1,200:1.

STEAM COMES TO THE MARKETPLACE

Like the engines of Hero and Huygens, the Papin engine was too cumbersome and slow for practical use. But it was not long before others refined his contraption into devices that were capable of producing economically useful work. In the seventeenth century, both the Marquis of Worcester and Thomas Savery designed steam-operated pumps, though it is not clear that the marquis actually built his engine. While Savery produced working models, they were not a commercial success. Nonetheless, some historians have credited Savery with the first working steam engine. More relevant than their technical or commercial accomplishments is that both Savery and the marquis won patents for their devices. Savery's came after he made a demonstration for the royalty at Hampton Court.

Late in the seventeenth century, inventors were tantalized by the prospect of a lucrative industrial monopoly and drove the quickening pace of technological innovation. Although the leading lights of the scientific revolution were highly educated, and many hailed from aristocratic wealth, the great engineers and inventors of the Industrial Revolution were almost without exception uneducated craftsmen, who were motivated mainly by the prospect of commercial gain. Thomas Newcomen, like his contemporary Savery, was typical. Newcomen's low social station did not prevent him from corresponding with Robert Hooke, one of the great scientists of his day, about the work of Papin and the Marquis of Worcester. Newcomen realized that the earlier designs suffered because of the slow cooling of their cylinders, which was accomplished externally. He designed an engine cooled by injecting cold water *internally*. Since Savery's patent was very broadly written and covered almost any design that Newcomen could have conceived, Newcomen was forced to join forces with Savery.

The historical record of their first device is almost nonexistent, but sometime in 1712, at the colliery at Dudley Castle, Worcestershire, the world's first functioning atmospheric steam engine began pumping water from the mine's depths. The key word here is "atmospheric." The Newcomen engine, depicted in Figure 5–4, operated solely by means of the ambient atmospheric pressure, as did Papin's. At rest, the piston resided at the top of the cold cylinder. Live steam from the boiler was injected

FIGURE 5–4   NEWCOMEN'S ENGINE

FIGURE 5–5   WATT'S ENGINE

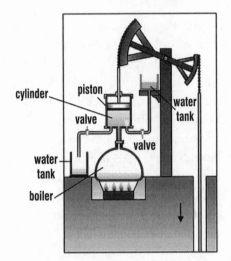

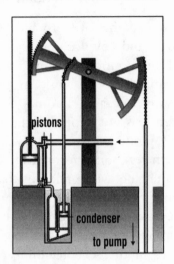

Source: Reproduced with permission of the Newcomen Society.

into the cylinder, displacing the cold air through the left valve in Figure
5–4. The cylinder, now filled with steam and with the piston at the top of
its stroke, was next injected with cold water from the right valve in the
figure, which condensed the steam and produced a near-vacuum. This
near-vacuum drew the piston down with great force, which was transmitted to the pumping mechanism. Steam was then again injected into the
cylinder, and the piston would rise gently. The next cycle was initiated
with another injection of cold water. Thus, the engine operated purely by
atmospheric pressure—the piston was not driven by the live steam, but by
the vacuum produced when the steam condensed.

Newcomen's pièce de résistance was incorporating automatic operation of the valves, whose opening and closing were controlled by the
motions of the main drive beam. The machine cycled twelve times per
minute and produced about 5.5 horsepower.[11] Although no more powerful than a waterwheel or windmill, it could do its work anytime, anywhere. Mankind could now deploy power at will, independent of
nature's whims. The new patent laws, which rewarded innovation and
refinement, drove the inventors far beyond the first primitive designs.
Within a few decades, Newcomen engines produced as much as seventy-five horsepower.

Newcomen's engine was the epicenter of a revolution in manufacture and transport that would forever alter the contours of world economic growth. It was not, however, economically viable. The design, which required that the entire cylinder be alternatively heated and cooled, was inherently inefficient, and because the engine was atmospheric, it was limited in force just 14.7 pounds per square inch of piston face. The engine consumed an enormous amount of coal, and so could only be used to pump out mines, where its fuel abounded. Worse, the engine produced power only on the downstroke, making it impractical for driving wheels and paddles. It was, in the words of one historian, a "hopeful monstrosity."[12]

Limited as it was, the Newcomen engine remained the state of the art, and thus little used, for more than two generations after its invention. A 1769 compilation of steam engines listed only sixty-seven.[13] While technically flawed, the engine's fundamental concept was sound, and succeeding generations of craftsmen gradually improved upon its power and fuel efficiency.

One such artisan was James Watt. Born in Scotland in 1736 into a poor merchant family, his difficult financial circumstances forced him to seek a trade. At age 19, Watt traveled to London, where he learned to make "philosophical instruments"—what we now call scientific apparatus. When he returned to Glasgow to establish himself in this business, the local guilds refused him entry. Fortunately, his innate mechanical talent was obvious, and Glasgow University gave him employment repairing and making instruments.

His new position gave him access to Scotland's greatest scientists, who familiarized him with the physics of steam. In 1764, fate presented him with one of the university's model Newcomen engines for repair. Watt immediately recognized that its inefficiency resulted from the alternate heating and cooling of the cylinder—it would consume far less coal if it could somehow run hot continuously. Shortly thereafter, while taking a now-fabled walk on Glasgow Green, he had a flash of insight: If the steam could be condensed *outside* the cylinder, the cylinder itself could remain hot throughout the cycle, greatly saving fuel. The next day, he returned to his laboratory and, using a small brass medical syringe, demonstrated the practicality of an external condenser. The critical external condenser in Watt's design is shown in Figure 5–5.

When Watt attempted to put his device into production, he ran into the same problem that would hamper Thomas Edison more than a century later. Invention was hard enough. Harder still for Watt was finding skilled workmen to produce his engines in great number. Hardest of all was obtaining money enough to build large numbers of the engines. Initially, Watt teamed up with a fellow inventor, John Roebuck, but the immense capital needs of the piston-and-cylinder engine, particularly for its expensive precision machining, forced them into bankruptcy.

Broke and needing to put food on the table, Watt found work as a civil engineer. Blessed by fortune not once, but twice, his luck turned a decade later, in 1774. In London on routine business, he met with Birmingham industrialist Matthew Boulton, who took an interest in his work. Also in that year, gun armorer John Wilkinson perfected a method for boring cannon that met the fine tolerances demanded by the piston-and-cylinder engine. Within months, Watt and Boulton had manufactured industrial-size engines that were made with Wilkinson's precision components. The first of these engines went to ventilate Wilkinson's blast furnaces in repayment for the cylinders he supplied.[14]

Nowhere did the concept of "synergy" apply better than to the interaction between steel and steam technologies. Steam improved the quantity and the quality of steel. Higher-quality steel allowed for more precise machining, as well as higher stress tolerances, of the pistons and cylinders, leading, in turn, to yet more efficient steam power.

Even the House of Commons cooperated. By 1774, there were only eight years left on Watt's original patent, not enough time to make the Boulton-Watt engine profitable. Parliament granted them another twenty-five years of patent protection. By the time the extension ran out, 496 of the devices were chugging away in England, powering mine pumps, blast furnaces, and factories.

The industrial opportunities created by the Boulton-Watt engine opened a floodgate of innovation. Watt designed engines that could produce rotary output—critical for factory and transport application—and that worked under positive steam pressure, not merely atmospheric (negative) pressure. Watt, though, was wary of using steam of much more than one atmosphere's pressure. Not so mine engineer Richard Trevithick. In 1802, two years after the parliamentary grant to Boulton and Watt expired, he patented an engine that operated at 145 pounds per square inch, ten times normal atmospheric pressure.

By the turn of the nineteenth century, mankind had decisively escaped the age-old limits imposed by muscle, water, and wind. The output of one person manning a factory machine or pneumatic coal hammer might be a few dozen times or even a hundred times that of his predecessors. Ships no longer depended on the vicissitudes of nature. More significant, the newfound ability to produce an abundance of mechanical energy would inspire inventions that previously were inconceivable. Two of these inventions—the railroad locomotive and the electrical generator—would soon transform the very substance of everyday life and in the process yield up the final piece of the global prosperity puzzle.

SPEED

A cornucopia of consumer goods has little value if it cannot be effectively moved from place to place. Clothing, food, and electrical equipment, no matter how efficiently produced, will remain prohibitively expensive if they cannot be transported cheaply and rapidly to their users.

Such was the case during the first half of the industrial revolution. In late 1821 when English writer Leigh Hunt and his family set off for Italy, the weather was so stormy that two months later, they had not yet cleared the English coastline and did not reach Livorno until the following July.[15]

During this same period, land travel was probably safer and more comfortable than sea passage, but not by much. As late as 1820, highway robbery in England was still common. On the Continent, matters were far worse. French shipments of merchandise routinely required security guards, and murder was not rare on Italian highways. Until the advent of the steam locomotive, Continental travelers routinely carried firearms.

Compounding the misery was the abysmal condition of the roads. Most were little more than heavily rutted dirt paths. Aside from limiting the speed of travel and causing discomfort, their uneven surfaces made them unsafe. A coach overturning even at low speeds could easily prove fatal to passengers. It would not be until about 1820 that John L.

McAdam transformed the science of road building by discovering that highways surfaced with finely crushed stone (macadamized) were smooth and resistant to rutting.

Sea travel may have been riskier than land travel, but before the invention of steam power, it was markedly cheaper, even when direct overland routes were available. Decades *after* the advent of rail travel, it was still less expensive to journey between London and Edinburgh by sea than by land.

A similar situation occurred in the New World, where the Appalachian Mountains posed a formidable barrier to inland travel. This is vividly demonstrated by the travel times shown in Figure 5–6. A coastal journey of five hundred miles by ship might take a week, while three weeks would be required to travel the same distance into the hinterland.

SLOW, BUT SURE, SAFE, AND CHEAP

The eighteenth century, however, had not been entirely without progress in transportation. Since ancient times, rulers had built canals to provide inexpensive, if slow, inland shipping. The advent of steam technology greatly increased the demand for fuel. Moving vast quantities of coal from distant and inaccessible mines is no small challenge. In 1767, the Duke of Bridgewater hit upon the idea of constructing a canal between his mines at Worsley and the textile mills situated thirty miles away at Runcorn. The canal was fabulously successful and operates to this day. Within two decades, Englishmen had constructed in excess of a thousand miles of canals.[16]

Yet this was nothing compared with the era of canal building that occurred in the U.S. in the early nineteenth century. Because capital was chronically short in the pre-Revolutionary period, the colonists did not greatly favor canals, whose initial construction is fabulously expensive. By the 1820s, however, the slowly expanding American economy began to produce an ever-increasing flow of capital, and businessmen began to dream of a vast system of inland canals for bulk transport. The completion of the Erie Canal in 1825 inaugurated the realization of this dream. One of the greatest construction projects of its age, the Erie Canal was called "an act of

FIGURE 5–6   TRAVEL TIMES FROM NEW YORK CITY IN 1800

Source: Reproduced with permission of publisher, John F. Stover, ed., *The Routledge Historical Atlas of the American Railroads* (London: Routledge, 1999), 11.

faith" by historian George Taylor. What else does one call the extension of a 364-mile artificial waterway westward from Albany to a vast wilderness?

The canal's story was epic. The federal government thought the scheme harebrained and denied support. This left it to a local politician, New York Governor De Witt Clinton, to commit New York State to back the enormous bond issues that were necessary to finance the canal. Today's libertarians forget that in underdeveloped nations (as the U.S. was in the early nineteenth century), few are willing to lend to private enterprises. The state is often the only party able to attract capital at reasonable rates.

Even before its entire length had been finished, the Erie was an enormous financial success. In spite of later competition from the railroads, its tonnage did not peak until 1880.[17] The canal's most visible legacy was the vast metropolis of New York City. Before the canal, Gotham had played second fiddle to Boston, Philadelphia, and later, even to Washington, D.C. The Erie Canal made New York City the entrepôt for the vast agricultural output of the Midwest, which flowed through the canal to the Hudson River and thence to the city's wharves for transshipment to its final destination, usually elsewhere on the East Coast or in Europe.

However successful the canals were, they were not a revolutionary improvement. For starters, they were useful only over relatively flat inland stretches—the maximum elevation of the Erie Canal was 650 feet. Nor did they offer great speed. Real change in transport awaited the application of steam to sea and land carriage.

STEAM ON THE HIGH SEAS

On the world's oceans, the sail did not yield easily to the steam engine. For more than a century after the Marquis Jouffroy d'Abbans built the first paddle-wheel steamer in 1787, sailing ships competed successfully against them. In fact, competitive pressures encouraged improvements in the technology of sailing ships that were almost as dramatic as those in steam propulsion. The clipper ship of the mid-nineteenth century could carry loads weighing up to several thousand tons while making twenty knots. Not until late in the nineteenth century would steam move most of the world's seagoing tonnage.[18]

The marriage of the steam engine to the maritime hull caused considerable difficulty. The top-heavy early engines made vessels unstable and gobbled huge amounts of coal. While frequent refueling was not a problem for river or coastal steamers, ocean transport was another story. One of the first steamers on the transatlantic route, the *British Queen*, carried 500 tons of cargo and 750 tons of coal.[19] Navies, which might be called upon for distant action on a moment's notice, initially shied away from the new technology. The largest ship of its day was the mammoth iron-hulled *Great Eastern*. Launched in 1858, it was driven by paddle, sail, and propeller, measured 692 feet long, and displaced 22,500 tons. Ultimately, frequent and expensive coaling stops doomed the *Great Eastern* commercially.

Steam power finally became practical with the perfection of the high-pressure marine engine and the screw propeller. Trevithick's original high-pressure engine design had proved too expensive and unsafe for practical use, but by 1870 pressures of up to 150 pounds per square inch were routinely employed. By the turn of the century, just before the advent of the oil turbine, the Royal Navy's standard Babcock and Wilson steam tube could generate 250 pounds per square inch.

ONE PRICE, ONE WAGE

The steam-driven increase in shipping volume was enough to "equilibrate" (bring into balance) the markets for the three fundamental economic inputs—land, labor, and capital—between England and America. In a world where workers and commodities do not move easily, large differences in the prices of commodities and wages will develop between countries, and even between neighboring cities. This produces uneven land prices, and if efficient communication is not available, even the return on investments will vary widely from place to place.

With the lack of adequate ocean transport, such unevenness of pricing was the state of the world economy before 1870. Because land was scarce in England and plentiful in America, land prices, and thus food prices, were much higher in Britain. On the other hand, because labor was plentiful in England and scarce in America, the wages paid to a British worker were far lower than those paid to his American cousin. Thus, a laborer's earnings bought far less in England, where wages were low and prices were high, than in America. (The same was true of capital. Because it was so much more plentiful in England than in America, its return was lower in England than in the U.S.)

The advent of steam transport leveled price and wage differences between the U.S. and England. In 1870 the price of beef was 93% higher in London than Cincinnati; by 1913 the differential was only 18%. Between those two dates, land rents increased by 171% in the U.S., but *fell* by 50% in England, a decline that paralleled an equally dramatic fall in land prices in Britain.

Not only did commodity prices, land prices, and rents reach equilibrium in the two nations, so, too, did real wages. This was not simply the result of cheap American foodstuffs. It was also a consequence of the increased ability of English workers to emigrate, which tightened the local labor market in Britain. Finally, the return on English capital improved as better information and transport provided it with more profitable overseas investment alternatives.* When we speak today of a "global economy," what we mean is a world in which wages and the prices of commodities and manufactured goods tend to converge among nations. The first giant steps in this direction were taken during the last half of the nineteenth century as steam power moved masses of goods and people across the world's oceans.

THE COMING OF THE RAILROAD

Steam's conquest of land transport was more rapid and far-reaching. Inventors immediately attempted to apply it to the road carriage. The task

---

* The theory that the convergence of commodity prices also produces convergence of prices for the three fundamental economic inputs—labor, land, and capital—is known as the Heckscher-Ohlin Model. First postulated by these two Swedish economists after World War I, it has since been confirmed by contemporary economists. This obscure theory is of no small importance in an increasingly integrated global economy. See Kevin H. O'Rourke and Jeffrey G. Williamson, "Late Nineteenth-Century Anglo-American Factor-Price Convergence: Were Heckscher and Ohlin Right?" *Journal of Political Economy,* 54 (Dec. 1994): 892–916.

was daunting, since a land vehicle offers even less engine space than a ship. In 1801, Richard Trevithick finally succeeded in powering a road carriage with one of his early high-pressure machines. By 1804, he was running a ten-mile tram, capable of hauling ten tons of iron and seventy men at five miles per hour, between the Penydarran foundry in Wales and a nearby canal. In 1808, he offered five-shilling rides to the London public near Euston Square.

The Michelangelo of the railroad locomotive was George Stephenson. Born into the poverty of the coalfields in 1781, he grew up near and in the mines, the son of an "engine man." Entranced by the symphony of steam, he, too, found himself managing a mine pump. Eventually, he met and consulted with Robert Hawthorne, the device's designer.

Stephenson's talent soon brought him to the attention of the British government. Coal production was a critical part of the war effort against Napoleon, and by the time he reached the age of thirty, Stephenson was managing the pumps at Newcastle's mammoth High Pit. Stephenson was illiterate, but his success afforded his son Robert an education, and the son soon taught the father reading and writing, as well as mathematics and science.

The coalfields provided the perfect nursery for the development of the railway locomotive. Coal cars had run on wooden rails for centuries in Germany and England. In the 1700s the wooden rails were slowly converted to iron tracks, and it was inevitable that the pit engines would replace the expensive and balky draft horses. A large share of that conversion fell to Stephenson.

The immediate catalyst for the development of a practical rail engine was an increase in the cost of horse fodder as a result of the Napoleonic Wars and an accompanying rise in the price of coal. Stephenson's initial designs were so underpowered that they often required a hefty human shove to get them moving. Such was the case with the *Blücher*, which provided the public with novelty rides in 1814. Stephenson and his son Robert continually improved their engines, with each being more powerful than the last. Their best-known creation, the *Rocket*, sped along at more than thirty miles per hour and captured the imagination of the British public. Actress Fanny Kemble's reaction was typical. Describing her first ride on the *Rocket*, she called it

. . . a snorting little animal which I felt inclined to pat. It set out at the ut-
most speed, thirty-five miles per hour, swifter than the bird flies. You
cannot conceive what that sensation of cutting the air was; the motion as
smooth as possible. I could either have read or written; and as it was I
stood up and with my bonnet off drank the air before me. When I closed
my eyes this sensation of flying was quite delightful and strange beyond
description. Yet strange as it was, I had a perfect sense of security and not
the slightest fear.[20]

In 1821, Parliament granted a consortium of businessmen permission to run a rail line from Darlington to Stockton-on-Tees. The coal-
field at Darlington had not been developed because of its remote
location, a problem that rail and steam would soon solve. Completed
three years later, the line made money almost immediately. A much
larger project that connected Manchester and Liverpool soon followed.
This line, linking the nation's industrial center with its port, was extraordinarily ambitious. Engineers would have to move massive
amounts of earth for grades and cuttings and build huge viaducts.
Stephenson would win the engine competition with the *Rocket*, which
pulled a heavy load sixty miles at speeds that averaged in excess of fourteen miles per hour.

The line opened on September 15, 1830, and although the ceremony
was marred by the first railway death—railway enthusiast and member of
Parliament William Huskisson was run over by the *Rocket*—it was apparent that the railroad had revolutionized modern life. A decade later, two
thousand miles of track were operating in England. Unlike the steamship, which only marginally increased speed and comfort, the railroad
changed the very nature of travel itself. Journey times that had been
measured in days and weeks were now counted in hours, and time itself
acquired a new modifier—"railway time"—to signify the sudden acceleration in the pace of everyday life (similar to the more recent "Internet
time"). Long-distance travel, previously restricted to the wealthy, became available to all. The English took 10 million stagecoach trips in
1835. In 1845, they took 30 million railway journeys; in 1870, they
took 330 million.[21]

By 1830, the steam engine sliced the journey between Glasgow and
London from several hard days to twenty-four easy hours. The *Railway
Times* exulted, "What more can any reasonable man want?"[22]

LIGHT

A particularly durable legend has it that not long after midnight on June 18, 1815, a lone carrier pigeon swooped low over the English Channel, bringing word to England of Napoleon's defeat at Waterloo. The momentous news was supposedly destined for consumption neither by the press and waiting public, nor even by the civil and military ministries, but rather for the eyes of one man, and one man only: financier Nathan Rothschild.

That morning, stock exchange members guessed that Rothschild likely knew the battle's outcome. Realizing that the market suspected his advance knowledge, Rothschild intentionally precipitated a panic by selling consols. The wily operator then quietly and methodically bought them back up, knowing that their prices would rise dramatically when news of victory reached the financial markets the next day.*

Such was the state of communication when the modern era began. The fact that even the most vital news took days to travel between adjacent nations meant that information was money in the bank to those who possessed it, and its lack calamitous to those who did not.

WARNING BECOMES ELECTRIC

Ever since the discovery of electricity, scientists dreamed of using it to transmit information, and beginning in the mid-eighteenth century, numerous attempts were made to do so. In 1746 French abbé Jean-Antoine Nollet

---

* The reality was far more complex. The Rothschilds did use carrier pigeons, but only for routine price data, not for critical communication between partners. The news of Waterloo was, in fact, relayed from Brussels newspaper accounts to the Rothschild offices by their private couriers two full days before the English government and public received it. Although Nathan Rothschild did make modest profits on the purchase of consols on the basis of this advance information, the unexpectedly swift defeat of Napoleon was a near-disaster for the House of Rothschild, which had expected a prolonged campaign and had consequently acquired vast amounts of gold, which fell in value with the end of hostilities. The legend of the supposed Rothschild coup at Waterloo, while suggestive of admirable financial prowess to the modern ear, had its origins in the contemporary writings of various anti-Semitic authors, most notably Honoré de Balzac. The sensibilities of nineteenth-century readers were deeply offended by the Rothschilds' supposed profiteering from the vicissitudes of war. For this very reason, Queen Victoria refused a peerage to Lionel de Rothschild. Niall Ferguson, personal communication. See also Niall Ferguson, *The House of Rothschild* (New York: Penguin, 1999), 14–15, 98–101.

linked two hundred monks with twenty-five foot iron bars. He stretched them over a mile, then administered electrical shocks to the first monk in the line. To his amazement, the last monk felt the shock at the same time as the first; electrical transmission appeared to be instantaneous.[23]

Shocked clerics aside, by the year 1800, electronic communication was still out of reach. There were three major problems:

- Reliable sources of electrical power were not available.

- Scientists found it extremely difficult to fashion electrical current into usable signals.

- As Nollet's experiment showed, the ability to detect and interpret those signals was crude in the extreme.

The problem of electrical generation yielded first. Before 1800, weak static electricity could be only erratically produced by rubbing materials together. In that year, Alessandro Volta correctly deduced that the twitching of Luigi Galvani's frog legs was caused by the contact of two different metals in a salt solution. Volta began to methodically test different pairs of metals and found that two combinations—zinc/copper and zinc/silver—yielded the strongest and most reliable current. By layering alternating sheets of these metals between brine-soaked flannel or paper, he was able to generate a continuous supply of electricity. He had effectively produced the first battery.[24]

The next barrier was the interpretation of the electrical current at the receiving end. This was no trivial task. Recall that abbé Nollet was reduced to verbal reports from shocked monks. During the early nineteenth century, the finger-on-the-wire technique was still the best available to telegraphers.

In 1820, Hans Christian Oersted, a Danish scientist, discovered that current flowing through a wire would deflect a compass needle. The flow of electricity could now be measured. All that remained was to fashion the current in such a way that it could provide Oersted's needles with an understandable message. By about 1825, a Russian by the name of Pavel Lvovitch Schilling induced an Oersted-type device to swing its needle right or left. Combinations of these impulses were used to indicate each letter or number. Schilling was even able to convince the czar to support his scheme, but Schilling died before he could build his device.

It remained for two separate teams of inventors—William Fothergill Cooke and Charles Wheatstone in England, and a group led by Samuel Morse in the U.S.—to create a telegraph that would finally work outside the laboratory.

Morse, who was born in Charlestown, Massachusetts in 1791, was an artist by training and profession. By the time he was thirty-four, he had won several prestigious commissions, including one for a portrait of Lafayette. But within his breast beat the heart of an inventor; he had already designed a novel pump and a machine for reproducing marble statues. While he was returning from Europe in 1832, a shipboard companion told him of Nollet and Oersted's experiments. Morse realized that a simple on-off code, read by Oersted's needles, could be used to transmit letters and numbers.

By the time he had completed the six-week sea voyage, he had arrived at the concept of the famous code that bears his name. A rank amateur, Morse was blissfully unaware that many before had failed at electrical telegraphy. Further, he simply did not have the technological expertise to produce a working device on his own. What he did possess was boundless energy, enthusiasm, and a compulsion to make electrical telegraphy a reality.

William Cooke was Morse's English kindred spirit. While Morse's epiphany was a code system that would work over a single wire, Cooke had the good fortune of personally attending a demonstration of Schilling's device in 1836. He immediately recognized its practical application. Within a few weeks, he had a working model, which consisted of three needles fed by three wires. (Since each needle could point right, left, or rest straight up, there were twenty-seven possible combinations. Thus, all the letters of the alphabet could be coded.) In modern terms, Morse had invented the software; Cooke had developed the hardware.

By then, Morse too was deep into hardware development, but both he and Cooke came up against the same problem. The signal would carry no further than several hundred yards. Neither inventor had any technical training—Cooke was an anatomist, and the portrait artist Morse had no scientific background at all—and neither one realized that his batteries produced too little voltage.

As any junior high school student knows today, the solution was to have several batteries hooked up in series. Neither Morse nor Cooke knew that by the 1830s scientists had driven currents through miles of wire with high voltage. One who had done so was Charles Wheatstone, distinguished professor of "experimental philosophy" (roughly, physics) at King's College in London. When Cooke called on Wheatstone, they immediately realized that Cooke's entrepreneurial drive and Wheatstone's technical expertise made them an ideal combination. They also took an immediate dislike to each other that would last their lifetimes: Wheatstone viewed Cooke as an ignorant businessman, and Cooke saw Wheatstone as an officious, academic snob. Within a few months, however, they had produced a five-wire/needle design that could rapidly transmit messages over long distances.

Although Morse had a four-year lead on Cooke and Wheatstone, he frittered it away designing an overly complicated sending device. He also failed to address the distance/voltage problem. At about the same time that Cooke and Wheatstone had built their first working model, Morse, who was reduced to teaching literature and art at New York University, came across Leonard Gale, who taught chemistry there, and Alfred Vail, a rich young man who knew a good thing when he saw it. The three teamed up, improved the battery design, streamlined Morse's code into its familiar form, and simplified the keying device for rapid operation with one finger.

ONE WIRE, ONE WORLD

Patents were filed on both sides of the Atlantic, and intense competition between the two teams ensued. At this stage, the Americans made a critical improvement—the relay. Essentially a second telegraph key that was powered by its own battery, it faithfully repeated and sent on all incoming signals. A carefully linked series of relays could transmit a signal hundreds or even thousands of miles.

In the end, the Morse relayed one-wire design proved the more workable of the two. It was difficult enough to keep one connection intact; maintaining the five simultaneous connections of the Cooke-Wheatstone device over great distances and long periods was nearly impossible. Cooke and Wheatstone gradually found that they could make do with fewer lines. They finally settled on the single-line technique as well.

On both sides of the Atlantic, the electric telegraph met a solid wall of skepticism. It was not hard to understand why. Unlike the steam engine, electrical telegraphy is difficult to convincingly demonstrate to others. In a typical public exhibition, the "telegrapher" sent messages from one room to another through a bramble of wiring, and the equipment at the receiving end displayed only a few flickering needles. On more than one occasion, newspapers and politicians accused Morse and Cooke of fraud. Although Congress eventually granted Morse $30,000 for a demonstration line between Washington and Baltimore, both the American and British teams wound up plowing their own assets into the first networks.

Cooke turned his attention to the most obvious customer: the railroads. In exchange for the use of its right of way, a railroad company got free telegraph service. In the early 1840s, Cooke built short lines along London's rail routes. The longest was the thirteen-mile link from Paddington to West Drayton.

Meanwhile, Morse, Gale, and Vail began stringing a forty-mile wire along the railbed from Baltimore to Washington. Congress suspected that the Morse team was bilking it, and accusations flew. The government appointed an observer named John Kirk, who proposed a test of the new system during the Whig Party convention that was to take place in Baltimore on May 1, 1844. From his post at the eastern terminus of the not-yet-complete line, thirteen miles from Baltimore, Vail was to telegraph the names of the nominees to Morse and Kirk in Washington. When Morse announced the convention's results more than an hour before the arrival of same news aboard the Baltimore train, all doubt about electric telegraphy evaporated.

A similar sequence of events unfolded in England. Three months after the American Whig convention, telegraphers transmitted the news of the birth of Queen Victoria's second son from Windsor to London well in advance of the train-borne courier. Soon, the new device began to astound the public with all manner of miracles: Criminals, who had grown accustomed to rail transport as a foolproof means of escape, were apprehended; relatives falsely informed of the death of a loved one were instantaneously reassured that they were alive; and cannons twenty miles away could be fired on command.[25]

In the same year, Cooke was able to convince the Admiralty to build an eighty-eight mile link between London and Portsmouth. Almost immediately afterward, John Lewis Ricardo, a financier and distant relative of economist David Ricardo, bought Wheatstone and Cooke's patents outright (instead of merely licensing them) for £144,000 and formed the Electrical Telegraph Company. The company proceeded to build a network linking England's major cities.

The new medium exploded and become, in the words of author and journalist Tom Standage, "the Victorian Internet." Telegraph mileage burgeoned. In early 1846, the only working line in the U.S. was Morse's forty-mile link between Baltimore and Washington. By 1848, there were about two thousand miles of wire, and by 1850, twelve thousand miles. In 1861, a transcontinental telegraph line was strung. Within days, the Pony Express was out of business.[26]

The crowning achievement of the era was the laying of the first transatlantic cable in 1858. Because it joined the American and European networks, almost all of the civilized world, from the Mississippi River to the Urals, was simultaneously astounded when the connection between the continents was opened on August 5. New Yorker George Templeton Strong wrote in his diaries,

> Yesterday's [New York] *Herald* said that the cable is undoubtedly the Angel in the Book of Revelation with one foot in the sea and one foot on land, proclaiming that time is no longer. Moderate people merely say that this is the greatest human achievement in history.[27]

The reality of the first transatlantic cable was a good deal less impressive. The line was not actually connected to the American system at its landing point in Newfoundland for several days. Traffic across the cable was painfully slow. Not until August 16 did Queen Victoria transmit a message ninety-nine words long to President Buchanan, and the world did not learn until much later that the message took more than sixteen hours to transmit. Shortly after the cable was opened, transmission quality deteriorated even further. By late August, entire days passed without intelligible cable traffic. On September 1, the signal finally sputtered and died.[28]

Engineers determined that a heavier and more durable cable was required, and in 1865, the only ship capable of carrying the thousands of miles of the bulky new cable—the *Great Eastern*—set about laying it.

The 1865 expedition also failed, losing its cable in two miles of water; multiple attempts to grapple it to the surface proved futile. The following year, however, the huge ship not only succeeded in laying a new line, but also recovered the old one, establishing two links. By 1870, the *Great Eastern* had stretched a cable to India, and the next year added Australia to the nineteenth century's worldwide web.

Considered from the perspective of human verbal exchange, nations shrank in size almost to nothing in the late 1840s, and by 1871 the globe itself became one. Vast local infrastructures sprang into place almost immediately. Tens of thousands of messenger boys and hundreds of miles of steam-powered pneumatic tubes connected a complex network of telegraph stations.

Consequently, the first telegraph service was prohibitively expensive. A transatlantic message cost about $100—a few months' wages for a working man. As with Rothschild's pigeons, the leading edge of communication technology carried only the most valuable information, which was almost always financial. In the early 1850s, the world's busiest line ran between the London Stock Exchange and the Central Telegraph Office. More than 90% of the early transatlantic traffic was business-related, almost all of it reduced to a compact code to lower cost. In 1867, telegraph operator E. A. Callahan invented a specialized machine that delivered a continuous record of stock prices. The machine's distinctive clatter earned it the name that survives to this day—the stock ticker.

With sublime irony, just as today's wired visionaries imagine mankind brought closer together in the blissful embrace of a Great Internet Peace, so too did eighteenth century journalists wax ecstatic about the telegraph's potential to end all human conflict. Unhappily, the telegraph did not end world conflict, just as the events of September 11, 2001, made it painfully obvious that bringing disparate cultures face to face in a wired world provides a less than sure-fire recipe for world harmony.

THE DAM BURSTS

The half century from 1825 to 1875 saw more thoroughgoing change in the way people lived their lives than any other period in history. Today, we think of our own time as being one of uniquely rapid technological change. Nothing could be farther from the truth. The average citizen of two generations ago would have little trouble understanding the computer, the jet airliner, or even the Internet. By contrast, a person of the 1820s transported through time to the year 1875 would have been rendered speechless after witnessing the swiftness of rail travel and the instantaneous global communication that had been brought about in a mere half century. Never before had mankind been wrenched into the future with such force and speed as it was in the decades following 1825. Nor is it likely to happen again.

What triggered the revolutionary changes of the early nineteenth century and the steady growth of wealth that has followed it, without sign of letup, for two hundred years thereafter? At the risk of stretching a metaphor, I believe that by 1800, the Western economy resembled a dam, behind which an increasingly swollen reservoir of potential was accumulating. This "reservoir" contained centuries of advances in English common law that began with Magna Carta, were magnified by the brilliance of Edward Coke and his successors, and were capped with the case law and statutes governing monopolies and patents. It also held the dazzling intellectual advances of the scientific enlightenment and the sequential improvements in the capital markets wrought by the Italians, the Dutch, and the English.

These accomplishments did improve individual well-being, but at a glacial pace; between 1500 and 1820, the per capita GDP of the average Western European grew at an average rate of about 0.15% per year.[29] Yes, robust property protection drove craftsmen to innovate, scientific rationalism provided them the tools to work with, and the capital markets supplied them the funds to develop and produce their wondrous inventions. What was lacking was the raw physical force needed to power their factories and transport their goods and the speed of communication necessary to coordinate the whole process.

The invention of the steam engine and telegraph breached, if you will, the dam, loosing a torrent of economic growth the likes of which had not been seen. That dam can never be rebuilt, and the torrent of Western growth will not soon be stilled.

CHAPTER SIX

Synthesis of Growth

IT IS *INSTITUTIONS*—property rights, individual liberties, the rule of law, the intellectual tolerance implicit in scientific rationalism, and capital-market structure—that matter. The last chapter's focus on the dramatic technological advances of the early modern period in no way minimizes this emphasis. Without the freedom of intellectual inquiry afforded Huygens and Papin, the rewards of patent and property protection available to Watt and Morse, or the capital-market financing provided to Cooke and Wheatstone, the great rail, telegraph, and electrical networks would not have been built.

The history of the Manchester-Liverpool railway line highlights the dependence of technological innovation on the capital markets. In 1825 a financial panic erupted midway through the line's construction, and work on it would have been abandoned without an emergency loan of £100,000 from the government.

The uses of intellectual property rights are diverse. As we saw in Chapter 5, the original inventor is often not the person best able to exploit his creation. The telegraph, for example, did not find a market until its patent rights changed hands. The licensers of the new telegraph technology—John Lewis Ricardo in England and Amos Kendall, a wealthy young entrepreneur, in the U.S.—marketed the telegraph far better than Cooke, Wheatstone, and Morse could. Kendall and Ricardo also made more money for Morse, Cooke, and Wheatstone than these three inventors could have earned on their own.

Even the subtleties of these institutions matter. At the beginning of the steam age, most observers thought that the steam-powered road coach had better prospects for success than the railway coach did. The first "road-steamers" worked as well as the first rail locomotives, and by the beginning of the eighteenth century McAdam and master road and bridge designer Thomas Telford had built an impressive network of smooth all-weather highways with money from Britain's turnpike trusts. Telford, who favored road transport, convinced steam engineer Goldsworthy Gurney to design a lightweight engine weighing "only" three thousand pounds to power the new road vehicles.

A rail network, on the other hand, would have to be built from scratch. Moreover, a railway line is by nature a monopoly undertaking that necessarily excludes the locomotives of other companies; the railroad interests would have to overcome the antipathy of the common law to monopolies. By contrast, road-steamers, with a multiplicity of owners operating on both public and toll roads, were more in keeping with the spirit of the common law.

In the end, parliamentary skullduggery and special pleading won the day. The rail and horse-and-coach lobbies, who argued that the fast-moving steam cars would be a safety hazard, forced through legislation that mandated prohibitive tolls for the new road contraptions, and killed the development of these vehicles. Even then, it was a narrow victory. Several years later, Parliament nearly repealed the legislation against road cars, but the death of Telford in 1834 sealed the doom of highway travel in England. Had the balance of institutional factors been slightly different, England likely would have developed a system of superhighways instead of a rail network.[1]

Of the four major factors that ignited sustained economic growth in the West—property rights, scientific rationalism, capital markets, and the technology of steam and telegraph—which were, and are yet today, the most important? Economic historians have long grappled with this question. Rosenberg and Birdzell, in *How the West Grew Rich*, favor the latter technological factors, since their advancement roughly parallels the growth of the world economy, while the protection of property rights has, if anything, deteriorated in the twentieth century.[2] Economic historian Jack Goldstone also emphasizes the steam and internal combustion engines as the primary factor in the nineteenth-century explosion of growth.[3] But others, like author Tom Bethell and economist Hernando de Soto, have no doubt that economic progress is impossible without property rights.[4,5]

A moment's reflection reveals that all are right and all are wrong. Modern economic growth can be likened to the structural lattice of a sky-scraper: Each element supports all of the others, and none will stand with-out all solidly in place.

The development of the steam railway and electrical telegraph most clearly demonstrate this concept. These key inventions were not possible without the incentive provided by property rights, a scientific mind-set, and financing from the capital markets. Again, even the subtleties of each institution matter. Bridgewater, for example, did not complete his canal until 1767, when falling interest rates after the Seven Years War enabled him to obtain final construction financing. The capital markets likewise benefit from secure property rights. Britain's modern financial institu-tions were born soon after the Glorious Revolution of 1688 curtailed the Crown's ability to steal. A rigorous scientific and mathematical intel-lectual framework (i.e., the science of economics) also bolstered the cap-ital markets. Halley's actuarial tables, for example, made possible the rapid growth of the insurance industry in the eighteenth century. With-out the insurance industry, businesses would not have been able to man-age risk, and absent the ability to manage risk, capital for new ventures would not have been available.

Last, and not least, the lifeblood of finance flows in the torrent of *infor-mation* that has been made possible by modern communications. Today, we take for granted an instantaneous knowledge of the supply and de-mand of almost all goods everywhere on the globe—where things are scarce, where things are plentiful. In the premodern era, consumers and merchants were weeks or months behind vital market information, and bore great inefficiencies as a result. (In the twentieth century, something of the sort occurred in socialist countries. Those nations directed the pro-duction of goods by fiat and thus blinkered themselves to the valuable in-formation that is inherent in market prices.) Efficient transport also lessens the need for, as well as the cost of, capital itself. A shorter interval between production and sale allows entrepreneurs to borrow less money over briefer periods. Where financial information does not flow freely and in-stantaneously, investors will not commit capital. Beginning in the late nineteenth century, the large publicly traded corporation became capital-ism's prime mover. Before then, such businesses—at first, exclusively trad-ing companies—required monopoly status in order to sustain operations and attract capital. Only the massive capacity for communication and transport offered by the telegraph and the steam engine made possible the survival of large business organizations that could operate around the world and obtain adequate financing without government protection.

The relationship of scientific rationalism to the other three factors is less obvious. Scientific inquiry can be subversive, for it challenges the status quo. This was particularly true in Western Europe at the start of the modern age, where a novel theory, or even an advance in scientific equipment, such as Galileo's telescope, could land you in the hot embrace of the Inquisition. Even in the modern era, there are still nations where disinterested intellectual inquiry can prove fatal. The scientific mind-set flourishes best in societies that most rapidly move information and cherish dissent and individual liberty, the fellow travelers of property rights. This link between individual liberty and scientific inquiry partly explains the paradox of how the U.S., with its narcissistic cult of the individual, continues to lead the world in scientific innovation despite a deteriorating educational system.

Last, the case for property rights is itself largely inductive and empiric, that is, based on scientific rationalism. Even a casual look around the world demonstrates that those nations that best protect property rights prosper most. The most effective way to stunt the wealth of nations is to interrupt the free and open traffic in goods and information. Marxist ideology, which by its very nature requires a massive leap of deductive faith, crumbles under the briefest consideration of empirical information.

Today, property rights appear to be the critical ingredient for economic growth. But this is a modern phenomenon. In today's world, the other three factors are now much more easily obtainable than property rights are. As we will see in Chapter 9, deeply ingrained cultural factors make securing individual freedom and property rights difficult in many nations. Contrariwise, both the ancient Greeks and the medieval English obtained property rights at a very early stage in their economic and political development, but because they were not blessed with the other three factors, they did not grow.

In the final analysis, it is as nonsensical to judge the relative importance of the four fundamental factors to a country's development as it is to ask whether the flour, the sugar, the shortening, or the egg is the most critical ingredient in a cake. All are essential; each complements the others. Without all four ingredients, there is no just dessert.

SECTION II

Nations

OVER THE PAST TWO CENTURIES, the world has become a vastly more prosperous place. This process has been uneven; some nations began to grow rapidly in the early eighteenth century, some not until much later, and some not at all. This has resulted in an enormous gap between our planet's haves and its have-nots. In A.D. 1500, Italy, the world's wealthiest nation, had a per capita GDP that was less than three times the per capita GDP of the world's poorest nations. In 1998, the per capita GDP of the U.S. was more than fifty times that of the world's poorest.[1] The pervasiveness of the media in contemporary life has pressed the noses of the world's least fortunate against the store window of Western prosperity. Bringing the world's poorest and wealthiest face-to-face magnifies the damage done by this imbalance and raises the temperature of the world's many cultural, political, and religious conflicts.

This section examines the origins of the widening gap between rich and poor—how some nations were first, some next, and some not at all. Representative countries will illustrate the process. Chapter 7 explores how modern wealth was first born in two countries: Holland and England. Chapter 8 focuses on three nations that followed on their heels: France, Spain, and Japan. There, we will identify the obstacles that impeded economic growth and show how these obstacles were eventually overcome. Chapter 9 lays out the anatomy of failure in the Muslim

world and in Latin America and dissects the critical interactions of religion, culture, politics, colonial heritage, and economics.

There is not enough space for many important stories, such as the
early development and resiliency of Germany or the depth of poverty
that plagues almost all of sub-Saharan Africa. This book's structure,
however, will at least provide a framework that can be applied to any
nation and point the interested reader in the right direction.

CHAPTER SEVEN

The Winners—
Holland and England

HOLLAND

The sustained growth of the Dutch economy began in the sixteenth century. More than two centuries before Malthus first elaborated his grim population trap, Holland had already escaped it. Although Holland's growth was far tamer than the explosive growth that occurred in England three hundred years later, Adam Smith, the founding father of economics, like most Englishmen of his time, had good reason to envy Holland's wealth:

> The province of Holland . . . in proportion to the extent of its territory and the number of its people, is a richer country than England. The government there borrow at two percent, and private people of good credit at three. The wages of labour are said to be higher in Holland than in England.[1]

By the end of the seventeenth century, England had just recovered from a brutal civil war and the Stuart restoration. Holland, in contrast, had been enjoying more than a century of republican, if oligarchic, government, and its per capita GDP was nearly twice that of its larger neighbor across the North Sea. Though the Dutch have never regained the military and economic dominance they held in the seventeenth century, they have remained to this day one of the world's wealthiest peoples.

So great was Dutch prosperity that even in 1815, after decades of embargo by England and the subsequent conquest and exploitation by France, its standard of living was still about the same as Britain's.

Angus Maddison's figures, shown in the table, summarize the Dutch economic triumph as well as any prose narrative.

Growth of Per Capita GDP in the Sixteenth and Seventeenth Centuries[2]

	1500	**1700**	**Growth Rate 1500–1700**
Holland	$ 754	$2,110	0.52%
England	$ 714	$1,250	0.28%
France	$ 727	$ 986	0.15%
Italy	$1,100	$1,100	0.00%
China	$ 600	$ 600	0.00%

While anemic by later standards, the 0.52% average growth rate sustained by the Dutch between 1500 and 1700 was a spectacular improvement over the economic stagnation that smothered Europe for a thousand years after the Fall of Rome.

Many humanists will no doubt be dismayed at the short shrift given Italy in this narrative. Were not the Italian city-states the most advanced in Europe in commercial, intellectual, and artistic achievement? Was not Italy the birthplace of the Renaissance? Yes, but the sad fact remains that excluding the Venetian Republic (and Florence before the Medici takeover), Italy was governed by the sword, not by the rule of law. *Condottieri* controlled the countryside, and well into modern times, travelers regularly hired armed guards.[3] Consequently, political, legal, and financial institutions at the national level never developed in Italy, and as its lack of growth shows, it increasingly became an economic backwater after 1500.

A MOST PECULIAR REPUBLIC

How exactly did the center of economic power shift north of the Alps? How did Holland manage to be first out of the blocks? What lessons do the rise and fall of Holland's commercial dominance provide for the modern world? In order to answer these questions, we must first examine the "facts on the ground" in Holland in the early sixteenth century.

During the late medieval period, the dukes of Burgundy gained control of the lowlands of Holland, and in 1506, Carlos I of Spain inherited these territories. Thirteen years later Carlos became the Holy Roman emperor, Charles V. The early sixteenth century, one of history's great watersheds, brought together five key players: Charles V, Francis I of France, Henry VIII of England, Pope Leo X, and Martin Luther. The first three of these men hotly contested the largely ceremonial post of Holy Roman Emperor, whose election was overseen by Leo. At the same time, the titanic struggle between Pope Leo and Martin Luther forever changed Christendom, and with it, the political, military, and economic history of the world. Holland's epic struggle for freedom against Charles' Habsburg heirs and Luther's heresy were to provide the historical and cultural backdrop for its ascension to economic power.

Holland's unique geography is central to its early economic rise. Holland is a low country, defined by its location at the North Sea outlet of the huge Rhine/Waal/Maas/Issjel river system. Three zones define Holland's topography:

- At the sea's edge—a group of barrier sand dunes, rising about twenty feet above sea level

- Behind the dunes—about half of Holland's current landmass, the so-called polders, which lie mostly *below* sea level

- Beyond the polders—sand plains that lie just *above* sea level and consist of a thin, nonproductive soil deposited over the centuries by the great rivers

Before about 1300, the present-day polders lay under water. Over the next three centuries, villagers used the newly invented windmill-driven pump technology to build the famous *bedijkingen*, or dikes, to reclaim the polders from the sea. The Dutch then dug and burned off the layers of peat that covered the newly dry land. In the process, they uncovered some of the richest farmland on the Continent.[4]

This peculiar bonanza carried with it the seeds of economic and social revolution. It created a web of wealthy, independent communities *without a preexisting feudal structure*. Not that Charles V, and his son, Philip II of Spain, did not attempt to impose one. Philip's invasion in 1568, which was meant to suppress the spread of Martin Luther's reformation into Burgundy, sparked a rebellion in its northern provinces that raged for eighty years—until 1648, when Spain formally granted the Dutch their independence.

Technically, "Holland" refers to the largest of the seven northern Dutch provinces. Before the war of independence, Antwerp had been the region's commercial hub and center of rebellion. With Antwerp's fall to the Spanish in 1585, Amsterdam, capital of the province of Holland, quickly assumed a leadership role. The six other major provinces—Zeeland, Utrecht, Friesland, Groningen, Gelderland, and Overijssel—had a combined population that was somewhat greater than that of Holland proper. But even though Holland contained less than half of the Dutch Republic's population, it dominated the others because of its disproportionate wealth. Holland supplied about 60% of the Republic's tax revenue and about 75% of the loans that were needed to support the insurrection.

Typical of the religious wars of the era, the Dutch revolt against Spain was an unspeakably barbaric affair. Originally, the rebels had hoped to unite all seventeen provinces of Burgundy, but cooler heads realized that it would be better to partition the Spanish Provinces into two states: a northern Protestant one and a southern Catholic one. The southern rump, containing Antwerp, was economically ruined by Spanish rule as well as by its separation from its prosperous northern neighbor. Control over the southern provinces passed from Spain to Austria after the War of the Spanish Succession in 1713, to France in the wake of the French Revolution in 1794, and back to Holland after Napoleon's defeat at Waterloo in 1815. Fifteen years later, the south rebelled against Dutch rule and finally gained its independence as the nation of Belgium.

The northern state came into being when the rebelling provinces coalesced into the loosely structured Union of Utrecht in 1579. It embraced a startling new concept, that of tolerance of all religions (or at least the Western ones): Protestantism, Catholicism, and, remarkably, Judaism.[5] This freedom of religion removed the shackles of the Aristotelian mind-set and allowed scholars and merchants to venture down intellectual and commercial paths that had been blocked for centuries without end.

Still more remarkable, the Dutch economic ascent began long before the start of the independence fight in 1568. The height of Holland's prosperity, in fact, came just as it was being emancipated from Spain in 1648. Moreover, the Dutch provinces battled for survival against the

Habsburg-Spanish behemoth as independent states, with no functioning central government. Historian Johan Huizinga marveled, "Where else was there a civilization that reached its peak so soon after the nation came into being?"[6]

Further, this evolving nation, because of the interplay of the rivers, sea, dikes, and the effects of military operations, was a constantly changing geographic and political landscape. At times, it bore little resemblance to the entity we now call Holland. The political history of Holland is beyond the scope of this book, but suffice it to say that before the nineteenth century, it was the provincial and municipal authorities who held the reins of power. At no time did the Dutch have a strong national government. Most often, these local officials were a small, self-appointed commercial elite. Not infrequently, the transfer of power was hereditary.

NEW LAND, NEW MEN

The creation of new land was singular; the creation of new men would prove revolutionary. As the Dutch built their dikes, they had to build drainage ditches to carry away the leakage. These ditches then became the boundaries of the newly created farms. The finished dikes left a dense structure of free peasants who controlled their own farms, free of manorial obligations. The strength of the old feudal system thus petered out as one moved north from the southern provinces toward the sea. During the early phase of reclamation, peat mining and burning provided welcome fuel for domestic consumption and export.

The reclamation projects also lowered the level of the land and caused its occasional loss to the sea. The maintenance of the dikes was an arduous task. Local and regional councils, largely self-governing, directed dike maintenance, whose most recognizable feature was the Dutch windmill.

The drainage councils buttressed an already independent Dutch body politic. This recalls the origins of the free Greek farmers—the geôrgoi—who worked the marginal hilly land overlooking the large feudal estates around the ninth century B.C. In ancient Greece, the highly motivated farmer on his small plot overcame the poor quality of his soil.

By contrast, the independent Dutch farmer worked reclaimed land of superior quality.

The new nation was favored not only with rich soil but also with peasants who were free from the dead hand of the feudal system and stifling Church dogma. For the first time since the Fall of Rome, the fruits of labor accrued largely to free republican citizens. The farmer who innovated successfully was fully rewarded. Dutch peasants could think and say what they pleased.

The battle against the sea was long, hard, and subject to frequent setbacks. In 1421 a flood inundated thirty-four villages and almost two hundred square miles of land, much of which was never reclaimed. In 1730, *Teredo limmoria*, a species of earthworm, infested the dikes, which had to be buttressed with extremely expensive stone facing.

But for the most part Holland's existence was a charmed one. After 1500 the so-called Little Ice Age lowered global temperatures and caused a drop in sea level as water was taken up by an expanding polar ice cap. Over time this greatly eased the burden of dike maintenance. In the sixteenth century there were fourteen recorded inundations in Holland; in the seventeenth, seven; in the eighteenth, just four; in the nineteenth and twentieth, only one each.[7]

HIGH PRICES, WIDE CANALS, AND FAT TIMES

The Dutch were fortunate in another important regard. Beginning about 1450, prices in Europe began to rise. When economists describe the price of a given commodity, they often talk about its "elasticity." Let's say that, for whatever reason, your income has just fallen. Although you will be likely to travel less often and to buy fewer electronic goods, you will probably not eat less. An economist would say that your supply-demand curve for food is highly "inelastic," since your demand for food is not much affected by its price. On the other hand, pleasure travel and consumer electronics are highly elastic commodities. If your income declines or if the prices of consumer electronics increase, you will buy fewer gadgets.

When prices began rising in the mid-fifteenth century, the cost of grain rose most dramatically. It was the most essential, and thus inelastic, of human commodities in the medieval period. In order of increasing elasticity are livestock, industrial crops such as flax and timber, and finally, manufactured goods, the latter of which are the most elastic of all. In other words, the prices of manufactured goods will rise the least as they grow scarce, and grain prices will rise the most.

During the late fifteenth century, skyrocketing grain prices greatly increased the value of farmland. This led to advances in civil engineering technology not seen since Roman times. The newly empowered Dutch farmer embraced a new type of windmill, the *bouvenkruier*, which required only that its top be turned (as opposed to the whole structure). Dutch engineers similarly advanced dike construction. The earliest windmill systems could pump out fields to a depth of only about a foot. By 1624 systems of advanced windmills operating in series could pump to depths of fifteen feet.

Dikes and windmills were expensive and did not repay their costs for decades. Large amounts of capital were required, and further, in order for these loans to "pencil out," they needed to be available at low interest rates. As we saw in Chapter 4, by the mid-sixteenth century, Dutch lenders could fund large construction projects at interest rates of 4% to 5%, and farmers could obtain mortgages at slightly higher rates. (Adam Smith's statement about 3% commercial and 2% government loans referred to a later period, and even then was somewhat exaggerated.) Between 1610 and 1640, Dutch investors sank an astonishing 10 million guilders—a fair chunk of their national wealth and far more than had been invested in the Dutch East India Company (VOC)—into drainage schemes.

Holland was fortunate in yet another key area: transport. Water conveyance, in general, was (and still is) cheaper than land carriage, particularly before the advent of steam power. No nation moved its goods as quickly and as cheaply as Holland did. The small, flat country was laced with canals and waterways, many of which were the product of reclamation activity. To this near-natural system of water transport the Dutch added a system of towpath-equipped canals, or *trekvaart*, that linked almost all of the major cities of coastal Holland.

Initially, Dutch canal transport was hobbled by the all-too-familiar toll-seeking behavior that was described in Chapter 1. In this case the offenders were municipalities that were bypassed by the proposed routes. In 1631, however, the major Dutch cities reached a kind of free trade agreement, and a canal boom began. Canal shipping was intimately bound to the mining of peat, which because of its bulk could only be transported inexpensively by boat. When peat demand was high and the trade profitable, canal building surged, and when prices fell, canal entrepreneurs abandoned projects, often with disastrous results for investors. By 1665, the Dutch built almost four hundred miles of *trekvaart,* giving Holland the world's best system of internal transport.[8]

By the year 1700, the Dutch were by far the world's wealthiest people, with a per capita GDP that was almost twice that of the nearest competitor, the English. In addition, the Dutch possessed an unrivaled system of finance, transport, and urban infrastructure. Holland's cityscapes were the most lovely in Europe, despite the fact that for much of this two-century period of rapid growth, the Dutch were fighting for their lives, first in a war of independence against the Spanish Empire, and later in conflicts with France and England.

Recall from Chapter 1 that one of the best ways to measure prosperity in historically remote times is by calculating the percentage of the population living in cities—the urbanization ratio. The higher this ratio is, the more prosperous the society is. By the mid-seventeenth century, the coastal region of Holland—Amsterdam, Haarlem, Leiden, The Hague, Delft, Rotterdam, Gouda, Utrecht—was known as the *Randstad,* or "rim city." They constituted a prototypical version of the U.S.'s Northeast Corridor that was home to about a third of the Republic's population. In 1700, 34% of the Dutch population lived in cities with a population greater than ten thousand. This far exceeded England's 13%, France's 9%, or Italy's 15%.[9]

GUILDERS ON THE CHEAP

The most important commodity price in any society is that of money—the prevailing rates of interest on loans and bonds. When money becomes dear (high interest rates), consumers are reluctant to spend, and businessmen are reluctant to borrow to expand their existing business or to create new ones. Society suffers. When money becomes cheap (low interest rates), consumers and businessmen are likely to borrow. The economy expands.

What determines interest rates? Many things. First and foremost is the state of the borrower's credit. A bank will lend to a trustworthy individual with excellent collateral at a much lower rate than it would offer someone of suspect character who had no visible assets. For the past seven hundred years or so, the largest borrowers in the Western world have been governments with pressing military needs. A government with little debt and a secure source of revenue from taxes and landholdings can borrow at low interest.

A large amount of previous borrowing raises a borrower's interest rates. Fearful that the borrower will not be able to repay the huge obligation, lenders demand a higher rate of interest to compensate for that risk. A government deeply in debt all too quickly finds itself in a fiscal death spiral, committed to paying large interest obligations, which increases the rate of interest it must pay on new loans, resulting in yet higher interest payments and eventual default.

The Dutch wars of independence sputtered along for nearly eighty years, and the enormous costs involved strained the provincial coffers. Holland almost always found itself on the right side of the borrowing equation. Although the Dutch situation was very tenuous—small, weak, newly independent states arrayed against one of the world's great empires—they had two large fiscal advantages. The first was a tax base of sales levies on everyday consumer goods. Further, that tax base was supported by a patriotic population willing to pay them. The second was the delightfully named Office of Ecclesiastical Property, which held confiscated Catholic Church land for later sale, usually at very high prices. The Dutch borrowing public, and later, foreign investors, considered both to be excellent collateral. Almost from the outset, Dutch interest rates were the lowest in Europe.

THE BIRTH AND "DEATH" OF DUTCH PROSPERITY

The sources of the amazing Dutch prosperity after 1500 now become obvious:

- A population that enjoyed robust property rights, matched only by those in England.

- The freeing of the Dutch from Church dogma by the Reformation. Dutch religious tolerance spared Holland from the worst excesses of the schism that scarred many of the early Protestant states, particularly in Germany.

- Copious funds for investment from Dutch capital markets that were energized by low interest rates and strong investor protection.

- A flat topography graced by easy and inexpensive water transport.

As has already been mentioned, for the entire period from 1500 to 1700, Holland's real per capita GDP annual growth of 0.52% was just one-quarter of the growth rate in the modern West. While a vast improvement over the preceding stagnation, this increase did not even begin to approach today's level of 2% sustained per capita GDP growth.

Further, much of that growth was fed by land reclamation and the rise in commodity prices. Once reclamation ended and prices leveled out, growth stopped. The relatively tepid pace of Dutch growth was due to the absence of technology that would not be available for another two centuries: steam-driven factory power, swift land transport, and electronic communications. Without these, the modern variety of rapid growth was beyond Holland's reach.

Dutch economic growth, steady but modest during its eighty-year struggle against Spain, came to a halt not long after Holland gained independence in 1648. Eighteenth-century Hollanders were acutely aware that their best days were behind them, and Dutchmen looked back nostalgically to 1648 as the apex of Holland's Golden Era. The evidence suggests that while wealthy oligarchs became progressively richer, the lot of the average citizen may not have improved much in the generations after independence. Moreover, by 1750, although they were still among the wealthiest people on earth, the Dutch were no longer significant players on the world's economic and military stage.

The reasons for Holland's decline are both controversial and complex. First, as we've already seen, even though the Dutch had great wealth on a *per capita* basis, competing countries had much larger populations. Worse, the Dutch rate of population growth was much lower than that of their larger rivals. In 1700, there were only 1.9 million

Dutchmen, versus 21.5 million Frenchmen and 8.6 million Englishmen. Because of its small population, at no time did Holland's aggregate GDP exceed 40% of England's GDP or 20% of France's.[10]

Second, any discussion of Holland's domestic and foreign commerce necessarily includes the word "monopoly." The Dutch jealously guarded the East Indies spice trade. One of the most notorious diplomatic fracases of the era revolved around the destruction of the English settlement on Amboina Island (in modern-day Indonesia) in 1623. The Dutch tortured its English settlers, inflaming Anglo-Dutch relations for decades. In Holland itself, monopolies stunted commercial activity. The Dutch government, for example, authorized only one company to produce navigational charts—an arrangement that lasted until 1880.

Third, Dutch prosperity did not rest on technological advance, the great engine of modern Western wealth. The provinces did have a patent system, but it was remarkably inactive. Shipbuilders did make real technological advances during the period, such as the fluit ship. But by and large technological innovation in Holland was sporadic. At the height of the mid-seventeenth-century golden era, the government granted about a dozen patents per year, and after 1700 it granted no more than a few annually.[11] Dutch prosperity came from trade, particularly with the Baltic region, which supplied grain for transshipment and timber to be cut in the new wind-powered mills. The highly profitable commerce with the East Indies rounded out Holland's cash flow.

Fourth, Dutch finance was a little *too* successful. The government could borrow so easily and at such low rates that by the eighteenth century Holland had buried itself in debt. Since the government backed loans with excise duties, tax rates were raised. Jacked up excise tax rates led to increases in prices and wages, making Dutch goods and services noncompetitive.[12]

Last, the Dutch political body was fragmented into seven semiautonomous states, a loose political confederation situated on the edge of a dangerous continent. The lack of a strong central bank and a vigorous national patent system carried obvious economic disadvantages. This lesson was not lost on the American Founding Fathers. The decentralized apparatus and resultant sorry political fate of eighteenth-century Holland served as an object lesson to the Federalist participants in the American constitutional debate, who saw Holland beset by "imbecility in the government;

discord among the provinces; foreign influence and indignities; a precarious existence in peace, and peculiar calamities from war."[13]

The Dutch economy of the eighteenth century was "lopsided." The vigorous and highly profitable trading sector produced far more capital than could be absorbed by the domestic economy, which was hobbled by a relative lack of technological advance and by monopolistic restrictions. The result was an enormous surplus of investment cash that steadily drove down domestic interest rates and raised domestic prices and wages to the point where the Dutch manufacturing sector could not compete internationally.

Holland became a "periwig" society. An increasingly narrow segment of the population subsisted mainly on investment income and produced little. Much of the excess capital was invested abroad, particularly in the United States, where between 10% and 20% of the Revolutionary War debt was held by the Dutch.[14] It was remarkable that a tiny nation reaching the end of its global importance could supply so much capital to the rest of the world.

The late-eighteenth-century Dutch dependence on income from foreign debt proved to be something of a curse. The repayment of the American debt was assured only by the vigorous intervention of Alexander Hamilton. With other debtor nations, the Dutch fared much worse. Dutch losses mounted as nation after nation, including France and Spain, went into default.

JEALOUS NEIGHBORS

Before the Congress of Vienna stabilized Europe in 1815, trade was a far-from-ideal method of economic growth. Not only was productivity growth in trade slower and less reliable than that in industry; it was also more vulnerable to interference from protectionism and military embargo.

Prosperous foreign trade breeds jealousy, distrust, and finally attack from poorer neighbors. For Holland, the seventeenth century's wealthiest nation, that was not long in coming. At mid-century, while Dutch power was at its peak, the British were barely emerging from the chaos of civil war. Their envy of Holland's prosperity was palpable, and they seized upon even the slightest pretext to disrupt Dutch trade. Said one English general, "What matters this or that reason? What we want is more of the trade that the Dutch have."[15]

The resulting commercial and military tension between Holland and Britain proved disastrous to the Dutch. Four Anglo-Dutch wars stretched over nearly a century and a half. The conflicts began just seven months after England's passage of the 1651 Navigation Act (which forbade third-party trade with England) and sputtered on to the end of the American Revolution, with a naval engagement off the English coast at Dogger Bank.

When not warring with England, Holland allied herself with the British against the French, who had grown particularly aggressive during the long rule of Louis XIV. In 1668, England, Holland, and Sweden formed the Triple Alliance against Louis, but by 1670 England's unstable king, Charles II, abandoned the alliance and left the Dutch to face French wrath alone. Two years later, both France and England attacked Holland.

The war against Holland was immensely unpopular in England, as was Charles II. At a critical juncture in the war in 1672, young Prince William of Orange opened Holland's dikes, flooded the polders, and blocked an invading French army. Not long after, the prince ascended to the post of stadholder as William III of Holland. England once again switched sides, and William gradually assumed control of the alliance's struggle against the French.

While prince, William had married Mary, the daughter of Charles II's much younger brother, the Duke of York. When Charles finally died in 1685, the duke ascended to the English throne as James II, making William not only the leader of Holland and marshal of the anti-French alliance but also an English royal son-in-law.

THE TORCH IS PASSED

James was a rabid Catholic, but the opposing Dissenters and parliamentarians were not alarmed by his religious beliefs. James was past fifty years old when he ascended the throne, and he would soon be succeeded by his Protestant daughter Mary. Or so everyone thought until James sired a son and heir in June 1688. Suddenly and unexpectedly, the specter of a long line of Catholic monarchs threatened England's Protestants.

Anglicans and Dissenters invited William to England to "negotiate" with James. William seized upon an audacious plan: He would invade England and depose James in order to better harness the British military in his battle against the French. He succeeded beyond his wildest dreams. After William landed at Torbay (accompanied by fifteen thousand of his fiercest soldiers), James' behavior became increasingly erratic, and his forces deserted him. In the aftermath of this English donnybrook—"The Glorious Revolution of 1688"—William and Mary jointly ascended the throne. This assured not only England's allegiance to the anti-French cause, but also her transformation into a democratic constitutional monarchy as well.[16]

The marital union of Holland and England gave the Dutch only brief respite. The Republic became embroiled in a series of Continental wars, mainly against the French. In the winter of 1794, Dutch luck finally ran out as the rivers of Holland froze solid, preventing a repeat of 1672's opening of the dikes. The ice locked much of the Dutch fleet in place and provided the revolutionary French army with a smooth highway into Amsterdam. Moreover, a populist "patriot" faction, unhappy with Holland's oligarchic political structure, did not object strongly to conquest by the forces of the Revolution. Defeat by Napoleon ended centuries of independence. Within a decade, the French would devastate Holland's economy with confiscatory taxes and bring to an end centuries of Dutch commercial leadership.

Even as Holland's economic and political beacon was beginning to dim, however, some of its best and brightest minds were already crossing the North Sea to help ignite a far greater explosion of wealth.

ENGLAND

William's assumption of the British crown marked not only the critical milestone on Holland's journey into global insignificance, but it also signaled the turning point in England's economic fortunes. With James II deposed, the center of world economic development abruptly shifted westward to England. Within a century of the Glorious Revolution,

Adam Smith would systematically identify the sources of economic growth in *An Inquiry into the Nature and Causes of the Wealth of Nations* (1776). For the first time in history the keys to prosperity were laid bare for all to see. In the historical blink of an eye, England would grasp them and put them to spectacular use.

It generally surprises the modern reader that before the eighteenth century, most European monarchs lacked regular public funding, and the Stuart kings (in order of succession, James I, Charles I, Charles II, and James II) were no exception. The monarchy met most of its needs privately, mainly through its landholdings, the impositions of customs duties, and, increasingly, the sale of monopolies. The Crown could occasionally induce Parliament to impose taxes, but only under extraordinary circumstances, mainly during wartime. In the pre–Civil War period, in fact, Parliament's limited power derived primarily from its ability to provide intermittent tax revenue to the Crown.

During the last years of Tudor rule, the exigencies of modern warfare necessitated dire methods. After the defeat of the Spanish Armada in 1588, Elizabeth sold a quarter of Crown property to raise money, and James I auctioned off yet more royal wealth to pay his armies.

The rest went under the rule of his son, Charles I, who then sought cash flow from every possible source: sales of monopolies, taxes of questionable legality, dispensations, sale of hereditary titles, forced loans that often were not repaid, and, finally, outright theft. In return, Parliament balked, a bloody civil war ensued, and Charles lost his head.

Cromwell's Parliament proved equally incapable of restoring political and financial stability, and the Stuarts were restored to the throne. Once again, the Crown proved fiscally inept, leading to Parliament's "invitation" to William to emigrate from Holland. The transfer of power resulted in one of history's most felicitous bargains, the Revolutionary Settlement. Parliament provided William with a stable tax base to finance his war against France. In exchange, William gave Parliament legal supremacy.[17] The Crown could no longer dissolve Parliament, and the notorious Star Chambers—Crown courts whose often barbarous rulings superseded those of common law—were abolished.

The Crown could no longer remove judges—only Parliament could do so, and only then for incompetence or corruption. Parliament, in turn, was firmly under the thumb of the electorate, albeit one severely limited

by wealth and gender. A new political system evolved: "The Crown demands, the Commons grants, and the lords assent to the grant."[18]

At a stroke, William and Parliament had solved the major political
and fiscal problems that beset the nation. The effect on England's financial markets was remarkable. The royal budget quadrupled, and within
two generations the Crown found itself able to float loans for previously
unimaginable amounts at rates that were almost as low as those in Holland. The flow of capital to the state pointed the way to a similar con-
duit for entrepreneurial capital. Ordinary Britons, no longer fearful of
royal default and seizure, gradually began to trust the capital markets, just
as the Dutch had before them. They were less likely, in the words of
economic historian T. S. Ashton, "to keep quantities of coin, bullion,
and plate locked up in safes or buried in their orchards and gardens."[19]

FARMS AND FACTORIES

Consider one very simple statistic, the percentage of the English labor
force engaged in agriculture (see Figure 7–1). This percentage provides a
rough measure of any society's prosperity. A nation in which 100% of
the labor force is engaged in agriculture and does not export food exists,
by definition, at the subsistence level.

Note that the fall in the relative size of the agricultural labor force
was a very gradual affair, occurring over several centuries. The most
rapid reduction occurred in the mid-1800s, more than a full century *after*
the Industrial Revolution ostensibly began.

Consider this small thought experiment: Start with a hypothetical nation that moves from a near-total agricultural economy into one in
which half of the workforce is employed in factories. To avoid food imports, the half remaining on the farm must double their productivity.

In reality, this process occurs only partly—food imports as well as increases in agricultural productivity close the shortfall in agricultural labor.
Still, if a nation is to prosper, an agricultural revolution is every bit as
important as an industrial revolution. Indeed, rising agricultural productivity means that fewer farm laborers are needed, forcing them to look
elsewhere for work.

FIGURE 7–1   PERCENTAGE OF BRITISH LABOR FORCE ENGAGED IN AGRICULTURE

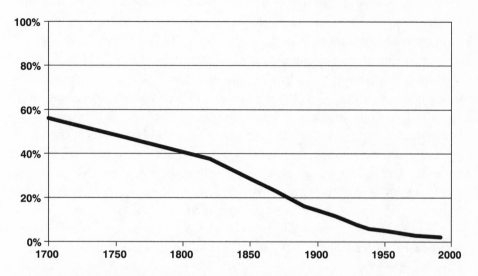

Source: Data from Maddison, *The World Economy: A Millennial Perspective*, 95, and Maddison, *Monitoring the World Economy, 1820–1992*, 39.

More important, both agricultural and industrial workers must have money left over after they've paid for food and shelter to buy the new industrial goods spewing forth. The economic history of the United States vividly illustrates this. In the two hundred years between 1800 and 2000, real per capita GDP in the U.S. increased thirtyfold, a remarkable accomplishment that reflected a period of unprecedented entrepreneurial efficiency and technologic innovation. Less well appreciated is the fact that the relative size of the agricultural labor force—that portion of the nation needed to feed it, and much of the rest of the world as well—fell from 70% to less than 2% during the same period. Thus, agricultural productivity increased thirty-fivefold, more than matching the stunning advances in industry and technology. In the second half of the twentieth century, U.S. industrial productivity increased by 2.6% per year, while agricultural productivity increased by 2.1% per year.[*]

---

[*]   From the U.S. Department of Labor, Bureau of Economic Affairs. "Productivity" in this case is defined as output per hour worked. Since it is nearly impossible to estimate hours worked before the nineteenth century, "productivity" is used synonymously, for the purpose of this book, with per capita GDP.

At the time of the American Revolution, England was self-sufficient agriculturally, with a rough equivalence between food exports and imports. In the absence of a reliable and reasonably priced source of food imports from turbulent France, England's agricultural productivity had to increase in order for her to industrialize.

The mechanical aspects of the agricultural revolution are straightforward enough: improved crop rotation schedules, harvesting schemes, and the like. The greatest gains came from improvements in mundane hand implements—seed drills and harvesting tools. Perhaps the most dramatic advance was the invention of the Rotherham triangular plow in 1830. Described by T. A. Ashton as "the greatest improvement in plow design since the late iron age," this plow required only two horses driven by a single man. It replaced the traditional rectangular device drawn by a team of six or eight oxen that required both an ox-driver and a plowman. In an instant, productivity in plowing more than doubled.

England became the first country to systematically and aggressively apply the scientific method to agriculture. In 1838, the Crown chartered the Royal Agricultural Society, which was modeled on the Bacon-inspired Royal Society. Five years later scientists founded the Rothamstead Agricultural Research Station and began to conduct the first systematic experiments on crop yields.

The creation of these organizations marked the start of a scientific approach to agriculture that paid almost immediate dividends in farming technique, particularly involving nitrogen supplementation. Intensive agriculture rapidly depletes the soil of nitrates, which are only slowly replaced by the conversion ("fixation") of atmospheric nitrogen back into plant-sustaining nitrates by bacteria. The Rothamstead Station quickly established that clover and legumes attracted nitrogen-fixing bacteria and concluded that farmers could double their yields simply by sowing clover between harvests.

The results of nitrate supplementation from animal fertilizer were yet more spectacular. Fertilizer from traditional sources—farm animals— is expensive, and it was not long before alternatives were found, first in the guano deposits from New World islands and later from synthetic nitrates.

THE PRIVATIZATION OF THE COUNTRYSIDE

These technological advances were only part of the story of the explosion of British agricultural productivity. Institutional advances were equally critical. Prime among these was the enclosure movement, which began in the medieval period and climaxed after 1650. Before that date, England, along with the rest of medieval Europe, operated largely under the "open field system," a relic of the feudal era in which vast swaths of land were held in common by the local farmers and lords.

As described so well by Garrett Hardin in "The Tragedy of the Commons," farming in the absence of clear ownership rights produces staggering economic inefficiencies, since farmers will not aggressively plow, fertilize, or otherwise improve common land.[20] (The modern correlate of this is a maxim attributed to Lawrence Summers, Harvard University president and former U.S. treasury secretary: "No one in the history of the world ever washed a rented car."[21])

After Runnymede, lords and villagers slowly fenced off, or "enclosed," common lands and placed them in private hands. By 1700, about half of all open land had been so privatized. Each enclosure required that the owners of four-fifths of the land in a given parish sign an enclosure petition, which was sent on to Parliament. The House of Commons voted thousands of these private acts during the seventeenth and eighteenth centuries.

In 1801, Parliament passed the General Enclosure Act, which streamlined the procedure. After 1700 enclosures rapidly accelerated, and by 1830 there was virtually no open land left in England. The greatest amount of land was enclosed in the period between the American Revolution and the Napoleonic Wars, as the dramatic rise in grain prices made privately cultivated cropland increasingly precious. By the mid-nineteenth century, the commons were nearly gone.[22]

Much literary and historical sound and fury has attended the enclosures, and although a minority of farmers were unjustly driven off their land, most historians now agree that the English concern for property rights and due process were, for the most part, observed, and that the process was on the whole fair and just. The number of small landowners increased significantly as the enclosure acts conferred ownership upon those whose families had tended the small common strips over the generations. For the first time, these smallholders enjoyed the *choice* of whether to sell or cultivate.[23,24]

This is not to say that the enclosures were not traumatic. But the rural and urban social chaos that followed on the heels of enclosures was not due to conscious exploitation of peasant farmers. Rather, the crisis arose from economic necessity: Enclosed land produces far more food than the commons does, requires fewer farmers per acre, and thus throws large numbers of farm laborers out of work.

This labor-sparing effect of enclosure was not a problem in the years leading up to the Napoleonic Wars, as high grain and corn prices brought a large amount of marginal land into production and kept farm employment high. After the Congress of Vienna concluded in 1815, however, it was a different story; prices fell almost immediately and remained low until the next great war came a century later. Marginal land went out of production, and out-of-work farm workers flooded the cities and factories.

The modern scientific approach to agriculture and the extension of well-defined property rights to a fresh group of small landholders combined to produce a new class of producer: the "improving farmer" who pursued ever-increasing crop yields through innovative agricultural techniques.

DIVISION OF LABOR

In a sense, there was no such thing as the Industrial Revolution or the Agricultural Revolution. Rather, there was a *productivity and specialization* revolution, as the glacial evolution of property rights, scientific rationalism, capital markets, and modern transport and communication gave farmers, inventors, and industrialists the incentive to innovate. These newly empowered capitalists produced a greater quantity and variety of almost everything. In the process, they raised the general standard of living of almost all Englishmen.

More than any other phenomenon, it is the degree of specialization that distinguishes the modern from the medieval. In the medieval world, there was one basic "job description" that applied to almost everyone:

working the land. During slack periods, peasants built and maintained their own shelter, assisted with the construction of manorial roads, spun their own yarn, wove their own cloth, and made their own garments. Early in the Industrial Revolution, most commercial weaving was not done in factories; rather, it was done by seasonally idle farming families in their own homes. In the premodern world, small communities, and even most families, were almost entirely self-sufficient.

By contrast, today it is inconceivable that any one community, let alone a single family, could produce even a small fraction of the goods and services it consumes. Every decade or so, the U.S. Department of Labor updates its *Dictionary of Occupational Titles*. The latest edition lists 12,740 separate job descriptions.

Modern prosperity can be thought of as an automobile's drive train, its engine being the four basic factors—property rights, scientific rationalism, the capital markets, and modern transport and communication—and the wheels the resulting productivity. The "transmission" that passes power from the engine (the four factors) to the wheels (GDP) is the degree of labor specialization. An economy with little specialization can only putt-putt along in first gear, while one with a high degree of specialization can travel at great speed.

By the coming of the Industrial Revolution, this process of specialization was already well advanced. Adam Smith immortalized it as the "division of labor." His exposition of this principle, applied to the manufacture of the lowly straight pin, is to this day unsurpassed:

> A workman not educated to this business (which the division of labour has rendered a distinct trade), nor acquainted with the use of the machinery employed in it (to the invention of which the same division of labour has probably given occasion), could scarce, perhaps, with his utmost industry, make one pin in a day, and certainly could not make twenty. But in the way in which this business is now carried on, not only the whole work is a peculiar trade, but it is divided into a number of branches, of which the greater part are likewise peculiar trades. One man draws out the wire, another straights it, a third cuts it, a fourth points it, a fifth grinds it at the top for receiving the head; to make the head requires two or three distinct operations; to put it on, is a peculiar business, to whiten the pins is another; it is even a trade by itself to put them into the paper;

and the important business of making a pin is, in this manner, divided into about eighteen distinct operations, which, in some manufactories, are all performed by distinct hands, though in others the same man will sometimes perform two or three of them.[25]

Smith described how even the simplest shop, employing ten workers to cover the eighteen separate steps in pin making, could turn out 48,000 pins per day—240 times as much as could be produced by ten unskilled workers separately.

How does this happen? The division of labor is the machinery that translates technological change into wealth. Here's how it works: The simplification of tasks broadens the available labor pool. Each worker is attracted to the job at which he is inherently most productive, then through experience becomes ever more proficient at it.

The division of manufacturing into many separate small tasks encourages technological innovation, as machines designed for a specific job are relatively easy to invent and refine. As innovators gradually improve these machines, the skill required to operate them generally decreases, which again broadens the labor pool and reduces the wages that must be paid still further.[26]

A modern example vividly demonstrates the principle. In 2001, Southwest Airlines logged 44.5 billion passenger miles using 31,600 employees.[27] Assuming that each employee worked two thousand hours that year, this comes out to 704 passenger miles per employee-hour worked—over ten times farther than you can transport yourself in a modern automobile with an hour of your own labor, and over two hundred times farther than you could using only your two feet.

The epitome of Southwest's labor force is the pilot, and the airline's signature technology is the Boeing 737. But for a complex division of labor that utilizes hundreds of different types of employees and a bewildering variety of mechanical and electronic tools, the pilot and aircraft would not be available to take you and your fellow passengers from Los Angeles to Baltimore for a few hundred dollars.

Human beings are inherently inventive. While intelligent and innovative individuals have existed in every place on earth since the dawn of history, their insights can translate into broader prosperity and growth only where there is division of labor.

THE WHOLE CLOTH OF WEALTH

The cradle of England's economic transformation was centered on the cluster of textile factories in and around Manchester. In the words of economic historian Eric Hobsbawm, "Whoever says Industrial Revolution says cotton."[28] Since time immemorial, farmers and their families had spun and woven linen from flax fiber. Farmers cultivated this crop widely throughout Europe; most grew small patches for their own needs, as well as for barter or sale. The other major source of cloth was wool, and for centuries, sheep were England's major source of trade.

England itself produced a small amount of domestic cotton, but quality was poor. The overland route supplied tiny amounts of expensive imported silk cloth for royalty and the wealthiest merchants, as well as high-quality cotton materials, chiefly calicoes from the Indian subcontinent. These fabrics were also expensive—not because of scarcity or high manufacturing costs, but because of high import duties. The opening of the maritime trade to India by way of the Cape of Good Hope by the Portuguese, Dutch, and English (via the East India Company) increased supply, but it was not enough to bring down prices significantly.

The production of linen, woolen, and cotton goods was a "cottage industry." Children picked the raw material clean, women spun the yarn, and men wove the cloth. Although skilled artisans manufactured the finest quality woolens, production was still a small-scale affair. There was little specialization of labor at any level of production, so costs remained high and output remained low. It's helpful to visualize the sequence of steps leading from raw cotton to finished cloth.

$$\text{Raw Cotton} \xrightarrow{\text{Carding}} \text{Cleaned Cotton} \xrightarrow{\text{Spinning}} \text{Yarn} \xrightarrow{\text{Weaving}} \text{Finished Cloth}$$

The key point of this scheme is that any improvement in cloth manufacture required roughly equal improvements in all three steps in the process: the carding of seeds and other debris from the raw cotton, the spinning of cleaned cotton into yarn, and the weaving of yarn into the finished product. An improvement in only one step served only to create bottlenecks in the other two steps.

This is precisely what occurred with the first modern advance in textile technology, the invention of efficient weaving machinery (the flying shuttle) by clockmaker John Kay in 1733. Although a dramatic improvement over the age-old frame loom, this device exacerbated an already acute shortage of women spinners. Cloth manufacture came to a halt at harvest time as farm women took to the fields to assist in the harvest. In 1748, Lewis Paul devised two machines for carding raw fiber, which previously had been done by laboriously dragging it across arrays of nails set into boards. Paul's invention, unfortunately, served only to further increase the demand on the already overtaxed spinners.

Spinning proved the toughest problem to solve, as the era's machine technology could not imitate the delicate twist that was produced between a woman's thumb and forefinger. The spinning wheel, derived from the ancient spindle, came into widespread use during the late medieval period, but it was used simply to wind the finished, spun thread onto the bobbin. Only a woman's delicate hands could first spin the thread.

In the late 1700s a series of inventions finally mechanized the process. Lewis Paul hit upon the idea of imitating the spinner's fingers with pairs of steel rollers, but his machine did not work well. Richard Arkwright added a second pair of rollers to his "water frame" in 1769, the first practical mechanical spinning device. James Hargreaves saw that a spinning wheel continued to operate after falling on its side and used that observation to impart a more even "twist" to the yarn. In 1779, Samuel Crompton combined Hargreaves's rotating wheel with Arkwright's rollers into his "self-actuating mule."

Crompton mounted this devilishly complex device on a carriage that moved backward and forward as it spun out thread. One of the basic principles of technological innovation is that complex productivity-improving devices usually demand less skill from an operator than the devices that preceded them. The sewing machine, for example, produces faster, straighter, and stronger hems than the most skilled seamstress using a needle and thread could, and the modern personal computer enables even a clumsy middle-aged author to produce documents that are more handsome than those that came from the finest printing presses of a hundred years ago. Ease of operation often results from complexity of design.

Early on, Crompton's mule demonstrated this principle. With relatively little training, a mill employee could produce smooth thread over a wide range of diameters, something that his or her more highly skilled predecessors could not.[29] Within a few short years factory owners had married the Watt-Boulton steam engine to the spinning machine, and the mechanical transformation of this critical operation was complete.

Manufacturers did not mechanize weaving as quickly. Initially, the vast amounts of mechanically spun yarn provided a bonanza for weavers. As late as 1813, only 1% of England's 250,000 looms were mechanically powered; the resistance of the weavers to mechanization and industrialization was to bring them to grief as the nineteenth century wore on.[30]

The production of cleaned cotton involved the laborious removal of the seeds, an expensive and grueling process. Eli Whitney's invention of the cotton gin in 1793 removed this impediment. Between 1790 and 1810 American cotton production increased from 1.5 million pounds to 85 million pounds per year. Whitney's invention realigned the landscape of the world economy in ways that few inventions have. Unfortunately, it also transformed the American political landscape as well. The cotton industry, and slavery along with it, suddenly became a paying proposition. Between 1790 and 1850, the number of slaves in the U.S. increased from 700,000 to 3,200,000.[31]

Cotton flooded the world market. Linen and wool, the old English staples, nearly disappeared. For the first time, the toiling masses of farmers and urban poor could own inexpensive cotton clothing. Cotton cloth fell in price from thirty-eight shillings per pound in 1786 to less than ten shillings by 1800. Textiles are highly "elastic" commodities; relatively small declines in price will result in large increases in demand. Just as the falling prices of personal computers proved a boon to sales, so, too, did the consumption of textiles explode in the early nineteenth century. Cotton was history's first true "growth industry." Over the same fourteen-year period, English cotton imports went up tenfold; and by 1840, fiftyfold.[32] A vast triangular trade arose around Liverpool, the port city of Manchester: Raw cotton came from America to Britain, finished cloth went from Britain to Africa, and, until outlawed in 1808, large numbers of slaves were shipped from Africa to America. The abomination of slavery aside, the availability of cheap cotton clothing had benefits that we are now only slowly beginning to comprehend. It is likely, for example, that cheap and available cotton underwear caused the dramatic fall off in infectious disease after 1850.

The most deadly diseases of the period—cholera and typhoid—are gastrointestinal and thus spread by fecal-oral contamination. They were also no respecter of social class. In 1861, Queen Victoria's beloved Albert, prince consort, would die of typhoid. These mundane cotton articles eliminated the irritation and inflammation that had been caused by infrequent changes of single-layered clothing, cut down on disease transmission, and saved millions of lives.[33]

THE NEW IRON AGE

The other major area of industrial advance was iron. In the premodern era, iron production required smelting with charcoal, and by the late eighteenth century, England's foundries had run out of nearby forests. Soon enough, Scottish trees had to be cut for the Midlands mills, and British engineers found it cheaper to import iron from Sweden. British foundries even found it cheaper to import Scandinavian wood because premodern water transport was much less expensive than land transport—shipping from the Baltic Sea cost about as much as twenty miles of land portage in England cost.

England had abundant coke, but substituting it for charcoal in the furnaces required a much more powerful ventilating blast. In 1775, Watt and Boulton adapted their steam engines to iron maker John Wilkinson's bellows for this purpose. A decade later Henry Cort introduced the "puddling" method, which made possible large-scale continuous production of high-quality wrought iron. Wilkinson then invented a steam hammer to finish the final product of Cort's process at 150 blows per minute.

Cort's innovation freed England from its dependence on increasingly scarce wood, depriving timber-rich Sweden of its historical advantage. Previously, imported Scandinavian steel was so superior to the English product that it took both domestic and foreign manufacturers a few years to get used to the idea of a superior British product. As with cotton, production soared. Between 1770 and 1805, costs plummeted and output increased almost tenfold. Immense quantities of iron and steel destined for the new railroads, bridges, and buildings poured forth from the expanded foundries.

The progress described in both cotton and iron manufacture did not end with Crompton's mule or Cort's puddling process. The ensuing decades saw the evolution of an almost continuous process of improvement. Foundries grew ever bigger, required less coal per ton of iron, and put out an ever-higher quality of product. Historian Phyllis Dean beautifully summarized this process of seamless innovation: "Machines and the machines that make machines have proved to be capable of an infinite sequence of improvement, and it is this process of continuing, self-generating technical change that is the ultimate cause of the sustained economic growth that we now take for granted."[34]

A less sanguine Dr. Johnson put it differently, "The age is running mad after innovation. All the business of the world is to be done in a new way; men are to be hanged in a new way."[35] For better or for worse, the world had started down a path of constant change and dislocation, but also of constantly increasing prosperity. There was, and is, no turning back.

THE "INDUSTRIOUS REVOLUTION"

The specialization of labor and an increase in productivity meant little unless they were accompanied by a specialization of consumption. The farmer who grew his own food and built his own house and horse cart provided no market for the products of the new factories. Neither did his wife, who spun and wove her own fabric and sewed the family's clothes. As the nineteenth century wore on, consumers switched from homespun but inefficient self-reliance to a cash-based system in which they engaged in a single highly productive job, then exchanged their salary for all their material needs. Jan de Vries named this transformation the "industrious revolution."[36]

No government, and certainly no all-seeing development czar, decreed that both the workingman and consumer would specialize, increase productivity, and create "takeoffs" in agriculture and industry. Rather, judges and parliamentarians, most of whom were landowners and businessmen, made case law and passed legislation that encouraged commerce and industry. Scientists, who previously had been hobbled by the Aristotelian mind-set, began to use the new Baconian scientific tools to unlock and apply to commerce the secrets of the universe. Finally, the new financial markets earned the trust of investors and supplied a river of capital to business ventures. A most happy English accident.

THE INDUSTRIAL REVOLUTION: JUST HOW BAD WAS IT?

The glories of the Industrial Revolution came at a price: child labor, hideous working conditions at low wages—the "dark satanic mills"—and alienation. What exactly did happen to living standards in England between 1760 and 1830? Over the years this issue has proven capable of making historians, economists, and ideologues squeal like so many hogs that have gotten stuck under a fence, the answer offered providing a sure indicator of the observer's political sympathies. Those on the left were resoundingly negative. According to an anonymous wag, life during the Industrial Revolution was nasty, *British,* and short.[37]

Friedrich Engels was a major beneficiary of the new industrial machine. The son of a Prussian cotton manufacturer, he became caught up in the revolutionary fervor that swept the Continent in the 1840s and soon fell in with another soon-to-be émigré, Karl Marx. Following the upheavals of 1848, both fled to England where Engels began managing one of his father's factories. His inherited wealth and managerial talents supported both Marx and himself in the coming decades.

Engels produced a shocking description of life at the bottom of the nineteenth-century social ladder, *Condition of the Working Class in England.* The young Engels—only twenty-four at the time—first painted an idyllic picture of life in rural pre-industrial Britain:

> So the workers vegetated throughout a passably comfortable existence, leading a righteous and peaceful life in all piety and probity; and their material position was far better than that of their successors. They did not need to overwork; they did no more than they chose to do, and yet earned what they needed. They had leisure for healthful work in garden or field, work which, in itself, was recreation for them, and they could take part besides in the recreations and games of their neighbors, and all these games—bowling, cricket, football, etc., contributed to their physi-

cal health and vigor. They were, for the most part, strong, well-built people, in whose physique little or no difference from that of their peasant neighbors was discoverable. Their children grew up in the fresh country air.[38]

The late eighteenth century swept away Engels' Arcadia, replacing it with the desolation, despair, and Augean squalor of England's industrial slums. A short, relatively innocuous passage from *Condition of the Working Class*, which directly quotes a government report, suffices to convey the scabrous effects brought by industrialism:

> It is notorious that there are whole streets in the town of Huddersfield, and many courts and alleys, which are neither flagged, paved, sewered, nor drained; where garbage and filth of every description are left on the surface to ferment and rot; where pools of stagnant water are almost constant, where the dwellings adjoining are thus necessarily caused to be of an inferior and even filthy description; thus where disease is engendered, and the health of the whole town perilled.[39]

A more balanced, if still grim, assessment is that of a modern observer, Joyce Marlow, who writes "The houses from which the people had come had not been palatial, but neither had they been built on top of sewage ditches in hundreds of rows, without gardens, without sight of a tree, without the smell of fresh air. . . ."[40]

Typical of later efforts from the left is an ideologically tainted piece by Eric Hobsbawm, who attempted to show that per capita food consumption decreased in London in the early eighteenth century. There was one slight flaw in his argument, namely that a falling food supply is inconsistent with the accelerating population growth that characterized the period. (Not only was population growing, but the *rate* of growth was rising as well.) Hobsbawm rationalized this contradiction by suggesting that while preindustrial society was more generously fed, it was also more *irregularly* fed and thus subject to periodic mass starvation. To the left-wing Hobsbawm, the latter seemed somehow a preferable state of affairs.[41]

There can be no question that the rise of industrial capitalism, whatever its net effect on the well-being of the average Englishman, was a disaster for many native peoples. In the words of Karl Marx:

> The discovery of gold and silver in America, the extirpation, enslavement, and entombment in the mines of the aboriginal population, the beginning

of the conquest and looting of the East Indies, the turning of Africa into a warren for the commercial hunting of blackskins, signalized the rosy dawn of the era of capitalist production.[42]

From the perspective of the modern West, the ideological fervor of Marx, Engels, and their later British acolytes—Hobsbawm, Beatrice and Sidney Webb, and George Bernard Shaw, along with entire generations of Oxford and Cambridge graduates—is a bit difficult to fathom. The same can be said of socialism's continuing appeal in many developing nations. Engel's description—generally held to be accurate, if a bit overwrought—of abject degradation and poverty in the midst of plenty makes the rage and lack of objectivity of the early socialists easier to comprehend.

The pervasive crowding and squalor of the era was no doubt responsible for the high death rates of the industrial underclass. The productivity of the new machinery also led to a surplus of labor. The number of house servants increased steadily throughout the 1800s, and the maid and the butler soon became a feature of even middle-class homes. By the beginning of the First World War, "domestic servants" made up fully 15% of the British labor force. Those who found such jobs were considered fortunate. Depravity and crime were often necessary to preserve body and soul. The often desperate condition of the workingman resulted in niches of slum employment that grace the English language to this day: mudlark, scavenger, guttersnipe, and woolgatherer.[43]

On the other side of the ideological divide, the right painted a far sunnier picture of life for the average working family. In 1948, T. S. Ashton answered the naysayers with this comparison of life in the England of the Industrial Revolution with that in the nonindustrialized Far East:

> There are today on the plains of India and China men and women, plague-ridden and hungry, living lives little better, to outward appearance, than those of the cattle who toil with them by day and share their places of sleep by night. Such Asiatic standards, and such unmechanized horrors, are the lot of those who increase their numbers without passing through an Industrial Revolution.[44]

Ashton's sentiments (although perhaps not his exact words) have aged well, but like later economic historians Walt Rostow, Phyllis Deane, and Harvard's legendary Alexander Gerschenkron, he confused cause and effect. The wretched masses of the third world suffer not because they are deficient in factories and machines but because they lack *institutions*—property rights, a scientific outlook, and capital markets—while at the same time their countries experience explosive population growth from their glancing encounter with the advances of modern medicine.

In recent years, scholars have turned down the temperature of the ideological debate about living standards during the Industrial Revolution and have focused on more objective biological measures of well-being. Studies of life expectancy have uncovered significant improvement in longevity between 1760 and 1820, which then remained static until 1860. Much the same pattern is seen in infant mortality rates, which decreased in the late eighteenth century, only to rise again in the early nineteenth. A favorite measure among cliometricians is data on human height.[*] These also show a pattern of improvement in the late eighteenth century that was followed by deterioration in the early nineteenth century.[45]

In the end, Engels and Hobsbawm were both partially correct: The preponderance of the modern evidence indicates that there was a slight deterioration in living standards in the later stages of the Industrial Revolution, at least at the bottom of the economic ladder. The Industrial Revolution was for many, and perhaps most, an unspeakably barbaric affair. England came far closer to civil strife and revolution during the economic fallout of the post-Napoleonic period than most contemporary observers were willing to admit.[46] Fortunately, the British political leadership, exemplified by brilliant visionaries like Robert Peel, himself the son of a cotton magnate, was flexible enough to respond with appropriate reform measures.

What Engels forgot, or likely never learned, was just how grim life was before Britain broke out of the Malthusian Trap. As bad as day-to-day existence in the early industrial slums was, it is indisputable that England's population rose rapidly during the period. Living conditions, almost by definition, must have been far worse two centuries before that, when every increase in numbers brought a reduction in living

---

[*] The study of skeletal remains has also proven invaluable in the investigation of economic trends in the ancient world. Ian Morris, "Early Iron Age Greece," preliminary draft, cited with permission of author.

standards that was severe enough to keep population in check. Between 1740 and 1820, the mortality rate fell from 35.8 per 1,000 to 21.1 per 1,000.[47] Engels' idyllic vision of life before the Industrial Revolution was the figment of a fevered imagination and a blind eye to the iron laws of preindustrial demographics.

The rapid growth of Britain's population after 1650 is indeed something of a mystery. The lack of accurate data clouds the issue. In most cases, scholars are reduced to computing the differences between recorded baptisms and burials. One important mechanism of population control was regulation of age at marriage. In prosperous times people would marry earlier and have more children; in lean times they would marry later and have fewer children. Beyond that, political ideology again intrudes. Left-wing demographers attribute the rapid population rise to the demand for cheap child labor, while right-wing scholars blame the Speenhamland System of poor relief, which rewarded poor families for bearing children. The most convincing explanation for the late medieval population rise involves improvements in sanitation and hygiene, which would argue for a gradual improvement in living conditions.[48]

Yet the problem is still a gnawing one: Throughout the period, per capita economic output rose along with population. Harvard economic historian Simon Kuznets explained this paradox with his "curve hypothesis": Inequality of wealth and income temporarily increases during periods of rapid industrialization, as those at its vanguard prosper at the expense of the rest of society.[49] The same sequence of events played out in the technology boom of the 1990s, which made thousands of computer-literate twentysomethings unimaginably wealthy (if only briefly) and produced great disparities of income.

Because of the uncertainties pertaining to inflation rates and standards of living, we will probably never know the precise contour of early modern English well-being and economic growth. Exactly at what point England's modern economic takeoff occurred and overall living standards took a turn for the better is matter of great controversy. The early historians of the Industrial Revolution—Phyllis Deane and William Cole—argued that rapid economic growth began as early as the late 1700s, while more recent work suggests that this did not occur until early in the twentieth century. This debate is well beyond the scope of this book. However, it is clear that the chaotic eighteenth century was filled with almost continuous great power conflicts. The ongoing carnage reached a climax between 1793 and 1815 with the advent of a new type of global mass warfare. The specter of starvation haunted even England during this later, terrible period, so it is hardly surprising that growth may have been muted in the years immediately before and after 1800. Miraculously, England doubled her population while at least preventing living standards from falling during a period that encompassed the Seven Years War, the American Revolution, the French Revolution and its wars, and the Napoleonic wars. Not until Europe stabilized following the Congress of Vienna and steam power and the telegraph were added to the economic brew could the modern variety of intensive economic growth take place.

In any case, this book's four-factor model helps us to understand why sustainable growth did not occur before the early nineteenth century, when steam-driven transport and electronic communication finally came into use. No matter how productive the manufacturing sector became, without the railroad and the telegraph, entrepreneurs could not efficiently market or transport their plethora of new goods to their ultimate consumers.

THE NON-INDUSTRIAL REVOLUTION

The birth of modern prosperity is usually associated with the Industrial Revolution. Although that term was first used by foreign commentators in the 1830s, historian Arnold Toynbee popularized it in an lecture series in Manchester in 1884. Traditionally, the Industrial Revolution refers to the period between 1760 and 1830.[50] The idea that an increasingly regimented mechanized way of living and production was the fount of Western prosperity seemed obvious to early- and mid-twentieth-century historians and economists such as Phyllis Deane, who wrote,

> It is now almost an axiom of the theory of economic development that the route to affluence lies by way of an industrial revolution. A continuous—some would say "self sustaining"—process of economic growth, whereby each generation can confidently expect to enjoy higher levels of production and consumption than its predecessors, is open only to those

nations which industrialize. *The striking disparity between the standards of living of the inhabitants of the so-called developed or advanced nations of the mid-twentieth century and the standards prevailing in today's underdeveloped or backward countries is essentially due to the fact that the former have industrialized and the latter have not.*[51] (Italics added)

By the 1960s, policy makers had identified industrialization as the sine qua non of global prosperity and saw forced industrialization as the one and only hope of the third world. MIT economist Walt Rostow popularized the term "takeoff": the point in a nation's economy when "the blocks and resistances to steady growth are finally overcome," and it industrializes. He placed the industrial takeoff of Britain shortly after 1800, of the U.S. in 1860, of Japan around 1900, and, most inaccurately of all, of Australia in 1950.[52]

Rostow felt that the prime requisite for economic takeoff was the existence of a political elite that would "regard the modernization of the economy as serious, high-order political business"—industrial transformation directed from the top down.[53] The words "private property" and "civil liberties" are nowhere to be found in Rostow's scheme of things, although in fairness, he did recognize the importance of scientific rationalism and religious tolerance. Reading Rostow, the mind's eye sees dozens of tiny nations poised on the brink of the planet's economic runway, each awaiting clearance to take off into industrialism's blue skies. (If Rostow's name stimulates recollection of American presidencies past, it should. He was indeed the same W. W. Rostow who was Lyndon Johnson's most hawkish advisor and believed right to the end that the war in Vietnam was going well because his numbers and charts were so encouraging.[54])

Even Alexander Gerschenkron, arguably the most illustrious economic historian of the last fifty years, saw industrialization as the be-all and end-all of economic development; a nation could simply not be prosperous and "advanced" without a large factory sector.[55]

The causes of modern wealth extend back almost to the dawn of civilization, and sustainable growth took place in Holland long before it occurred in England. Other modern examples also contradict the industrial-centered hypothesis. The wealth of Australia in the late eighteenth century is particularly telling. In the Deane/Rostow/ Gerschenkron scheme of things, Australia was a "backward" agricultural nation, with only a small industrial sector. How, then, was it able to maintain one of the world's highest standards of living at a time when other agricultural nations were mired in poverty?

Another key Rostovian precondition for "takeoff" was an increase in the rate of investment above 10% of national income. Here again, the MIT professor confused cause and effect. Except in totalitarian societies, it is individuals who choose the proportion of national income invested, not governments. Investors provide capital only when enterprises promise high returns. Modern econometric research clearly demonstrates that vigorous modern economies have high savings rates *because* they offer a wide variety of profitable opportunities, and not the other way around.[56] In any case, the British savings rate during the Industrial Revolution was much less than Rostow's 10% minimum.[57]

How could these formidable scholars have gotten things so wrong? First, they underestimated, as so many did before 1980, the importance of institutional factors, particularly property rights and rule of law. Second, they simply did not have access to accurate historical data. Only in the past few decades have economists attempted to reconstruct the contours of economic growth going back centuries and even millennia. This more recent information suggests that in the late nineteenth century the U.S. was still largely an agrarian nation, but one with a per capita GDP that was nearly identical to England's. At the same time, as we've already seen, Australia, which by Rostow's reckoning had not "taken off" until half a century later, briefly possessed the world's highest per capita GDP.

We could just as well credit the rise in national wealth to automobiles (as Rostow indeed did), to telephones, to Rolex watches, or to Louis XV chairs. Like industrialization, these items, luxury goods or not, are the artifacts of prosperity, not its root causes. Even the man in the street now realizes that industrialization per se is not the cornerstone of economic development. The collapse of the Soviet experiment, which was founded on forced industrialization, and the abject failure of most large foreign-sponsored infrastructure projects in the third world demonstrate that there is more to prosperity than simply building factories and dams. The remarkable late-twentieth-century "postindustrial" wealth of the most advanced nations, whose information- and service-based economies have mushroomed even as their manufacturing sectors have withered and migrated to lower-wage countries, gives the lie to the importance of industrialization as the root source of prosperity.

Also discredited is the more recent "import substitution" theory of economic development, which suggests that developing nations must protect their nascent industries with tariffs and other trade barriers. Recent data suggest that such policies serve only to decrease the long-term competitiveness of these infant industries and slow overall economic growth.[58]

England was the first nation to sustain high rates of economic growth, both in terms of aggregate GDP, as well as per capita GDP, because of her nearly insurmountable lead in developing all four of our institutional factors. In the end, however, England's long economic history, no matter how glorious, became a burden. As late as the eighteenth century, the statute books bulged with a mass of medieval regulations. One example was the Statute of Apprentices, which originated in Elizabethan times, but was not repealed until 1814. Surveying this statute, Adam Smith wrote:

> It has been adjudged, for example that a coach-maker can neither himself make nor employ journeymen to make his own coach-wheels; but must buy them of a master wheelwright. . . . But a wheelwright, though he has never served an apprenticeship to a coach-maker, may either himself make or employ a journeymen to make coaches; the trade of a coach-maker not being within the statute, because (it was not practiced) in England at the time when it was made.[59]

The woolen trade was hidebound with such rules, and one of the reasons behind the cotton industry's explosive growth was that as a new commodity, it went unregulated. Industrialists could avoid trade and apprentice rules by carrying on business in grim "new towns" like Birmingham and Manchester, where these rules did not apply and where the justices of the peace who enforced the old regulations did not sit.

The English monopolistic tradition was also slow to disappear. The East India Company kept its lock on trade with India until 1813, and on trade with China for decades after that. The East India Company's monopoly, by crippling other British companies desiring to trade with the Far East, did more harm than good to English commerce. The Bubble Act, which was passed in 1720 in the wake of the South Sea episode to discourage speculation, hobbled innovation by requiring a parliamentary charter for the formation of joint-stock companies. Parliament did not repeal the Bubble Act until 1825, and it did not streamline the process for forming joint-stock companies until 1856.

The Bubble Act also forbade use of many of the "speculative tools" that were blamed for the 1720 market debacle, including short selling and futures. We now know that these devices enhance market stability and lower the cost of capital. Their absence made the British financial markets exceedingly volatile over the ensuing century.

Like the rest of Europe, England was highly mercantilistic, not sweeping away its protectionist bulwark until long after the Battle of Waterloo. We've already touched on the repeal of the Corn Laws; Parliament did not void the Navigation Acts until 1849. The steamship is of little use to trade if governments are overly protective of their domestic agriculture and industries. Not until England swept away its protectionist legislation would the last block in prosperity's foundation—effective transportation—be securely in place.

THE NEW JERUSALEM

Not only did the American colonies possess all of Britain's institutional advantages, they also escaped most of her curses. American capital formation was particularly unhindered. Shortly after the Constitution was ratified, the U.S. created the world's most advanced patent system. All that was lacking was capital itself and workers. Both would soon be freely flowing from within and without. By 1855, the U.S. had more inhabitants than England did; by 1870, its economy was also larger than Britain's.

Figure 7–2 shows the growth of U.S. per capita GDP after the ratification of the Constitution. In contrast to the uncertainty of growth in England in the early nineteenth century, the U.S. experienced productivity growth of about 2% per year almost from the very beginning—far faster than on the other side of the Atlantic.[*] Much of the early growth of U.S. productivity was of the catch-up variety—Maddison estimates

---

[*]   The closeness of the fit of the graph of per capita GDP in Figure 7–2 to the 2% trend line is uncanny. Recall from Chapter 1 that the growth of per capita GDP of the world's major developed nations during the twentieth century also clusters very tightly around 2%.

FIGURE 7–2   REAL U.S. PER CAPITA GDP

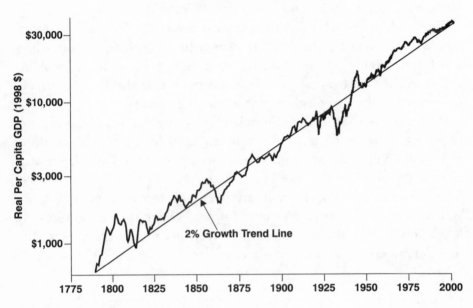

Source: U.S. Department of Commerce.

that in 1820, per capita GDP in the U.S. was only 73% of that in the U.K. and that American productivity did not surpass England's until the early twentieth century. Because of immigration and a higher birth rate, however, the raw size of the American economy exceeded England's long before that.[60]

An abundance of land and resources blessed the new country, but its huge continental geography, even with its long rivers, was not at all favorable to economic prosperity, particularly compared with that of England or Holland. From the very start, the U.S. inherited from England a far more valuable commodity: the world's best institutions. It chose those that encouraged liberty and commerce, discarded those that did not, and invented some all of its own. Only its own peculiar flaws, particularly the institution of slavery, which would precipitate a devastating civil war, could delay its assumption of the dominant place among the world's nations.

CHAPTER EIGHT

Runners-Up

THE BURGEONING PROSPERITY of Holland and England soon spread to the rest of Western Europe, and later, to East Asia. Whether or not a country became rich depended on deeply rooted institutional and cultural factors. From among the dozens of nations that achieved prosperity in the wake of Holland and England, I shall single three out for analysis: France, Spain, and Japan.

Figure 8–1 shows the growth of per capita GDP in these three countries alongside that of England. Because of its proximity to England and its post-Revolution reforms, France followed closely on the heels of its cross-channel neighbor; Spain and Japan took more than a century longer. The economic stories of all three countries center on the obstacles to growth that were in their path, how these obstacles were overcome, and what lessons can be drawn for today's developing world.

THE RULER AND THE RULED

Beginning in Holland and in England, merchants and the petty aristocracy gradually curbed the ruler's prerogatives and fundamentally changed the relationship between state and citizen. This shift slowly spread to the rest of Western Europe. The process unfolded neither smoothly nor uniformly. The *ancien régime* under Louis XIV, for example, reached heights

FIGURE 8–1   PER CAPITA GDP (INFLATION-ADJUSTED)

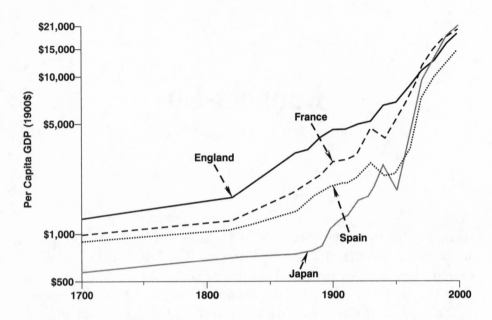

Source: Data from Maddison, *Monitoring the World Economy, 1820–1992* and Maddison, *The World Economy: A Millennial Perspective*, 264.

of political and economic absolutism that were not seen until the advent of modern communism and national socialism.

For thousands of years, the primary goal of any ruler was to maximize his own wealth. The divine right of kings yielded only under the greatest of duress, as occurred at Runnymede in 1215. Premodern Europe was a maelstrom of constant warfare among small states—"nation" is too grand a word to describe all but the very largest. Estimates vary, but in the medieval period, as many as a thousand sovereign principalities were scattered across the Continent. The clever prince or duke learned that if he taxed laborers and merchants too heavily, they were liable to take their business a few miles up the road, where levies lay lighter on the purse.

Slowly, rulers began to identify their own well-being with that of their subjects and learned not to pluck too many feathers from the goose. States that neither taxed their subjects too heavily nor seized their property too often found themselves with fuller treasuries and larger armies than states that did. Nations that could not refrain from plundering their subjects grew weaker, and, in many cases, disappeared. Gradually, through this Darwinian process, states with enlightened taxation, rule of law, and secure property rights prospered and prevailed over their less advanced neighbors, and Europe became a good place to get rich. The fragmented European political landscape thus provided a dramatic contrast to the centralized Turkish and Chinese states, where entrepreneurs discomfited by ill-advised government policy had nowhere else to go.

The wise ruler collects taxes in ways that do not interfere with free market incentives. From an economic and social perspective, the optimal levy is the excise, or sales, tax. The most common modern version of the excise levy is the European-style value added tax, which is essentially a national sales tax that does not "cascade" through the intermediate steps of the production process as ordinary sales taxes do. Income taxes are moderately "distorting," as are property taxes, since both decrease incentives to earn and invest. The worst path to state revenue runs through the sale of competition-throttling monopolies.

More important than the type or perhaps even the rate of taxation is its method of administration. Nothing corrodes economic health more than the arbitrary seizure of assets, whether by those wearing a robber's mask or a badge of office. Similarly, nothing demoralizes a society more than the wholesale exemption of entire social classes from taxation. The certainty of a 30% tax on income is easily tolerated; a 30% chance of arbitrary and complete appropriation or the exemption of 30% of the population from payment will impoverish a society and foment revolution.

WEALTH AND THE SWORD

Before the modern era, the very idea that a nation could grow wealthy and powerful through commerce was almost unheard of. For millennia, the road to riches lay through victory and plunder. Before the rise of a tepid prosperity in Renaissance Italy and the more robust variety in Holland, few rulers understood the value of commerce and industry, let alone made it a national priority. Conquest alone produced riches. When the booty ran dry, a characteristic death spiral played out. In order to make up for lost revenue, the ruler increased taxes on his primary wealth producers—farmers. Unable to pay the increased levies, farmers sold or simply abandoned their plots. This drove down tax revenues, leading to yet higher tax rates and the abandonment of yet more farms. From late Hellenistic Greece through Rome after Constantine to the late Ottoman Empire, the signature characteristic of the decaying state was a depopulated countryside.

The very first step towards prosperity, then, is a ruler's awareness of the link between his welfare and that of his subjects. The modern developed nation is a "service state" that actively provides public goods that enhance commerce. To name a few, these are:

- Education for its young
- Police protection to ensure public safety and property rights
- Justice administered by independent courts to assure citizen loyalty
- Roads to transport labor and products

Deciding, then, who led and who lagged on the journey to prosperity centers on determining when and where the ruling aristocracy first grasped the importance of the following elements that provide the foundation for national wealth: the rule of law, the security of private property, the separation of powers, a vigorous private commerce and trade, the switch in state revenues from monopoly rents toward a broad-based excise-tax system, and the provision of public safety, education, and roads.

WHY DID FRANCE LAG?

In an influential essay, economic historian N. F. R. Crafts concluded that England beat France to the Industrial Revolution by chance.[1] He argued that both nations possessed the intellectual and social infrastructure necessary for modern growth, and that therefore, England's victory was a "stochastic"—that is, random—event. If the eighteenth century could be played over and over, Crafts suggested, France would have won the economic contest at least as often as England did.

Undoubtedly, a strong random element permeates history. What would have happened had a stray microbe or bullet put an early end to Hitler, Wellington, or Louis XIV? Nonetheless, even the briefest survey of Europe's institutional history reveals that in the race to the Industrial Revolution, the French never really stood a chance.

At least superficially, the French matched the English in all four of the critical economic factors. By all rights, France *should* have joined England and Holland in the vanguard of world prosperity. Were not French property rights secured by a strong central government and a highly organized judiciary? Could not France, home of Descartes and Pascal, have just as well claimed itself to be the home of the scientific enlightenment? Would not France's record of technological innovation prove just as impressive as England's? Did not the court at Versailles obtain vast amounts of capital from a public hungry for *rentes*? Was not the French system of roads and canals, constructed under Henry IV and Louis XIV, superior to the collection of rutted paths and ragged quays in seventeenth-century England?

The answer to each of these questions is a ringing affirmative. Yet the start of France's economic takeoff lagged England's by more than a century. Why? The answer to this riddle lies in the *efficiency* with which each of the four growth factors operated under the *ancien régime*.

WHAT A FRENCHMAN REALLY WANTS

By the beginning of Henry IV's reign in 1589, feudalism was nearly dead in France. Clear and alienable title to land and possessions had spread widely, and commerce grew apace. But while the French property system conferred ownership, it did not supply incentive. The problem lay with what economists call "rent-seeking behavior"—the propensity to use special privilege, as opposed to enterprise and hard work, to earn money. Familiar modern examples include excessive fees for required vehicle inspections, union featherbedding, and extravagant pay and benefit schemes for top corporate executives. Rent seeking is a basic feature of human nature, and all societies suffer from it to some degree. Economic damage occurs only when rent seeking consistently becomes more attractive than earning an honest living. Such was the case during the *ancien régime*.

To grasp how rent seeking evolved in premodern France, we need to understand her tax structure. The primary source of revenue was the *taille,* a tax on land and buildings. Nobility and clergy were exempt from the levy, so by default it fell on peasants and small businessmen. The purchase of noble status or the taking of vows thus paid handsome dividends in both spiritual and material terms. The Crown did attempt to extract revenue from the nobles and clergy, first with the *gabelle* (the salt tax) and the *aides* (taxes on luxury items such as wines, soap, and candles), and later with a complicated head tax, the *capitation.* The inequality of the tax burden slowly forced peasants to sell off their land, but they often remained on it as tenant farmers. Property accumulated in the hands of absentee noblemen who, from the safety of Versailles, dispatched agents charged with extracting seigneurial and sharecropping dues—*sans merci*—from the land's former peasant owners and their offspring. By the time of Louis XIV's death, France had regressed to a near-feudal state, which would provide the primary source of dry tinder for the Revolution.[2] The Crown found it difficult to collect such a wide range of complex levies and so became increasingly dependent on tax farmers—private businessmen who collected revenues for the government in return for a share of the take.[3]

This system was cumbersome, odious, and devastating to the nation's commercial vigor. Beginning in the time of Henry IV, the newly wealthy dreamed of setting their sons up as bureaucrats and tax farmers in the same way that today's modern professionals yearn to send their offspring to Ivy League universities. For its part, the Crown, which was chronically short of capital for military adventure and court extravagance, gladly exchanged future revenue for present cash. Businessmen in France did not find it particularly difficult to succeed, but under such a system, family entrepreneurial spirit rarely lasted more than a single generation. One historian described the French mind-set:

> While in Holland and even in England a merchant, manufacturer, or financier, having made his fortune, had no other desire but to see his sons extend the range of his business, in France the dream of every self-made man was to buy his eldest son an official post; if he was at the top of the ladder, he would make him a Councillor in one of the

Parliaments of the *Chambres de Comptes*; if he was a small shopkeeper, he would make him a clerk.[4]

As families exchanged productive activity for purchased titles and official sinecures, upwards of 80% of a village's surnames might disappear from its tax rolls in a single generation.[5] Property rights work their magic by supplying *incentive*. France possessed superficially robust property rights, but saw its citizens' incentives drained by institutions that encouraged rent-seeking behavior. To this day, the Frenchman still aspires to the status of *fonctionnaire*—roughly, a bureaucrat endowed by the state with considerable status, benefits, and perks. Yet again, the fall of a great power had turned on tax policy.

Although England's Stuart kings also used the sale of monopolies as the royal road to revenue, the English were rank amateurs in this area, granting exclusive rights to the importation of this commodity or the sale of that finished product to the first courtier to grab the monarch's ear. Under the reign of Louis XIV, the French would take the state exploitation of monopoly rights to new heights.

THE VERSAILLES PROBLEM

The most evocative adjective available to describe such regimes is "dirigiste," which is derived from a French root meaning "to steer." The French centralizing instinct arose out of the debilitation and chaos that followed the Hundred Years War (actually lasting 116 years, from 1337 to 1453, and fought over the control of Norman France). Although England won most of the war's great battles—Crécy, Agincourt, and Poitiers—victory went to France after Joan of Arc broke the siege of Orleans. By the end of the conflict, the English held only Calais.

In the aftermath of the war the French state—little more than a patchwork of feudal fiefs loosely held together by King Charles VII— was in a shambles. Charles slowly began to assert power on a national level, beginning with the establishment of national taxes and the sale of offices.[6] Under Henry IV, the craft guilds, given monopoly power over their industries, choked competition and stunted innovation. Over the ensuing two centuries, successive monarchs concentrated power in the

Crown. This process reached its pinnacle as Louis XIV gathered French nobles in the splendid imprisonment of the Versailles Court. This unified the nation politically, but it also isolated the aristocracy from their social and commercial roots in the provinces and fractured the nation's commercial life.

The extravagancies of the Court, which need not be recounted here, consumed fully 6% of the national budget. The Court's indirect costs were far higher. The nation's elite, obsessed with gaining the Sun King's favors at Versailles, became detached from its commercial interests back home.[7]

Louis' best-known *contrôler général* (finance minister) was Jean Baptiste Colbert. Hardworking, sincerely focused on France's welfare, and honest by the standards of his time, he commanded the French economy nearly as completely as Louis manipulated the nobility. Above all a mercantilist, Colbert believed that the economic health of a nation derived from the gold in its coffers, which in turn depended on its balance of trade. When exports flowed strongly and imports could be held down, wealth accumulated. When exports waned, gold left the country and weakened it.

Mercantilism thus was a zero-sum game that played out to the detriment of all nations. Its most pernicious quality was succinctly described by another ardent mercantilist, Sir Francis Bacon, who observed that "the increase of any estate must be upon the foreigner."[8] Economic progress has historically involved much trial and error. Adam Smith's penetrating wisdom saw that trade does not occur unless it is mutually agreeable and that the mercantilist *guerre d'argent* benefits almost no one. The truth of this notion had eluded the brightest minds of previous eras, including Colbert's, just as it continues to elude the minds of today's foes of globalization.

Colbert wished to strengthen exports, and so he decided that France should establish preeminence in all of the great luxury export items of the age: tapestries, glass, and porcelain (at the time, these were dominated by the southern Netherlands, Venice, and China, respectively). In 1667, he imposed punitive import tariffs on these items. He saw factory workers as the cannon fodder of a vast industrial army and forbade them to strike. He directed functionaries "to drive fear into the workers' hearts."[9]

Edict after edict mandated production methods in infinitesimal detail. One particular type of cloth was to contain 1,376 threads; another, 2,368 threads. Specific widths were demanded for each type as well. The regulations pertaining to cloth dyeing alone ran to 317 articles. The rules defined three different types of dyers, each with its own guild. The three groups were to be strictly separated from one another. Colbert's ministry published forty-four codes pertaining to different industries and appointed a corps of inspectors to ensure that they were followed to the letter.[10,11,12]

This was only the beginning. By Colbert's death, fifteen separate inspectorates functioned. When inspectors found that existing regulations did not apply to all stages of manufacture, the *contrôler* expanded the codes and appointed yet more inspectors. By 1754, the number of inspectorates had swelled to sixty-four.

The guilds egged on the regulators. When the button makers' guild discovered to its alarm that cloth buttons had supplanted its bone-based product, the *contrôler* called out the inspectors to fine the offending tailors and even to enter private homes so that those wearing the contraband items could be punished. Sheep could be sheared only in May and June, black sheep could not be slaughtered, and carding devices had to be made from a particular kind of wire and contain a certain number of teeth.[13] Colbert's system, with its arcane and all-encompassing trade regulations, choked off innovation and provided almost endless opportunity for corruption.

All states require revenue; the manner in which they collect it often determines the very life and death of nations. Even today, in many countries in Africa and Asia, the sale of government offices and monopolies, with the attendant crippling of competition and growth, provides an all-too-easy source of government revenue. Premodern France and Spain fell headlong into this trap.

The English and Dutch, as we've already seen, were not above exchanging monopoly status for financing, but over time they became increasingly reliant on excise levies that fell on all. After 1700 the road to wealth in Britain and Holland no longer wound through a government post; increasingly, citizens grew rich by engaging in manufacture, commerce, or trade.

The English and Dutch trading companies did indeed enjoy monopoly status, but in return for the privilege the companies bore substantial risk. Even today, patent law grants limited monopoly power, but that, too, is accompanied by the risk undertaken by the inventor. In any case, the 1624 Monopoly Act largely ended the granting of arbitrary monopolies in England by the Crown. France, by contrast, did not curtail its monopolies until after the Revolution. The 175-year gap between these two events goes a long way towards explaining France's lag in prospering economically.

HOW TO RUIN RATIONALISM

Few would deny that the French fully participated in the scientific enlightenment. Because it glorified the nation, Versailles valued groundbreaking science. Nor can we argue that the French were inherently less intelligent, curious, or ambitious than the English were. By the same token, we cannot assert with a straight face that English scientific, technologic, and intellectual accomplishments in any way exceeded those in France. The list of influential *philosophes,* commencing with Descartes, on whose shoulders Newton metaphorically stood, is at least as long and distinguished as that of the great English scientists of the period. Likewise, the French equaled the English in the adoption of steam power, rail transport, and telegraphy.

Yet, subtle but key differences in attitude toward intellectual and technological advance arose on either side of the English Channel. Religious intolerance had long been a staple of French political life. When Henry IV, a Protestant by birth, ascended the throne as the first Bourbon king in 1589, he was forced to convert to Catholicism before he could claim the crown. He justified his conversion by exclaiming, "Paris is worth a mass." While king, Henry sought to cast oil on the turbulent religious waters. In 1598, he issued the Edict of Nantes, which gave protection and a degree of autonomy to Protestant Huguenots. Louis XIV, who despised Protestantism, revoked the edict in 1685. At a stroke, the Sun King stripped France of her brightest scientists and most talented craftsmen, most of whom fled to England and the Low Countries. Denis Papin, builder of the first model steam engine, was one such refugee.

The great industrial innovations of the seventeenth and eighteenth centuries issued from gifted craftsmen, not scientists, and therein lay another French disadvantage. In France, scientists remained an elite class, coddled by the Court and ensconced in their academies. These luminaries only rarely interacted with the general population, craftsmen, or inventors. In England, by contrast, academics and artisans freely communicated and intermingled. Professor Wheatstone may have barely tolerated the upstart Cooke, but that did not prevent the two from collaborating. More often than not, respected scientists like Hooke and Halley freely gave their time and advice to poorly educated craftsmen like the engine man Newcomen and the clockmaker Harrison. In the words of economic historian Joel Mokyr:

> In Britain, the bridge between natural philosophers and engineers was broader and easier to cross than in other countries, and more than anywhere else, Britain could count on able people who could effortlessly move between the world of abstraction, symbol, equation, blueprint and diagram and the world of the lever, the pulley, the cylinder, and the spindle.[14]

Almost two decades after publishing his "stochastic" thesis, Crafts defended it by suggesting that the British may have had an advantage over the French in "microinventions," which are incremental technological improvements in existing machines, but the French were their equal in the production of "macroinventions," which are revolutionary devices that arise by serendipity and chance.[15] True, perhaps, but irrelevant. On those occasions when the French did beat the English to an invention—micro or macro—they repeatedly showed themselves unable to capitalize on and produce it. The signature macroinvention of the Industrial Revolution was the spinning machine. From 1686 until 1759, French economic regulations forbade the production, the importation, and even the *wearing* of printed cotton calicoes, the quintessential end product of the new devices.

Even had the French invented the spinning machine, their micromanaged industrial and capital systems would have prevented the widespread use of this revolutionary machine. Incredible as it seems today, in the eighteenth century, France executed over sixteen thousand peasants and small businessmen—most hanged or broken on the wheel—for violating the cotton regulations.[16] Aghast at the carnage, reformers championed the guillotine as a more humane method of capital punishment.

CAPITAL FLEES FRANCE

France's difficulty with the third area, the capital markets, was more subtle. Though France held abundant capital, the entrepreneur could not unlock this bounty. The successful businessman, rather than invest in his own firm, aspired to the state of *rentier,* the happy, passive recipient of income from *rentes* issued by the Crown (and later, from foreign investments). The preferred financial vehicle of the middle and lower classes was the *bas de laine*—the wool sock that was filled with gold and silver coins and customarily resided under the mattress. These two traditional vehicles—*rentes* and the *bas de laine*—crowded out the needs of entrepreneurs, which in any case stayed relatively small. During the nineteenth century, French investors sent approximately three-quarters of all their savings either to the national and local governments or abroad.[17]

Religious intolerance also caused great mischief in the capital markets. John Calvin was, of course, a Frenchman. His belief that the salvation of the soul lay through the believer's profession and his approval of loans at modest interest gave rise to powerful Protestant banking houses in La Rochelle, Nîmes, Lyons, and Paris. Since the Crown would not sell offices to Protestants, they were "forced" into commerce, and Protestant banks flourished through the generations. Louis XIV's revocation of the Edict of Nantes forced Protestants to choose between conversion and exile. In the typical case, some family members might move to Amsterdam, London, Hamburg, or Danzig, while others became Catholic and remained in France. The separated family branches would keep in close contact, much as the Rothschilds would later do. Even so, the Crown's stupidity in such matters inflicted great damage upon French capital markets.[18] (But not as much damage as was done in the technological sector, where Protestant craftsmen and inventors, whose businesses were much more portable, fled en masse.)

OF ROADS AND TOLLS

France's own geography also placed it at a disadvantage to England. France is a large, continental nation, while no point in the United Kingdom lies more than seventy miles from the sea. From a purely mechanical perspective, France rose to the challenge of her unfavorable geography. France's road system was no worse than England's. Moreover, French mercantilism had some salutary features. A positive trade balance required effective transport (as well as uniform systems of weights, measures, and currency). This resulted in a long Crown tradition of canal and road building. Henry IV's finance minister, the Duke of Sully, envisioned a vast network of canals in the north that would divert trade from the Habsburg routes.

Sully actually began work on one part of the proposed system, a canal linking the Seine and the Loire, which was not finished until decades after Henry's death. Colbert improved the waterway and began to execute the rest of Sully's grand design, which, again, was not finished until long after the deaths of both Colbert himself and the Sun King. An even grander project—the *Canal de Deux Mers*—connected the Mediterranean Sea with the Garonne River (and thus with the Atlantic Ocean). The canal was completed in 1691, but the high cost of building and maintaining its one hundred locks rendered it uncompetitive with the sea route.[19]

Sully and Colbert pursued road building with the same fervor. During the reigns of Henry IV and Louis XIV, serviceable roads linked Paris to all French frontiers. Transit times were cut in half, and by the end of the seventeenth century, fast coaches could travel from Paris to Lyon in "only" five days. By the mid-eighteenth century, France had Europe's best system of inland transport.

But along with the beginnings of an efficient road and canal system, Colbert inherited a Rube Goldberg scheme of internal tariffs. This system divided the nation into customs zones, and traffic among the zones was subjected to a crushing burden of tolls. Adding insult to injury, the hated tax farmers administered this vast and arcane system.

During the reign of Henry IV, a load of salt transported the 270 miles from Nantes to Nevers was subjected to tolls that came to four times the actual value of the cargo.[20] This system splintered the country into roughly thirty trade zones, destroying any semblance of a unified national economy.[21]

Colbert recognized the need to dismantle the internal tariffs, but entrenched local princes, who derived substantial income from the tolls,
blocked him at every turn. Colbert eventually carved out a large cus-
toms-free region in the heart of France, the *Cinq Gross Fermes* (five great
farms). He then relegated the outer provinces to free trade with their
foreign neighbors, but not with the *Cinq Gross Fermes.*[22]

Metaphorically speaking, Colbert spent his mornings toiling on his
networks of canals, while in the afternoons the local gentry sabotaged his
creations with internal tariffs.* After the *contrôler* died in 1683, all fiscal
restraint was lost. By the end of Louis XIV's reign three decades later,
the state had doubled the tolls on the roads and rivers it controlled, and
the nation that had once been Europe's breadbasket could not import
desperately needed corn because it lacked the necessary credit. While
England prospered under the rule of law, France was bled white by the
"reign of the Farmers-General."[23,24]

APRÈS LE DELUGE

What of France after the overthrow of the *ancien régime?* Whatever the excesses of the French Revolution, two of its reforms resuscitated the nation's
moribund economy. First, the Constituent Assembly, in one fell swoop,
abolished all internal tolls.[25] Second, the revolutionary land settlement confirmed the peasant farmers' title to their holdings, transferred ownership to
many tenants, and finally permitted the enclosure of common lands. At the
same time, the settlement allowed farmers to subdivide their property. This
resulted in the modern-day pattern of large numbers of tiny farms—the
so-called *morcellement.*[26] The atomization of French farming locked an inap-
propriately high proportion of the populace into an increasingly inefficient
agricultural sector, which in turn strengthened the constituency for the protectionist measures that swept France in the late nineteenth century.

---

* Internal tolls did even more damage in Germany. The scenic Rhine castles so beloved by
modern tourists were constructed for the purpose of intimidating the river traffic below. One
medieval observer labeled the river tolls, typically levied about once every ten miles, "the raving
lunacy of the Germans." One literally did not lose sight of one toll station before spying the next.
See Heckscher, 56–60.

Between 1853 and 1888, while the English were rolling back tariffs as fast as they could, the French increased the import duty on grain ninefold, and that on cattle, fortyfold. Late-nineteenth-century French political discourse was neatly reduced by one wag to, "everyone has promised to protect everybody."[27] Not only did *morcellement* deprive French industry of much-needed skilled labor, but it also yielded Europe's costliest food, caused by the combination of inefficient farming and protectionism. This, in turn, drained Frenchwomen's purses and starved the capital markets. Not until the twentieth century would France cast off her mercantilist past and roll back the crippling tariffs that had dogged her, in one form or another, since the time of Sully and Colbert.

DOOMED FROM THE START

In a way, Crafts was right—England's economic victory over France was a chance event, although not in the sense he originally meant. Lady luck did cut the cards, but the deck was an *institutional* one; once the seventeenth century's respective institutional hands had been dealt, the pot belonged to England. Then, as now, every nation pursued the same objective: to maximize state revenues and power. During the seventeenth century, the Dutch and the English trembled at their mercantilist, centrally planned French neighbor in the same way that the West quavered before the apparent Soviet economic colossus during the twentieth century.[28] Few in Holland and England felt certain that their "system"—equality under the law, separation of powers, decentralized commerce, and avoidance of unnecessary regulation—would prevail. As well as we can know the mind of any official at Versailles, Colbert had nothing but the best interests of France at heart when he unleashed his disastrous scheme of industrial centralization.

It would be yet another century until the Great Game's referee, Adam Smith, declared the outcome and the rationale. Only after the fact did it become obvious to all who had eyes that it was France, with her flawed system of property incentives, lack of communication between scientists and craftsmen, stunted capital markets, and suffocating internal tariffs, who held the losing hand.

SPAIN—ALL THE WRONG STUFF

In the great Western European economic race, Spain brought up the rear. If ever a great nation wished to intentionally throttle its economic growth and geopolitical influence, it could not have done so more effectively than premodern Spain did.

Like the Romans before them, the Spaniards made conquest and plunder—not industry, trade, and commerce—their primary economic goal. The marriage of Ferdinand of Aragon and Isabella of Castile in 1469 united two of Europe's great nations. Their daughter Joan then consummated another great dynastic union by marrying Philip, son of Maximilian of Austria and later Holy Roman Emperor.

The offspring of that marital alliance, Carlos I, inherited the Habsburg Empire, which at his ascension to the throne included all of Spain, southern Italy, Burgundy (Holland, Belgium, and portions of northern France), Austria, Hungary, and various small German states. Carlos succeeded his grandfather as Holy Roman Emperor, and, as Charles V, found himself at the head of the most wealthy and feared state in Europe. Although the rest of the continent trembled in dread of this colossus, it was doomed by its peculiar fiscal and institutional architecture. Within a century it would collapse upon itself, prey to the tender mercies of former victims.

The events of 1492 proved momentous for both the New World and the Old World. In that year, Habsburg Spain chose to persecute and expel its most advanced and industrious populations—the Jews and the Moors. The treatment of the Muslims was particularly appalling. The terms of Spain's earlier conquest of Granada gave them freedom of worship, but that right was almost immediately abrogated by the Church. The Inquisition forced most Muslims to convert to Christianity, the new Christians and their descendants becoming known as Moriscos.

During the sixteenth century, the Inquisition threw the Moriscos out of Granada and scattered them throughout Spain, before finally expelling them altogether from the empire in 1609. The tragedy was magnified as the Muslim regimes of North Africa martyred many of the newly arrived Moriscos because they were Christian. Spain itself suffered as a result of its treatment of the Moriscos: The Moors and Morsicos ran sophisticated irrigation projects that helped to produced great quantities of grapes, berries, rice, and sugar. Within a few generations of their expulsion, these fell into disrepair.

OF CONQUEST AND COMMERCE

This long march of folly continued. Ferdinand's orders to conquistadors embarking for the New World could not have been more explicit: "Get gold, humanely if possible, but at all hazards—get gold."[29] And gold they did get, great mountains of it. Soon after Columbus's four missions, explorers found a relatively small amount of the glittering metal in Hispaniola (the island containing what is now Haiti and the Dominican Republic), the first Spanish colony. Subsequent mining operations essentially exterminated the native population. Within a few decades, explorers found far larger sources of gold and silver in Mexico and in the Andes. The brutal tale of Spanish conquest in these two locations astonishes to this day.

Between 1519 and 1521, about two thousand Spaniards, led mainly by Hernán Cortés, conquered Mexico. Their main enemy, the Aztecs, fought every bit as valiantly and brutally as the Europeans had. Indeed, the brutality of the Aztecs ultimately proved to be their downfall. Local tribes that had smarted under the Aztec lash provided the Spaniards with tens of thousands of willing allied troops, without whom victory would have been impossible. In 1548, the Spaniards found the first large ground-level silver veins near Guanajuato, which eventually proved to be the richest precious metal deposit of all time, supplying one-third of world production.

A nearly identical sequence of events played out in 1532 in the high Andes. After more than a decade of planning and reconnaissance, Francisco Pizarro led a force of two hundred men over the mountains and subjugated an Inca nation of more than 3.5 million people. In the process, Pizarro captured and held for ransom the Incan emperor, Atahualpa. The conquistadors collected a ransom of gold objects that filled a room that was seventeen feet wide, twenty-two feet deep, and nine feet high. Then, they duplicitously garroted the Incan emperor. The Incas, on their part, demonstrated an exquisite sense of the Spanish mind-set. In retaliation for their emperor's execution, they murdered a

Spanish hostage by pouring molten gold down his throat with this taunt: "Drink thy fill; for here's enough to content even the most covetous."[30]

Compared with the Spanish triumph over the Aztecs, the conquest of the Incas was a short and relatively bloodless affair, at least from the European perspective. Little more than a decade later, in 1547, an Incan herder named Gualci came upon the great Potosí deposit in Bolivia, later described by the Spaniards as "a mountain of silver."

A FATAL RIVER OF WEALTH

Although the silver mines were for the most part privately operated, the Spanish Crown tightly controlled the entire process—from the refining of the metal to the final arrival of bullion at the House of Trade in Seville. The government owned the great mine at Huancavélica, which produced the mercury that was essential for extracting silver, and used the mercury mine to keep tabs on the silver refiners. Locally refined bullion first found its way to the colonial royal assay offices, where smelters cast it into bars and plate and "quinted" the silver (stamped it to indicate that it was liable to taxation). Spanish authorities severely punished holders of unquinted metal.

In Mexico, conquistadors conveyed the bullion overland to Vera Cruz for shipment to Spain. South American metal followed a more complex route that involved transport down from the mountains by llama, the only possible means of conveyance, to the Pacific Coast, shipment north to Panama, and then transshipment across the isthmus to the Caribbean ports of Nombre de Dios and Porto Bello.

These three Caribbean ports and the surrounding ocean—the storied Spanish Main—saw the greatest flow of wealth in history. Generally, one heavily guarded convoy per year left from both Panama and Mexico. Charles V was said to clap for joy at their safe arrival in Spain, and contrary to popular impression, he was not often disappointed. Pirates intercepted and stole the entire silver armada only twice, the Mexican fleet by the Dutch in 1628 and the South American fleet by the English in 1656. More common was the straggling ship that made easier prey, especially for the English, who during one month in 1569 brought

FIGURE 8–2 FLOW OF GOLD AND SILVER FROM THE NEW WORLD TO SPAIN

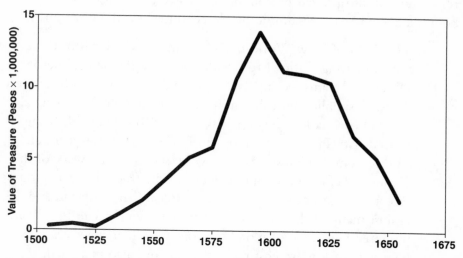

Source: Data from Earl J. Hamilton, "Imports of American Gold and Silver Into Spain, 1503–1660," 464.

twenty-two Spanish ships into Plymouth. In the end, foul weather took far more ships than piracy did.[*]

Figure 8–2 shows the value of the precious metals shipped through the House of Trade—the sum total of all legal Spanish imports, which peaked in the late sixteenth century. The amount of illegal bullion is controversial, and scholars have suggested that the peak of New World silver shipments did not occur until the mid-seventeenth century. This is beside the point, however. Figure 8–2 is an accurate representation of the *official* tally, and this is what the Spanish treasury depended upon.

---

[*]   Three sources on the Spanish conquest of America are highly recommended. Victor D. Hanson's *Carnage and Culture* (New York: Doubleday, 2001) provides a vivid description of Cortés's remarkable victory over the Aztecs. William H. Prescott's *History of the Conquest of Peru*, published in 1847 and reprinted by the Heritage Press in 1957, does the same for Pizarro and the Incas. For a highly entertaining and readable account of the mining and transport of precious metals from the New World to Spain, see Earl J. Hamilton's "Imports of American Gold and Silver Into Spain, 1503–1660," *Quarterly Journal of Economics* 43 (1929): 436–72. The MIT Press has graciously allowed me to post this article at http://www.efficientfrontier.com/files/hamilton-spain.pdf. I also thank JSTOR for facilitating the availability of this material.

The massive infusion of wealth strengthened and emboldened the Spanish Crown. It also proved profoundly corrosive to Spanish society. The bounty crippled Spain economically for centuries, for three reasons.[*]

+ The flood of New World treasure came on the heels of the elevation of King Carlos I to Charles V, Holy Roman Emperor. His exalted status fed his ambitions, and the new wealth, unfortunately, supplied him the means to carry them out. During almost all of Charles's reign and that of his son, Philip II, Spain warred with France, England, and Holland. At times it fought all three simultaneously. Spain saw herself as the bulwark of the Counter-Reformation and defender of the true faith. Religious fervor imbued her struggles against Holland and England and against many of the smaller German states with a sense of divine purpose. This sense of moral mission was a fiscal disaster. The new style of warfare cost more than anyone had imagined. Spain rapidly outspent her revenues and began running huge and constant deficits. The 1552 campaign at Metz alone cost ten times the annual silver levies, and the doomed armada sent against England in 1588 cost five times Spain's total annual revenues. When Charles V abdicated in 1555, he left a deficit that amounted to nearly one hundred times annual silver revenues. The Crown defaulted with astonishing frequency—in 1557, 1575, 1576, 1607, 1627, and 1647—all the while awash in a torrential flow of gold and silver.

+ The New World bonanza focused the energies and ambitions of the nation on conquest and treasure. When the silver ran out, its loss left Spanish society devoid of industrial and commercial instincts. In the words of one nineteenth-century historian:

> The rich enjoyed in ease the wealth which they had inherited, or derived from the Indes. The poor nobles turned to the church, or followed the profession of arms, or sought unimportant offices . . . resigning themselves . . . to suffer hunger, naked-

---

[*]   The enormous flow of New World silver also produced a great inflation, as a swollen money supply chased a fixed amount of goods. This in no way detracted from the fact that Spain, the source of that money supply, prospered greatly from this state of affairs relative to her neighbors.

ness, and misery rather than humiliate themselves by living by the work of their hands.[31]

The parallel between sixteenth-century Spain and present-day Saudi Arabia, both nations whose stupendous natural wealth discouraged hard work at home and financed religious adventurism abroad, requires little comment.

♦ By 1550 Spain already lagged far behind the Protestant northern Europe in the development of property rights, scientific rationalism, capital markets, and transport and communication—the four factors required for prosperity. The Spanish Crown's newfound mineral wealth and power led to the ossification of all four of these factors.

THE FOUR FACTORS IN SPAIN

We've now set the scene for the economic calamity that was Habsburg Spain—a society cursed with plunder-derived wealth that strengthened and further entrenched its rent seekers. At the same time, Spain had snuffed out any commercial instincts that remained in the country. The dependence on New World mineral wealth and its exploitation for military adventurism affected the development of the four traditional growth factors. We shall consider each of them in turn.

1. Property rights. Spain's feudal history and the initial flow of easy New World treasure blinded it to the importance of effective economic incentives. Even the Tudors and Stuarts in England dimly appreciated that their economic interests were aligned with those of their subjects; the Habsburgs were oblivious to the importance of their subjects' well-being. Why bother with commerce, industry, and the well-being of the populace when silver from the Americas, plunder, and tribute from the Low Countries furnished an endless flow of wealth?[32]

In addition, after 1200, the Spanish Crown developed a most unusual source of revenue. During that period, the sheep industry had come under the domination of the nation's largest landowners—two dozen or so families known as *grandees*.[33] In the thirteenth century, the Crown granted this consortium of grandee sheep ranchers (later known as the *Mesta*), a grazing monopoly in exchange for tax revenues. As the American gold and silver mines played out in the seventeenth century and the Low Countries slipped from Spain's grasp, the sheep monopoly became the Crown's primary source of revenue.

After the expulsion of the Moors and Moriscos, huge swaths of southern Spain fell fallow. This attracted the attention of the *Mesta*, who saw great potential for winter pasturage in the south's milder climate. The Crown granted grazing privileges to the *Mesta* not only on the old Moorish property but also along migratory routes and on land that had not previously been cultivated. In order to protect these grazing rights, local farmers were forbidden to enclose their commons. The migratory sheep deforested the countryside, devastated agriculture, and devalued land. The *Mesta*'s herders burned trees to improve pasturage, which led to extensive soil erosion. Migrating animals even grazed on town commons.[34] In short, "the privileges of the *Mesta* suggest the hunting privileges of a medieval aristocracy. They discouraged agriculture, and those who opposed them found it easy to argue that they doomed to barrenness some of the finest districts of Spain."[35]

In the premodern period, the sale of monopolies supplied an all-too-easy source of revenue—an addictive quick fix that satisfied current needs but stunted long-term economic growth. In effect, the *Mesta* stole from Spaniards the agricultural advantages of enclosure that had invigorated the English and French countryside.

Nor was the *Mesta* the only malfunctioning quarter of Spanish property institutions. As in the New World, much of Spain proper was acquired as the result of conquest, particularly from the Moors. The court rewarded huge tracts of land to distinguished military figures and royal favorites. By custom and by law, this land was "entailed"; that is, it was passed down through primogeniture (to the eldest son) and could not be sold. This system encouraged indolence, kept huge estates intact for centuries, and forbade the sale of land to those who might improve it (not unlike, for example, what occurs in present-day Zimbabwe or Indonesia). A malicious ruler hell-bent on sowing the seeds of economic destruction could not have contrived a better way of doing so.

The never-ending wars of the seventeenth century, combined with the loss of New World silver and the independence of the Low Countries, launched Spain into a downward fiscal spiral. Philip II clawed for revenue wherever he could. He sold titles and indulgences (a favorite being certificates of legitimacy for the sons of the clergy) and imposed forced loans in the form of *juros* (government bonds). Next, he suspended payments on the *juros,* and soon enough, he began to steal outright, seizing gold and silver from private individuals. As the Spanish population declined in size and a larger and larger portion of it found shelter from taxes by joining the clergy and buying into the nobility, an ever-increasing tax burden fell upon an ever-smaller cadre of farmers and merchants. This sequence of events was nearly identical to that which occurred during the decline of the Roman Empire.[36] The loss of confidence caused by these dislocations precipitated the collapse of trade—even with Spanish America—by 1640.[37]

By the seventeenth century, all private economic incentive had evaporated. In the words of historian John Elliott, "The nature of the economic system was such that one became a student or a monk, a beggar or a bureaucrat. There was nothing else to be."[38]

2. Scientific rationalism. The Habsburgs throttled intellectual life in the same way that they crippled the nation's finances. In the early sixteenth century the enlightened inquiry of Erasmus flourished in Spain. But the transformation of the Spanish Empire into the arsenal of Counter-Reformation terror under Philip II reversed Spain's scholarly traditions. The Inquisition arrested academics, forbade students to travel abroad, and effectively quarantined the nation from the infectious heresies sweeping across Europe north of the Pyrenees.[39]

The Inquisition was not a Spanish invention. It evolved slowly from existing Church structures after A.D. 1000. In time, it enforced theological discipline over all of Europe. As late as 1696, an unfortunate medical student at Edinburgh named Aikenhead was hung by the Inquisition for heresy.

The institution came into full flower in Spain after the marriage of Ferdinand and Isabella, who established a *national* Inquisition, independent of papal supervision and restraint. The Spanish Inquisition became a powerful self-sustaining and self-funding bureaucracy—a state within a state. It competed with the Church itself for lucrative dispensations and at times even attacked high-ranking clergy. Although the Inquisition's primary victims were heretics—Jews, Moslems, and, later, Protestants—it also took aim at more secular targets, including Enlightenment

philosophers and scientists who were unfortunate enough to find themselves within Spain's borders.

By such means, the empire successfully protected its inhabitants from
participating in and enjoying the fruits of the seventeenth-century triumph
of scientific rationalism. Two hundred years would pass before Spaniards
would rejoin the front ranks of world science in significant numbers. Perhaps the most damaging consequence of Spain's intellectual backwardness
was its tolerance of a succession of increasingly inept monarchs. This brutal appraisal of the Habsburg bloodline was oft-quoted in eighteenth-century Europe: "Charles V was a warrior and king, Philip II only a king,
Philip III and Philip IV not even kings, and Charles II not even a man."[40]

3. Capital markets. The harm done to Spain's financial markets
by Habsburg adventurism and extravagance may have been more damaging than all its wars. The huge quantities of gold and silver that
passed through the House of Trade remained only very briefly on
Spanish soil before leaving the country again. The first way station for
much of the New World silver was France, whose laborers, drawn by
Spain's wealth and high wages, climbed south across the Pyrenees. An
old adage said that "it was to enrich the French that the Spaniards
worked the mines of El Dorado."[41]

Paradoxically, by the mid-sixteenth century, gold and silver coins
had all but disappeared from Spain. In their place, the Crown minted a
flood of poor quality copper coinage that the populace, tradesmen, and
even royalty viewed with suspicion. In an environment of huge government deficits, constant defaults, and debased coinage, interest rates
soared. As early as 1617 the Spanish Council of Finance complained
that with the nation awash in *juros* yielding as much as 10%, private enterprises could not offer returns high enough to attract capital.[42] In
modern parlance, the huge government debt had "crowded out" the
private sector. By 1673, the Crown was paying interest of 40% per year
on its debt, compared with loans that were floated at rates as low as 3%
the same year in Amsterdam. Two economic historians, perhaps with
the example of Spain in mind, have dryly commented, "The trends and
levels of interest rates were very different (among the nations of Europe), and often foreshadowed much of the future economic and political power of each country."[43]

4. Transport and communications. If an abundance of mineral riches is a curse, nature can bestow one gift of incontrovertible value upon a nation, and that is a relatively flat, island landscape that is laced with navigable rivers. France may have suffered geographic disadvantage versus England in this regard, but Spain was even worse off: Cursed with a vast hinterland that was mountainous and arid, she had almost no usable waterways.

Only occasionally did Spain address its geographic limitations. Philip II's transfer of the empire's capital to Madrid required that the Tagus River be made navigable all the way from Lisbon. (Portugal at that time was part of the empire.) By 1580, engineers had dredged the first stretch, two hundred miles upriver to Alcantara. By 1588, they extended the project another two hundred miles to Toledo, just south of Madrid. Unfortunately, in that year, Spain lost the armada off England, and Spain's priorities shifted. By the time of Philip III, the section of the river between Alcantara and Toledo had silted up.[44] Another vital transportation project, a proposed canal between the Tagus and the Monzanares, was submitted to a committee of clerics. In a stunning demonstration of the sixteenth-century Habsburg inability to overcome medieval logic, the clergymen invoked divinity in vetoing the canal. "If God had intended for the rivers to be connected," they reasoned, "He would have made them so."[45]

Spain's preference for the mule and the narrow path spread to the New World and persisted for many centuries. No less a court luminary than Count Olivares, Philip IV's great prime minister and alter ego, lamented that the foreigner must surely think his country barbaric "when he sees us having to provision all the cities of Castile by pack animal—and rightly so, for all Europe is trying out internal navigation with great profit."[46]

A NATION DESPOILED

Habsburg Spain's history is a chronicle of waste. At its height, Spain proper produced only one-tenth of the empire's income. Its economic system poisoned everything it touched. While Dutch northern Burgundy prospered, Spanish southern Burgundy withered.[47] The Habsburgs wrote the script for the destruction of great national wealth and power: Pursue conquest and treasure over agriculture, industry, and trade. Next, finance that pursuit to the hilt, tax unmercifully, fix prices, and default often. Finally, close borders and minds to outside influences and neglect the transport and communications infrastructure.

Spain burdened itself with ruinous economic institutions and passed these on to its colonies in the Americas. Latin America was consigned to be the poor relation of the New World, just as Spain had been in the Old.

More than that, sixteenth-century Spain's great wealth and power encouraged mercantilism, the curse of the later European economy. Spain's neighbors reasoned that if the accumulation of gold and silver was good for Spain, it must be good for them as well. Since Spain's competitors could not secure specie as easily as Spain could via plunder, they would have to do so through trade.[48]

THE LONG ROAD BACK

The reform of Spanish institutions was a long, painful process. The replacement of the Habsburgs with the Bourbons in the wake of the War of the Spanish Succession (1701–14) cleared away only a portion of the deadwood. In 1766, Charles III decreed that all municipal lands be appraised and distributed to "the neediest inhabitants," but powerful landowners and herders thwarted him at every turn.[49]

Spain did not attempt serious property reform for another century, during the early post-Napoleonic period. The *Cortes* (parliament) repeatedly passed complex and far-reaching land reform acts disentailing both church and private lands, only to be reversed each time by a newly resurgent Crown. A typical early example was the abolition of the vestiges of feudalism by the *Cortes* in 1811. Three years later Ferdinand VII annulled the move. Soon after, the king took just six months to nullify an enclosure decree that was strongly supported by Spanish economists. During the early nineteenth century, the Crown even brought back the Inquisition, which had been abolished by Napoleon.

This seesaw battle between *Cortes* and Crown raged throughout most of the nineteenth century. Only very slowly did Spain divest the Church of its huge holdings and privatize common land, and it took the rise of Franco for the nation to begin freeing itself from the economic shackles that had kept it Europe's poor cousin for five hundred years.

But the scars of the Habsburg regime remained. As late as 1930, 4% of Spain's landowners owned two-thirds of the country's agricultural land, and the wealthiest 0.1% held one-third of the land.[50] Not until the twentieth century did Spain finally modernize its property institutions and join the ranks of the liberal democracies.

As early as the seventeenth century, Spaniards were acutely aware of their institutional shortcomings. A school of economic critics, the *arbitristas,* clearly saw the problems and even accurately prescribed solutions: tax reform, the defanging of the Church, restoration of the power of the *Cortes,* tax relief for laborers, and navigation and irrigation projects.[51] Unfortunately, the names of these critics—González de Cellerigo, Sancho de Moncada, Fernández Navarrete—are far less recognizable today than Spain's most famous fictional character of the same period: Don Quixote de la Mancha.

FORCE MAJEURE—THE IMPORTATION OF PROSPERITY INTO JAPAN

If ever a nation entered the modern era totally lacking the institutions necessary for economic development, it was Japan. The vast majority of its citizens were utterly bereft of the most basic individual liberties and property rights. The Japanese peasant existed solely to support a vast, idle, parasitic warrior class. Between the seventeenth and nineteenth centuries, Japan sealed itself off from the outside world and replicated the worst aspects of European high feudalism.

The Land of the Rising Sun is not rich in farmland. Three-quarters of its land surface is mountainous; only 16% of it is arable. Every last square foot was needed to support a population that on the eve of industrialization had grown to ninety million.[52]

THE AGRICULTURAL DEATH SPIRAL IN FEUDAL JAPAN

Japan is a relatively new nation. Evidence of the first hunter-gatherer societies does not appear there until the fifth millennium B.C. These first inhabitants, known as the *Jomon*, evolved into Japan's modern aboriginal population, the Ainu. Just before the birth of Christ, Korean farmers arrived on the southern island of Kyushu. Over the next several centuries, they worked their way southward on that island, then up the Inland Sea and northeast across the main island of Honshu. These agriculturalists reached the far northern island of Hokkaido in the first century A.D., intermarrying with the native *Jomon* along the way. Japan laid the foundations of an oppressive feudal society with the Taiko "reforms" of A.D. 645–50, which declared that all land was government property and provided stipends to nobles and warriors. A thousand years later, this almost total lack of private peasant-owned land would spell the doom of Japan's ruling classes.[53]

The ruling warrior class levied taxes on peasants in the form of obligations of grain, cloth, and labor. These obligations were *fixed*—the same amount of rice was due from each farmer, whether there was bounty or famine.[54] This system, which during lean years imposed an impossible burden upon the peasant farmer, lasted well into the modern era and produced great social instability. (Some flexibility was built into the system, but not nearly enough. In the event of a total crop failure, levies might or might not be temporarily reduced.)

This system of fixed levies was pernicious in the extreme. Imagine an income-tax system in which a worker is obligated to pay $10,000 per year, *whether he is working or not*. Slowly but surely, most will fall into debt and ruin. Sooner or later, the nation's economy will collapse.

After the early Taiko reforms, the government granted some private land to nobles, to temples, and to those who reclaimed new arable soil. Often, these plots were exempt from taxation, which only increased the burden of those tilling the "public land." This began the all-too-familiar spiral of onerous taxation of peasants, decreased output, and depopulation. There was little centralized authority, and the ability to tax emanated from the point of the sword. By the mid-fourteenth century, anarchy was the norm.[55]

Gradually, Japanese society, under its oppressive samurai warrior-rulers, evolved into three distinct social classes—the imperial family, the samurai themselves, and the commoners. The last were further divided into three groups, according to status: farmers, who were held in the highest esteem, followed by artisans, and, on the lowest rung, traders and businessmen. The high status of farmers was purely theoretical. Brutally taxed and subject to arbitrary physical abuse and execution by the daimyo (the local samurai feudal lord) and lesser samurai, their existence could only be described as miserable. The Tokugawas, according to one historian, "thought highly of agriculture but not of agriculturalists."[56]

A NATION OF PARASITES

On the eve of Japan's late-nineteenth-century industrialization, about 85% of the population worked the land, and at least 6% were nonproductive samurai. The remainder belonged to the artisan and trading classes.[57] The huge number of samurai—the equivalent of the United States supporting a domestic military establishment of 15 million men—proved to be the undoing of feudal Japan. For most of Japan's history, the samurai held the reins of power, and the imperial family and its retainers were mere figureheads imprisoned in the imperial court at Kyoto. The samurai consisted not only of the top rungs of the Tokugawa shogunate (*shogun* roughly translates as "generalissimo") and the lesser daimyo but also of the vast number of warriors whose services were no longer needed in a Japan that had no significant internal or external enemies. The ruling daimyo grew increasingly wary of the large numbers of their unemployed brethren and slowly gathered them up into castle towns, where they could be more easily observed and controlled. The status and wealth of the average samurai slowly deteriorated. By the end of the Tokugawa period, it was not unusual for a down-on-his-luck warrior to sell his treasured swords and titles to a commoner. Much worse, a samurai might even engage in trade.

The condition of commoners could only be described as desperate. The daimyo forbade peasants to move or to sell possessions and viewed them purely as a source of revenue, extracting as much as half of their meager crop yields.[58] The status of Japanese serfs was even more wretched than that of their European counterparts, who at least enjoyed the nominal protection of the Germano-Roman feudal code. The Confucian system, which governed day-to-day activity in Japan, provided little in the way of ground rules or credible sanctions for miscreant lords.

FROM CHAOS TO ISOLATION

As in other non-Western societies, the introduction of firearms served to unify Japan. Those who first obtained the powerful new weapons procured a "first mover advantage." Three remarkable successive daimyo—Oda Nobunaga; his greatest general, Hideyoshi; and Hideyoshi's deputy, Tokugawa Ieyasu—used firearms to establish political stability and national unity. Nobunaga first stitched together a complex skein of fiefdoms, but was assassinated in 1582. Hideyoshi completed the task and then attempted to conquer Korea as well. This proved disastrous. His death in 1598 provided a rationale for abandoning this ill-advised adventure, and his successor, Tokugawa Ieyasu, created the shogunate that came to bear his name. The samurai, incensed that a peasant wielding a gun could effortlessly dispatch a skilled swordsman, had the new weapons outlawed. Japan's history of unending political and military chaos haunted Ieyasu, and he became obsessed with establishing stability. He succeeded beyond his wildest dreams. Edwin Reischauer, historian and onetime U.S. ambassador to Japan, characterized Ieyasu's shogunate, which lasted 250 years, as "a state of absolute peace, internal and external, that has never been matched over a comparable period of time by any other nation."[59]

The Tokugawa ended centuries of political chaos, and the return of political stability was in itself enough to produce a modicum of growth. Between 1600 and 1820, Japan's per capita GDP grew by 0.14% per year—nowhere near even the tepid rate of Dutch growth, but impressive for an isolated feudal state.[60] But that prosperity came at a terrible cost—the sealing off of Japan from the rest of the world and the freezing in place of the rigid feudal structure.

After 1641, the shogunate limited contact with the outside world to two tiny trading posts—one each for the Chinese and Dutch—that were situated near Nagasaki.[61]

The outward manifestations of the Tokugawa structure remain to this day—the new shogun moved the capital from Kyoto to Edo (Tokyo), where his fortress castle layout forms the heart of the modern imperial grounds—and modern Japanese society still bears much of the Tokugawa stamp.

THE COUNTRYSIDE SAVES JAPAN

The Tokugawa did make economic progress, but this was in spite of, and not because of, the extraordinary degree of peace and order it provided. They removed the samurai to crowded castle towns; in reaction, much of the nation's businessmen fled these rigidly controlled fiefdoms for rural districts, where the heavy hands of taxation and guild regulations did not stifle commerce.

Besides a relative absence of strict feudal rule, the countryside had other advantages. These included an abundance of waterpower and an agile cadre of farmers used to the money economy and able to alternate between agriculture and factory work. Both advantages of the country-side—a versatile labor force and waterpower—are key requisites for industrialization. By the time the Meiji Restoration overthrew the shogunate in 1868 and brought Japan's Industrial Revolution, the countryside provided a well-trained rural workforce ready to man the new European-style factory machines. In 1880, just eight years after the British built the first railway line between Yokohama and Tokyo, a native force of laborers trained in this "rural industrial school" built a far more demanding link in the hilly country between Kyoto and Otsu.[62]

Thus, economic activity in Japan tended to flow to wherever the samurai were absent. The essential paradox of Tokugawa rule was that its chief victims were the samurai themselves. Forced to reside in the impoverished castle towns, they provided the easiest target for revenue-starved daimyo, who gradually ratcheted down samurai pensions, which amounted to about half of government expenditure. When time ran out for the shogunate in 1868, disaffected samurai occupied the front ranks of the Meiji vanguard.

Simultaneous with the Spanish economic self-immolation half a world away, the Tokugawa methodically throttled all four factors that might have led to economic prosperity in Japan. Their rigid social structure deprived almost the entire populace of any semblance of property rights and inhibited the development of efficient capital markets. Just as royalty was doing in France and Spain, the shogun and daimyo employed the sale of trade, industrial, and guild monopolies as a major source of tax revenues. More often than not, this revenue was not part of any codified structure. Most payments were made in the form of "contributions" and "thank-money," which created a corrupt governmental culture that survives to this day.[63]

The shogun owned fully one-third of Japan's arable land, with the remainder being divided among more than two hundred daimyo. The shogun and daimyo occasionally granted small parcels of land to individual farmers, but these farmers were not permitted to sell their plots. (Nor could commoners, upon pain of death, use silk, consume tea, or even let their gaze fall upon certain daimyo.) Peasants could, however, borrow against their land. Perversely, even if a peasant's land could not be sold, it could still be foreclosed. The foreclosure problem spun out of control during the twentieth century and precipitated General Douglas MacArthur's land reforms after World War II.[64]

The elimination of foreign contact prevented the acquisition of Western scientific enlightenment; this self-imposed trade embargo negated the natural advantage of an island topography that in some ways was as favorable as England's. Japan was leagues behind the west. By the mid-nineteenth century, her per capita GDP was one-quarter of England's and one-half of Spain's, and the country had a hopelessly outmoded military.

BLACK SHIPS

The iconic image of Japan's modern transformation depicts the arrival of Commodore Matthew Perry's black ships in Tokyo Bay in July 1853. Like all emblematic historical stories, it is an oversimplification. Substantial reform did not arrive with Perry. Rather, it began decades before Perry's shocking first appearance and continued for more than fifty years.

Western power had alarmed the Tokugawa as early as the 1839–42 Opium War in China. Even earlier in the nineteenth century, many Jap-

anese aristocrats acquired Western learning—the Dutch had educated
thousands in an influential school that opened in 1838. It was Perry's
second appearance in Tokyo Bay in 1854, not his first the year before,
that opened up trade with the U.S.

After Perry's expeditions, other nations demonstrated Western naval
superiority in far more lethal and spectacular fashion than did the Americans. The devastating British naval bombardment of rebellious southern
daimyo at Kagoshima in 1863 and by a multinational force and at
Shimonoseki in 1864 made much more of an impression than Perry's
visits. Last, and not least, the final collapse of the shogunate did not occur for more than two decades after the black ships appeared.[65]

During its last years, the shogunate in fact initiated many innovations
that were completed by the succeeding Meiji Government. The last
Tokugawa shoguns sent diplomats and students to study in the West,
borrowed capital from France and the U.S. to finance dockyards and industrial projects, and offered high official posts for the first time to talented commoners.[66]

Too little, too late. When a nation first opens itself to trade, it experi-
ences "price convergence"—a euphemism for a highly destabilizing
state of affairs that produces big winners and losers. The prices of a
nation's commodities, and with them, the prices of the three classical
inputs—labor, land, and capital—converge with those in the rest of
the world.*

Since the prices of Japan's major export products—rice, tea, and
silk—were far below world levels, these commodities rose in price, and
many landowners and merchants became rich, while consumers of these
commodities, particularly the samurai living in the castle towns, suffered.
At the same time, the availability of cheap foreign cotton and industrial
equipment caused a dramatic fall in their prices, severely harming Japan's

---

* The Heckscher-Ohlin model, again (see footnote, page 178). Price convergence is often used
as a tool to evaluate world trade patterns. For example, the fact that the prices of commodities did
not dramatically change during the Age of Discovery (the century after 1492) indicates that little
substantive trade took place during that era. See Kevin O'Rourke and Jeffrey G. Williamson, "Late
Nineteenth-Century Anglo-American Factor-Price Convergence: Were Heckscher and Ohlin
Right?" See also, by the same authors, "The Heckscher-Ohlin Model Between 1400 and 2000:
When It Explained Factor Price Convergence, When It Did Not, and Why," NBER Working
Paper 7411, 1999, available at http://www.j-bradford-delong.net/pdf_files/W7411.pdf.

domestic producers of these goods. Peasants and samurai alike blamed the shogun, who was caught between the powerful domestic interests that were damaged by the new international trade and the foreign cannon. In 1868, a group of disaffected and highly capable southern samurai overthrew the Tokugawa regime. At nearly the same time, the reigning emperor died and was replaced by a young successor.

Reform tore through feudal Japan like a razor through silk and introduced the four factors into that nation in thoroughgoing fashion. Within a few years, the new regime had destroyed the institutional basis of the feudal state. Feudalism's death conferred solid, if rudimentary, individual and property rights. For the first time, the law broke up the guilds, abolished legal distinctions between classes, and allowed peasants to move, to sell or partition their land, and to plant whatever crops they desired.

The Japanese enthusiastically embraced Western culture and, with it, scientific rationalism. The new government sent its best and brightest abroad to Germany, England, France, and the U.S. to plumb the mysteries of engineering, military science, government, and finance. It also laid the foundation of its sharply pyramidal and intensely meritocratic modern public educational system. No longer would command of government and industry be left to the lazy and incapable sons of the samurai and daimyo.[67]

Finally, Japan established the foundations of a modern service state, giving the capital markets and transport and communication a much-needed boost, and introduced uniform coinage and paper money, as well as railway, telegraph, and postal services. As a symbol of Japan's radically new outlook, the new government changed the name of the ancient capital from Edo to Tokyo and moved the imperial court onto the grounds of its old Tokugawa fortress.

THE DEATH RATTLE OF THE SAMURAI

The Meiji then skillfully handled the most dangerous task faced by any revolutionary regime—dealing with the remains of the old aristocracy. Initially, the Meiji paid the daimyo one-tenth of their former tributes and taxes as salary. A few years later, they cut off payments entirely. The Meiji converted the samurai stipends into bonds with below-market interest rates, which drastically reduced the traditional income for the samurai.

In 1877, a coalition of recalcitrant southern samurai instigated and led the shogunate's last stand—the Satsuma rebellion. The insurrection was easily crushed by an army of conscripts. The humiliation of the samurai at the hands of rag-tag peasants demonstrated the utter impotency of a warrior class that had long been out of touch with its military roots.[68]

Even foreign domination of trade proved a blessing. Deprived by the Europeans of the ability to erect tariff barriers, the rigors of foreign competition toughened Japanese companies.[69] Forces from within also served to decrease state control over industry. The shogunate's experimentation with Western-style industrialism left the new nation with a large number of inefficient government-owned factories and mines. After the Restoration, the Meiji rapidly privatized these facilities, which wound up in the hands of a relatively few owners, the *zaibatsu*. The power of these oligopolies would not be broken until after World War II. The one ominous exception to privatization was the production of munitions, which remained under tight government control.[70] The application of the Western "crowbar" combined with domestic privatization provided a powerful "anti-Colbertian" stimulus to Japanese trade and growth.

Because Japan was so backward, even the simplest technological advances produced sizable gains. Before the Meiji Restoration almost all plows were pulled by humans, resulting in meager crop yields. By 1904 more than half of all cropland was broken by the ox-drawn plow. Such is the oft-times mundane nature of economic growth. Between 1870 and 1940, real per capita GDP grew at 1.9% per year. While robust, the economic growth seen during the post-Meiji period pales in comparison to the growth that took place after World War II.

JAPAN ACQUIRES A BAD HABIT

Japan learned the lessons of the black ships a bit too well. During the Meiji period, she made the same geopolitical mistake that Spain had made and sought prosperity through military conquest. Japan first embarked on wars against China in 1894 and Russia in 1904 that not only were successful but also were cheap and economically invigorating. Real per capita GDP growth in Japan rose to 2.16% per year between 1890 and 1910, the two war decades.

These victories whetted the Japanese appetite. In 1931, Japan invaded China and raised tensions with the West. Military spending increased from 31% of the national budget in 1931–32 to 47% in 1936–37 and required a massive increase in government debt, as had occurred in Habsburg Spain. When Korekiyo Takahashi, the capable finance minister, objected to the high level of military expenditures, the army assassinated him.[71] Japan's military and economic courses were set, and their final ends were not happy.

THE MACARTHUR "MIRACLE"

Between 1940 and 1998, which includes the disastrous Second World War, real per capita GDP increased at a phenomenal annual rate of 3.51%. What lit the fire under Japanese growth in the second half of the twentieth century? Two things. First, the post World-War II years were a "golden period" for world economic growth in general. Humanity had emerged from two disastrous world wars in little more than a generation; sandwiched between them was the greatest economic depression in history. Even tired old England saw its real per capita GDP grow at 1.83% during the postwar period. Second, the American Cold War strategic umbrella allowed the Japanese to nearly eliminate the military spending that had previously brought on ruin.

Many credit Japan's postwar "miracle" to the democratic and economic reforms wrought by the Allied military occupation led by General Douglas MacArthur. The great warrior did indeed force three major areas of institutional change upon the defeated nation: He broke up the *zaibatsu*, resuscitated the prewar democracy, and forced through extensive land reform.

Laudable as these three actions were, none proved of major economic importance. The *zaibatsu* did not greatly stifle competition. Modern econometric research has established that once a government affords rule of law and rudimentary individual liberties, further advancement of democracy does little for economic progress and may even harm growth.

Prosperity stimulates democracy, not the other way around.* Had Mac-
Arthur not extended the franchise to women, decentralized the police
apparatus, enacted humane labor laws, and pushed through a myriad of
other worthwhile political reforms when he did, these changes would
have occurred on their own later as prosperity created a more demanding electorate. Although some historians have termed the origins of
modern Japanese power and prosperity "binational"—a combination of
homegrown and imported American institutions[72]—in point of fact,
many of the reforms forced upon Japan by the Allied occupation had
been underway for more than seven decades.

LAND, LANDLORDS, AND PEASANTS

This was especially true of land reform. The Meiji introduced rudimentary liberties, property rights, and clear titling of land, resulting in the redistribution of land from large aristocratic holdings to small private
owners by way of the "Coase mechanism" (see Chapter 2). This glacially
slow but stable process allowed hardworking small farmers to gradually
buy up property from the enervated heirs of wealth and privilege, as had
happened earlier in premodern England.

The processes of land redistribution in England and Japan, however,
differed radically. The clear title and free alienation available under the
Meiji notwithstanding, fixed rice levies in Japan dictated that in lean years
rich creditors gradually siphoned land away from capital-poor nobles and
small landowning peasants. The Restoration reforms saw the fixed rice tax
converted to a fixed money tax of 3% to 4% of the land's assessed value.
This oppressed small farmers even more than did the old system, which
had at least allowed a modicum of flexibility when crops failed.

Before the twentieth century, there were no industrial jobs to employ
defaulted farmers, who were thus forced to remain on the land as tenants.
Between 1871 and 1908, the amount of this tenanted land increased from

---

* This topic will be covered in some detail in Chapter 10. For those wishing a more thorough
treatment, see Robert J Barro, *Determinants of Economic Growth*, 2d ed. (Cambridge: MIT Press,
1999).

30% to 45% of the total and remained at that level until the end of the Second World War. By the time General MacArthur arrived, rural Japan was divided into two bitterly opposed camps: a great mass of tenant farmers and a tiny elite of wealthy absentee landlords.

Meanwhile, seventy-five years of Meiji structural reform had dramatically changed the social face of Japan. Universal conscription and education did not spare the sons of landlords, and a wealthy land heir often found himself serving in a military unit under the command of a better-educated tenant farmer. The newly literate and influential tenants became increasingly dissatisfied with their situation. During the interwar years, land reform was a hot-button political issue; during the 1930s, the support of the military-dominated government enabled landlords to maintain the upper hand.[73]

From a strictly economic viewpoint, the landlord-tenant ownership system is highly efficient. The landlord's incentive to improve agricultural output is identical to that of the small owner-farmer; in addition, the landlord possesses superior capital resources with which to improve the land. Under the landlord-dominated system, Japan's agricultural productivity rapidly accelerated after the Restoration.

From a social perspective, however, Japan's tenant-landlord conflict was a disaster. The poor only got poorer, and the rich only got richer. MacArthur believed that the landlord class formed a bedrock of fascism and militarism, and his occupation forces set about destroying it. The occupation compensated large landholders, but at prewar prices. Because of rampant postwar inflation, these payments, made in devalued yen, amounted to confiscation. (In a nation where the average farm size was 2.5 acres, anyone owning more than ten acres was considered a land baron.)[74,75] While sharecroppers and tenant farmers may elicit more of our sympathy than wealthy landlords do, it is also true that MacArthur's land reform did real violence to the property system. As Reischauer piquantly observed, "Revolutionary reforms are easier and more fun to make in someone else's country."[76] Whatever the net social and political effects of the land reform in Japan were, they ultimately became economically irrelevant. In an increasingly industrialized nation, the structure of land ownership loses importance.

MacArthur's final lesson to the Japanese turned out to be an unwitting demonstration of the awesome power of the rule of law in a liberal democracy. On April 11, 1951, President Harry Truman fired him. The

Japanese were astonished to see that a tart letter from an unimposing civilian leader could topple so powerful and revered a warrior.

Of greater moment is the fact that the American military umbrella allowed Japan to spend just 1% of its GDP on defense. That the Japanese economy grew at all during the first four decades of the twentieth century in the face of crushing military demands on both capital and manpower was the real "Japanese miracle." Freed from the ball and chain of militarism, Japan's economy could not help but grow vigorously from the ashes of World War II.

To summarize, then, the postwar growth spurt came as the inevitable consequence of several mundane factors.

- The Japanese, along with much of the rest of the world, were destitute after thirty years of war and economic catastrophe. When industry runs far below capacity and capital must be diverted from consumption to restore and modernize plant and equipment, the result will be vigorous economic growth.

- The American military presence freed Japan from the clutches of the demon that most reliably derails great nations—excessive military expenditure.

- Seventy years before MacArthur arrived, the Japanese had established primitive but adequate property institutions and had adopted Western-style science, capital markets, transportation and communication.

Nor did it hurt that Japanese culture emphasized hard work, saving, and literacy and that the nation had more than fifty years of experience with parliamentary democracy before MacArthur "imported" it.

"THE RISING SUN"

During the 1980s, it became fashionable to assume that Japanese economic growth would continue unabated until the country dominated the world. (Just as in the 1960s, when the rest of the developed world nervously eyed the *Wirtschaftswunder*—the German equivalent of Japan's postwar miracle.) This, too, was never a serious likelihood. First, once property rights and rule of law are in place, a depressed economy will of its own accord grow like Topsy; the trick is much more difficult for one that is running at full tilt. Second, these institutional blessings are a one-time thing—once property rights and rule of law have been established, growth must be found in other areas. Finally, the U.S. is rapidly growing tired of subsidizing the defense of a wealthy Japan. Soon enough, Japan will regain the desire to provide adequately for its own military needs. Pray that she does not once again do so too well.

CHAPTER NINE

The Last

THE TIME HAS COME to consider those nations that were left behind. The first two chapters in this section proceeded in more or less linear fashion, with traditional generation-by-generation accounts of economic development in Holland, England, France, Spain, and Japan. Since the losing entries in the world economic sweepstakes are actually events that failed to occur—the greyhounds that refused to run, if you will—their stories cannot be told as a traditional historical narrative.

The history of economic failure is about the resistance of traditional cultures to change. As such, it is not as easily examined in the fashion of a nation-by-nation analysis. Rather, to understand why some nations failed to become prosperous, we shall examine two broad, culturally defined regions—the Ottoman Empire and the modern Arab world it gave rise to, and Latin America.

In the first half of this chapter we'll discuss how the four growth factors—property rights, scientific rationalism, capital markets, and modern communications and transport—fared in the Ottoman Empire, whose disintegration gave rise to the boiling cauldron of poverty and resentment of the modern Middle East and the Balkan peninsula. In the second half of the chapter, we'll examine certain aspects of the capital markets and property rights in Latin America, and particularly how its Spanish colonial legacy, discussed in Chapter 8, continues to cripple Latin America's economic growth.

Until very recently, ideological fashion dictated that disparities in the distribution of the world's wealth resulted from differences in natural wealth and their exploitation by the twin Marxist bogeymen—colonialism and imperialism. At chapter's end, we'll dissect this theory with both statistical evidence and powerful anecdotal examples.

We cannot cover all of the world's failed nations, particularly in Africa and Asia, for there are far too many. The interested reader can easily apply the four-factor dynamics of the Middle East and Latin America to the rest of the underdeveloped world.

WHY DID ISLAM FALL BEHIND?

We'll now apply our four-factor paradigm to one of the primary geopolitical divides in today's world: that between the secular West and the more traditional and devout Muslim societies. We'll explore the roots of Arab despair in the sorry history of the four factors in the Ottoman Empire. In the next chapter, we will follow this analysis with a data-intensive sociological approach that suggests that the growing gap in economic status between the Muslim and Western worlds has little to do with religious doctrine, and everything to do with local culture.

From the perspective of the early twenty-first century, it is all too easy to label Islam as "backward," unable to provide its adherents with even the most basic tools necessary to achieve the level of individual freedom and prosperity that is taken for granted in the West. But turn back the clock five hundred years, or even a thousand years, and the mirror image of today's imbalance is seen—a vibrant, powerful Muslim culture that was seemingly poised on the brink of overrunning a jumble of impoverished, backward Christian nations.

After the first flush of Muslim conquest in the seventh century, Islam rapidly broke up into a number of warring caliphates, and an all-encompassing, coherent Islamic state did not return until the conquest of Constantinople by the Ottoman Turks in 1453. At the height of the Ottoman Empire, only China rivaled it in size, power, cultural accomplishment, and scientific sophistication.

Consider that even before the Ottoman ascent, Arab astronomy had no equal in the world. By the eleventh century, Ibn al-Hytham, known in Europe as Alhazen, had formulated theories of optics and the heavens that were far beyond anything seen in the European Dark Age.[1] In 1550, the Turks built a lighthouse on the Bosporous that was 120 steps high, larger and more advanced than any in Europe.[2]

Since animal skins for parchment were scarce on the Arabian peninsula, early Muslim scribes borrowed paper technology from China and greatly improved upon it. Islamic scholars translated ancient Greek documents long before the Fall of Constantinople in 1453 brought these texts to the attention of Renaissance Italy.[3] The Arabs imported a numerical system from India that contained a revolutionary concept—the use of zero as a place-keeper—without which almost all of modern mathematics would not exist. Just as the Greeks invented geometry and Europeans invented the calculus, so, too, the Arabs invented *al-jabr,* or, as we know it today, algebra.[4] E. L. Jones best summed up the gap between medieval Christendom and Islam: "Large, well-lighted cities with universities and great libraries in Muslim Spain stood in contrast to the virtual hutments and Spartan monasticism north of the Pyrenees."[5]

Just as the early Arab caliphates, such as that of Jerusalem's reconqueror, Saladin, evoked awe and fear in Christendom, in the sixteenth and seventeenth centuries the Ottoman Empire seemed to be a colossus that was on the verge of devouring the West. Its size and influence were immense. It was as large and rich as the Roman Empire had been at its height and was invested with the same sense of superiority and permanence as its ancient predecessor. The geography of the Ottoman realm has powerfully stamped the modern world. The empire included many of the lands central to current geopolitics: Saudi Arabia and the Gulf States, Jordan, Syria, Palestine/Israel, Egypt, much of Iran, the Balkans, and most of North Africa. All of the hopes, aspirations, anger, and frustration that emanate from this volatile region today are firmly rooted in the history of this great empire, its capital sitting on the southeastern edge of the European continent itself. For a time, pashas ruled in Budapest and Arab corsairs routinely attacked the British Isles. On one occasion in 1627 the Ottomans raided as far northwest as Iceland for that most valuable of commodities—European slaves.[6]

THE LONG OTTOMAN DECLINE

In the seventeenth century, the Turks twice besieged Vienna; the turning point in European fortunes came in September 1683, when the Austrians broke the second Turkish onslaught. Within little more than a decade, Peter the Great had captured a bridgehead on the north shore of the Black Sea, which had previously been a Turkish lake. By 1699 the Treaty of Carlowitz formalized the reduction in the size and status of the Turkish Empire.

The rapidity with which Napoleon conquered Egypt in 1798 stunned the Ottomans. In reality, the young Corsican general's invasion was a bumbling, incompetently planned affair that was executed without proper knowledge of the terrain or climate. Within a few years his forces were easily ejected by another young military man, Admiral Horatio Nelson. The significance of these events, according to historian Bernard Lewis, "was all too clear; not only could a European power come and act at will, but only another European power could get them out."[7] Within a century the Ottoman Empire became "the sick man of Europe," kept alive by the British and French as a counterbalance to the power of Habsburg Austria.

When civilizations and cultures find themselves in eclipse, they use one of two rationales to come to terms with their decline. The first rationale poses the hard but constructive question, What did we do wrong? The second seeks scapegoats and asks, Who did this to us? To their credit, the Ottomans asked the first question, rather than the second.[8] Unfortunately, they arrived at the wrong answer.

By the seventeenth century, the Ottomans realized that their military technology lagged far behind the West's. They attempted to remedy the situation through the wholesale importation of weapons and advisors. For two centuries after the Treaty of Carlowitz, a steady stream of military officers and munitions specialists from Austria, Germany, and France made their way to Istanbul, and the Turks expended a huge amount of treasure on the latest products of the Western armories. The Ottomans adopted Western uniforms and even imported Western military music.

As Ottoman diplomats and commercial legations fanned out through Western Europe to assess the enemy, the enormous output of the newly built factories astonished them. One Turkish ambassador suggested that the empire purchase "five factories for snuff, paper, crystal, cloth, and porcelain . . . then in the course of five years (we shall surpass them), since the basis of all their current trade is in these commodities." A strategy worthy of Professor Rostow: Build factories and they will come. But the flaw in simply building modern factories without developing other Western institutions is a bald one: Without solid legal, intellectual, and financial foundations, the mere construction of Western-style factories assures failure. The few facilities that were built by the Turks soon fell into disrepair and ruin.[9] Without clearly defined property rights and strict limits on the actions of the sultan and the imams, no rational businessman would make the enormous effort necessary to build and maintain a large enterprise, and no rational investor would lend him the capital to do so.

There was yet another, even less productive, way to respond to the question, "What have we done wrong?" To many, the answer was, Return to the old ways. That is, retreat even further into religious conservatism. Beyond the areas of military science and factory production, the Ottomans were profoundly incurious about the West. It speaks volumes about both cultures that the Europeans, led by the English, rapidly established Arabist departments at their great universities, but the Ottomans did not reciprocate with "Western studies" programs at theirs.

This lack of intellectual curiosity partly derives from the Muslim doctrine that views Judaism and Christianity as imperfect way stations on the road to the True Faith: "What was true in Christianity was incorporated into Islam. What was not so incorporated was false."[10] Westerners remained unenlightened infidels, even if they possessed greater wealth and better weapons.

Sometime around the fifteenth century, Muslim scholars froze interpretation of the Koran. This quiet catastrophe—a doctrine known as *taqlid,* the meek acceptance of previous interpretation and the closure of Islam to all future reinterpretation—crippled Islam as a dynamic social and economic force.[11] It was as if the U.S. Supreme Court had stopped all reinterpretation of the Constitution in 1857 after the Dred Scott decision, which declared that blacks could not claim citizenship, nor could Congress prohibit slavery.

The prohibition of free intellectual inquiry inherent in *taqlid* speaks to the second factor necessary for economic prosperity: scientific rationalism. A society that is inherently not curious about the outside world and unwilling to challenge its own assumptions is one that does not innovate. A society that does not innovate cannot advance or prosper.

THE AGRICULTURAL DEATH SPIRAL IN TURKEY

The Ottomans knew that they were failing, just as the Europeans knew that they were succeeding. But neither side really understood why. The inferiority of the Turkish military and economy was merely a symptom of a much broader disease. In Chapter 8, we emphasized the importance to agriculture, commerce, and industry of the character of the state, particularly its method of tax collection. Enlightened rulers provide their citizens with critical services such as police protection, public health precautions, roads, education, and an independent judiciary. States that do so prosper; states that do not fall behind.

States whose revenue depends upon conquest and plunder inevitably fail. When the booty runs out, the same sequence of events that we encountered in Hellenistic Greece, Rome, and pre-Tokugawa Japan ensues. To raise sufficient amounts of revenue, the state raises taxes. Higher taxes make once-fertile farmland economically nonviable, depopulate the countryside, and throttle the economy. The Ottoman Empire, even more than the Roman Empire before it, was a plunder machine without a productive domestic economy. As such, the Turks were doomed. In 1675, an observer noted that two-thirds of the farmland was abandoned in one region of European Turkey.[12]

Holland and England were the first nations to make the conscious connection between becoming a service state and gaining power, both military and economic. France soon followed them, while Spain and Japan lagged for centuries before finally catching on. The Ottomans never saw the connection; nor has most of the rest of the Muslim world.

THE FOUR FACTORS IN THE OTTOMAN EMPIRE

Let's now take a moment to examine the state of the four growth factors in the Ottoman Empire.

- **Property rights.** Rulers in traditional societies do not greatly respect the rule of law or the sanctity of property. Surely, the most flagrant violation of property rights is slavery. The Ottomans curtailed their lucrative slave trade in the nineteenth century only under Western pressure. They did not forbid slavery within their own borders until the twentieth century. Yemen and Saudi Arabia did not abolish it until 1962.[13] To this day, estimates of the number of slaves in Sudan, Somalia, and Mauritania range as high as 300,000.[14]

+ **Scientific rationalism.** Islam, which had initially glorified intellectual inquiry, inexplicably turned against it sometime around 1500. One small vignette will suffice to illustrate the Ottoman attitude toward science. In 1577 the empire built a great observatory near Istanbul. It was the Arab answer to Tyco Brahe's Uraniborg observatory, with equipment and staff that equaled its Danish counterpart. Almost immediately upon its completion, the sultan had it destroyed on the recommendation of his religious advisors.[15]

+ **Capital markets.** The Islamic prohibition against the payment of interest stifled commerce. Moreover, since the sultan could seize property at will, capital was scarce, and banking was nonexistent. As has been mentioned, it would take the Europeans to set up the first Turkish banks in the nineteenth century.

+ **Transport and communication.** Here, the European lead was not great. While communications and transport were underdeveloped in the late medieval and early modern Ottoman Empire, they were not much better in Europe.

THE FOUR FACTORS IN THE MODERN MIDDLE EAST

In the modern Muslim world, the institutional terrain is radically different. As we discussed in Chapter 1, three of the four factors—scientific rationalism, capital markets, and modern transport and communications—are readily available, even in the Middle East. In order to grow and prosper, the only remaining requirements are property rights and the rule of law.

But today the concept of Western-style rights is deeply unpopular in the Middle East. That unpopularity even extends to the legal profession.[16]

The extreme measures taken against criminals under *shari'a*—stoning and amputation—give the impression of strict rule of law. Most of the nations in the modern Middle East function as police states, and strict legal enforcement means little if the power of the state is itself unchecked. The hallmark of the lawless society—the high walls, topped with barbed wire and glass shards, that ring the homes of the wealthy and even government offices—looms everywhere in the Muslim world.

Geographers and archaeologists have even made a credible case that the great expanse of the Middle Eastern deserts is in part a consequence of the absence of clear-cut land title. Under Roman rule, much of North Africa was once wooded and fertile, and became dry and barren only with the coming of the Islamic empires. The population and agricultural output of North Africa were much higher in Roman times than it was even under the Ottomans, more than a thousand years later.

The "technology" of irrigation is almost as old as history. The earliest Mesopotamian civilizations were hydraulic societies, and the Romans successfully cultivated large areas of the North African desert with vast irrigation projects. With the loss of secure property institutions in the wake of the Arab and Ottoman conquests, these irrigation schemes were gradually abandoned, and the region's population fell. Astonishingly, in many cases modern archeologists have been able, with little effort, to reestablish water flow under artesian pressure from many of the old Roman irrigation systems, which have been dormant for over a thousand years.[17]

The Arab tradition of nomadic herding follows logically from the absence of well-defined property rights. The goat is highly mobile and can forage anywhere—ideal characteristics in a realm where no one has clear ownership of land and the caliphate stands ready to seize the possessions of the farmer or the herder. (Thus, perhaps, the old Arab proverb, In movement there is blessing.) The goat, which crops vegetation close to the ground, is a particularly efficient despoiler of the land. Whither goes the goat, so follows soil erosion, and so spreads the desert.

When real property is not secure, it will not be irrigated, tilled, or fertilized. Decade after decade, the Arab version of the Tragedy of the Commons—overgrazing by the ubiquitous and ravenous goat—offers up more and more marginal land to the desert.

THE VILLAGE AND THE MOSQUE

In the Muslim world escape from the economic trap will mean replacing the traditional governing system based on the family and religion with that of a trusted, secular, and service-based state. Separating Caesar from God is not an impossibility in the Muslim world. It has already been largely, if tenuously, accomplished in both Turkey and Malaysia.

The modern-day Muslim world is no more backward than the bulk of continental Europe was three centuries ago, and in many regards, such as access to transport, communication, and capital, it is in a better position. Beginning in the sixteenth century, Western Europe slowly began to overthrow religion as its organizing principle. In other words, Western Europe began to acquire a civil society. If the Muslim world truly wishes to enter the modern era, it, too, must do that. The process will require centuries, not decades or years. Simple regime change, whether by internal or external impetus, is at best a cosmetic procedure, as the British and French discovered after World War I, when they created unsuccessful parliamentary regimes in the former Ottoman territories.

We can only guess at just how this might occur in the modern Middle East. One path is a growth model, discussed at length in the next chapter, in which the development of property and individual rights leads to greater prosperity, followed by increasing citizen empowerment, and, finally, democratic reform. It is the village and the patriarch that are much more in need of reform than are the imam and the mosque.

Bernard Lewis suggests another, more intriguing possibility. He points out that early Islam was egalitarian and nonhierarchical, in contrast to the Christian pyramid of priest, bishop, archbishop, cardinal, and pope. Much later, the Turks appointed a series of religious officers, culminating in the grand mufti, who was roughly the archbishop of Istanbul. In the past few decades the Iranians have created out of thin air an entirely new bureaucracy of ayatollahs that imitates almost exactly the modern Catholic apparatus. Perhaps, hopes Lewis, "They may in time provoke a Reformation."[18]

Whatever the path, the necessary cultural transformation will come to the great expanse of the Muslim world, but it will take many sorrowful, impoverished generations. In 1853 the Japanese gazed upon Commodore Perry's black ships and drew the correct conclusions. Today, the black ships of Western-style wealth and power, and the institutions that support them, are no less visible to the Muslim world. The conclusions it draws will determine its fate.

LATIN AMERICA—AN UNFORTUNATE HERITAGE

It is no accident that England's cultural and colonial offspring—the U.S., Canada, Australia, and New Zealand—rank among the world's wealthiest nations. Nor is it a coincidence that Spain and Portugal's offspring have not done well. The last chapter explored the dysfunctional characteristics of premodern Spain's politics and economy, particularly its underdeveloped property rights system, and touched upon the criminally exploitative nature of the Spanish colonial machine. Not surprisingly, Spain's descendants suffered from her brutal stewardship and flawed institutions.

Of the four factors promoting growth, Latin America had relatively little problem with two. Latin America came of age long after the Reformation finally broke the shackles of Church dogma. After the fall of the Inquisition, scientific rationalism flourished in all of the New World, English-speaking and Spanish-speaking. Likewise, during the late nineteenth century, Europe and the U.S. liberally financed the establishment of Latin shipping, railroad, and telegraph systems. Along with international financing and the telegraph came sophisticated capital markets. By the turn of the twentieth century, Buenos Aires boasted one of the world's great stock exchanges. In fact, the largest Argentine companies did not even trade there. As an indication of their importance, the shares of Argentina's great telegraph and railroad companies were actually bought and sold on the London Exchange.[19]

Latin America's central economic problem, typical of the modern age, rests with its property institutions. The "liberation" of South America from Bourbon Spain in the wake of the Napoleonic wars superficially resembled the American Revolution, and the new republics adopted governmental institutions that were modeled on those of the U.S. Behind that democratic façade, however, were all of Spain's flaws. The Habsburg legacy denied the newly independent nations the culture of individual liberties and property rights that were enjoyed in the U.S. and England, and the new Latin political institutions reflected the totalitarian and violent Habsburg past.

In the U.S., the outbreak of revolution was a spontaneous event, sparked by scattered groups of fiercely independent small landowners. Not until British troops had made it back to the safety of Boston after a headlong retreat from enraged small landowners at Concord and Lexington did the Founding Fathers realize that they needed to plan a more organized struggle, and quickly.

South America's wars of independence, on the other hand, were led from the top by adventurous members of the large landholding elite— the spiritual, if not the literal, descendants of the original conquistadors. As in the U.S., oppressive taxation (in this case, the huge levies necessary to support the Napoleonic wars) sparked the dry tinder of revolt. The American Revolution was a bloody affair, but the South American struggles were of a completely different order. The rebel armies looked nothing like their counterparts in North America. Volunteer soldiers were almost unheard of; Bolívar's armies were filled with mercenaries, treasure hunters, and conscripts, many of the latter in manacles. Some of the rebel forces were little more than roaming bands of thieves commanded by competing warlords.

South America's wars of liberation featured mass slaughter, brutal summary executions, and the public display of severed heads. Simón Bolívar, the George Washington of South America, ruled as a virtual dictator of Venezuela and the Transandean nations. Bolívar could behave with cruelty—upon liberating Caracas in 1813, he executed as many as he killed in battle. In terms of downright brutality, however, he could not hold a candle to his vice president, Francisco Santander. The drama that followed the fall of Bogotá in the summer of 1819 was typical. Bolívar secured the city, imprisoned the royalists in their garrison, and moved on to the West, leaving Santander in command. As soon as Bolívar disappeared over the horizon, Santander put all thirty royalist officers in the compound before a firing squad, and then he commissioned the composition of a song to commemorate their executions. For good measure, he shot a passerby who on behalf of the officers urged mercy. These events set the tone for the wars of liberation and for much of South America's subsequent history. This violent streak found its modern expression during the 1970s in the mass executions by the right-wing dictatorships of South America's southern cone.

The Spaniards themselves were even worse than the rebels. One of the most bizarre actors in the Andean scene was a royalist commander named Josè-Thomas Bove, who, though of Spanish blood, despised white people. Bove planned to kill off as many Caucasians as possible and replace them with settlers of mixed blood. His weapons of choice were spears for white men and whips for their women.

The murderous lawlessness, looting, and general mayhem of Latin America's revolutionary origins began nearly two centuries of widespread political instability. The immediate post-independence history of Mexico vividly illustrates the point. In February 1821, a local Spanish commander, Agustín de Iturbide, sealed the fate of colonial rule by turning his coat, entering Mexico City, and declaring independence from Spain. Not content as constitutional leader, he led a coup against his own government the next year and proclaimed himself emperor.[20] Over the next nine years there were four more coups in Mexico.

PROPERTY SOUTH OF THE BORDER AND THE STORY OF AN OBSCURE ECONOMIST

The lack of stable government constitutes only half of the story. Just as England's cultural offspring prospered from the inheritance of a robust system of property rights, the former colonies of Spain and Portugal suffered from its absence.

If we want to understand the problem with property rights in Latin countries, we must delve a bit further into the fundamental nature of these rights. Chapters 2 and 7 briefly touched on the fact that property rights must not merely be available, they must be *efficient*. That is, they must not be too expensive to obtain, maintain, or enforce. Abraham's purchase of land from Ephron was inexpensive. Abraham's enforcement costs were limited to wine and finger food for the witnesses. Once obtained, Abraham's right to the land was undisputed, and with it the authority to deal with squatters and poachers. Just as important, his rights to the property were *alienable*—he was free to sell the land to whomever he chose.

Now, fast-forward four thousand years. In the mid-1950s, a University of Chicago economist named Ronald Coase began to explore the arcana of government regulation of conflicts among private parties. Consider, for example, a corn farm adjacent to a cattle ranch. The cattle wander, as is their wont, into the cornfields and eat the farmer's crop. Economists call this a "negative externality," similar to the industrial pollution from a thousand miles away that befouls your drinking water or the noise from a neighbor a hundred feet away that disturbs your quiet.

Coase realized that there were two possible ways to settle this sort of conflict. The first, and most obvious, way required that the cattleman pay for the damage. The second, and less intuitive way, allowed the cattle rancher to request payment from the farmer in exchange for fencing in his cattle. In the first case, the liability is the cattleman's; in the second, the farmer's. Coase's genius lay in realizing that it did not matter who initially "owned" the liability. In each case, the end result would be the same—an identical amount of money would change hands, only it would move in opposite directions. The two possible outcomes were economically equivalent.[*] Economists and legal scholars soon recognized that the same was true of property rights; *it is less important how equitably property is initially distributed than how efficiently and clearly the rights to it are defined.* For Coase, only three things mattered:

- That ownership and liability be clearly defined
- That property and liability can be bought and sold at will
- That the expenses of negotiating, selling, and enforcement are low

So long as these three conditions were met, property would eventually find its way to those who could make the most efficient use of it, and liability would be extinguished by the person to whom its elimination was worth the most. In such a universe, the government has no regulatory role beyond defining and enforcing property rights. All property transactions take place between private individuals.

---

[*] Ronald. H. Coase, "The Problem of Social Cost," *Journal of Law and Economics* 3 (October 1960): 1–44. Coase's name is known mainly among economists and lawyers. This paper is one of the most cited articles in the economic literature; in 1991 he was awarded the Nobel Prize in economics for this and related work.

Imagine, for example, that all of the property in a country with efficient and secure property rights was suddenly transferred to a few dozen families. Within two or three generations, that concentration of ownership would begin to dissipate as the dissolute heirs of the original owners, in need of money for high living, sold the land to those who could use it far more efficiently than they could. Within a century or two, widespread smallholdings would be the rule, with large estates remaining largely among families that had managed them wisely.

This is exactly what happened in England following the Norman Conquest. An increasingly efficient system of property rights allowed the gradual dispersion of English landholdings that were initially owned by a small number of Norman families. Coase and his followers were correct—in the long run, exactly who owns something is less important than how clear and alienable the title to it is. In plain English, the health of a society depends far more upon clearly understood and enforced rules than upon the apparent "fairness" of wealth distribution. In even plainer English, rule of law matters more than "social justice."

Similar to the situation in Norman England, about two dozen grandees owned most of the land in Spain after the expulsion of the Moors. Spain then "exported" this same concentration of landholdings to its Latin American colonies. In Mexico, for example, when millions of small farmers died from smallpox in the sixteenth century, their property passed into the hands of Spanish *haciendados*. Their huge plantations dwarfed even those of the grandees in the mother country.[21] Because of the flawed property mechanisms inherited from Spain, most land in Mexico wound up in enormous, poorly managed hereditary estates until well into the modern era.

Things turned out differently in Spain and her colonies than in post–Norman England. On both sides of the Atlantic, the backward state of Spanish property institutions prevented the breakup of large states through the normal dynamics of free property markets. Given the empire's ill-functioning property institutions, neglect by Spain actually conferred long-term advantage—Costa Rica, long considered a backwater of the colonial regime, escaped the accumulation of land into huge estates and so became Central America's only economic success story.[22]

Modern-day Latin America meets none of Coase's three conditions. The easiest way to understand the efficiency of property rights is to consider the purchase of a piece of land. In the U.S., the most complex and difficult part of the process usually involves the negotiation of price. Once this is agreed upon, a title search inexpensively establishes the legitimacy of the seller's ownership rights, a check is written, and the transfer registered at the county office. Done.

Not so in Latin America. In researching the Kafkaesque world of Latin property law, economist Hernando de Soto found that it requires 728 steps in Lima, Peru to properly purchase a house.[23] In such a world, none but the wealthiest individuals and largest businesses can afford to obtain clear title. The farmer cannot sell his land because the buyer cannot be certain that he is getting unencumbered ownership. In such a society, the only way to keep property in the family is to divide it among the sons. After several generations, this progressive division of the land results in a squabbling group of starving distant cousins. Nor can the farmer borrow to improve his property. The bank has no assurance that it will be able to foreclose should the farmer default on its loan. Similarly, businesses cannot obtain capital. Investors are unwilling to provide it if they are unsure of their residual rights. De Soto depicts third-world nations as treasure troves of "dead capital": property that *could* attract vast amounts of investment if only clear title allowed it to be unlocked as collateral.

Populist political rhetoric in Latin America contributes to the poisonous economic atmosphere. Where the avenging specter of "the people" hangs heavy in the air, improving a property or a business serves only to make it a fatter target for confiscation. Peasants who receive land purchased or expropriated by the government wind up in the same situation as any other small landowner. They are unable to sell the property, are unable to borrow against it, and are fearful that the next coup will reverse the gift.

The West did not help. For decades, developed nations encouraged land reform through government decree, and in so doing they engendered a system that bestowed upon the peasant property that he could neither sell nor improve. The West forgot the lesson that it learned centuries ago: The most effective way to promote prosperity and democracy is through "English-style land reform"—the distribution of land to small farmers through secure property rights and free and open markets for land. Expropriations and forced sales of property in the name of "the people," however well intentioned, serve only to corrode the very institutions that are necessary to raise a disenfranchised population out of poverty.

OF CRONIES AND CAPITAL

The chaotic state of Latin American property markets also shackles its capital markets. Mexico provides a well-studied example. Until 1890, the only source of financing for most Mexican farmers and businessmen was the family. The "impersonal" sources of finance commonplace in the Western world—small bank loans for individuals, stock and bond issues for larger companies—simply did not exist. Even after Mexico's first bank opened in 1864, collateralized business loans were available only at very high interest rates—at times above 100% per year.[24] This condition persisted until the late 1930s. At the outbreak of World War II, only fourteen stocks traded on the Mexico City stock exchange.

Without powerful political connections, the nineteenth-century Mexican businessman soon found himself battered by competitors who *did* have friends in high places. During the early and mid-nineteenth century, tenures in government offices were measured in months, making it difficult for even the wealthiest to protect their property. After the ascension of dictator Porfirio Díaz in 1877, the situation grew less complex, but it did not improve. During the *Porfiriato*, which lasted until 1910, almost every major Mexican company had a government minister, or a relative of one, on its board to assure government approval when it issued stock or floated bonds. Since stock and bond capital was available only to those with government connections, this greatly reduced the number of banks and made capital scarce for smaller businessmen and farmers.

Since Latin American nations did not see themselves as "service states," they ignored the institutional infrastructure of the capital markets—laws governing credit, loans, mortgages, and incorporation. Mexico did not have even rudimentary commercial and property statutes on its books until near the end of the nineteenth century. Where no legal framework protects the investor, the rate of return required by the lender or investor is so high that capital effectively becomes unavailable.

The corruption of Latin politics originated in Habsburg Spain and was perpetuated by political instability. A heritage rife with conquest, plunder, exploitation, and forced extraction of mineral wealth does not greatly value efficient capital markets. The modern scourge of the Andean nations—the drug industry and the lawlessness that accompanies it—is a symptom, not the disease.

It is no coincidence that the two wealthiest and most democratic Spanish-speaking nations—Chile and Spain herself—got that way by passing through repressive right-wing dictatorships that emphasized secure property rights. Chile's case is particularly instructive. Augusto Pinochet's economic policies were directed by the "Chicago Boys"— economists trained in the Windy City and heavily influenced by Ronald Coase and Milton Friedman. The selection of right-wing dictators, of course, is a dangerous game, since you are more likely to wind up with a Perón, a Marcos, or a Duvalier than a Pinochet or a Franco. And Pinochet and Franco were no picnic.

The economic prospects for Latin America, with its pockets of budding property institutions, relatively easy access to capital, and embrace of Western culture, seem brighter than in the Muslim world. However, Latin prosperity is far from a foregone conclusion. South America's poorest nations—those of the Andean *cordillera*—and some of the wealthier ones as well, are still in the thrall of their corrupt, violent, and economically defective Iberian colonial heritage. It will be generations before the last nations escape from it.

The failed states of Latin America and the Muslim world raise issues of religion and culture that must be met head on if the ever-widening gap between our planet's wealthiest and poorest nations is not to lead to some sort of Armageddon; we will deal with the interactions among culture, religion, and economic growth in the next chapter.

NATURAL WEALTH AND IMPERIALISM

In the nineteenth century, serious institutional defects delayed economic development in France, Spain, and Japan. In the modern world, these same institutional flaws have derailed prosperity in the Muslim world and in most of Latin America. No analysis of why some nations lag others is complete without mentioning two factors that are *not* important:

1. Natural resources. There may well be an inverse correlation between wealth and natural endowment. Cast your gaze upon the Habsburg Empire, as well as modern Nigeria, Saudi Arabia, and Zaire, and it is difficult not to conclude that abundant natural resources are a curse. The production of wealth from commercial enterprise born of risk taking and sweat encourages healthy governmental institutions and begets further wealth. The production of wealth from a limited number of holes in the ground, owned or controlled by the government, begets rent seeking and corruption.

It is hard to consider Singapore, Holland, and Switzerland and not wonder if their lack of natural resources did not confer an advantage upon them. True, England sat on a "mountain of coal," but she also had to import most of her iron ore and nearly 100% of her cotton, the Industrial Revolution's key raw materials. (Iron ore came from Sweden, while the cotton had to be shipped around the Cape of Good Hope.) France, on the other hand, had not one, but two easy sources of cotton: her West Indian colonies and an efficient Mediterranean route to the Levant. Yet, England developed the cotton-based textile industry first.

Finally, few developed nations so lacked natural resources as did Japan. The meteoric rise of its economy after 1868 throws into sharp relief the utter irrelevance of natural resources to economic development. The only natural endowment that matters is a topography that is favorable to internal transport. Great mineral wealth corrodes the very institutions that promote long-term prosperity.

2. Imperialism. Guilt and self-loathing have become the great growth industries of the modern West. If some nations are rich and others are poor, it seems, it cannot possibly be because the former produce more than the latter do, but rather because the former have stolen from the latter. Beginning with Marx, academics and the chattering classes began to explain English (and Western) prosperity in terms of imperialist exploitation. This misconception survives to this day among those who are able to contort logic into equating the sneaker-wearing executives of the Nike Corporation with the jackbooted troops of Her Majesty's armed forces.

Even a moment's reflection reveals, however, that this left-wing sacred cow is largely irrelevant. While colonial governments could be unimaginably brutal and exploitative, they also often brought material prosperity through the importation of the rule of law.

FIGURE 9–1   1995 PER CAPITA GDP VERSUS POPULATION DENSITY IN 1500

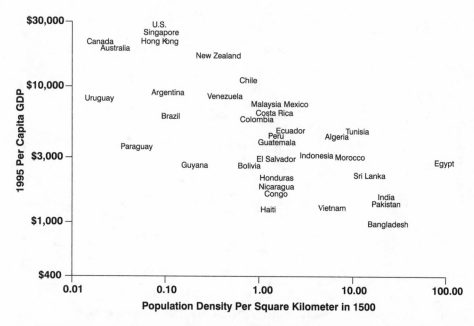

Source: Daron Acemoglu, Simon Johnson, and James A. Robinson, "Reversal of Fortune: Geography and Institutions in the Making of the Modern World Income Distribution," *Quarterly Journal of Economics* 117 (2002):
1286–89, and Daron Acemoglu, Simon Johnson, and James A. Robinson, "The Colonial Origins of Comparative Development: An Empirical Investigation," *American Economic Review* 91 (Dec. 2001): 1398.

In recent years, economists have begun to focus on and understand
the interplay among colonialism, economics, and national institutions.
Since 1500, there has been a "reversal of fortune" in the developing
world. The wealthiest nations of 1500 that would later be colonized—
the Mughals of India, the Aztecs, and the Incas—are now among the
poorest, while the poorest nations of 1500 that were later colonized—
the rest of the Americas, Australia, and New Zealand—are now among
the richest.[25] Figure 9–1 shows the population density (a well-accepted
proxy for per capita GDP in preindustrial societies) of colonized nations in 1500 versus their present-day per capita GDP. Figure 9–2
shows the even more fascinating relationship between mortality resulting
from European settlement and later economic development—nations
with high death rates among Caucasians suffered subsequent low economic growth.

FIGURE 9–2   1995 PER CAPITA GDP VERSUS SETTLER MORTALITY

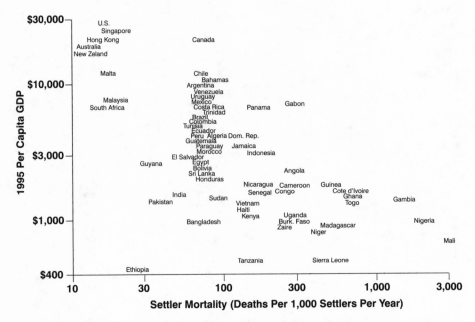

Source: Daron Acemoglu, Simon Johnson, and James A. Robinson, "The Colonial Origins of Comparative Development: An Empirical Investigation," 1398.

These two graphs suggest that densely populated colonies that suffered high mortality among Caucasians attracted few settlers. A low population density and high mortality among Western settlers meant two
things: first, weak western institutions and rule of law, and second, that
those few settlers that braved such adversity and survived tended to confine themselves to highly profitable extractive and exploitative activities,
particularly mining—think Leopold's Congo. Nations with low native
population density and low Caucasian death rates, such as North America, Australia, and New Zealand, attracted a large European influx and
thus benefited from Western institutions and an agricultural-industrial
economic base. In these locations, the large numbers of English settlers
relative to the number of local inhabitants produced a "clear field" for
European culture and institutions to flourish by allowing the settlers to
systematically annihilate a colony's original inhabitants. (A highly cynical

observer might note that a fifth factor is necessary for prosperity in colonial nations—genocide.)

Both of these types of colonialism could be barbarous, but neither type, especially the latter, impoverished the surviving native peoples much beyond their original condition. Colonialism itself did not produce poverty; rather, the form it took made the difference between later poverty and wealth. When engaged in by large numbers of settlers who concentrated on agriculture and industry, prosperity followed. When engaged in by a few disease-ridden settlers who enslaved the native population in pursuit of mineral wealth, poverty and backwardness were the inevitable result. Even in this case, the economic advantages of colonialism could be substantial. Most Westerners, for example, do not realize that India is made up of several linguistic communities, with no mutually intelligible native language. Consequently, that nation's very existence would have been doubtful without the sword's point introduction of English as a lingua franca.

As to its perpetrators, colonialism probably did more harm than good. By far, England's richest colony was America. If the imperialist hypothesis holds any water, then England should have been devastated by American independence. Quite the opposite occurred—economic growth exploded in both nations when the British defeat equalized trade relations. Even at the height of the British Empire, England's colonies absorbed less than a quarter of her output. Exports to unprotected markets like Europe and the U.S. provided the bulk of Britain's export trade.[26]

In a world where imperialism actually matters, the planet's wealthiest nations should be those that remained largely free of Western rule, such as Bhutan, Mongolia, Ethiopia and Russia, while those nations that remained under the colonialist system the longest, such as Hong Kong and Singapore, should be the poorest. Imperialism, then, is the end effect of vast discrepancies of wealth and military capability among nations, not their cause.

Institutions, not the bounty of nature or freedom from imperialist domination, separate the winners from the losers in the global economy. First and foremost, it is the degree of respect and reverence for the Rules of the Game—rule of law, equality under the law, and respect for the civil liberties of all—that determines the wealth of nations.

Consequences

IN THIS SECTION, we plumb the historical concepts that have been discussed in the previous nine chapters for modern relevance. During the past decade, tensions in the world have shifted in focus from the ideological to the religious; Chapter 10 will explore the frontiers of sociological and economic research for lessons on the relationship between religion, wealth, ideology, and democratic development.

The overwhelming popular impression of life in the modern West, particularly in the U.S., is that it is an increasingly harried, insecure, and stressful existence. Just what is the use of growing rich as a nation if wealth does not make us happier? In fact, there is a trade-off between economic growth and happiness, which we will examine in Chapter 11.

Whether or not money buys happiness, it certainly influences geopolitical power. Chapter 12 will relate the interwoven strands of wealth, conquest, and influence over the past five hundred years of world history, particularly as it pertains to increasing American hegemony in a "unipolar" world.

Although the sustained economic growth of the past two centuries has been unprecedented, it spans but a moment in history. Were all of human history represented in a day, the prosperous modern era would occupy less than ten seconds. How sustainable is the modern growth regime, and, more important, how *stable* is a world in which per capita wealth doubles each generation? In the book's final pages, we'll muse about prosperity, the escalation of human wants, and the outlook for continued growth.

CHAPTER TEN

God, Culture, Mammon, and the Hedonic Treadmill

Money does not buy happiness, but at least you can suffer in comfort.

—Lillian Bernstein, *Author's Mother*

THE USES OF WEALTH

The premise of this book is that prosperity flows naturally once a society acquires the four crucial factors—property rights, scientific rationalism, capital markets, and modern transportation and communication. All well and good you say, but is there any way of objectively verifying this hypothesis? After all, nations don't lend themselves easily to controlled scientific experiments.

The perceptive reader will notice that although this book contains lots of GDP figures and many graphs, nowhere have I collected data for *all* nations and made comparisons with, for example, measures of the rule of law. Does such comprehensive quantitative information actually exist, and if so, what does it tell us?

And while we're at it, just what is the good of all this wealth anyway? As the world grows more and more prosperous, does it become a more or less happy place? How do social policy and political policy simulta-neously affect the prosperity and overall happiness of a society? What, precisely, is the relationship between wealth and happiness?

Over the past several decades, sociologists, political scientists, and econ-omists have accumulated a great amount of data for more than a hundred nations that correlates wealth and growth with a multitude of political, economic, and sociological characteristics. We can think of every country as an "experiment of nature," each with different social and institutional endowments. With careful statistical analysis, we can draw some cautious conclusions about prosperity's causes and effects. Out of this blizzard of numbers emerges a fascinating relationship between prosperity, psycholog-ical well-being, democracy, and sociological measures of traditional values and personal empowerment. Wealth, it turns out, does not make us much happier, but it does greatly strengthen democracy.

In the late 1950s political scientist Seymour Lipset first undertook this kind of objective analysis. Lipset's major interest was democratic devel-opment. At the time, an academic debate simmered over the relative im-portance to democracy of political, economic, and religious factors. For example, adherents to the theory of religious determinism pointed out that almost all democracies were of Judeo-Christian origin, while their opponents cited fascism in Italy and Germany. What bothered Lipset was that neither side seemed willing to analyze *all* of the available data. From a statistical perspective, political and economic systems are very "dirty"; any sociologist worth his salt can find plenty of exceptions to even the most fundamental sociological principles.

Lipset started with a simple measure of democratic development and then performed a statistical analysis of all the possible factors that might affect that development. The most important factors proved to be wealth and educational level, which seemed to support democratic institutions.[1] In the decades since the publication of Lipset's pioneering article in 1959, sociologists, economists, and political scientists have followed his lead. In this chapter we'll examine the small but exciting slice of that re-search that relates to the toughest part of the world wealth puzzle—the nexus between money, happiness, democracy, religion, and culture. We must tread carefully here. It is easy to be fooled when social and political factors seem to correlate. A medical analogy will suffice to explain. De-cades ago, studies of housepainters showed that they had below-average

I.Q. At first, researchers concluded that there was something in paint that damaged the brain. This turned out not to be the case. Careful analysis showed that the I.Q. effect was not "dose dependent," that is, it did not become more severe with increased occupational exposure. Rather, house painting, being a rather boring occupation, tends to attract those with low I.Q. The chain of causation was the reverse of what was expected: Low I.Q. "caused," if you will, house painting.[2]

OF RICH PROTESTANTS AND POOR MUSLIMS

We cannot avoid addressing the relationship between religion and economic growth. Western prosperity sprang from Protestant northern Europe, and the temptation to wield faith as an analytic tool in comparative economics is strong indeed. Certainly, when philosopher and sociologist Max Weber cast his eye over the globe more than a century ago, he found a religious explanation irresistible. One of sociology's founders, he suggested in *The Protestant Ethic and the Spirit of Capitalism* that the Reformation triggered modern capitalism, and that the Calvinist emphasis on self-denial and hard work made Protestantism the engine of world prosperity.[3]

The same observation strikes the modern observer. Why, too, are the Muslim and Hindu nations among the world's poorest? Surely, the world's major religions must each carry with them, for better and for worse, a great deal of economic baggage. Yet, as we shall soon see, the data show this *not* to be the case. Wealth and poverty correlate more closely with sociological and cultural factors than with religion.

Real problems plague Weber's hypothesis, and among modern economists and sociologists, Calvinism's role as the prime mover of Western prosperity has lost favor. For starters, Calvin's Geneva was hardly a bastion of capitalist free enterprise. Although the august pastor ended the ancient prohibitions against lending at interest, his nearly continuous meddling with interest rates and commodity pricing did real harm to Geneva's economy. Geneva was advanced and enlightened for its time in other ways as well, particularly regarding public education. However, it remained an economic backwater for centuries after Calvin.[4] Not until three centuries after the Reformation would Protestant nations begin to allow Adam Smith's invisible hand to work its magic. By the time Weber's book was published in 1905, Catholic Austria and France had joined the ranks of the world's most prosperous countries.

The dominance of the Arab caliphates and of the early Ottoman Empire over an impotent and backward medieval Europe vividly demonstrated that Christianity provided no intrinsic political and economic advantages over Islam. Moreover, modern data show that the economic difference is cultural, not religious. This lack of a religious correlation cannot be emphasized enough. Culture is determined by geography, not by place of worship. Sociological surveys demonstrate, for example, that while a German Catholic is likely to have more conservative and traditional values than a German Protestant does, he will resemble a Catholic from South America, or even Italy, far less. The same holds true in the most parochial parts of the third world, where the data demonstrate that the outlook of a Muslim from India or Africa will resemble that of his Christian or Hindu countrymen more than that of Muslims in other nations.[5]

Most spectacularly of all, a Bosnian Muslim resembles more closely a Parisian sophisticate in dress, mannerism, and sensibility than he resembles his Saudi co-religionist. Yet another variation on this theme is the cultural gap between Israel's Sephardic and Ashkenazic populations. Sephardic culture closely reflects that of the Arab world, while the Ashkenazi culture is highly westernized. Says Bernard Lewis,

> . . . in many of their [Sephardim and Ashkenazim] encounters what we see is a clash between Christendom and Islam, oddly represented by their former Jewish minorities, who reflect, as it were in miniature, both the strengths and the weaknesses of the two civilizations of which they had been a part.[6]

Maxine Rodinson, one of Islam's most thoughtful observers, flatly states that nothing in Islam's precepts is inherently anticapitalist.[7] Even a cursory look at the most advanced nations in the Muslim world, such as Malaysia and Turkey, demonstrates that this is so. More to the point, nothing in the religion of devout Muslims from the Middle East, Pakistan, and India prevents them from effectively wielding the tools of entrepreneurial capitalism after they emigrate to the secular West.

This is not to say that religion has no influence at all on economics. At least theoretically, Christianity possesses a unique doctrinal advantage relative to other faiths: It clearly expresses the separation of church and state: "Render therefore unto Caesar the things which are Caesar's; and unto God the things that are God's."[8]

From the conversion of Emperor Constantine through Calvin's Geneva this separation was honored more in its breach than in its observance. From the early Roman era until well after Martin Luther, the Church's stance toward entrepreneurial capitalism was only slightly to the right of that of Karl Marx. As we saw in Chapter 1, both Augustine and Aquinas were patently hostile to business, and over the course of the first millennium, the Church evolved a doctrine that was increasingly opposed to moneylending and capital formation. The early Church's anticapitalist mentality may well have been the major cause of medieval Europe's backwardness in comparison to the Islamic world of the time. Ironically, without the financial infrastructure provided by the Jews to Europe, the Turks probably would have overrun it. The extent of anticapitalist antipathy in Europe is made clear by Barbara Tuchman:

> To ensure that no one gained an advantage over anyone else, commercial law prohibited innovation in tools or techniques, underselling below a fixed price, working late by artificial light, employing extra apprentices or wife and under-age children, and advertising of wares or praising them to the detriment of others.[9]

Hinduism is the one major world religion whose precepts directly handicap its adherents' economic status. Its stultifying caste system subdivides humankind into a hierarchy that blesses the wretched condition of its lower classes and denies prosperity in this world in exchange for a shot at the brass ring in the next.*

Religion simply provides a lens through which a society's traditions are filtered. The varying treatment of women in the Muslim world illustrates the point. In some Islamic societies, women and men function

---

* India's modern constitution forbids the practice of untouchability. The Indian government also operates the world's largest affirmative-action program, which is aimed at members of the lower castes. See Shashi Tharoor, *India: From Midnight to the Millennium*, (New York: Perennial, 1998), and Francis Fukuyama, *The End of History and the Last Man*, 228.

together in the workplace as equals, while in others, tradition bars women from the workplace. Superficially, it appears that Islam wastes one-half of its human capital and so harms the economies of Muslim nations. In reality, the narrow cultures of traditional societies do most of the damage in these countries. In the Arabian Peninsula and elsewhere, Islam and the Koran are simply smokescreens that are employed to rationalize the taboos of an isolated desert society that predated the Prophet by thousands of years. Had the Arabs been converted to Judaism or Christianity instead of Islam, it is likely that modern-day Saudi Arabian society would still be as fundamentalist as it is today.

THE PYRAMID OF HAPPINESS

That said, Weber's conjecture about the connection between Protestantism and prosperity proved invaluable. The science of sociology he helped invent has shed much-needed light on the religious and cultural factors that affect political structure and economic growth. Indeed, one of the strongest correlations with happiness is the perception that an individual has control of his life. The solid connection between individual autonomy and happiness has been substantiated by surveys done in scores of nations, from Argentina to Zimbabwe.[10]

In the 1950s, psychologist Abraham Maslow popularized his "hierarchy of needs." This construct, together with more recent sociological research, provides a powerful paradigm with which to examine the relationship between wealth and democracy.

As a young academic, Maslow noted that certain human urges took precedence over others. The most basic need is breathing. If someone deprives you of air, you will become distressed in less than a minute. Starving for air will blot out all other impulses—thirst, hunger, even pain. Only after you resume breathing can these other sensations be attended to. Maslow's great contribution was to define the hierarchy of these needs.

After you have satisfied these immediate "physiologic" needs of oxygen, water, food, warmth—you can proceed to address safety needs: personal security and a steady job. And after these have been largely satisfied, belonging needs—the love of a spouse, family, and community—can be met. Next come esteem needs—the respect (as distinct from mere love) of your peers, as well as self-respect.

The higher up the pyramid you ascend, the more internally secure you feel. The highest point on the hierarchy became the Holy Grail of the New Age: "self-actualization." Maslow was rather vague about what the term actually meant, but he did describe the characteristics of those who had attained this exalted state, such as Lincoln and Gandhi. They lacked egotism, differentiated means from ends, solved rather than complained, and filtered out the corrosive effects of peer pressure.

Individuals who dwell near the bottom of Maslow's pyramid run purely on instinct and are not much given to abstract thought. They have little personal choice, and their well-being suffers accordingly.

Maslow's pyramid provided sociologists around the world with a framework with which to measure and interpret various kinds of psychological and sociological data, particularly measures of well-being. The largest such efforts are the World Values Survey (WVS) and the Eurobarometer Survey. The WVS originally conducted studies in ten European nations in 1981, but the results so stunned researchers that they expanded it to sixty-five nations, encompassing 80% of the world's population. The Institute for Social Research (ISR) at the University of Michigan currently coordinates this effort.

The ISR does not focus primarily on religious and national groupings, but upon easily defined and measurable personal characteristics. Its investigators have used these techniques to plumb the links among personality, culture, religion, politics, and prosperity.

THE SCALES OF DEMOCRACY

Just how do social scientists evaluate the interaction of culture, well-being, wealth, and democracy? They proceed in the same way that any scientist would—by formulating hypotheses and collecting data with which to test those hypotheses. The bread-and-butter tool in this complex area involves conducting surveys of many sociological variables across many nations. One such variable is the "survival/self expression" (S/SE) scale, which the WVS devised to measure a person's attitudes toward independent thought and expression. Roughly speaking, S/SE measures an individual's ascent up Maslow's pyramid. Investigators ask subjects, for example, whether they value self-expression more than physical security, if they have ever signed a petition, and how much they trust other people. A preponderance of "yes" answers results in a high S/SE score, and many "no" answers yields a low S/SE score. The higher the score, the higher up the Maslow pyramid the subject has climbed, and the happier he tends to be.

Sociologists Ronald Inglehart of the University of Michigan and Christian Welzel of the International University Bremen looked at the correlation of the S/SE score with the strength of democratic institutions, and they found a high correlation between a nation's average S/SE score and the vigor of its democracy.

It should come as no surprise that S/SE correlates with democracy. The real question is, which is the chicken and which is the egg? It is just as easy to imagine that democracy leads to increased self-expression as to imagine that self-expression leads to greater democracy. Their data demonstrate a surprising relationship: *The link between the two is wealth itself.* Inglehart and Welzel teased out this chain of causation with a statistical tool known as "lagged cross-correlations." Specifically, they determined that the correlation of S/SE in 1995 with the democracy index in 2000 was much higher than the correlation of the S/SE in 2000 with the democracy index in 1995. (The democracy index was calculated by combining the Freedom House score for civil and political rights with a corruption index from Transparency International.)

In other words, present democracy correlates well with prior S/SE score, while prior democracy does not correlate nearly as well with present S/SE score. These data suggest that a population that is empowered, self-actuated, and able to make free choices strengthens democracy, not the other way around. This does not *prove* that personal empowerment (high S/SE) produces democracy, but it is highly consistent with that conclusion.

Next, Inglehart and Welzel examined the relationship between the S/SE and personal wealth.[*] Once again, they found a strong correlation between wealth and the S/SE, and once again, the same lagged cross-correlation technique suggested that it was wealth that led to a higher S/SE, and thus to a stronger democracy, and not the opposite.

Obviously, this model oversimplifies an enormously complex process. Yes, democracy strengthens a citizen's sense of empowerment. But the reverse—that citizen empowerment produces democracy—is a far more powerful dynamic. This is consistent with recent history. The late twentieth century demonstrated the impossibility of exporting democratic institutions to nations with a silent and fearful populace. The recent experience in Bosnia and Kosovo, where the maintenance of even a creaky governmental apparatus will require a massive and long-term armed presence by United Nations peacekeepers, bears this out. The same applies to the atrophied state of "democracy" in impoverished nations like Pakistan. India provides a less extreme case. Its democratic institutions are weak, at least by Western standards, because of a servile caste system. Although legally abolished, the caste system still exerts a powerful cultural influence.

At the time of this writing, the U.S. and its allies believe (or say they believe) that they can transplant democracy to Iraq. The above discussion suggests that this may be a dangerous delusion. Moreover, if democracy in Iraq is a delusion, then democracy in Afghanistan is a fevered dream.

---

[*] Welzel and Inglehart used an index of wealth that they call "power resources." This differs from simple per capita GDP in that it combines standard indexes of wealth with educational level and life expectancy, among others, and also measures the evenness of their distributions among the population. The power resource parameter has a much higher correlation with the S/SE than simple per capita GDP does. Ronald Inglehart, personal communication.

THE THEORY OF EVERYTHING

We can combine the thesis of this book with the Welzel/Inglehart Hypothesis to generate the following diagram:

Property Rights ⎫
Scientific Rationalism ⎬→ Prosperity → Citizen Empowerment → Democracy
Capital Markets ⎪
Transport and Communication ⎭

Admittedly, this model is not without flaws. The above-pictured paradigm moves, albeit less well, from right to left. That increasing democracy benefits the empowerment of citizens and the four factors, for example, is beyond dispute. However, the data of Welzel, Inglehart, and others leave little doubt that the primary impetus in this model sweeps left to right, not right to left. While democracy is highly desirable on its own merits, the data demonstrate that its direct economic benefits are at best debatable.

What about educational level, Lipset's other major determinant of democracy? Education strengthens democracy primarily through its economic effects. A badly educated society cannot master new productivity-enhancing technologies and so dooms itself to poverty. But even a highly educated populace can suffer the same fate without efficient economic incentives. In both cases—nations that are poor because they are badly educated, and well-educated nations that are poor because of inadequate property institutions—the resultant poverty will stunt democratic development.

Communism produced a bumper crop of well-educated nations that failed to advance both their economies and their bodies politic. The most spectacular failure among these nations is Cuba, which in the forty years following its revolution dramatically advanced education at all levels and reduced illiteracy from about 35% to less than 2%. During the same period, however, per capita real GDP in Cuba fell by one-third, in spite of massive subsidies from the USSR—a singular accomplishment in an era when the per capita real GDP of the rest of the world more than doubled. The above analysis also suggests that Cuba's poverty per se helped Fidel Castro hone his country into one of the world's most repressive states.

The track records of non-Communist nations, especially among the newly powerful economies of Asia, also support the hypothesis that democracy flows from prosperity. Most often, prosperous countries become democracies, not the other way around. An early example occurred in Japan, where the Meiji allowed a cosmetic representative apparatus that quickly developed into a vibrant parliamentary system as the nation grew more prosperous. At the dawn of the Meiji era, a high property requirement qualified less than half a million Japanese to vote. Increasing prosperity empowered Japanese peasants and forced the government to gradually liberalize to the point of universal (male) suffrage in 1925. During the 1930s, democratization suffered a setback as the government fell victim to what was, in effect, a slow, rolling military coup. But without question today's vigorous Japanese democratic institutions resulted primarily from the country's brisk postwar prosperity, and not the other way around.[11]

IN PRAISE OF DESPOTS

The current combination of economic liberalization and political repression in China appears more likely to succeed than its Russian mirror image. A rare "double example" of this phenomenon occurred in Chile, where Salvador Allende and his Marxist agriculture minister, Jacques Chonchol, cleansed the constitution of its property rights clause, appropriated land, and maimed the country's economy. This set the stage for the rise of a fascist tyrant, Augusto Pinochet, who repaired the economic damage by reestablishing property rights and freeing the markets. The new prosperity strengthened the nation's democratic institutions and brought about the dictator's eventual downfall. A similar transformation from a property-respecting right-wing dictatorship into a liberal democracy occurred in Spain. When Laureano Lopez Rodo, one of Franco's economic ministers, was asked when Spain would be ready for democracy, he famously replied that democracy would arrive when the average income exceeded $2,000 per year. When Franco's dictatorship finally fell in 1975, the average income in Spain was $2,446.[*]

---

[*] In a field as messy as political science, theory often requires the aid of coincidence: It did not hurt that Franco died in 1975, leaving the democratically inclined Prince Juan Carlos in charge. See Fukuyama, 110.

Johns Hopkins University political scientist Francis Fukuyama drew a similar conclusion in his solidly reasoned if controversially named *The End of History and the Last Man*. He noted that Philippine democracy had failed to accomplish meaningful land reform because of a powerful land-owning minority. He wondered if "dictatorship could be much more functional in bringing about a modern society, as it was when dictatorial power was used to bring about land reform during the American occupation of Japan."[12]

The connection between prosperity and democracy adds an interesting dimension to the assertion by Nobe Prizel-winning economist Amartya Sen that famine does not occur in functioning democracies because a free press and ambitious politicians are strongly motivated to uncover and rectify hunger.[13] While no doubt true, the absence of hunger in functioning democracies is also a byproduct of the fact that prosperity itself simultaneously encourages democracy and provides a dandy cure for hunger.

TRADITIONALISM AND RATIONALISM

The WVS measures a second key sociologic parameter, the strength of "traditional values." Whatever their religion, fundamentalist societies stress traditional values, such as prohibitions against abortion, divorce, and homosexuality. Strongly traditional societies are usually authoritarian, devout, and male-dominated.[14]

The WVS determines this "traditional/secular rational" (T/SR) score by soliciting agreement with such statements as "God is very important in my life," "I have a strong sense of national pride," and "I favor more respect for authority." "Yes" answers place the subject toward the "traditional" (T) end of the scale (that is, they indicate a negative T/SR score), and "no" answers place them toward the "secular-rational" (SR) end of the scale (i.e., they indicate a positive T/SR score).

Societies with high T/SR scores tend to be wealthier than societies with low T/SR scores. However, the effect of the T/SR score on wealth is not as strong as that of the S/SE score. In essence, the T/SR score measures the degree of "falsifiability" of a community's body of knowledge, a concept that was discussed in Chapter 3. A society with a high score will gladly accept challenges to almost all of its knowledge base, while a society with a low score will hold fast to its beliefs no matter how persuasive the contradictory information is.

A low T/SR score correlates strongly with an agricultural economy, although the U.S., to a certain extent, and Latin America are exceptions. Personal beliefs change more slowly on the farm, which values family and community stability highly, so the association of low T/SR scores with a large agricultural sector is hardly surprising. The S/SE score, on the other hand, correlates strongly with the size of the service economy. Service workers spend their workdays expressing opinions and making hundreds, even thousands, of decisions, a milieu that encourages autonomy and personal expression.

Combining S/SE and T/SR scores cleanly separates the world into religious/cultural groups. Figure 10–1 charts nations on a two-dimensional grid, with the T/SR score on one axis and the S/SE score on the other. Protestant European nations cluster in the upper right of the graph, with high S/SE and T/SR scores. We can describe these wealthy nations as "outspoken secularists." The English-speaking nations tend to be in the mid- to bottom-right of the graph. They are "outspoken conservatives." The ex-Communist nations—"silent atheists"—cluster in the upper-left, while the south Asian world, which consists mainly of Muslim nations and India, occupies the bottom-left. They are "silent fundamentalists."

Figure 10–2 overlays per capita GDP onto this scheme. This graph speaks volumes about the relationship between wealth and personal/cultural values—the rich are indeed different. As one travels from left to right along the x-axis (that is, S/SE), wealth increases. In wealthy societies, individuals are not only happier; but they feel free to speak out, challenge the government, and make their own life choices.

Along the y-axis (that is, T/SR), from bottom to top, this relationship becomes less clear—traditional societies tend to be less wealthy, but the relationship between wealth and T/SR is not as strong as that between wealth and S/SE (that is, a move from right to left crosses two or three of the wealth demarcations, while a move up crosses only one or two). While Weber may have been right about the association of prosperity and Protestantism, it was because Protestants were, well . . . protesting. Piety had nothing to do with it.

FIGURE 10–1 THE INTERACTION OF RELIGION, CULTURE, SELF-EXPRESSION, AND TRADITIONAL VALUES

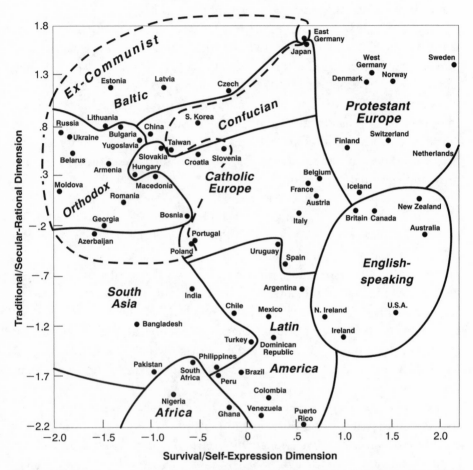

Source: Reproduced with permission from Ronald Inglehart and Wayne E. Baker, "Modernization, Cultural Change, and the Persistence of Traditional Values," *American Sociological Review* 65 (Feb. 2000), 29.

The U.S., with its low T/SR score clearly seen in Figure 10–1, stands out as an anomaly among wealthy nations. This belies the American conceit of living on the leading edge of social progress. Not only does most of northern Europe have higher S/SE scores, but the T/SR score of the U.S. is about the same as Bangladesh's.

The poorest and unhappiest places on earth are those that are clustered in the lower left of Figures 10–1 and 10–2—impoverished, tradi-

FIGURE 10–2   THE INTERACTION OF PROSPERITY, SELF-EXPRESSION, AND
TRADITIONAL VALUES

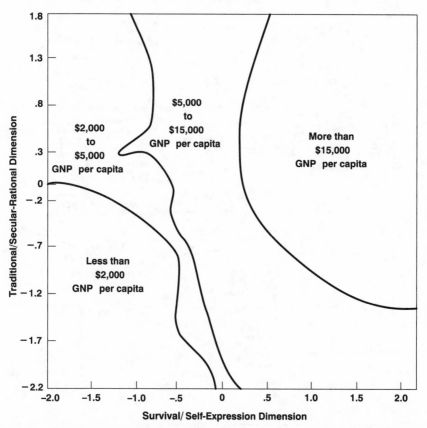

Source: Reproduced with permission from Ronald Inglehart and Wayne E. Baker, "Modernization, Cultural Change, and the Persistence of Traditional Values," *American Sociological Review* 65 (Feb. 2000), 30.

tional societies where unhappy citizens neither freely express their views nor execute their life choices.

The schemas of Figures 10–1 and 10–2 are not entirely the result of age-old static forces. Without fifty years of communism, the Baltic nations and the Czech Republic would most likely have found themselves in the upper right corner of the graph along with the rest of their northern European brethren. Data collected over long periods of time reveal that significant changes can occur in both S/SE and T/SR over relatively brief periods, as is shown in Figure 10–3.

FIGURE 10–3   CHANGES IN SELF-EXPRESSION AND TRADITIONAL VALUES OVER TIME

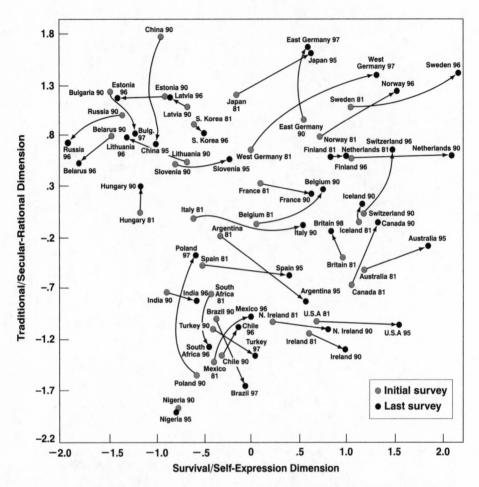

Source: Reproduced with permission from Ronald Inglehart and Wayne E. Baker, "Modernization, Cultural Change, and the Persistence of Traditional Values," *American Sociological Review* 65 (Feb. 2000), 40.

The movements seen in Figure 10–3 are systematic and not simply random fluctuations or experimental error. Over time, almost all of the developed nations significantly increased their S/SE scores, while those in the developing world moved relatively little. Among ex-Communist countries, Figure 10–3 reveals an even more striking finding. As most of these nations experienced economic collapse, their S/SE scores fell. This reinforces the point that prosperity influences S/SE, which is a proxy for personal happiness, and not the other way around. Since S/SE drives democracy, this does not bode well for the ex-Soviet world.

The clustering of nations by culture in Figure 10–1 shows that culture influences wealth, S/SE, and T/SR, more than religion does. This is confirmed by sophisticated statistical techniques showing that S/SE and T/SR scores correlate with many factors, including a Communist history and the proportions of the population working in the service, industrial, and agricultural sectors, independent of wealth or religion.[15]

As we've already discussed, the S/SE score correlates best with wealth. The degree to which people trust others seems to be the key factor that connects wealth and S/SE. As individuals grow wealthier and ascend Maslow's pyramid, they become more accepting and trusting of strangers. Economists and sociologists have grown increasingly aware of the "radius of trust" phenomenon—how far outside the confines of the immediate family a person is willing to believe the words of others and to depend upon their actions. Fukuyama points out that even within nations, the radius of trust can vary greatly. He blames Sicily's poor economic condition relative to the Italian north on the minuscule southern radius of trust: "Southern Italy is the home of the Mafia and bribe politics. You cannot explain the difference between northern and southern Italy in terms of formal institutions."[16] The Inglehart/Welzel Hypothesis suggests that the reverse is actually the case—wealth extends the radius of trust, not the other way around.

THE SCIENCE OF ECONOMIC GROWTH

It was not long before economists got into the act. The economic approach to the effect of culture and institutions centers on a widely used compilation of statistics known as the Summers-Heston dataset.[*] I'm indebted to Professor Robert Barro, who has done much of this work, for supplying the graphs from the second edition of his *Economic Growth* to illustrate these data.

---

[*]   Named after its original compilers, economists Robert Summers and Alan Heston. These data are also referred to as the Penn World Tables.

The basic technique involves sophisticated statistical analysis of a wide range of factors that are believed to influence economic growth, such as educational level, fertility rates, life expectancy, amount of public and private investment, and so forth. The effects of all of these factors can be measured, which in turn leaves a part of the economic growth that cannot be explained by them. Economists then correlate this "unexplained part" of the growth with the factor of interest.

Even if you're unfamiliar with the statistical techniques of multiple regression that are involved, the graphs are not difficult to understand. Let's examine, for example, the relationship between the *growth* of per capita GDP and total GDP itself that is shown in Figure 10–4. This graph demonstrates a high negative correlation between the two. Simply put, the economies of poor nations tend to grow faster than the economies of rich nations. In plain English, poor nations have a tendency to

FIGURE 10–4   ECONOMIC GROWTH VERSUS WEALTH

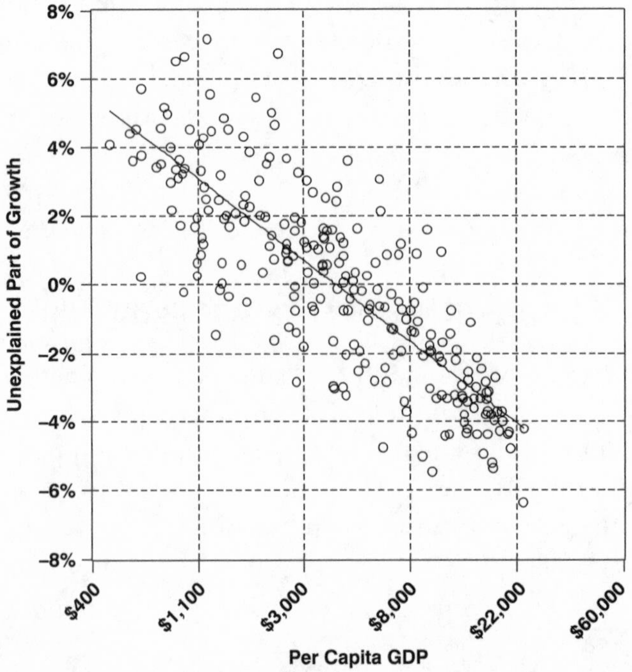

Source: Reproduced with permission of the authors and modified from Robert J. Barro and Xavier Sala-i-Martin, *Economic Growth*, 2d ed. (Cambridge, MA: MIT Press, 2004).

catch up to rich ones, as happened after 1960 in the East Asian Tiger nations, which experienced real growth rates as high as 6% per year.

Pundits have declared the sustained high growth rates seen in these initially poor nations to be "miracles." They were no such thing; rather, they were the normal course of events following the acquisition of open markets, rule of law, and secure property rights by a poor modern nation. If this seems familiar, recall that we've already screened this movie in Chapter 8 with the story of the Japanese "miracles" following the Meiji restoration and World War II.

Once such nations approach a Western standard of living, they no longer grow as rapidly. During the early years of the Cold War, high growth rates in the Soviet Union seemingly corroborated Nikita Khruschchev's famous boast to the U.S., "We will bury you." (He was speaking economically.) That serious analysts during the 1950s and 1960s were genuinely concerned about the strength of the Soviet economy seems almost comical today, but such was the fever pitch of Cold War paranoia. Of course, we need not have worried: The high Soviet growth rates, to the extent that they weren't fictitious, represented the natural course of events in a backward but developing nation, not that of a looming juggernaut.

Recall "the daughter-in-law who doesn't speak." The introduction of even the most basic modern technologies into a preindustrial society works miracles. Growth comes more slowly to nations that are at the leading edge of technology. Two percent productivity growth, while impressive in an advanced nation, is disappointing in an underdeveloped one.

We've repeatedly emphasized the importance of property rights and the rule of law. How well do the empirical data stack up? Figure 10–5 shows the effect that the "rule of law" index from the *International Country Risk Guide* has on the "unexplained" growth part.

The real-world relationship is somewhat messy because the index measures the strength of the legal system more than it gauges the protection it provides private property. For example, in 1982, the scale assigned the then-Communist nations of Hungary and Poland ratings of six and five, respectively, on a seven-point scale (corresponding to scores of 0.83 and 0.67 in Figure 10–5). Even so, the overall trend is clear: The overwhelming majority of countries with high ratings exhibit positive unexplained growth, and the majority of nations with low ratings have

FIGURE 10–5   ECONOMIC GROWTH VERSUS RULE OF LAW

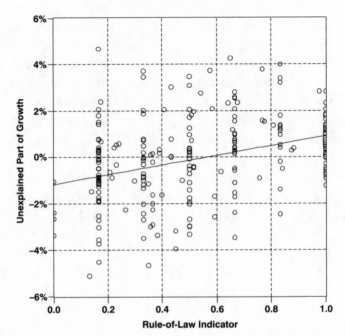

Source: Reproduced with permission of the authors and modified from Robert J. Barro and Xavier Sala-i-Martin,
Economic Growth.

low unexplained growth. Other researchers have confirmed these findings. More recently, economists Robert Hall and Charles Jones found a
fairly high statistical correlation between what they called "social infrastructure"—institutions and government policies supportive of property
rights and the rule of law—and worker productivity.[*]

Economists Bradford DeLong and Andrei Schleifer performed a
clever historical study in which they examined the effect of property
rights upon economic growth in Europe over a period of several hundred years. Since precise long-run political and economic data are hard
to come by, they did the best with what they had. First, the authors sim-

---

[*]   At the macroeconomic level, "worker productivity" is GDP per hour worked and is thus an
excellent measure of average wealth. See Robert E. Hall and Charles I. Jones, "Why Do Some
Countries Produce So Much More Worker Output Than Others?" *Quarterly Journal of Economics*
114 (1999): 83–116.

ply labeled national governments in any given century as either absolutist or nonabsolutist, reasoning that the latter would protect property better than the former. Next, they measured the population increase of the largest cities in those nations as a rough proxy for economic growth.

The correlation between type of government and urban growth was stunning—almost without exception, urban populations grew much faster in nonabsolutist nations than in absolutist ones. DeLong and Schleifer ascribed the shift in the economic and demographic center of Europe from south to north that occurred after 1500 as the direct result of the rise of nonabsolutist, property-respecting governments north of the Alps.[17]

Another important determinant of growth, and one of great political importance, centers on the size of government. The war cry of the political right trumpets the negative effect of government spending on economic growth. Just how bad is it, really? Figure 10–6 demonstrates that a mildly negative effect of big government is just barely visible and not as

FIGURE 10–6   ECONOMIC GROWTH VERSUS SIZE OF GOVERNMENT

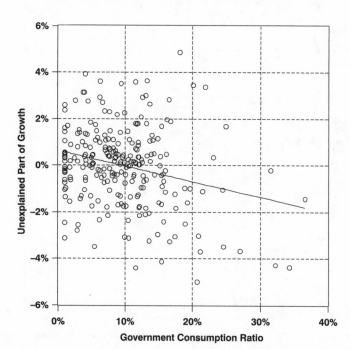

Source: Reproduced with permission of the authors and modified from Robert J. Barro and Xavier Sala-i-Martin, *Economic Growth*.

impressive as the rule-of-law graph. Without the computed trend line shown on the graph, the effect of big government is invisible.

Economists have found a stronger relationship between growth and the investment ratio—the percentage of GDP that is invested by both the government and private sector, as shown in Figure 10–7. The positive correlation of growth with investment exemplifies reverse causation; growth produces increased investment, not the reverse. Professor Barro has teased this out statistically by looking at lagged correlations, similar to those used by Welzel and Inglehart, to establish the flow of causation from wealth to self-expression to democracy. In the case of growth and investment, prior growth correlates better with later investment than prior investment correlates with later growth. Therefore, growth leads to investment, not the opposite.[18] This is consistent

FIGURE 10–7   ECONOMIC GROWTH VERSUS INVESTMENT LEVEL

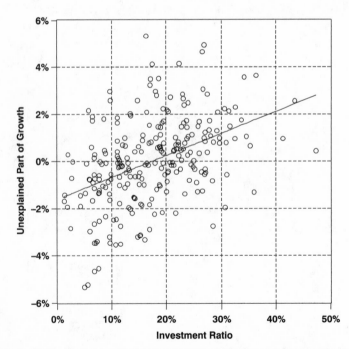

Source: Reproduced with permission of the authors and modified from Robert J. Barro and Xavier Sala-i-Martin, *Economic Growth*.

FIGURE 10–8   ECONOMIC GROWTH VERSUS DEMOCRACY

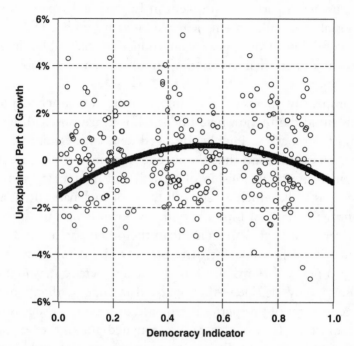

Source: Reproduced with permission of the authors and modified from Robert J. Barro and Xavier Sala-i-Martin, *Economic Growth*.

with theory—private parties choose to invest only when high growth promises high returns.

Finally, there is democracy itself. The relationship to growth, shown in Figure 10–8, is curious, in the shape of an inverted-U. Up to a point, democratization helps. The elimination of the most onerous features of totalitarianism supports growth.[*] But once the government further advances democratic institutions, growth actually suffers.

Professor Barro suggests that the detrimental effects of advanced democracy are caused by the soak-the-rich propensities of populist regimes,

---

[*]   Here, Professor Barro uses the Gastil indicator of civil liberties to measure democratic development. See Raymond D. Gastil, *Freedom in the World* (Westport, Connecticut: Greenwood Publishing Group, 1982).

but other causes are not hard to imagine. Democracies tend to subsidize failing industries, a particular problem in Europe and Japan. Democratic institutions also provide an emancipated citizenry with a wide variety of socially useful but economically unproductive charitable, intellectual, and political outlets that are not open to citizens in more repressive countries.

The propensity to invest also suffers from "too much democracy." Economists find the highest investment ratios in nations with intermediate levels of democracy. Highly advanced democracies tend to decrease the return on capital, and thus the incentive to invest.

The cause-effect relationship of growth and democracy shows up in Barro's data as well, which agree with those of Inglehart and Welzel and also confirm the original Lipset hypothesis: Prior economic growth correlates better with later democracy than the other way around. Prosperity is primarily responsible for democracy, while democracy itself does little for prosperity.[19] Barro also found that democratic development can trail prosperity by decades—the lagged data suggest that, on average, about a generation of prosperity is required to produce a successful democratic transition. In Chapter 8, we touched upon the explosion of Spanish wealth during the Franco dictatorship and the highly successful democratic transition that followed it. Liberal historians have pointedly ignored this sequence of events.

Similarly, vigorous democratic institutions did not evolve in Chile, Taiwan, and Korea for decades after those nations began to approach a Western level of wealth. The process grinds with glacial slowness; enthusiasm about the prospects for democracy in China, even after nearly a generation of rapid economic growth, requires both optimism and patience.

Can supply-side tax cuts, increased spending on education, or other sorts of politically driven economic and social tinkering increase growth in an advanced, prosperous liberal democracy? Barro is dubious:

> It would probably be feasible to raise the long-term growth rate by a few tenths of a percentage point by cutting tax rates and nonproductive government spending or by eliminating harmful regulations, [but] there is no evidence that increases in infrastructure investment, research subsidies, or educational spending would help a lot. Basically, 2% per capita growth seems to be about as good as it gets in the long run for a country that is already rich.[20]

WHY DOES IT MATTER?

At some point, the thoughtful reader will begin to question this book's obsession with the material aspects of this world. What is the use of economic growth if Western man's worldly success does not appear to have purchased the average citizen even a modicum of happiness, let alone existential or spiritual fulfillment? Ever-increasing prosperity has brought with it higher levels of drug abuse, job insecurity, and family disruption, to say nothing of the envy and resentment that a substantial portion of the third world, most particularly its Muslim population, feels for rich Western nations. To paraphrase John Kenneth Galbraith, there are other, more important measures of an individual's worth and purpose beyond the question, "What have you done today to increase the nation's gross domestic product?"

As with the debates over living standards early in the Industrial Revolution, such discussions often degenerate into ideological fisticuffs over the effects of globalization, neocolonialism, and the role of the state. In such a political minefield, we gain insight only by forming hypotheses and testing them with objective data.

The time has now come to examine the relationship between wealth and happiness itself. Has the rapid increase in the wealth of the West harmed or improved the well-being of its inhabitants? More bluntly, is all this wealth making us any happier? Is it even possible to answer such questions?

In recent decades, psychologists and sociologists have obliged us and developed widespread and sophisticated measurements of human satisfaction. Over nearly half a century, a great mass of research has observed human well-being as mankind has grown ever more prosperous. A typical example, the General Social Survey, samples various sociologic measures in the U.S. Consider the following question from the Survey:

> Taken all together, how would you say things are these days—would you say that you are very happy, pretty happy, or not too happy?

Since 1970, the number of Americans who answered "very happy" has held fairly constant at about 30%. The World Values Survey (WVS) and Eurobarometer Surveys have provided even more detailed and systematic data on well-being.

THE SCIENCE OF HAPPINESS

Many will object to the application of a one-size-fits-all barometer of happiness across the broad canvas of the world's disparate cultures. Researchers have found, however, that all societies explicitly embrace and
define the concept of happiness and well-being in nearly the same fashion.
That should not be a surprising finding. After all, at base we're all human.

In the rest of this chapter, we shall use the term "well-being" in its
psychological, as opposed to its economic, sense—that is, as a synonym for
happiness. Sociologists have found that in almost all societies, the same
four indicators predict well-being: economic status, employment, health,
and the state of the family.[21] Of the family-related factors, marital status
proves the most critical. Late night comedians aside, married people are, as
a group, far happier than single people. Unemployment causes unhappiness, even when income from other sources is adequate. That is to say, the
deleterious effects of unemployment upon well-being are independent of
income; stripping a worker of his job will, on average, make him much
less happy, even if his employment income is completely replaced. In the
words of one researcher, "an enormous amount of extra income would be
required to compensate for people having no work."[22]

In addition, quantitative measures of happiness have real value as pre-
dictive tools. Individuals with elevated happiness scores have very low in-
cidences of psychosomatic illness and work loss, above-average longevity,
and even higher than normal brainwave activity in the left frontal area.[23]

Another frequently raised objection to happiness surveys is that they
fail to take into account the different cultural and linguistic translations
of "happy" and "satisfied." Switzerland provides a superb laboratory in
which to study this concern, with its German-, French-, and Italian-
speaking populations. Data show that all three linguistic groups have
significantly higher happiness scores than their cultural cousins in Germany, France, and Italy. This makes it unlikely that language plays a
significant role in happiness surveys, at least among the three different
Swiss nationalities.[24]

Political and military stress also make people unhappy. Multiple studies demonstrated a drop in well-being in the U.S. between the late
1950s and the early 1970s, most likely related to Cold War tensions. In
the late 1970s, as the specter of nuclear Armageddon began to recede,

well-being returned to baseline levels.[25] Yet, even when sophisticated statistical testing is used to separate out these important attributes, economic status remains a powerful driver of happiness and well-being.

Some have also questioned the causality of economic status and happiness. Is it not possible that the happy become the most successful? No. In the first place, in all societies studied, people identify wealth as important to their happiness. Second, the recent dramatic drop of average measured well-being in ex-Communist nations that experienced economic crisis demonstrates that poverty causes unhappiness, not the other way around.

ARE WE HAVING FUN YET?

Figure 10–9 shows the trend in perceived well-being in four representative European nations over the quarter century between 1973 and 1998. It plots the percentage of respondents from these nations who described

FIGURE 10–9   SATISFACTION INDEX

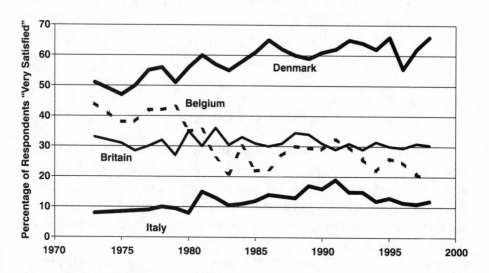

Source: Data from Ronald Inglehart and Hans-Dieter Klingemann, "Genes, Culture, Democracy, and Happiness," in *Culture and Subjective Well-Being*, E. Diener and Mark Suh, eds. (Cambridge: MIT Press, 2000), 167.

themselves as "very satisfied" (as opposed to "fairly satisfied," "not very satisfied," or "not at all satisfied").

Strikingly, Europeans have not gotten much happier during a period when real per capita GDP increased by about 60%. Even more puzzling are the extreme differences between the Danes, with an average of 60% of their population very satisfied, and the Italians, who average only about 11%. Britons fall about halfway between the two. Figure 10–9 also shows that Belgians became more depressed during that quarter century. What was the source of this melancholy? The answer likely has to do with the eruption of the cultural and linguistic (French-speaking versus Dutch-speaking) tensions in Belgium in the past few decades, which resulted in a more fragmented political apparatus. This is similar to the drops noted in happiness in the U.S. during the Cold War and in the ex-Communist world after 1990.

Sociologists cannot explain these differences among nations by economics alone—the gaps in per capita wealth among these four nations remained relatively small throughout the period. Clearly, there must be cultural factors involved. Stereotypes—the good-humored Dane and the dour Belgian—take us only so far; the low scores of the outwardly ebullient Italians come as a bit of a surprise.

Japan supplies the most dramatic example of money's failure to buy happiness. Between 1958 and 1987, a period when per capita GDP in Japan increased fivefold, the Japanese happiness scale did not budge.[26]

NATIONS, SAD AND HAPPY

We gain a different perspective on happiness when we examine the relationship between per capita GDP and average perceived well-being. Figures 10–10 and 10–11 graph yet another satisfaction scale—a composite index of happiness and satisfaction from the WVS—versus per capita GDP. Over a sufficiently wide range, national wealth correlates loosely with national mood.

The left side of Figure 10–10 shows a large spread in happiness among poor nations that is attributable to the inclusion of ex-Communist nations. When we eliminate the ex-Communist countries, most of

FIGURE 10–10   WELL-BEING VERSUS PER CAPITA GDP

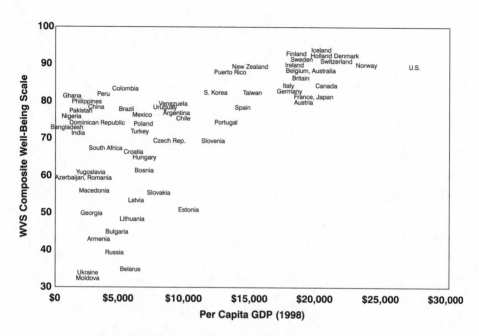

Source: Data from Ronald Inglehart and Hans-Dieter Klingemann, "Genes, Culture, Democracy, and Happiness," in *Culture and Subjective Well-Being,* 172–73 and Maddison, *The World Economy: A Millennial Perspective,* 264, 276–79.

whom experienced large drops in happiness as a result of the sudden worsening of political, social, and economic conditions, the correlation becomes tighter, as Figure 10–11 illustrates. The formerly Communist nations that have made the transition to a market economy and democracy most successfully—Poland, the Czech Republic, and Hungary—have happiness measures that are at the bottom of the Western range, but are still higher than those of their ex-Communist peers.

Fragmentary evidence suggests that the deterioration in the national mood in the ex-Communist nations is a relatively recent affair. For example, in the Tambov region of Russia, a composite happiness score fell from 70 to 39 between 1981 and 1995. Scores for the Hungarians, who have experienced much less social and economic dislocation than the Russians have, fell much less—from 74.5 in 1981 to 62 in 1990, before rising slightly to 65 in 1998.[27]

FIGURE 10–11   NON-COMMUNIST WELL-BEING VERSUS PER CAPITA GDP

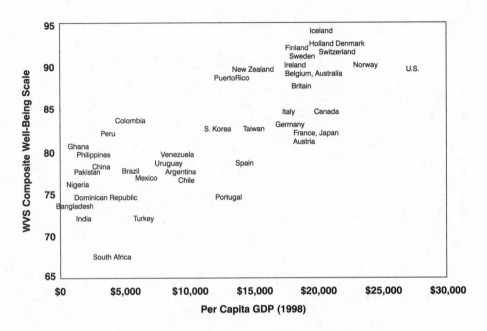

Source: Data from Ronald Inglehart and Hans-Dieter Klingemann, "Genes, Culture, Democracy, and Happiness," in *Culture and Subjective Well-Being*, 172–73 and Maddison, *The World Economy: A Millennial Perspective*, 264, 276–79.

The effect of national wealth on national well-being that is seen in Figure 10–11 is relatively small. The right side of the graph, which displays nations with per capita GDP above $15,000, demonstrates almost no relationship between wealth and happiness—only below this level does wealth become a factor.* As we've already noted, the data demonstrate that national wealth and national well-being correlate only loosely. For example, Colombians are happier than Austrians, despite the four-fold difference in per capita GDP.

---

* Those familiar with economics will recognize that the utility of wealth is logarithmic—that is, happiness is gained only with geometric increments of wealth. The arithmetic scale used on the x-axes in Figures 10–10 and 10–11 distorts this effect; the theoretical increment of happiness obtained by increasing per capita GDP from $15,000 to $30,000 is only one-fifteenth of that obtained by moving from $1,000 to $15,000.

WELL-BEING BY THE POUND

Within nations, however, wealth matters a great deal. In study after study, without exception, the richest individual citizens prove to be the most satisfied and the poorest citizens, the least satisfied. Figure 10–12 displays the substantial difference in happiness between the wealthiest and poorest citizens in twelve representative nations.

Figure 10–13 details this phenomenon with even small income grada-tions—in this case, in the U.S. in 1973. Note the smooth and curvilinear relationship—the gains in happiness are greatest at low incomes, then taper off at higher incomes. Some sociologists have interpreted this kind of graph, as well as the apparent lack of a wealth effect on happiness in wealthy nations that was observed in Figure 10–12, as demonstrating a "threshold effect." In other words, once a certain level of income is reached (roughly $8,000 in the year of this study, 1973), survival and safety needs have been met, and further increases of wealth do not result in a further improvement in well-being.

This is probably not the case. Economists have long hypothesized that people perceive wealth "logarithmically," according to proportion-ate increases in income. Theoretically, they say, you should gain a simi-lar increment of well-being each time your income increases by a given

FIGURE 10–12   PERSONAL HAPPINESS RATING VERSUS WEALTH

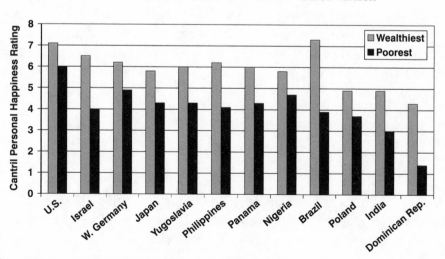

Source: Data from H. Cantril, *The Pattern of Human Concerns*, 365–77.

FIGURE 10–13   INCOME VERSUS HAPPINESS IN THE U.S., 1973

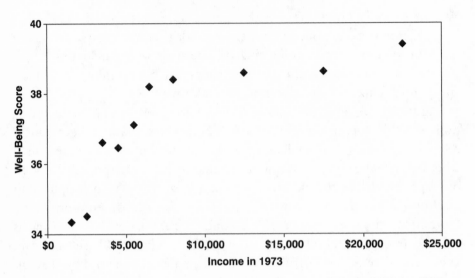

Source: Data from Ed Diener et al., "The Relationship Between Income and Subjective Well-Being: Relative or Absolute?" *Social Indicators Research* 28 (1993): 208.

factor—if you receive a certain increase in happiness by doubling your income from $50,000 to $100,000, you will obtain a similar increase by doubling it yet again to $200,000. Figure 10–14 demonstrates that this is indeed the case—one of the rare examples in which human beings actually behave as economists predict. This graph is identical to Figure 10–13, except that it represents wealth logarithmically on the horizontal scale, as opposed to the more conventional arithmetic representation in Figure 10–13. The economists were right after all—well-being increases with the *logarithm* of wealth.

YOUR WIFE'S BROTHER-IN-LAW

Money, then, does buy happiness, but only in a relative sense. Absolute wealth matters less than wealth relative to your neighbors. According to Karl Marx:

FIGURE 10–14   INCOME VERSUS HAPPINESS IN THE U.S., 1973, LOGARITHMIC SCALE

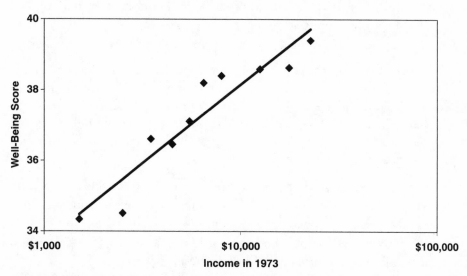

Source: Data from Ed Diener et al., "The Relationship Between Income and Subjective Well-Being: Relative or Absolute?" *Social Indicators Research* 28 (1993): 208.

A house may be large or small; as long as the surrounding houses are equally small it satisfies all social demands for a dwelling. If a palace rises besides the little house, the little house shrinks into a hut.[28]

Or, as more tartly put by H. L. Mencken, a wealthy man is one who earns more than his wife's brother-in-law.[*]

Just how we define our peer group is an important subtlety. All people gauge their wealth primarily against that of their friends and neighbors. The person earning $100,000 per year in an economically depressed rural community is likely to be far happier than someone earning the same amount—even adjusted upward for purchasing power—on Manhattan's

---

[*]   This is more than a joke; a woman is 20% more likely to be employed if her sister's husband makes more than her husband. See David Neumark, and Andrew Postlewaite, "Relative Income Concerns and the Rise in Married Women's Employment," University of Pennsylvania, unpublished data, 1996. Yet another piquant description of this phenomenon comes from economic historian Charles Kindleberger: "There is nothing so disturbing to one's well-being and judgment as to see a friend get rich." See Kindleberger, *Manias, Crashes, and Panics*, 4th ed. (New York: John Wiley & Sons, 2000), 15.

Upper East Side.* This "neighbor effect," one of the bedrocks of human nature, applies in many other areas, as well. Economist Paul Krugman describes his unhappiness as a well-paid, highly-respected academic with a secure position in one of the world's great universities:

> I had a very pleasant job that paid quite well and received lots of invitations to conferences around the world. Compared with 99.9% of humanity, I had nothing to complain about. But of course that isn't the way the human animal is constructed. My emotional reference group consisted of the most successful economists of my generation, and I was not generally counted among their number.[29]

Modern telecommunications may be breaking down the local nature of the "neighbor effect." As recently as fifty years ago, Stalin and Mao successfully insulated a quarter of the world's population from the knowledge of its own destitution. Today, North Korea may be the last nation on earth able to turn this appalling trick. In an increasingly globalized society, the wealth of those at a distance acquires real significance. Closer to home, the modern media makes inner-city slum dwellers or even the comfortable members of the middle class more aware of their poverty relative to the lifestyles of the rich and famous that they will never meet. Abroad, the denizen of the Arab street must face up daily to the material shortcomings of his lifestyle as compared with that in the West.

It is not too much of a stretch to say that the wealthy among us are the cause of our unhappiness. The wealthier they are and the closer their proximity, either real or electronic, the more miserable they make us feel. If this is true, then societies with the smallest inequalities of wealth should be the happiest. Is this actually the case? Yes. The nations at the top of the WVS combined subjective well-being scale—Iceland, Netherlands, Denmark, Switzerland, Finland, Sweden, Ireland, and Norway—all have avowedly redistributionist tax policies and narrow income distributions.

---

* Not all of the data are consistent with this hypothesis. For example, Diener et. al. failed to demonstrate a primarily relative wealth effect. However, they also failed to validate the alternative hypothesis—that well-being was related to the satisfaction of nonrelative survival needs. See Ed Diener et. al., "The Relationship Between Income and Subjective Well-Being: Relative or Absolute?" *Social Indicators Research* 28 (1993): 208.

FIGURE 10–15   WELL-BEING VERSUS INCOME INEQUALITY

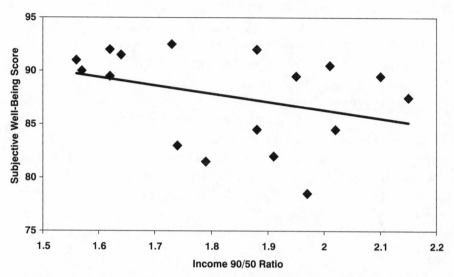

Source: Data from the Luxembourg Income Study, http://www.lisproject.org/keyfigures/ineqtable.htm, and Ronald Inglehart and Hans-Dieter Klingemann, "Genes, Culture, Democracy, and Happiness," in *Culture and Subjective Well-Being*, 172–73.

A good way to measure the "neighbor effect" calculates the ratio of the income of those at the 90th percentile to those at the median—the 50th percentile. Figure 10–15 shows the WVS well-being scale versus this measure. The downward-sloping trend line illustrates a loose negative correlation between wealth inequality and happiness. More sophisticated analyses, like those described above on the Summers-Heston dataset, demonstrate the same phenomenon.[30]

Even within nations, differing degrees of income inequality influence happiness. Israel's diversity of communal organizations provides a laboratory for the study of the income inequality-happiness dynamic. In 1977, a group of sociologists at Hebrew University in Jerusalem studied two *moshavim*—cooperative societies. The first, which they labeled "Isos," paid all of its members equally, while the second, "Anisos," paid its members according to production and rank. The average Cantril score, which measures happiness on a scale of zero to ten, was 7.88 in Isos and 7.25 in Anisos.[31]

Although this difference was small, this was nonetheless a highly significant result for several reasons. First, the Cantril ratings were tightly clustered in both groups, making this difference statistically significant. For example, 20% of Isos members rated themselves as a perfect "ten" on the Cantril scale, while none of the Anisos members did. Second, South American immigrants dominated the Isos membership, while the Anisos membership was primarily European. Since South Americans tend to score lower than Europeans on well-being and S/SE measures, the higher well-being score in the South American-dominated Isos community is particularly striking. Third, Anisos members were better educated than Isos members were, a factor that also correlates with happiness. Finally, the average income at Anisos was one-third higher than at Isos. The fact that all four of the above indicators *should* have made the Anisos residents happier makes it all the more remarkable that they were not.[32]

To summarize:

- Within a single nation or society, wealth is an important, but far from the only, determinant of happiness.

- Across nations, this is less true. National wealth only loosely correlates with national happiness; at the global level, cultural and historical factors become more important.

- Because of the relative nature of wealth perception—the neighbor effect—increases in aggregate national wealth that result from economic growth do not make nations any happier. Although a nation's wealthiest citizens tend to be its happiest, the neighbor effect dictates that the nation as a whole does not get happier as it gets richer. Neither, however, does a nation become more unhappy as it grows wealthier. The fellow travelers of increasing productivity—increasing demands on time, stress, and lower job security—seem not to have taken much of a toll. (It might be argued that increasing wealth does make people happier, which is exactly counterbalanced by the stresses of modern life.) In 1995, economist Richard Easterlin asked the rhetorical question, Will raising the incomes of all increase the happiness of all? The answer is clearly no.[33] What is good for the individual is not necessarily good for the nation as a whole.

THE MOVING TARGETS OF POVERTY AND WEALTH

Modern man is on a sort of "hedonic treadmill." As nations grow wealthier, they must produce an ever-increasing amount of goods and services to maintain the same degree of satisfaction among citizens.[34] A description elicited a generation ago from an Indian farmer earning $10 per month provides a simple illustration of how this phenomenon operates:

> I want a son and a piece of land since I am now working on land owned by other people. I would like to construct a house of my own and have a cow for milk and butter. I would also like to buy some better clothing for my wife. *If I could do this, then I would be happy.*[35] (Italics added)

Note that the farmer did not even mention the modern devices considered essential for happiness by today's third-world inhabitants—the refrigerator, television, and motorbike. His material frame of reference was as different from that of his modern counterparts as the modern Chinese peasant's frame of reference is from the average Westerner's.

If the concept of wealth is a moving target, so, too, is the definition of poverty. Even the poorest of today's Americans would have been considered quite well-off in 1500, while in another five hundred years, the lot of today's average Westerner will seem a miasma of penury and barbarism. The question of whether the proportion of the world's population living in poverty is growing or shrinking must be qualified—do we mean poverty in the *absolute* sense or poverty in the *relative* sense?

In the *absolute* sense, we are winning the battle. As seen in Chapter 1, even if we discard per capita GDP as meaningless, life expectancy, literacy, and child mortality rates among the earth's most wretched have improved dramatically over the past several decades, just as the specter of mass starvation largely disappeared from the globe half a century ago. (The world's last great mass starvations, in China and India during the mid-twentieth century, were more manmade than natural. The more recent famines in sub-Saharan Africa have been stopped well short of their full deadly potential by an international system of trade and aid supported by modern transportation.)

In a *relative* sense, we are just as clearly losing the battle. The gap between the wealthiest and the poorest nations and the disparities of wealth within nations have dramatically increased during the past century. The poor and their advocates will draw scant comfort from the fact that the real incomes of society's most impoverished people have actually risen and their quality of life has improved during the modern era.

This modern variety of poverty, then, depends solely upon the degree of income dispersion; we can ameliorate it only if we redistribute wealth. The forced leveling of income, within limits, will reduce poverty and improve a society's overall well-being, but we will have to sacrifice some growth in the process. In the next chapter, we shall explore the trade-off between growth and economic egalitarianism and examine how it has been handled on opposite sides of the Atlantic.

CHAPTER ELEVEN

The Great Trade-Off

THE GREAT PARADOX OF ECONOMIC GROWTH is that the same mechanisms that create great wealth also give rise to great inequalities in its distribution. Private property provides a powerful incentive to produce wealth for oneself while simultaneously denying that same wealth to others. Wealth does trickle down to the rest of the population, but oft times not fast enough to avoid political strife and worse.

It cannot be any other way. If individuals cannot keep what they earn, they will not produce. If, on the other hand, those who produce the most are allowed to keep what they earn, inequalities will increase, and as inequality rises, societal well-being deteriorates. This is particularly true in a technologically minded world where an individual's unique talents can be "scaled up" to an almost infinite degree by the ability to instantaneously transmit his or her output across the globe. The trade-off between vigorous economic growth and income inequality are both necessary consequences of the emphasis on property rights and the rule of law.

Property rights, even without the income inequality that they engender, are not an unalloyed blessing. They are often expensive to maintain. Rendered in the jargon of economics, property rights necessitate "enforcement costs": an extensive judicial system, police, and, at times, even a military and national security apparatus. Not infrequently, these costs exceed the economic benefits that are gained by securing alienable property.

The history of the beaver-hunting Montagnes Indians in colonial Labrador provides an instructive illustration. For thousands of years, the cost of establishing individual property rights across endless tracts of beaver habitat greatly outweighed the modest economic benefits brought by these animals. By default, the tribe considered the beavers to be communal property, to be hunted by all. As late as the mid-seventeenth century, the first Europeans to visit the Montagnes noted the absence of private property rights over beaver ranges. Then, the Hudson Bay Company arrived and offered astronomical prices for the pelts. That changed everything. Suddenly, the establishment of property rights over hunting grounds became a paying proposition.[1]

The Plains Indians never did establish property rights over their hunting grounds because buffalo and other game were of little economic value. Even if they were, the ranges of the hunted animals were so vast that the enforcement costs would have been prohibitive. In modern society as well, some property rights may simply be too expensive to maintain—downloadable music and Sylvester Stallone movies come most easily to mind.

Enforcement expenses vary greatly among societies. In relative terms, property can be protected far more cheaply in the United States than it can be in Afghanistan. In Kansas City, all that is needed is the local police, while Kabul requires the services of the U.S. Army's Special Forces. In Kansas City, most people perceive themselves as stakeholders—law-abiding citizens with a strong interest in the safety of everyone's possessions, not simply their own. In Kabul, they do not. Where stakeholders abound, few steal, enforcement costs are low, and property is easily secured. Where the populace is disaffected and highly distrustful of authority, the cost of protecting property rights mushrooms, and the economy suffers accordingly.

This phenomenon, which I call the "stakeholder effect," provides the likely reason for the seeming imperviousness of the Western economies to seven decades of progressively increasing government spending and intrusion. Yes, the dead hand of the state claims an ever-larger portion of the economy, but most of that increase takes the form of middle-class entitlements. Spending by individuals—whether their own money or money redistributed to them through the various social welfare systems—distorts markets much less than direct government spending for goods and services does. When the public spends money that is redistrib-uted to them by social welfare programs, the spending reflects the true economic value of the goods and services, while government spending does not. In other words, 30% of GDP redistributed to citizens in the form of transfer payments distorts prices much less than the same amount spent directly by the government on goods and services does.[*] People who are not starving or lacking in shelter tend not to steal.[2]

THE NEW ROBBER BARON ERA

The stakeholder effect is far more fragile than we imagine. As Harvard Law School professor Mark Roe points out, Argentina had the world's eighth-highest per capita GDP at the turn of the last century. Its debt obligations ranked among the most secure in the world, and commenta-tors opined that its political stability was as high as Britain's. Boatload af-ter boatload of Europeans immigrated there.

Although it was not obvious at the time, all was not well in Argen-tina. Like the rest of Latin America and Spain, its land ownership was highly concentrated among a few wealthy landowners, and when the Great Depression hit, millions of landless tenant farmers streamed into the cities searching for work. The destitute millions became sitting ducks for the demagoguery of Juan Perón, who pandered to them shamelessly and derailed a once-flourishing economy.[2]

If wealth and income inequalities grow large enough, the average citizen's well-being will suffer to the point that he no longer feels like a stake-holder—as happened in Argentina. The cost of enforcing property rights will then skyrocket, and at some point economic growth will begin to suffer.

---

[*] This is analogous to the "Deadweight Loss of Christmas" phenomenon. The cost of Christmas presents, on average, exceeds the value to their recipients—i.e., the average recipient would be willing to pay less for each present than the giver actually spent for it. One researcher estimated the total "deadweight" of Christmas presents at $4 billion to $13 billion in the U.S. during the 1992 season. More important, the deadweight losses of the Medicare, Medicaid, and public housing programs are estimated to be between 9% and 39% of expenditures (which themselves totaled 23% of the 2003 fiscal year federal budget.) See Joel Waldfogel, "The Deadweight Loss of Christmas," *American Economic Review* 83 (Dec. 1993): 1328–36.

Just how far down this road has the U.S. traveled? Economists Thomas Piketty and Emmanuel Saez recently examined the broad sweep of income inequality in the U.S. over most of the twentieth century. Figure 11–1 shows the portion of national income earned by the top 1% of income-tax-return filers, before and after capital gains on stocks and property are included. The picture drawn by Piketty and Saez conforms to the popular image of the distribution of twentieth-century American wealth: extreme inequalities at the end of the era of robber barons in the early twentieth century which were reversed by the redistributive tax po-lices of successive Democratic and Republican administrations. Inequality then returned in the 1980s.

Just how much more unequal things have gotten depends on which parameter one examines. The graph of the top percentile in Figure 11–1 suggests that the nation has not yet surpassed the inequality of the early twentieth century. Our perspective changes when we exclude invest-ment earnings and look only at salaries. Here, the inequalities are worse than they were during the era of the robber barons, especially in the cor-porate chief executive's suite. In 1970, the average CEO of a large cor-

FIGURE 11–1   PERCENTAGE OF INCOME EARNED BY TOP 1% OF TAX FILERS

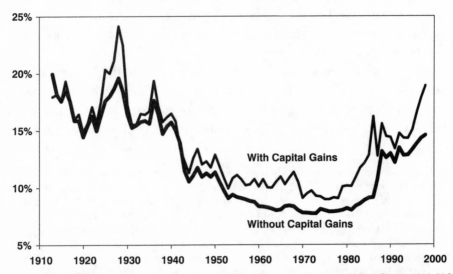

Source: Adapted with permission of the authors from "Income Inequality in the United States, 1913–98," Thomas Piketty and Emmanuel Saez, NBER Working Paper 8467.

poration earned about forty times the wage of the average worker, approximately the same as the income ratio between those at the top and at the bottom of the social scale in late-seventeenth-century England that was described by the early British demographer Gregory King. By 1998, the average CEO collected over *one thousand times* the salary of the average worker. The understated conclusion of Peketty and Saez is that

> the current top wage earners should be able to accumulate amounts of wealth much larger than in the earlier decades. If progressive taxation of income and estates does not counteract this new phenomenon, inequality in wealth and capital income should also start to increase sharply during the next few decades.[3]

The political right romanticizes the laissez-faire of nineteenth-century America as the golden age of capitalist enterprise, free of confiscatory taxation and government interference in private enterprise. The plain facts belie this notion. In the modern West, economies prospered even as tax rates soared and government regulation of industry ballooned. Only the devastation of war temporarily slowed the pace of economic growth. Liberal democracies do have it within their power to smother prosperity, but only by income redistribution and government spending on a near-Communist scale, as occurred in England in the 1960s and 1970s.

History teaches that significant wealth inequality is not as benign as a moderately uncomfortable tax burden is. Large discrepancies in wealth and income can derail seemingly prosperous economies—as happened in Perónist Argentina.

BLOOD ON SAINT PETER'S FIELD

Even the most stable, liberal, free-market nations are not immune from such catastrophes. Post-Napoleonic Britain came closer to prosperity-ending upheaval than is commonly realized. In the early stages of the Industrial Revolution, English workers, attracted by high factory wages, crowded into the fetid slums of the Midlands. During the Napoleonic Wars, weekly pay for semiskilled machine operators reached sixty shillings per week, enough to make the awful conditions of the industrial tenements bearable. The price decreases of the post–Napoleonic period were accompanied by a collapse of wages to a weekly average of twenty-four shillings and the strengthening of England's Corn Laws, which forbade the import of grain and kept domestic grain prices artificially high. This combination of low wages and inflated food prices drove tens of thousands to destitution, many to the brink of starvation and beyond, and destabilized the political landscape.[4]

While England's House of Commons may be the mother of parliaments, it was hardly a representative one, even as recently as the early nineteenth century. An extremely narrow voting franchise skewed parliamentary representation in favor of Britain's South and West. Tory party whim could easily buy, sell, or even cancel elections. The desperate condition of the new urban working class drove demands for parliamentary reform and rallied a growing group of radical politicians.

The reactionary government of Liverpool and Castlereagh, haunted by the memory of the French Revolution and terrified at the prospect of a Jacobin uprising on English soil, misinterpreted the reform movement and imagined insurrection everywhere. In March 1817 the government suspended habeas corpus for nearly a year. The suspension temporarily curtailed radical agitation, but at its restoration, a series of strikes sent Lancashire into turmoil. On the warm, cloudless day of August 16, 1819, reformers marched through Manchester's outskirts and held a meeting in a field near Saint Peter's Church to choose a new parliamentary member. His "election" was illegal, and the rally featured the renowned radical orator, Henry Hunt. Attendance at the rally was enormous, particularly for that era. The best estimates had about 90,000 at the scene, perhaps 60,000 of whom were in Saint Peter's Field itself.

The authorities, already on the alert for caches of nonexistent weapons, surrounded the field with fifteen hundred troops. The orderliness of the procession and gathering bewildered the troops, who panicked and decided to arrest Hunt. With a further turn of twisted logic, the authorities decided that force would have to be used to make the arrest because of the large number at the rally. Swinging swords cleared a path through the tightly packed throng towards Hunt, and the situation rapidly spun out of control. Several hundred bystanders were injured, but the absence of firearms—sabers and truncheons were the weapons of choice—kept the death toll to only eleven.

One of the victims, a veteran of Waterloo named Richard Lees, remarked that at least on the Belgian battlefield, it had been man-to-man;
what happened that day on Saint Peter's Field was murder, pure and
simple.[5] Lees died of his wounds shortly after making that statement.
The massacre was quickly named "Peterloo" and became a cry for political reform. The poet Shelley, in *The Masque of Anarchy*, rhymed:

> I met Murder on the way—,
> He had a mask like Castlereagh—[*]

The violence shocked England and energized the Whigs, the reform
party. In 1833, the Factory Act charged the government with overseeing
industrial safety. In that same year, the first emigration officers ensured that
those making the transatlantic voyage to America were well provisioned.
In 1846, after decades of political skirmishing, Parliament finally repealed
the Corn Laws and ushered in an era of freer international trade, which
reduced the prices of consumer goods, particularly grain.

Three short years later, Parliament struck the Navigation Acts from the
statute books, which eased the lot of the workers by again driving down
grain prices. Despite the cries from the railroad companies of "interference
with property," the Railway Acts moved to improve transportation safety.
Medical health officers oversaw hygiene in the industrial slums, and Parliament dramatically increased the degree of bank regulation. In a brilliant
act of social engineering, Lord Mayor (and later prime minister) Robert
Peel of London organized the first municipal police force. In the
mid-1800s, England witnessed one of the most aggressive extensions of
government authority over commerce and private life ever seen in the
Western world. Nineteenth-century Britain never was the gauzy Valhalla
of laissez-faire that has been romanticized by modern libertarians.[6]

HOOVER, MACARTHUR, ROOSEVELT, AND THE BONUS MARCHERS

A similar sequence of events occurred in the U.S. a century later during
the depths of the Great Depression, when unemployment stood at

---

[*]   Note to American readers: This does indeed rhyme.

one-quarter of the civilian population. In July 1932 Rexford Tugwell, an aide to presidential candidate Franklin Delano Roosevelt, observed:

> By this time, the millions who had no jobs whatsoever were in an advanced stage of desperation. Private charities had practically exhausted their resources, and public agencies were rationing their meager appropriations. Not only wages, but salaries too were being reduced when there were any jobs at all. People with debts faced settlements with no way to meet them. They had to resign themselves to foreclosures of pledged collateral, which might represent the savings of years, perhaps their business properties or homes.[7]

The resemblance of the American scene to that in Germany, where unemployment was even worse and the streets were filled with murderous brown-shirts, was not lost on Tugwell:

> We had no time to study these events carefully, but it was evident that they portended something sinister. Besides, they had a frightening similarity to occurrences at home, which had begun to have the same immediacy.[8]

Millions, out of work and with no prospects, left home to "ride the rods" on freight trains and camped in small groups or in huge, unsanitary Hoovervilles that sprouted across the country. Events came to a head in late July, when unemployed World War I veterans converged on Washington, D.C. to demand that a bonus, promised for 1945, be paid early. President Hoover, fearful of incipient revolution, ordered Army Chief of Staff Douglas MacArthur, assisted by two young aides named Eisenhower and Patton, to clear the protesters from Pennsylvania Avenue and from their adjacent encampment in Anacostia Flats. Hoover's orders to MacArthur, relayed through Secretary of War Patrick J. Hurley, were clear:

> The president has just informed me that the civil government of the District of Columbia had reported to him that it is unable to maintain law and order in the District. You will have United States troops proceed immediately to the scene of the disorder. Surround the affected area and clear it without delay.[9]

Once again, the forces of a liberal democracy advanced on a peaceful crowd with drawn sabers. This time, though, through an accident of military technique—mounted troops, as these soldiers were, can intimidate unarmed opponents with their horses and use the flat edges of their swords without inflicting serious injury—the fuse barely avoided being lit. But the sight of regular army troops attacking unarmed veterans sickened the nation, and whatever chance Herbert Hoover had for reelection disappeared that hot afternoon. Roosevelt, who had been nominated four weeks earlier at Chicago Stadium, concluded that Hoover was finished and was able to take precious time from his campaign to begin planning on the New Deal.[10]

Both Britain and the United States themselves came closer to revolution during those times than many would care to admit.* In the two decades following the Battle of Anacostia Flats, a progressive tax structure and redistributionist social programs lessened economic inequalities in the U.S. Although the data of Piketty and Saez show that economic inequalities have begun to increase in recent decades, the resulting disaffection clearly hasn't reached the crisis proportions of the post-Waterloo and Great Depression eras. Yet.

PUSHING THE ENVELOPE

There exists a trade-off, then, between economic growth and social cohesion. We can conceive of a "stability envelope" within which a society provides property rights and curbs taxation to the extent necessary to assure growth of its economy, but not to the point where inequalities of wealth are extreme enough to create social and political instability. The United States appears to be cautiously probing the "right edge" of that envelope, exploring just how much income and wealth inequality can be tolerated in the interest of encouraging optimum growth.

The rest of the developed world seems to dwell at the "left edge" of the envelope, determining just how much economic growth can be sacrificed in the name of encouraging optimum equality and happiness.

---

* For an excellent survey of the near-revolutionary conditions in early-nineteenth-century England, see R. J. White, *Waterloo to Peterloo* (London: Heinemann, 1957).

The Scandinavian nations and the U.S. supply a case study in the limits of government spending. Between 1924 and 1995, the portion of the Danish GDP that was funneled through the state rose from 11% to 51%. In the U.S., this figure runs at about 30% of GDP, the total spent by federal, state, and local budgets.[11,12] Given the recent painful retrenchments in the level of government services in northern Europe in the past few decades, the Europeans seem to have approached the upper limits of taxation.

How is it possible that the economies of northern Europe, which are taxed at fully 50% of their output, are able to sustain nearly the same degree of prosperity as an American economy that pays only 30%? Three reasons stand out:

- The European social welfare system has created a solid reservoir of stakeholder-citizens who willingly observe their society's norms, respect the rule of law, and pay their taxes. The mechanisms behind this are diverse—from the obvious fact that an unemployed worker on the dole is far less likely to steal to the more subtle benefits wrought by the stakeholder effect on tax collections and fulfillment of commercial contracts. All of these beneficial effects of high social welfare spending result in a very low cost of enforcing property rights, which largely mitigates the damage to economic incentive from high taxes.

- Although both American and European government expenditures are extremely high by historical standards, they consist mainly of transfer payments, and thus have a very low "deadweight loss"—the wastage that occurs when the purchaser and consumer are not the same person. Military expenses, on the other hand, have a very high deadweight loss. Thus, the 15% to 25% consumption of GDP by the militaries of the Habsburg Empire and Soviet Union proved far more damaging than the 50% of government spending by northern Europe's welfare states, whose defense spending is a negligible portion of GDP.

- Finally, the Europeans "tax smarter" than the U.S. does. The European tax system is surprisingly regressive but is economically more efficient than the U.S. system is. It relies more on consumption-based taxes like the value added tax and less upon economically inefficient taxes on income, dividends, and capital gains than the U.S. does.[13]

Have Americans grown more tolerant of income inequality during the past century? To the extent that this may be true, it is only a result of the redistributionist safety nets that began appearing with the New Deal, without which the U.S. would long ago have experienced severe social and political instability. We should not, however, grow too complacent. Tolerance of wealth inequality decreases dramatically during tough times, as happened during the Depression. Perhaps this is just one more turn in a long, never-ending economic and political cycle of the sort postulated by Kondratieff, where periods of laissez-faire alternate with periods of redistributionist vigor as the excesses of one regime bring about the reforms of the next.* The best we can hope for is that the world's great liberal democracies, both the newly emerging and the long established, will manage this eternal cycle in a reasonably orderly fashion.

INFLATION VERSUS JOBS

The "hard data" approach to happiness also clarifies the trade-off between inflation and unemployment. Easy money makes for higher inflation and lower unemployment, while tight money has the opposite effect. Readers of a certain age will recall the "misery index" of Jimmy Carter's presidency—the sum of unemployment and inflation. As we saw in the last chapter, unemployment is a powerful engine of misery. Does inflation cause as much pain? No, it does not. A study of the effects of unemployment and inflation on happiness in twelve European nations and the U.S. found that each percentage point of unemployment increased unhappiness by more than twice as much as an identical rise in inflation did.[14] A detailed discussion of the relation among monetary

---

* Nikolai Kondratieff was a Russian economist who in the 1920s wrote of recurring sixty-year economic cycles, or "waves," involving output and investment. Kondratieff concluded that these waves meant that capitalism's ills in the 1930s were temporary and self-correcting; Stalin was not amused and sent him to the Gulag, where he died in 1938. See Nikolai Kondratieff, *The Long Wave Cycle* (New York: Richardson and Snyder, 1984).

policy, inflation, and unemployment lies far beyond this book's scope, but policy makers in the developed world and developing world would do well to consider that inflation causes far less emotional suffering than unemployment. Contrariwise, those who favor a European-style social welfare state should consider the corrosive effect on public morale of the high unemployment levels inherent in such systems.

RICH NATIONS, POOR NATIONS

The last trade-off we'll consider is just how the developed nations can assist the developing nations to grow. There is only so much money, only so much effort, and only so many people that can be spared for such enterprises. Over the past half-century, the most advanced nations have acted in two ways toward less wealthy peers. Private and nongovernmental agencies have supplied, in spotty and indiscriminate fashion, "humanitarian" aid, usually medical or agricultural. At the governmental and international level, large loans have been granted for infrastructure projects. Another avenue of aid is political assistance. From time to time wealthy nations, particularly the U.S., encourage and observe free elections (except in nations ruled by despots who are friendly to the West).

How can the developed nations most efficiently deploy these limited resources? Paddy Ashdown, the U.N. High Representative for Bosnia and Herzegovina, puts the answer succinctly: "In hindsight, we should have put the establishment of the rule of law first, for everything else depends on it: a functioning economy, a free and fair political system, the development of civil society, public confidence in police and the courts."[15]

In other words, before a nation builds roads, establishes clinics, and constructs dams, it must first train lawyers and judges. Then, patience in tank-car quantities is required. Before democracy will bloom in that nation, its economy must grow for decades. Attempts to plant the seeds of a democracy in the soil of an impoverished traditional agrarian or nomadic culture are doomed. Aid projects may build schools and factories, but if property rights and the rule of law are ignored, these facilities will fall into disrepair and disuse, just as occurred in Ottoman Turkey two centuries ago and in Africa thirty years ago.

Should we worry that an emphasis on free-market reforms will increase income inequality in developing nations? No. Inadequate rule of law allows governing elites and cronies to engage in highly profitable rent-seeking behavior and, at times, outright theft. Even in Mexico, which has an avowedly redistributionist tax system, those at the 90th percentile of income earn 11.6 times more than those at the 10th percentile, versus 5.5 in the U.S. and 3.0 in Sweden.[16]

It is often argued that developing nations cannot "afford" free-market reforms because of the detrimental effects on those at the bottom of the social scale. At least in its early stages, the improvement of economic institutions reduces income inequality merely by making it harder to steal. In poor nations, then, there is no trade-off.

It does little good to offer economic assistance of any sort to countries without adequate rule of law. The best illustration of this is Nigeria, which since 1980 has exported more than 15 billion barrels of oil, earning far more than could have been donated by the West—and yet saw its per capita GDP fall by one-fifth in the ensuing twenty-three years. The only useful thing that the West can donate to the world's underdeveloped nations is its institutional heritage, without which every other form of aid is wasted.

CHAPTER TWELVE

Mammon and Mars: The Winner's Curse

Victory goes to whoever is left with the last escudo.

—Don Bernadino de Mendoza, *Theoria y practica de la Guerra*

Chapter 10 concluded that wealth may not necessarily improve a nation's well-being, but that it does facilitate development of democratic institutions there. Now, we will concern ourselves with another important benefit of prosperity: great power. It is no exaggeration that economics is the stuff of the life and death of nations. An understanding of economic development provides deep insight into the history of major power politics and explains the shape of the modern world.

Wealth's twin offspring, democracy and power, make world hegemony by one or more of the world's large liberal democracies an increasing certainty. First, the complex historical connection between wealth and power will be surveyed; then, the surprising geopolitical advantages wielded by populous liberal democracies will be explored.

The connection between wealth and power in the modern world is simple. Distilled to its essence, modern warfare is largely an industrial endeavor, and the most productive nations generally prevail. The story of military productivity is as old as history. In ancient Greece, hoplite tactics and the panoply provided the Greek soldier with an insurmountable advantage over his Persian opponent. At the outset of the Hundred Years War, the longbow, deadly accurate at two hundred yards and with a firing rate of up to twelve projectiles per minute, devastated the elite of the French at Crécy and Agincourt. Then, technology reversed the tides of fortune as siege catapults supplied the French margin of victory.[1] As in any industrial contest, productivity provides the decisive factor. The products may be different, but the nature of the competition is all too similar—he who turns out the deadliest equipment at the lowest cost and in the greatest quantity wins.

Just as Crompton's spinning mule gave England victory in the Industrial Revolution, so did its military counterpart—the machine gun—allow the British to prevail in many nineteenth-century colonial battles—such as in the Battle of Omdurman in Sudan, where eleven thousand Dervishes were slaughtered at the cost of a few dozen British soldiers. Similarly, Nazi Germany's command of aerial combat and tank warfare in Poland, the Netherlands, and northern France allowed it to swiftly defeat the larger combined economies of France and England.

Victory, of course, requires more than the mere development and purchase of military hardware; it is not the bat maker who wins at Yankee Stadium. Beaches must be stormed, lethal fixed positions assaulted, seas braved in floating ammunition dumps, and deadly aerial combat engaged in. But without high-quality baseball bats, even the Yankees are doomed.

Besides raw wealth, advanced weaponry, and brave, well-led soldiers, geopolitical dominance also requires the *will* to spend both treasure and blood in the pursuit of national power. In totalitarian states—in reality, most nations throughout most of history—this is not a formidable barrier. The rulers of Habsburg Spain and the former Soviet Union impoverished their populaces and converted their peasants into cannon fodder without a second thought. At the other extreme, modern Europe and nineteenth-century America (with the exception of the Civil War) preferred wealth to power and thus directed the bare minimum of their economic output into arms. Surprisingly, England at the height of its power belonged in the latter category. Because its forces were so much more advanced than those of its colonial opponents, Britain ran its empire on a shoestring, with military expenses below 3% of GDP. More-over, at no time was GDP in England much more than one-tenth of total world output (compared with the two-fifths American share in 1945 and the one-fifth share today). As late as 1880, the number of British men under arms was less than half that in France, one-third that in Russia, and even smaller than that in Germany and Austria.[2]

Occasionally, a nation can trump a military opponent's wealth. In a small, localized conflict, a poor, backward nation in possession of a disciplined, motivated army fighting on its home territory and willing to sustain huge casualties can best a far larger and wealthier foe. This most often happens during wars of national liberation—in Algeria, in Indochina twice, and, lest we forget, in America during the revolutionary war.

In the premodern period, distance provided safety, nowhere more so than in the American fight for independence, where the British labored under the insurmountable disadvantage of having to ship "every biscuit, man, and bullet"[3] across the cold, stormy Atlantic. For almost two centuries, America's physical isolation offered the sort of security that nations sitting in the heart of the European cauldron could only dream about.

In the nineteenth century, things slowly began to change, as steam allowed the West to project power more effectively across the ocean and even far inland by way of navigable rivers, such as Africa's Congo and China's Yangtze. Mountainous areas, most notably in Afghanistan, proved more resistant, but by the twentieth century, even this extreme a geographic disadvantage could be overcome. Those who predicted that U.S. troops in Afghanistan would meet the same sorry fate that the British had met before them failed to realize that the cruise missile, the long-range bomber, the aircraft carrier, and the helicopter had effectively neutralized the Afghan fighter's traditional allies—physical remoteness and difficult terrain.

That said, de Mendoza's analysis—that victory went to whoever was left with the last escudo—proved fundamentally correct. In the prolonged global conflicts between grand coalitions that have characterized the modern era, technological, motivational, and geographic factors "averaged out" over many nations and far-flung battlefields, and economic heft almost always provided the margin of victory.

The Second World War epitomized the concept of war as industrial competition. At the conflict's beginning, the aggregate GDP of the initial

Allied powers—Britain and France—barely exceeded that of the initial Axis powers—Germany and Italy ($475 billion for the Allies versus $400 billion for the Axis, expressed in 1990 dollars). With Germany's superiority in fighting morale, armored vehicles, and air forces, Nazi troops quickly overran Poland in September 1939 and France in May 1940. After that, England stared into the frightening maw of Germany's far larger economy and military machine, and Britain's very survival seemed far from certain. In the days immediately following the Fall of France, Britain nearly capitulated. Only Churchill's skillful maneuvering during sessions of the inner cabinet against his defeatist opponent, Lord Halifax, prevented an ignominious end to nine centuries of English independence.[4]

Britain muddled along for nineteen months more before the U.S. entered the war in 1941. This changed the economic tally of the combatants to $1,750 billion (the U.S., Britain, and USSR) versus $600 billion (Germany, Italy, and Japan). Churchill, as he so often did, extracted the single, essential truth from the confused strategic outlook permeating the dark days after Pearl Harbor: "Hitler's fate was sealed. Mussolini's fate was sealed. As for the Japanese, they would be ground into powder. *All the rest was merely the proper application of overwhelming force.*"[5] (Italics added)

The Battle of Midway, to cite a familiar example, is often identified as a "turning point,"[6] or the "decisive"[7] engagement of the Pacific war. Even though the Allies had broken the Japanese ciphers and ascertained enemy intentions, the outcome of the battle was not a foreordained victory for the U.S. A hopelessly uncoordinated American attack finally found three of the four Japanese aircraft carriers momentarily undefended and with flight decks laden with fuel and bombs just as American dive-bombers arrived overhead. Military historian B. H. Liddell Hart calls Midway an example of the "'chanciness' of battles fought out in the new style by the long-range sea-air action."[8] The conventional military wisdom has it that an American loss at Midway would have devastated Allied prospects in the Pacific and allowed the Japanese to fight on for years, or even have forced the U.S. to sue for peace.

Even a cursory look at the numbers, however, tells a different story. Both sides began the war with half a dozen large fleet carriers. Japan threw all six into the Pearl Harbor attack; four of these were subsequently lost at Midway. By the end of 1942 four of the U.S. carriers had also gone to the bottom (*Lexington* at Coral Sea, *Wasp* to submarine attack, *Hornet* near Guadalcanal, and *Yorktown* at Midway itself). Thus, by late 1942 both sides were down to just two fleet carriers, with one of them usually in port for repair and resupply at any given time. In the ensuing three years, the Japanese produced only two more fleet carriers, while the U.S. built sixteen. The Japanese also built fourteen smaller carriers, while the U.S. churned out 118 (although many of these served on convoy duty in the Atlantic).[9]

By late 1943, Admiral Nimitz was able to deploy a dozen fleet carriers for the invasion of the Gilbert Islands, giving the U.S. absolute control of the sea and air. Had the Japanese won decisively at Midway, the tally would still have been nine fleet carriers for the Americans to five for the Japanese. In any case, the United States could repair a loss of three large American carriers within six months, while the Japanese took more than a year each to produce their last two. With a similar margin in other capital ships, submarines, and aircraft, the "proper application of overwhelming force" spelled certain doom for Japan. The war in the Pacific was decided as much in American shipyards as it was on the bloody islands and high seas.

While victory requires more than just the last escudo, wealth has always been of central military importance. The fortunes of the great powers can be traced directly through their economic circumstances.

THE DOWNFALL OF CROESUS

Legend has it that Croesus, the fabulously wealthy king of the Lydians, sent his minions to Delphi to inquire of the oracles whether or not he should attack the Persians. The oracles replied that "if he should send an army against the Persians, he would destroy a great empire." Thus emboldened, Croesus attacked. He learned in battle that the oracles had gotten things exactly right—the empire destroyed was *his*.[10]

Hegemony often carries with it the seeds of its own destruction. Economists have long been aware of the "winner's curse": The winning bidder at an auction often overpays and winds up worse off than if he had "lost."[11] In geopolitics, the winner's curse has proven to be almost a law of nature, for the simple reason that wielding and maintaining great power requires astronomical expenditure. True, the acquisition of territory can supply a healthy initial flow of treasure, but after the plunder tapers off, expenses multiply as the "winner" must garrison, suppress, and defend ever more distant lands—resulting in what historian Paul Kennedy calls "imperial overstretch."[12]

During the period from A.D. 1500 to the present day, conflicts have only become more expensive. The major combatants in a sixteenth-century war might spend £10,000,000 over the course of the entire conflict. By the time of the Napoleonic War, the major combatants spent more than £100,000,000 in each and every year, and during the "French Wars" from 1793 to 1815, total British expenditures exceeded £1.6 billion.*

War expenditures grew at a far greater rate than that of the economies that supported them. Between 1600 and 1820, England's economy grew only sixfold, France's less than threefold, and Spain's did not even double. Although the rare premodern prince may have been cognizant of the dangers of military overexpenditure, Adam Smith, in a 1755 lecture, formalized the deleterious effects of war and the crushing levies needed to support it:

> Little else is requisite to carry a state to the highest degree of opulence from the lowest barbarism, but peace, easy taxes, and a tolerable administration of justice; all the rest being brought about by the natural course of things.[13]

It is unfortunate that the Habsburgs and Bourbons did not have the counsel of the wise, dour Scot. Chapter 8 touched on Spain's skyrocketing military obligations and the country's chronic defaults. At the time of Philip II's death in 1598, the Spanish Crown owed 100 million gold ducats, ten times the cost of the ill-fated armada of 1588 and fifty times the annual bounty of New World silver, which was at that moment near its peak.

Philip's extravagant adventurism proved a mere prelude to the disastrous Thirty Years War (1618–48), a European religious slaughter that

---

* All of the amounts quoted are in current pounds sterling—i.e., the actual monetary amounts at the time. The £10,000,000 quoted as the cost of a sixteenth-century conflict was the equivalent of about half a billion dollars today; the £1.6 billion cost of the French wars, about $60 billion today. Between these two periods, there was relatively little inflation. See Roger G. Ibbotson and Gary P. Brinson, *Global Investing* (New York: McGraw-Hill, 1993), 251–52.

sucked huge amounts of men and treasure into Germany and the Low Countries from all sides and doomed the underfinanced Habsburgs. By 1650, the flow of precious metals from the New World fell by more than 80%, and Spain had lost its revenues from Holland. All that was left to Spain was its own meager domestic economy.[14]

With burgeoning commitments and expenses and rapidly dwindling resources, no amount of strategic brilliance and fighting valor—which Spain had in ample amounts throughout her decline—could save it from the fact that it had run out of escudos. Soon enough, both Portugal and the Netherlands gained their independence from Spain and humiliated it at the peace table. Again, Paul Kennedy: "The Habsburgs simply had too much to do, too many enemies to fight, too many fronts to defend. . . . The price of possessing so many territories was the existence of numerous foes."[15]

The Habsburgs routinely outspent their revenues by a factor of two or three. During times of mortal crisis, such flagrant military overspending may be necessary for survival, but doing so for decades at a time spells doom regardless of the fortunes of battle.[16]

Who took Spain's place? Holland was simply too small to compete against the larger nation-states that were slowly organizing around it. Relative to her larger neighbors, Holland had already passed the pinnacle of wealth and power by the time it won independence at the end of the Thirty Years War. England, which otherwise should have profited by Spain's downfall, was at that point just beginning to sort out the unhappy aftermath of its murderous civil war: a series of disastrous parliaments, protectorates, and later Stuart monarchies.

All this should have left France best placed to fill the power vacuum left by the Habsburg implosion, but it, too, had overspent during the long conflict. Spain and France fought for eleven years after the Peace of Westphalia was concluded in 1648, and by the time they signed the Treaty of the Pyrenees in 1659, France was financially prostrate, its tax rates out of control, its population impoverished, and its credit ruined.

France would not learn to control its martial appetite for many more generations. Louis XIV proved just as reckless and profligate as the Habsburgs had been. The perceptive Colbert well understood the magnitude of the fiscal mayhem wreaked by the Sun King's military adventures, but generally failed in his attempts to restrain him; the only conflict that the *contrôler* supported was the 1672 expedition against Holland, France's opponent in the great mercantilist game.[17]

Louis's baldest and most expensive folly was the War of the Spanish Succession. When the pathetic last Habsburg, Charles II, died in 1700, Louis placed his grandson Philip of Anjou on the throne as Philip V, occupied the southern Netherlands, and monopolized for France all trade with Spanish America. At a stroke, Louis had accomplished the impossible by uniting almost all of Europe into a grand coalition—against him. The inevitable conflict stripped France of large amounts of territory and trading concessions in the New World, separated the two Bourbon monarchies, gave Gibraltar to the British, and saddled the regime of the dying Sun King with a vastly increased debt.

France's financial shambles after the War of the Spanish Succession set the stage for the era's financial Götterdammerung, in which Scotsman John Law convinced the French Crown to allow him to assume France's crushing debt burden in exchange for shares of his Mississippi Company. The speculation in the Mississippi Company triggered history's greatest financial explosion, the combined Mississippi and South Seas bubbles in Paris and London in 1719–20.[*]

Three generations later, the Sun King's great-grandson, Louis XV, would engage England in the Seven Years War, the world's first truly global conflict, and once again drain France's coffers. England would go on to take the rest of Canada from France, as well as end France's influence in the West Indies and India. Talleyrand best captured the congenital Bourbon inability to restrain their adventurist streak with his characterization of the *ancien régime—Ils n'ont rien appris, ni rien oublié.* ("They have learnt nothing, and forgotten nothing.")[18]

England, too, escaped neither fiscal distress nor military folly. Even its limited involvement in Holland during the Thirty Years War strained Britain's puny economy. Parliament and the Crown constantly bickered over wartime expenditures, and when Charles I arbitrarily appropriated

---

[*]   Relative to GDP, the South Sea Bubble was far larger than even the recent Internet mania. The best estimate puts the total equity capitalization of the English stock market in 1720 at about £500 million, or about seven times GDP. At the height of the Internet craze, the total value of all publicly traded U.S. companies was only about twice GDP.

funds for naval construction (the infamous Ship Money), he triggered a civil war that would cost him his head.[19]

Half a century later, the War of the Spanish Succession also saddled England with considerable debt. As in France, a speculative commercial venture, the South Sea Company, assumed the huge burden of government war loans, which, like Law's Mississippi venture, experienced its own bubble. Since England's debt was smaller and its capital markets healthier, the South Sea Bubble in 1720 did less damage than the Mississippi Bubble did in Paris. England, too, engaged in an expensive military folly in the eighteenth century—the American Revolution—whose outcome was preordained by the geographic realities of the conflict.

The French could not resist meddling in the American Revolution, and Louis XVI would repeat the mistakes of his grandfather and his great-great-great-grandfather; France's war against the British (simultaneous with the American Revolution) would cost it as much as its three previous wars had cost.

The British and French governments once again called upon the sophisticated financial markets to produce loans to close the gap between the huge costs of modern warfare and their relatively weak national economies. At the end of the American Revolution, both Britain and France had similar national debts—in the range of £200,000,000.

Once again, the fates of nations turned upon mundane fiscal details, in this case, the level of interest rates. With its superior capital markets, England could borrow at half the rate of interest that France could. Hence, Britain's cost of servicing the resulting loans was only half as great as France's was. England could easily carry the burden, but France could not. France's insolvency triggered a momentous series of events: Louis convened a rare meeting of the States General in 1789, which sparked the French Revolution. Contemporary observers were not blind to the connection between finance and victory. According to Bishop Berkeley, credit was "the principal advantage that England hath over France."[20]

The Revolution devastated the French capital markets, which were shaky in the best of times. In 1797, Napoleon renounced two-thirds of the government's debt, which destroyed confidence in the government's credit and sent interest rates soaring beyond 30%.[21] How, then, did Napoleon pay for his gargantuan *levee en masse* army? The old-fashioned way: by conquest and plunder. The audacious Corsican burdened his defeated foes with crushing reparations and taxes, often in excess of 50% of a conquered nation's revenues. Painfully aware of his predicament, he observed, "My power will fail if I do not feed it on new glories and new victories. Conquest has made me what I am, and only conquest can enable me to hold my position."[22]

For a time, it worked. France prospered, and falling interest rates nearly equaled those in England. But France could not escape history's oldest trap. When the plunder ran out, its finances quickly went flat, depriving the military of its oxygen. The famous *élan* of the empire's newly emboldened peasant troops evaporated when the brutal new style of total war followed Napoleon back to French soil. Soon enough, Napoleon was sent packing to Elba.

In the nineteenth and twentieth centuries, the cost of warfare continued to grow faster than government revenues. Even extraordinary wartime levies failed to meet expenses, and governments had to float huge loans to sustain their fighting. As in previous centuries, what separated the winners from the losers was the ability to borrow. The bourse became coequal with the bivouac.

Over the past two centuries, the British and American capital markets discharged their battlefield missions admirably. The performance of the American financial machine during the twentieth century's two world wars was every bit as impressive as that of its military machine. Figure 12–1 paints a broad-brush portrait of an economy that successfully absorbs the massive costs of war with the help of good credit and healthy financial markets. The black line shows the amount of military spending as a percentage of GDP (left scale). First, note how low American military spending has been—less than 1% of GDP through most of its history, and less than 10% during the Cold War. During our three major conflicts—the Civil War and two world wars—spending peaked at 47% of GDP in 1945.

Very high military expenditures necessitate borrowing, and the U.S. government tapped the bond markets to make up the shortfalls. The gray line shows how the debt burden, also expressed as a percentage of GDP (right scale), took decades to work off after each conflict. The debt curve shows two increases that were unassociated with wartime—the

FIGURE 12–1   U.S. MILITARY EXPENDITURES AND DEBT AS PERCENTAGE OF GDP

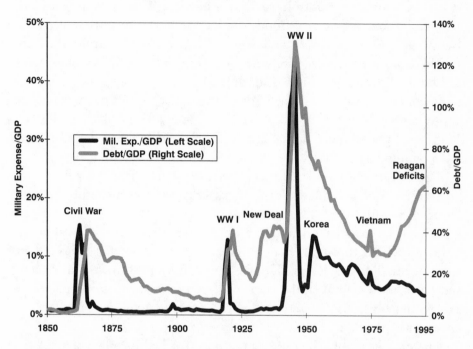

Source: Data on U.S. GDP are from the U.S. Department of Commerce; data on military expenditures are from the Material Capabilities dataset of the Correlates of War Project, University of Michigan, http://www.umich.edu/~cowproj/; data on national debt are from the U.S. Treasury Department.

first to pay for the costs of the New Deal, the second to pay for the Reagan administration's combination of tax cuts and modestly increased Cold War military spending.

With each successive conflict, America accomplished its wartime borrowing with less disturbance of the capital markets and a smaller rise in interest rates than in the one before. During the Civil War, the government, unaccustomed to placing large amounts of bonds, had to rely on the private sector to do so (mainly in the person of investment banker Jay Cooke, whose genius lay in establishing a vast network of brokers who sold the bonds to ordinary investors). The borrowing came at a relatively modest cost, with government bond yields rising to just 6% from the prewar level of 4.5%.

By the twentieth century, the government had grown adept at selling its debt not only to institutional buyers but also directly to private citizens in the form of Liberty Bonds (to pay for World War I) and Savings Bonds (for World War II and after). Consequently, during the First World War, interest rates barely budged from the prewar baseline of 4%, and by the Second World War, both the government and large corporations could borrow gargantuan sums without affecting interest rates at all. When the national debt peaked at a staggering 131% of GDP in 1945, U.S. government bonds sold at a 2.5% yield, about the same as at the beginning of the war.[23]

The rest of the world did not fare so well. In nearly every other nation, an inexorable sequence of financial stress and exhaustion played out in both world wars. The murderous fiscal demands of continuous high-intensity conflict on multiple fronts corroded each national economy and forced the weaker states into debt to their richer allies. These weak states (Russia, Austria-Hungary, and Italy in World War I; Italy and Japan in World War II) were unable to feed and equip their forces and would be forced to retreat, or, as happened to Russia in 1917, to drop out of the war entirely.

The process would then spread to states that had initially appeared robust—by late 1918, Germany had so concentrated its economy on munitions that its GDP dropped by almost one-third from prewar levels, its industrial output fell even more, and its population found itself poised on the brink of starvation.[24,25] Figure 12–2 graphs Germany's twentieth-century military spending, again as a percentage of GDP. Note how much higher the wartime spikes rose in Germany than in the U.S.—84% of GDP in the First World War, 139% during the Second World War. In addition, this level of spending was sustained over a longer time period—Germany fought in World War II for almost six years, and as early as 1938 military spending consumed one-third of GDP. Even the giant American capital markets could not have sustained such an effort; certainly, Germany's less-developed capital markets were not up to the task.

By the conclusion of both world wars, the U.S. was the last man standing, economically as well as militarily, while England was deeply in debt to the U.S. The final turn in Lord Keynes's long and distinguished career was his punishing mission in April 1946 to an international monetary conference in the U.S. in pursuit of favorable terms for England's war debt.

FIGURE 12–2   GERMAN MILITARY EXPENDITURE AS PERCENTAGE OF GDP

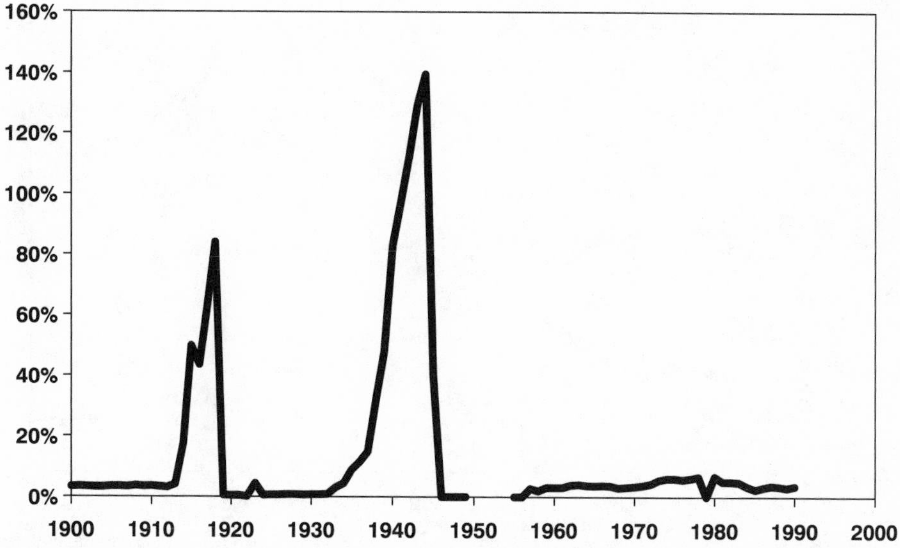

Source: Data on military expenditures are from the Material Capabilities dataset of the Correlates of War Project; data on German GDP are from Maddison, *Monitoring the World Economy, 1820–1992*, 180. Deflator from Ibbotson Associates.

He was ultimately successful in his quest, but he returned to England a broken man and died two weeks later.[26] The British Empire ended not with the bang of battle but with the whimper of insolvency.

De Mendoza's bon mot, then, needs to be modified slightly. Victory goes not so much to he who has the last escudo as to he who can borrow it at the lowest rate of interest from his own citizens.

PROSPERITY, DEMOCRACY, AND HEGEMONY

Both democracy and military power spring from the same source: economic prosperity, spread widely among the populace. The close association of entrepreneurial vigor and military innovation strengthens the link between wealth and power—demonstrated most recently by the extraordinary performances of the American military machine in Afghanistan and Iraq.

FIGURE 12–3   U.S. AND U.K. GDP AS PERCENTAGE OF WORLD GDP

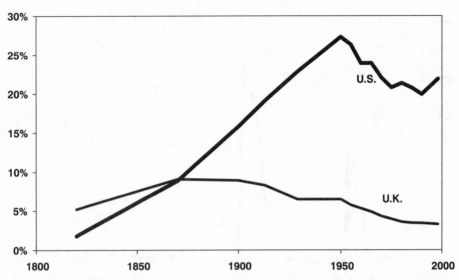

Source: Maddison, *The World Economy: A Millennial Perspective*, 263 and Maddison, *Monitoring the World Economy, 1820–1992*, 182, 188, 227.

The cause of England's decline in power is clearly visible in Figure 12–3, which shows the U.S. and U.K. shares of world GDP: The relative dominance of the British economy, once the world's largest, has slowly faded away. This is not to say that England has become poorer—far from it. Between 1870, when Britannia was at the height of her powers, and her greatly diminished world status in 1998, British real per capita GDP increased almost sixfold.[27] England's strategic misfortune was that the rest of the world grew yet more rapidly.

Likewise, Figure 12–3 makes obvious the foundation of rising American power, shaped by the triple threat of a high birth rate, massive immigration, and snowballing productivity. It helps to add some flesh and blood to a single thin line on a graph: Between the Civil War and the Spanish-American War, the U.S. production of grain increased more than threefold; rail mileage, by more than sixfold; and coal output, by ninefold. By the turn of the century, European leaders and journalists were already beginning to howl about unfair competition from cheap American food and manufactured items. While kings and prime ministers openly discussed combining against the American behemoth, only the most disastrous of historical misfortunes could have prevented America's ascension to world primacy in the twentieth century.[28]

Raw GDP alone carries insufficient geopolitical weight—if global heft is desired, wealth must be combined with technologic advance. The cases of Russia and China illustrate that economic size in the absence of modern industrial and military technology stands nearly useless. During the second half of the nineteenth century, Russia possessed one of the world's largest economies and by far the largest number of men under arms. Throughout most of history, China had the world's highest GDP simply by virtue of its huge population and the relatively narrow per capita gaps in wealth of the preindustrial world. Even now, China has the world's largest standing army and one of its largest economies.[29]

The military balance in the modern Middle East also demonstrates that technological advancement can make up for deficiencies in raw GDP. There, Israel has dominated its four "frontline" neighbors—Egypt, Jordan, Syria, and Lebanon—since its birth as a nation in 1948, despite the fact that the aggregate economies of the four Arab nations are more than twice the size of the Jewish state's.* Those seeking an oversimplified economic formula for geopolitical power might consider a measure that takes both technological advancement and raw economic size into account. A relatively simple "power index" might involve multiplying total military spending by per capita GDP.

The rise of U.S. geopolitical power during the twentieth—the "American"—century follows as the nearly inevitable consequence of the rise of its economic power and technologic prowess. Since the U.S. and the U.K. had the world's highest per capita GDPs, and along with them, the most sophisticated militaries, for almost all of the nineteenth and twentieth centuries, the message of Figure 12–3 is clear: In the modern world, geopolitical power becomes the province of large, prosperous, free-market nations. Totalitarian nations may temporarily acquire territory and global influence as well, but absent the solid economic foundation that only a free-market economy can provide, that power must inevitably crumble.

---

* Maddison, *Monitoring the World Economy: A Millennial Perspective, 1820–1992*, 307, 308, 311. This gap shows no sign of narrowing, since the Arab economies, with their far lower per capita GDP, are growing approximately at the same rate as Israel via the "catch-up" phenomenon. See Chapter 10 for the inverse relationship between per capita GDP and economic growth.

BULLETS AND BALLOTS

What of democracy and power? Modern liberal democracies possess a subtle, yet powerful, geopolitical advantage: Their political structures provide an effective brake on the kind of imperial overstretch that doomed Habsburg Spain, the *ancien régime*, Nazi Germany, and the Soviet Union. While adventurist politicians can seduce democratic electorates into unwise military action, voters do not indefinitely tolerate the casualties, crushing increases in taxation, and reductions in government services that result from intense and prolonged military action. Eventually, something has to give.

Modern liberal democracies also check military adventurism through a second mechanism: With increasing wealth and individual liberties come a lower tolerance of war casualties. The 618,000 Civil War combat deaths represented nearly 4% of the U.S. male population. This exceeded the total loss of life in all of America's subsequent wars. (In yet another example of economic determinism, once that conflict became a war of attrition, the Confederacy's puny industrial base doomed its armies to eventual defeat.) By the 1970s, the war in Vietnam, supposedly a battle for survival against communism, became intolerable after 58,000 lives were lost—despite the fact that the U.S. population was eight times larger than it was in 1865.

In addition to its braking effect on military adventurism, the connection between wealth and the aversion to bloodshed impels military innovation. Twenty years ago, slack-jawed incredulity would have met the assertion that the defeat of one of the world's largest standing armies, such as Iraq's, no matter how ill-equipped and trained, and involving widespread armored engagements, helicopter assaults, and tens of thousands of aircraft carrier launches, many of them at night, could be accomplished with the loss of little more than a hundred U.S. lives. This dazzling quest for efficiency was motivated in no small part by a defense establishment that was acutely conscious of the public's growing dislike for military funerals.

The trajectory of post–World War II American relative wealth shown in Figure 12–3 is intriguing. The U.S. share of world economic output peaked in 1945 as the U.S. emerged victorious from World War II. Angus Maddison estimates America's share of the world's economic output immediately after World War II at about 30%, while others have placed it closer to 50%.[30] One would expect the relative economic dominance of the U.S. to decline as the rest of the world rebuilt after the war, but two unexpected things occurred. First, the decline in U.S. economic dominance was relatively small. Over the past three decades, the American portion of world GDP has remained nearly constant, at about 22%. Second, and more remarkably, U.S. geopolitical dominance seems not to have corroded with the inevitable retreat from its 1945 relative economic peak.

In an influential article in *Foreign Affairs*, Dartmouth professors Stephen Brooks and William Wohlforth starkly described a "unipolar" world, the likes of which have never been seen before in history. It is characterized by an American hegemony that is based on a technologically superior military machine and paid for by the world's largest and most vigorous economy. In contrast to the ruinously expensive Roman, Habsburg, and Bourbon militaries, American global superiority costs a mere 3.5% of GDP—far less than even the 10% spent on American defense in the Eisenhower years. The authors even managed to quote Paul Kennedy: "Being Number One at great cost is one thing; being the world's superpower on the cheap is astonishing."[31] Further, Brooks and Wohlforth discounted the social and military impact of terrorism as nothing more than the modern reincarnation of politically motivated mass murder—a story that is as old as history itself.[32] We can put the terrorism threat into perspective in other ways. Even were the worst-case scenarios of nuclear terrorism realized, it would not cost the tens of millions of lives snuffed out by the ogres of the previous century: Hitler, Stalin, Mao, and Pol Pot.

Too much is made of the anger of the Arab "street." Displeasure, if it is to have geopolitical meaning, must be transmitted through efficient vehicles of violence. Few consider that the events of September 11, 2001 also forced a reevaluation of the Muslim world among Americans. An ideologically committed American can act on his beliefs through military enlistment far easier than his rock-throwing counterparts in Rawalpindi, Cairo, or Jakarta can position themselves to harm the Great Satan.

Brooks and Wohlforth expect U.S. world dominance to last for at least several decades. How does America maintain its power despite the decline of the U.S. economy relative to that of the rest of the world? Quite simply, everyone else has either given up the game or was never in it in the first place.

In the first category stood the Soviet Union, its economy hobbled by a system of perverted incentives and run by a collection of sadistic ideologues. For two generations, the USSR funneled more than one-sixth of her puny national output into an elephantine military.[33] With the arrival of the CNN era, the USSR could no longer hide its own poverty, and the West's wealth, from a demoralized populace.

Because of the opacity of Soviet finances, we cannot translate the former USSR's military expenditures accurately into dollar terms, but it appears that the "arms race" was relatively close. In any given year, U.S. and Soviet defense expenditures were approximately equal, and, indeed, a rough equivalency in military power existed throughout the Cold War.[34] The same inaccuracies apply in attempting to gauge the USSR's GDP, with the most optimistic estimates putting the Soviet economy at about 40% the size of that of U.S.[35]

Figure 12–4 plots Russian military expenditure during the twentieth century, again as a percentage of GDP. The data underlying this plot are admittedly flawed. Historians can only wonder, for example, if proportionate Soviet military spending was really higher during the Cold War than in the Second World War. But the underlying conclusion is clear: The USSR spent in excess of 15% of its GDP on defense for almost half a century. During the Cold War, the Russians weren't worried just about the U.S. threat. By the 1960s, their disagreements with the Chinese forced the Soviets to garrison the Sino-Soviet border with more than forty army divisions. Cold War expenditures strained even the vigorous American system—it can only be imagined what the same burden did to the far smaller Soviet economy over those decades. The USSR finally collapsed when the regime's last economic prop—oil revenues—crumbled with the worldwide fall of petroleum prices in the mid-1980s.[36]

Meanwhile, the European nations, who were exhausted by generations of conflict and disinclined to surrender national sovereignty to an adequately funded all-European military command, elected not to match their economic power with military might. They thus became geopolitical geldings. One of the stranger images of recent history remains that of a

FIGURE 12–4   RUSSIAN MILITARY EXPENDITURE AS PERCENTAGE OF WORLD GDP

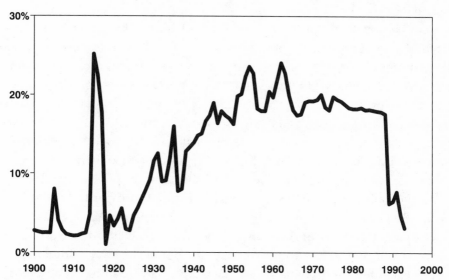

Source: Data on military expenditures are from the Material Capabilities dataset of the Correlates of War Project; data on Russian GDP are from Maddison, *Monitoring the World Economy, 1820–1992*, 186–87. Deflator from Ibbotson Associates.

prosperous, happy, and impotent Europe unwilling to lift even a collective finger to stop the pillage, rape, and murder just across their borders in Bosnia and Kosovo, leaving it to that notorious warmonger, William Jefferson Clinton, to finally send in the F-18s. Japan shares with its developed European peers a vigorous, modern free-market economy, Smith's "tolerably administered justice," and an intense desire to avoid significant conflict and military expense for the foreseeable future.

Other nations, such as China and India, certainly aspire to regional power, but they are also economic and institutional weaklings, possessed of poorly equipped and ineffective, if large, militaries. They are unlikely to challenge American global hegemony anytime soon. The fall in Chinese military spending relative to GDP is a fascinating and often ignored story. Mao's successors learned from the Soviet example and quietly decreased military spending as part of the post-Deng economic reforms. Any appraisal of Chinese defense appropriations poses the same challenges that the former USSR does—estimates of current military spending range from $15 billion to $60 billion—but even the

high estimate is only a few percent of total GDP, down from an estimated 17% in the early 1970s.[37]

Brooks and Wohlforth confined their analysis to U.S. hegemony, but
beyond their enthusiastic prognosis for a new *Pax Americana*, an even
larger point emerges: World-power status is open to *any* large, successful,
free-market nation willing to devote even a modest portion of its innovative energy and wealth to its military. This simple fact identifies many
nations as great-power candidates, and many more will qualify in the future. That no other large, prosperous nations will aspire to—and attain—world power status over the next century is inconceivable.

Figure 12–5 summarizes the relationship among prosperity, democracy, and military power. As seen in Chapter 10, prosperity born of secure property rights and the rule of law promotes democratic
development; wealth begets democracy, not vice versa. The very same
prosperity also gives rise to military and geopolitical power. Crudely put,
states that value the rule of law and property rights tend to become both
democratic and powerful at the same time. In addition, wealthy democracies resist the imperial overstretch that has plagued totalitarian nations
throughout history. In doing so, liberal democracies protect their wealth
and power. Finally, the aversion of wealthy democratic states to battle
casualties spurs the development of advanced military technologies.

This connection between free-market economics, democracy, and
military efficiency suggests a conclusion that goes beyond Brooks-
Wohlforth: Regardless of the duration of American hegemony, it seems
likely that for the foreseeable future prolonged great-power status will
become the exclusive domain of populous, innovative liberal democracies, the only nations that will be able to expand their economies, develop their weaponry, and adequately fund their militaries. Further, the
politically empowered electorates of these nations will hold military expenditure to a tolerable level—say less than 10% of GDP—and thus resist imperial overstretch.

Using a different line of reasoning, Francis Fukuyama came to much the
same conclusion. Fukuyama points out that in the modern world, liberal
democracy has no serious competitors, nor the prospect of any in the foreseeable future—hence the book's deliberately provocative title. History has
defeated monarchism and discredited fascism and communism. Islam, while
a growing force in many parts of the world, has limited appeal outside the

FIGURE 12–5

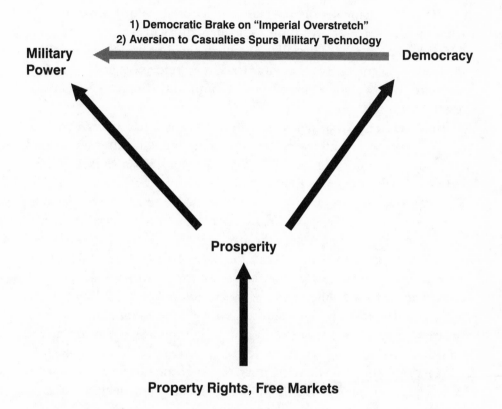

1) Democratic Brake on "Imperial Overstretch"
2) Aversion to Casualties Spurs Military Technology

Military Power

Democracy

Prosperity

Property Rights, Free Markets

Muslim heartland. But Fukuyama's explanation is largely noneconomic. Only liberal democracy, he states, best satisfies humankind's desire for pride and self-worth. The author often (rather too often) invokes the Greek term for such feelings: *thymos*.

Of course, thymos is simply another name for the upper reaches of Maslow's pyramid, the province of those with full bellies and a roof over their heads. Not many of Fukuyama's thymotic men are found in subsistence societies. Only in places where basic material and safety needs have been met—no small task that—does thymos, and ultimately, liberal democracy, thrive. An otherwise repressive state that respects property rights must ultimately prosper, that prosperity must ultimately empower its citizens and encourage their thymotic impulses, and those thymotic impulses must ultimately lead to greater democracy.

Totalitarian states may briefly attain world power, but in the modern world, this happens only where a dictatorial coup hijacks a large, successful, free-market economy, as happened in Japan and Germany in the 1930s. The historical parallels between these two nations are striking. Both saw previously backward regimes reformed politically and economically shortly after 1870, and both saw dramatic economic growth as a result.

While neither prewar Japan nor Germany was a Jeffersonian democracy, both nations greatly expanded the voting franchise after the turn of the century. From 1870 to 1913, Germany and Japan evidenced the world's second-fastest and third-fastest growth in per capita GDP, respectively, behind the U.S. As a result, both became regional powers. Even before World War I, Germany reigned as Europe's leading industrial power. At Germany's unification in 1871, voting rights were granted to all males over the age of 25. Between 1930 and 1934, Hitler concentrated political power through a complex process that used democracy against itself. Subsequently, Germany and Japan fell into dictatorship, and with the inherent democratic resistance to imperial overstretch gone, lunged at world power before being crushed in the Second World War.

Like Napoleon, the modern militarily aggressive totalitarian state is faced with a terrible choice. It must either take battlefield gambles, as Germany and Japan did, and eventually rouse its economically more powerful democratic competitors out of their torpor and into arms, or risk having its economy stagnate under the weight of excessive and prolonged arms expenditures, as happened in the Soviet Union.

If China and Russia continue to move in a liberal democratic direction, nothing would prevent them from successfully challenging U.S. hegemony as fellow Western-style superpowers. Were the European nations merely to take their militaries seriously and submerge their sovereignties in the same way that they have merged their currencies, they could accomplish the same thing even more quickly. Though neither of these scenarios seems immediately likely, history teaches us that dominance by one nation does not last forever. It is probable that the next fifty to one hundred years will see the decline of American influence. From which direction the challenge will come is not yet clear.

What seems more likely is that as long as the world's great liberal democracies can summon the will, their inherent economic advantages guarantee their aggregate geopolitical dominance. While many disagree, perhaps correctly, with the current American preemptive, unilateralist stance, the mere fact that at least one democratic power is willing to challenge the world's totalitarian states is reassuring. No matter how much the eight-hundred-pound U.S. gorilla alarms the rest of the planet, a world with no liberal democratic superpower willing and able to rise to the inevitable totalitarian challenges would be a far more frightening place.

CHAPTER THIRTEEN

The End of Growth?

VIEWED FROM THE PERSPECTIVE OF THE PAST FEW CENTURIES, technologic progress, and the economic growth it creates, seems an unrelenting, never-ending engine—an economic perpetual motion machine showing no signs of fatigue, let alone stopping. Yet even a rudimentary grasp of human history gives pause. In the larger scheme of time, two hundred years are not even the blink of an eye, and what seems timeless and inexorable to one generation crumbles into sand in the next.

In a provocative essay at the conclusion of *The First Modern Economy*, Jan de Vries and Ad van der Woude's masterful economic history of Holland, the authors point out that Dutch economic growth, which began in earnest in the mid-sixteenth century, simply petered out two centuries later.[1] Is the story of Holland's eighteenth century stagnation a warning shot across the bow of the Western world, itself just now reaching the bicentennial of the birth of sustained economic growth? To paraphrase Professor Robert Barro, Is two percent and two hundred years all that a wealthy nation—or planet—gets?

Questioning modern economic growth is a treacherous game; in the 1970s, an entire generation of pessimists, led by the Club of Rome, embarrassed themselves when they invoked strict limits to growth as the inevitable consequence of fixed resources.[2] Surely, they said, with population growth and limited supplies of land, food, timber, and petroleum, the game must eventually be up. While the Club and its acolytes did Thomas Malthus proud, they ignored the adaptability and creative genius of the human species. When a commodity becomes scarce or expensive, innovators devise better and cheaper substitutes. As recently as a hundred years ago, the only reliable stores of value were property and gold. Over the course of the twentieth century, measures of wealth beyond land and specie appeared, as if by magic. A century and a half ago, serious thinkers predicted that our cities would soon be cast into darkness. After all, the world was running out of whale oil.

Even a cursory glance at economic history shows a gradual, general decline in the real prices of commodities. The average person pays a far lower portion of his or her income for food and clothing than was the case a century ago, and the same is true of the prices of the raw materials used in industry.

Economic historian Simon Kuznets pointed out that a slowdown in economic growth can come from either of the two basic economic forces: supply or demand. He believed that supply, driven by man's innate curiosity and industry, could not be the source of stagnation. Demand, he decided, was growth's more likely assassin.[3] As individuals became wealthier, they would prefer leisure to work and consumption—people would surely lose interest in the empty pursuit of material wealth. In one of economic history's sublime ironies, Professor Kuznets died in 1985, the same year that the Home Shopping Network appeared on nationwide cable television.

FAILURE MODES

Demographic forces deserve consideration as a threat to growth. In the coming decades, increasing life expectancy and the ever-growing costs of educating and training the young will squeeze the remaining working population. The number of producers will fall; an ever-shrinking proportion of those in the work force will be left to support an ever-larger population of dependent young and old. In recent decades, the national budgets of the world's most advanced nations have become appendages of their social welfare programs. Fully 60% of the U.S. federal budget for 2003 consisted of expenditures for the "big four" social programs: Social Security, Medicare, Medicaid, and General Assistance. Of the remaining

40%, 18% went to defense and 8% paid interest on the national debt, leaving 14% for "everything else"—law enforcement, the judiciary, education, veteran's benefits, and the nation's infrastructure items (the FAA, weather service, highway and airport subsidies, and so forth).

Over the next few generations, the 60% of the budget going to the big four social welfare programs—over half of which involve medical expenses—are forecast to grow far faster than the overall economy, and it is not difficult to imagine fiscal doomsday scenarios in which the government, faced with nearly $50 *trillion* in unfunded liabilities, is forced to default, ignite ruinous inflation, or impose crippling taxes.[4]

More likely, however, will be a combination platter from the "menu of pain": a smorgasbord consisting of equal parts low-level intergenerational conflict, an agonizing reassessment of the Social Security and Medicare programs, and high European-style taxation.[5]

Although the short-term dislocations will be painful, the long-term effects of this demographic shift will not be that great. Using a complex algorithm, researchers Robert Arnott and Anne Casscells have estimated that the effective "dependency ratio"—the number of young and old supported by each worker—will rise from 0.55 to 0.76 during the twenty years between 2010 and 2030, after which it will level off. This will temporarily slow growth by about 0.6% per year for two decades—bothersome, to be sure, but temporary and hardly the end of prosperity as we know it.[*]

Ecological, economic, and demographic forces do not thus seem likely impediments to growth. The next obvious candidate, then, is military catastrophe. The industrialization of violent death places astonishing destructive forces in the hands not only of armies but of individuals as well. Moreover, growth itself destabilizes societies. Both within nations and among nations, growth produces winners and losers, and with the growing disparity of wealth between them comes the possibility of social discord and war. In 1700, the per capita GDP of the wealthiest nation, Holland, was five times that of the poorest. By 1998, the per capita GDP

---

[*]   An increase from each worker's supporting 1.55 people, including himself, to 1.76 over a period of twenty years implies a 0.6% drag on per capita GDP growth: $(1.51/1.37)^{(1/20)} = 0.006$. See Robert D. Arnott and Anne Casscells, "Demographics and Capital Market Returns," *Financial Analysts Journal* 59 (Mar./Apr. 2003): 20–29. Also, R. Arnott, personal communication.

of the wealthiest Western nations was more than forty times that of the poorest sub-Saharan Africa countries.[6]

While domestic and international turmoil may theoretically make the world a more dangerous place, exactly the opposite seems to be happening. For thousands of years before 1950, armed conflict between European states was commonplace; today, a major war between even two members of the Organization for Economic Cooperation and Development—the world's wealthiest and most powerful countries—seems highly unlikely. Similarly, the terrorist threat, while frightening on an emotional level, does not rise to quantitative significance. Even if terrorists can regularly execute events on the scale of September 11, they will cause carnage that is orders of magnitude less than that resulting from AIDS, alcohol, tobacco, road accidents, or Big Macs. In the first half of the twentieth century, the damage was far worse. On an average day between September 1939 and August 1945, approximately 25,000 people met violent deaths. That comes to one September 11 every three hours, twenty-four hours a day, for *six years*.

The simple mathematical implications of sustained productivity growth over future generations are staggering—had world per capita GDP started growing at 2% per year when Christ was born, it would now be sixty *quintillion* dollars—that's six followed by nineteen zeros—instead of the current $8,000 per head. Even a growth rate of 1% would have resulted in a current per capita GDP of about $200 billion. While it is possible that we are on the cusp of a long future blessed with unimaginable wealth, no great amount of cynicism (or even a graduate degree in history) is needed to forecast stumbles and falls. Only the precise nature of catastrophe remains unknown. And, as suggested in Chapter 10, even if vigorous growth persists in the very long term, it will likely not make us much happier.

THE WEALTHY AND THEIR ENTITLEMENTS

The greatest potential threats will probably come from the imperatives of growth itself. As societies become wealthier, their tolerance for risk and adversity decreases. Poor relief first became a public charge in England and

Holland only in the late premodern period. In 1750, the idea of universal public education, had it been raised, would have seemed an extravagant use of scarce government funds. By 1900, it had become the norm. In 1870, only socialists advocated that governments finance unemployment and retirement coverage. By 2000, all Western nations provided these benefits. Universal government-sponsored health care graduated from pipe dream to expensive Western reality in less than a generation, except in the U.S., where the cries for extension of government-mandated health care to all have become deafening.

It's doubtful that the citizens of increasingly wealthy nations will consider universal medical care the final frontier of government mandates. As wealth grows, so will the percentage of GDP that is consumed by government (30% in the U.S., including federal, state, and local expenditures, and higher still in most other Western nations), as it pursues an ever-growing list of entitlements. The economic drag produced by the growing list of entitlements may give rise to a sort of Malthusian "growth equilibrium" in which any rise in wealth is almost immediately choked off by an increased demand for government services.

SCIENCE FICTION

Nor should we worry only about growth-killing bogeymen. Is Barro's "two percent speed limit" an economic constant, like the speed of light?[*] What if biological modifications to the human species allow for increases in the growth rate of productivity? The most probable route to higher growth rates would likely involve tinkering with growth's primary engine—the human brain.

Advances in genetic engineering will soon allow parents—as well as the state—to increase the intelligence of their offspring. Imagine that an OECD nation gains control of baby making and thereby raises the average I.Q. of its population to 120 or 140. The hard part then will be the

---

[*]   This upper limit of growth refers only to wealthy, technologically advanced nations. Developing nations, as well as developed nations recovering from wartime destruction, can temporarily grow at a much faster ("catch-up") rate.

preservation of individual liberties and the rule of law so that economic incentive is left intact. Very shortly, that nation will begin to outperform its neighbors by a few percentage points of GDP each year, doubling its economy relative to its competitors with each generation. At some point, other nations might have to choose among three unattractive alternatives regarding their burgeoning neighbor: destroy it, adopt its genetic policies, or do neither and thus be consigned to a progressively inferior economic and military status.*

As the old joke goes, it's very hard to make predictions, particularly about the future. These speculations are not much more than science fiction. While the variety of possible modes of economic failure in the future is limited only by one's ability to imagine them, betting against Western Civilization has not been a paying proposition for the past five hundred years. The accuracy of even the most talented dystopian prophets—Orwell, Huxley, and Bradbury—has been unimpressive. A century from now, the world will likely be a far more prosperous place, and a thousand years hence, the earth's inhabitants will judge the current century to have been an impoverished, cruel, and deprived Dark Age. Will per capita economic growth over the next hundred or thousand years continue at the modern 2% real rate? Will it be slower? Will it be faster? We simply do not know.

---

* It is also possible that parents will voluntarily embrace intelligence-enhancing genetic engineering techniques, leaving the state out of the process and thus avoiding the dire geopolitical consequences discussed above.

CHAPTER FOURTEEN

When, Where, and Whither

IN THE 250 YEARS SINCE ADAM SMITH FIRST IDENTIFIED "peace, easy taxes, and a tolerable administration of justice" as the necessary conditions for prosperity, economists have refined his simple recipe. In the modern era, it has become apparent that technological progress is the ultimate fount of growth. By tracing the course of innovation through conception, development, production, and ultimate consumption, we can arrive at a working model for understanding economic growth. If we can understand growth, so, too, can we glimpse the dim outlines of the fates of nations.

This book's primary message is that a nation's *institutions*—not its natural resources or its cultural endowment, not its sense of power or its sense of economic and political victimization, not even its military prowess—that determine its long-term prosperity and its future. The path to prosperity winds through the four institutions that were discussed in Chapters 2 through 5. The lack of each of these institutions has constituted a gate, or barrier, if you will, that has impeded human progress. When all four of these institutions were in place in a country, the barriers to human genius, creativity, and ambition were breached. Innovation flourished, and the prosperity of that nation followed.

First, governments must provide technology's creators with adequate incentives. If, as in ancient China, the reward for innovation is confiscation by the state, little progress will be made. Thus, the prime requisite for prosperity is the protection of property rights, Smith's "tolerable administration of justice."

If the fruits of enterprise are not reasonably secure, few will innovate and produce. If the worker cannot retain most of his wages, he will not toil. Property can be threatened from many directions—from the criminal, from the despot, and, in extreme cases, even from the well-intentioned bureaucrats of a welfare state or a central bank unable to control spending and monetary inflation. The key concept is that only governments split by the separation of powers and circumscribed by the rule of law can effectively enforce property rights, for the simple reason that the naked fiat of any ruler, no matter how wise and just, corrupts and loses its legitimacy. Without the legitimacy emanating from the impersonal apparatus of a judicial system that is divorced from the ruling apparatus, no edict is enforceable. A law that does not apply equally to all citizens, the ruler included, is no law at all.

Although rule of law was first applied in ancient Greece and republican Rome, the Roman Republic's demise snuffed it out for more than five hundred years. It did not reappear until the medieval period in England. The sorry political experiments of the twentieth century have added to our understanding of Smith's deceptively simple phrase. The mere existence of an efficient judicial machine is not enough; the judiciary's power must be wholly separate from that of the ruler, and it must apply equally to all.

Taxation must be, in Smith's words, "easy"—the state cannot take too much. How much is too much? The success of the U.S. and the social experimentation of Europe's welfare states provides a rough approximation: A prosperous nation can easily tolerate the consumption of 30% of its economic output by the state, as in the U.S., but once the government take approaches 50%, as in many of the nations of northern Europe, economic growth begins to suffer.

Second, innovators must have the proper intellectual tools. Just as the most skilled carpenter is hobbled without his hammer, his saw, or his level, so the inventor is impotent without an effective intellectual model with which to interpret his surroundings. Before about 1600, even the most brilliant Greek, Roman, Chinese, Indian, and European natural philosophers were not in the correct intellectual frame of mind. The soul of Western man lies not in the great literature, art, and architecture that sprang from its Greco-Roman roots, but rather in the simple willingness to subject his most cherished beliefs to the harsh light of empirical scrutiny. Today, this is what truly separates the West from the rest of the world. Glorious as Greek logic and science were, they did not yield easily to the hard facts of the real world, and they reliably failed to provide mankind with useful models of nature.

The proper tools alone—an empirical bent of mind buttressed by the scientific method—are not sufficient. Societal and religious tolerance is also required. Innovation is a highly subversive process, and societies that discourage dissent are hamstrung. For more than five hundred years, the Catholic Church stifled intellectual and scientific innovation. While Martin Luther's revolt produced its own suffocating orthodoxy, it broke the Church's monopoly on Europe's intellectual life and in the long run freed the creative energies of an entire continent to explore whither they would.

A counterfactual analysis in which the Church doesn't wind up the steward of the Greco-Roman intellectual legacy provides an interesting thought experiment. To its credit, the Church set up the first great European universities in the early medieval period and kept alive the learning of the Greeks and Romans. Without the Church's protection of this ancient knowledge, the darkness that descended upon the West after A.D. 476 may well have lasted much longer and been far deeper. It is just as easy to make the opposite case—that the Church's monopoly on academic inquiry strangled Europe's intellectual development. Without the Church's dead hand, man might well have walked upon the moon centuries earlier than he actually did.

Third, once inventors and entrepreneurs possess adequate incentive and intellectual tools, they must have access to large amounts of financial capital in order to bring their inventions to the greater public. That, in turn, requires earning the trust of those who have that capital. Beginning in the sixteenth century, the Dutch municipal governments and later the English Crown convinced their respective investing publics that lending money to them was a good idea. Once the public became comfortable with loans to government, ordinary citizens also began to provide private enterprises with capital. In the nineteenth century the advent of limited liability for corporations made possible the establishment and capitalization of the huge impersonal companies that, for better and for worse, power the modern West.

Fourth, and last, there must be reliable and rapid communication with which to direct the flow of capital and to advertise the new goods, as well as transport capable of physically conveying these products across the nation and, increasingly, over the whole world. Since time immemorial, the puny physical output of man and animal limited the speed and power of human enterprise. While the waterwheel and the windmill did increase the amount of power available for manufacturing in certain favorable locations, they did nothing to speed the flow of goods and information. But in a historical heartbeat, Watt's steam engines would increase the volume and speed of shipping by a factor of ten. A century later, the magic of the telegraph would make global communications instantaneous.

Figure 14–1, which illustrates the historical flow of the four critical institutions—property rights, scientific rationalism, efficient capital markets, and modern power, transportation, and communication—summarizes the thrust of Chapters 2 through 5. This historical schematic shows just why the world's economy exploded early in the nineteenth century, as the last of the factors developed and matured.

Historically, secure property rights and rule of law, while necessary, have not proven sufficient by themselves to ensure prosperity. The Athenians and the late medieval British acquired robust rule of law and secure property, yet they did not experience vigorous economic growth.

FIGURE 14–1

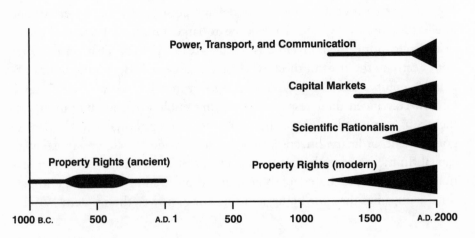

In hindsight, they lacked the other three factors: the proper intellectual tools, adequate financial capital with which to produce their inventions on a large enough scale, and transport and communication with which to convey and advertise their end products.

While a sophisticated system of property rights provided the Greeks and the medieval English with relatively little economic benefit, property acquired critical importance in the modern world as the other three factors—scientific rationalism, capital markets, and modern power generation, transport, and communications—came into being. Not only did the other three factors become available in the modern era, *they became available for the taking*. Physics, engineering, economics, and law can be taught at any university or gotten from any bookstore. Capital can be obtained from across town and, if not at hand there, from a foreign bank. Roads can be built, and automobiles, aircraft, computers, and cell phones can be easily purchased. But the protection of property enjoyed in most of the modern West and celebrated by Coke, Locke, and Smith does not come so easily. Today, across the globe, it is what most reliably separates the haves from the have-nots.

WHERE

The first section of this book, then, explained why growth occurred *when* it did. Once we have framed the question of growth with the four critical factors, we could address the question of *where*. The book's second section examined the pattern of growth in several nations in terms of our four institutional factors. A nearly one-to-one relationship was found between the presence of the four factors and the economic takeoff of each nation.

By about A.D. 1500, Europe, with its hundreds of states and principalities, became an unwitting hotbed of competing institutions and ideologies. It is no accident that the two nations with the most advantageous combinations of these factors—England and Holland—became the birthplaces of modern prosperity. The development of property rights, scientific rationalism, the capital markets, and transportation and communication in sixteenth-century Holland, albeit rudimentary, sustained slow but steady growth for almost two centuries. Although steam power and transport were not yet available to the Dutch economy, Holland was endowed with the one natural feature that is of undoubted economic benefit—a flat topography laced with navigable waterways. At the opposite extreme, all four of our factors were essentially absent from Japan and Spain before the late nineteenth century; not surprisingly, the economic development of both nations did not begin until then.

In today's world, just as in 1800 or 1900, where the four factors flourish, so does prosperity. Both Hong Kong and Singapore, with their English common law heritage, acceptance of Western rationalism, booming capital markets, and advanced transport, thrive. It does not hurt that the two were winners in the geographical lottery as well—both small island nations that have superb and strategically situated natural harbors.

As you inherit your good looks, brains, and athletic ability to a certain extent from your parents, so does a nation benefit from good institutional "genes." Where the institutional inheritance has been bountiful—the New World lands settled by England, and in places such as Hong Kong and Singapore, whose citizens drew the common law to their bosom—prosperity has flowed. And where the "genes" have been disadvantageous, as with South America's dysfunctional Iberian traditions of conquest, gratuitous brutality, religious fervor, and a rent-seeking mentality born of a temporary bounty of mineral wealth, backwardness and poverty have been the inevitable consequences.

At the extreme, sub-Saharan Africa suffers from an almost complete lack of all four factors. African tribal structure invests its chiefs with both executive and judicial power. This lack of separation of powers denies these nations the fundamental requirement for the rule of law and the maintenance of property rights—an independent judiciary. Add to this sorry brew the intellectual torpor of a traditional culture and the virtual absence of capital markets, and the result is a recipe for economic stagnation. The resultant poverty inevitably looses the Four Horsemen. That the tragedy of HIV looms largest on the world's least economically advanced continent is no accident.

Africa also has a fifth disadvantage. Despite its embarrassment of mineral riches, the continent lacks the one economically important physical endowment: the presence of navigable waterways. The smooth African coastline offers less shelter than Europe's shores do, and most of its rivers are studded with waterfalls, guarded at their entrances by impassible sandbars, and bereft of the snow-fed runoff that would keep the water levels high year round, as happens in Europe, Asia, and North America. As a general rule, African waterways carry useful levels of traffic only during the rainy season.[1]

WHITHER

Once we have acquired the four-factor framework for understanding economic growth and have learned how to apply it to specific nations and cultures, what does it tell us about the prospects for continued prosperity, democracy, and the geopolitical state of the world?

All four of our factors are now solidly established in the world's developed nations, and it would take a world-ending catastrophe—one essentially eradicating all of humanity from the face of the earth—to destroy their imprints.

This is not too strong a statement. While World War II may have physically destroyed Japan and Germany, their westernized institutional souls and knowledge base went untouched, and their economies quickly recovered. (As we saw in Chapters 1 and 8, the Japanese and German "economic miracles" were not merely the result of the magnanimity of the victors—Germany exhibited a similar recovery after the First World War and the vindictive Treaty of Versailles.)

Never again will mankind lose these essential technological and institutional "recipes." We cannot simply misplace the knowledge of cement, as occurred for thirteen centuries after the destruction of the Roman Empire. Its formula, as well as the designs for all of our essential technologies, are diffused among too many millions of people, books, and computer hard drives for them ever to be completely lost, as occurred to most of advanced civil technology with the Fall of Rome. Further, the West has so incorporated the institutional basis for its prosperity into its behavioral norms that continued growth has become both inevitable and ultimately resistant to all but the most final of human catastrophes.

The relationship between economic growth and democracy developed in Chapter 10 is a profoundly optimistic one. If, as recent sociological research suggests, prosperity is the primary driver of democratic development, not only is the continuing spread of liberal democracy a foregone conclusion, but so also is the geopolitical power that is conferred by this wealth machine. This means that a relatively benign hegemony will be practiced by the world's largest liberal democracies. *New York Times* columnist Thomas Friedman wryly refers to this as the "McDonald's Theory of War and Peace": Until very recently, no two nations possessing McDonald's franchises have ever gone to war with each other.[2] Globalization does not come without cost, of course. The world's increasing interdependency leaves it far more vulnerable to contagions of all varieties, be they social, environmental, financial, or microbiological.

Chapter 10 does supply a less than optimistic forecast for mankind's aggregate happiness in a world growing ever more prosperous. However, even the most cynical observers of our increasingly materialistic culture must admit that its worries and insecurities pale in comparison to those inherent in the subsistence-level existence shared by 99% of humanity before 1820.

For the first time in human history, vast regions of the world are experiencing a continuous and dramatic increase in wealth and an accompanying improvement in living standards. The sources of this wealth—secure property rights, scientific rationalism, vigorous capital markets, and modern transportation and communication—have become so embedded in the Western way of life that they have easily survived the worst cataclysms of the last century—even in those Western nations that suffered the most physical damage. For better or for worse, the human race has entered an era in which economic growth spurred on by technological innovation has itself becomes the leading actor on the world's stage. To rewrite Santayana, those who fail to learn from economic history will be left in its wake.

Notes

PREFACE

1. Jared Diamond, *Guns, Germs, and Steel* (New York: W. W. Norton, 1999), 13–14.

INTRODUCTION

1. Dava Sobel, *Longitude* (New York: Penguin, 1995), 11–14, 57–59.
2. Stephen E. Ambrose, *Undaunted Courage* (New York: Simon and Schuster, 1996), 52.

CHAPTER ONE

1. "Conversations, The Long View; Covering 50 Years of War, Looking for Peace and Honoring Law," *New York Times*, 16 Dec. 2001.
2. Angus Maddison, *The World Economy: A Millennial Perspective* (Paris: OECD, 2001), 30, 264.
3. Ibid., 172, 231.
4. Douglass C. North, *Structure and Change in Economic History* (New York: W. W. Norton, 1981), 14.
5. Phyllis Deane, *The First Industrial Revolution*, 2d ed. (Cambridge: Cambridge University Press, 1979), 207.
6. Deane, 12–13.
7. T. S. Ashton, *The Industrial Revolution, 1760–1830* (Oxford: Oxford University Press, 1967), 5.

8. E. L. Jones, *Growth Recurring* (Ann Arbor, Michigan: University of Michigan Press, 1988), 29–31.
9. Ashton, 42.
10. Angus Maddison, *Explaining the Economic Performance of Nations* (Cheltenham, England: Edward Elgar Publishing, 1995), 433.
11. Ibid., 438–39.
12. Ibid.
13. Maddison, *The World Economy: A Millennial Perspective,* 18.
14. E. L. Jones, *Growth Recurring,* 73–86, 149–67.
15. J. A. Goldstone, "Efflorescences and Economic Growth in World History," Working Paper, 2002.
16. E. L. Jones, *The European Miracle* (Cambridge: Cambridge University Press, 1987), 49.
17. Maddison, *The World Economy: A Millennial Perspective,* 264.
18. Adam Smith, *An Inquiry into the Nature and Causes of the Wealth of Nations* (Chicago: University of Chicago Press, 1976), II: 436.
19. Eli F. Heckscher, *Mercantilism,* 2d ed. (New York: Macmillan, 1954), 140.
20. Barbara Tuchman, *A Distant Mirror* (New York: Alfred A. Knopf, 1978), 5–6.
21. Ibid., 19–20.
22. Ibid., 5–6, 9.
23. William Manchester, *A World Lit Only by Fire* (Boston: Back Bay Books, 1992), 6.
24. Paul Johnson, *The Birth of the Modern* (New York: HarperCollins, 1991), 865.
25. Manchester, 53.
26. Tuchman, 25.
27. Ibid., xix.
28. Matthew 22:21.
29. Manchester, 35.
30. Tuchman, 26.
31. Ibid., 26–28.
32. Ibid., 287, 339.
33. Manchester, 203–4.
34. E. William Monter, *Calvin's Geneva* (New York: John Wiley & Sons, 1967), 17, 83, 101, 152, 155.
35. Sidney Homer and Richard Sylla, *A History of Interest Rates* (New Brunswick, New Jersey: Rutgers University Press, 1996), 29–30.
36. Both quoted in Tuchman, 37.
37. Homer and Sylla, 69–72.
38. Laurence B. Packard, *The Commercial Revolution* (New York: Henry Holt & Co., 1927), 2–3.
39. Hechscher, 45.
40. Paul Johnson, 169.
41. Douglass C. North and Robert P. Thomas, *The Rise of the Western World* (Cambridge: Cambridge University Press, 1981), 102–119.
42. Robert Woodward, *Maestro: Greenspan's Fed and the Economic Boom* (New York: Simon and Schuster, 2000), 126.
43. Paul M. Romer, "Increasing Returns and Long-Run Growth," *Journal of Political Economy* 94 (Oct., 1986): 1002–1013.
44. Diamond, 45.
45. Charles C. Mann, "1491," *Atlantic Monthly* (Mar. 2002): 41–53.

46. Douglass C. North and Robert P. Thomas, "The First Economic Revolution," *Economic History Review* 30 (May 1977): 240–41.
47. Thomas Malthus, *An Essay on the Principle of Population as it Affects the Future Improvement of Society, with Remarks on the Speculations of Mr. Godwin, M. Condorcet, and Other Writers* (London: Printed for J. Johnson, 1798), from http://www.ac.wwu.edu/~stephan/malthus/malthus.0.html.
48. Walt W. Rostow, *The Stages of Economic Growth* (Cambridge: Cambridge University Press, 1961).

CHAPTER TWO

1. P. J. O'Rourke, *Eat the Rich* (New York: Atlantic Monthly Press, 1988), 233.
2. Leon Trotsky, *The Revolution Betrayed* (New York: Doubleday, Doran & Co., 1937), 76.
3. Genesis 23:16.
4. Robert C. Ellickson and Charles DiA. Thorland, "Ancient Land Law: Mesopotamia, Egypt, and Israel," unpublished paper.
5. Victor D. Hanson, *The Other Greeks* (Berkeley: University of California Press, 1999), 1–22.
6. Ibid., 31, 35.
7. Aristotle, *Politics,* VI: 4.
8. Quoted in Hanson, 97.
9. David Johnson, *Roman Law in Context* (Cambridge: Cambridge University Press, 1999), 2–11, 30–44.
10. Marcel Le Glay et al., *A History of Rome* (Oxford: Blackwell, 1991), 96–97.
11. Bernard H. Siegan, *Property Rights* (New Brunswick, New Jersey: Transaction Publishers, 2001), 1.
12. Heckscher, 277–78.
13. Raghuram G. Rajan and Luigi Zingales, "The Great Reversals: The Politics of Financial Development in the Twentieth Century," Working Paper, 2002, 37. For a detailed discussion of the differences between common and civil law, see René David and John E. C. Brierley, *Major Legal Systems in the World Today,* 2d ed. (New York: Free Press, 1978).
14. A translation of the 1215 Magna Carta can be found at http://www.bl.uk/collections/treasures/magnatranslation.html.
15. Siegan, 5–11.
16. Quoted in Siegan, 9.
17. Ibid., 10.
18. Ibid.
19. Heckscher, 279.
20. Siegan, 12.
21. Ibid., 13.
22. Ibid.
23. Ibid., 15.
24. Ibid., 19–26.
25. Ibid., 17.
26. Heckscher, 286–87.

27. *Encyclopedia Britannica* (New York: Encyclopedia Britannica, 1911), 16: 844.
28. Tom Bethell, *The Noblest Triumph* (New York: St. Martin's Press, 1998), 86–87.
29. John Locke, "An Essay Concerning the True Original Extent and End of Civil Government," 1690, 222. Accessible at http://odur.let.rug.nl/~usa/D/1651-1700/locke/ECCG/governxx.htm.
30. Ibid., 87.
31. Ibid., 140.
32. Bruno Leoni, *Freedom and the Law* (Los Angeles: Nash, 1972), 10.
33. Hernando de Soto, *The Mystery of Capital* (New York: Basic Books, 2000), 179–182.
34. North, 5–6.
35. Etienne Balaszs, *Chinese Civilization and Bureaucracy* (New Haven: Yale University Press, 1964), 18.
36. Ibid., 22.
37. Ibid., 27–43.
38. Siegan, 22–23.
39. Bruce W. Bugbee, *Genesis of American Patent and Copyright Law* (Washington, D.C.: Public Affairs Press, 1967), 38.
40. Ibid., 130.
41. Garrett Hardin, "The Tradegy of the Commons," *Science* 162 (1968): 1245.

CHAPTER THREE

1. R. H. Popkin, ed., *The Philosophy of the 16th and 17th Centuries* (New York: Free Press, 1966), 63.
2. Ivar Ekeland, *Mathematics and the Unexpected* (Chicago: University of Chicago Press, 1990), 7–8.
3. Howard Margolis, *It Started with Copernicus* (New York: McGraw-Hill, 2002), 27–37.
4. A. C. Crombie, *The History of Science,* 2 vols. (New York: Dover Publications, 1970), I: 81–99.
5. Margolis, 91–102.
6. Ibid., 15–63.
7. Crombie, II:179–82.
8. Colin A. Ronan, *Edmond Halley: Genius in Eclipse* (New York: Doubleday, 1969), 10–23.
9. Max Caspar, *Kepler* (New York: Dover Publications, 1993), 190.
10. Francis Bacon, *The New Organon,* ed. Fulton Anderson (Indianapolis: Bobbs-Merrill, 1960), vii–xi.
11. Karen I. Vaughn, *John Locke* (Chicago: University of Chicago Press, 1980), 5.
12. Bacon, xix–xx.
13. Johan Huizinga, *The Waning of the Middle Ages* (Garden City, New York: Edward Arnold, 1954), 28.
14. Bacon, 49.
15. Ibid.
16. Ibid., 50.
17. Frank E. Manuel, *A Portrait of Isaac Newton* (Cambridge: Harvard University Press, 1968), 119.
18. Ibid.
19. Steven Shapin, *The Scientific Revolution* (Chicago: University of Chicago Press, 1998), 145.

20. Crombie, II:185–89.
21. Caspar, 34–38.
22. Ekeland, 6–14.
23. Crombie, II:189.
24. McClellan and Dorn, 224.
25. John J. Norwich, *A History of Venice* (New York: Alfred A. Knopf, 1982), 510–16.
26. McClellan and Dorn, 232.
27. Ibid., 233–34.
28. Manuel, 23.
29. Ronan, 1–27.
30. Ibid., 80–90.
31. Jay Pasachoff, "Halley and His Maps of the Total Eclipses of 1715 and 1724," *Astronomy and Geophysics* 40 (Apr. 1999): 18–21.
32. F. Richard Stephenson, "Historical Eclipses," *Scientific American* (Apr. 1982): 154–63.
33. McClellan and Dorn, 253.
34. Ronan, 150.
35. Nathan Rosenberg and L. E. Birdzell, *How the West Grew Rich* (New York: Basic Books, 1986), 246.
36. Crombie, II:176.

CHAPTER FOUR

1. Jean Strouse, *Morgan: American Financier* (New York: HarperCollins, 2000), 15.
2. Ibid., 314.
3. Quoted in Ashton, 9.
4. Ibid., 9–10.
5. Homer and Sylla, 4.
6. Rosenberg and Birdzell, 38.
7. Jonathan B. Baskin and Paul J. Miranti, *A History of Corporate Finance* (Cambridge: Cambridge University Press, 1997), 313.
8. Ibid., 38.
9. Charles A. Kindleberger, *A Financial History of Western Europe* (London: George Allen and Unwin, 1984), 19–20.
10. Baskin and Miranti, 318.
11. Kindleberger, 36–39.
12. Norwich, 3–13.
13. Geoffrey Poitras, *The Early History of Financial Economics, 1478–1776* (Cheltenham, England: Edward Elgar, 2000), 228.
14. Larry Neal, *The Rise of Financial Capitalism* (Cambridge: Cambridge University Press, 1993), 7.
15. Poitras, 229–231.
16. Homer and Sylla, 128.
17. J. de Vries and A. van der Woude, *The First Modern Economy* (Cambridge: Cambridge University Press, 1997), 113–19.
18. Neal, 18.
19. de Vries and van der Woude, 134–58.

20. Baskin and Miranti, 100.
21. Ibid., 101
22. David Ormrod, *The Dutch in London* (London: Her Majesty's Stationery Office, 1973), 17.
23. Homer and Sylla, 159.
24. John C. Burch and Bruce S. Foerster, "Big Bucks for Big Business," *Financial History*, 76 (Winter 2003): 16–17.
25. Joel Mokyr, ed., *The British Industrial Revolution* (Boulder, Colorado: Westview Press, 1999), 109.
26. Ashton, 68.
27. Roger G. Ibbotson and Gary P. Brinson, *Global Investing* (New York: McGraw-Hill, 1993), 149.
28. Baskin and Miranti, 59.
29. Neal, 8–9, 17.
30. Baskin and Miranti, 65.
31. Ibid., 104.
32. Ibid., 130, 141.
33. James Buchan, *Frozen Desire* (New York: Farrar, Straus and Giroux, 1997), 208–19.
34. Baskin and Miranti, 128.
35. Walter Bagehot, *Lombard Street* (Philadelphia: Orion Editions, 1991), 2.
36. Ibid.
37. Ibid., 3.
38. Ibid.
39. Ibid., 5.
40. Victor D. Hanson, *Carnage and Culture* (New York: Doubleday, 2001), 269.

CHAPTER FIVE

1. "The Daughter-in-Law Who Doesn't Speak," *Wall Street Journal,* 26 July 2002.
2. T. K. Derry and Trevor I. Williams, *A Short History of Technology* (New York: Dover Publications, 1960), 243.
3. Adapted from Abbott P. Usher, *A History of Mechanical Inventions* (New York: Dover Publications, 1954), 165.
4. Ibid., 157.
5. Derry and Williams, 243.
6. W. R. Paton, *The Greek Anthology*, 3 vols. (London: William Heinemann, 1916), 418.
7. Derry and Williams, 251.
8. Ibid., 253.
9. Ibid., 313.
10. Ibid., 315.
11. Usher, 351.
12. Mokyr, ed., *The British Industrial Revolution,* 21.
13. Usher, 252.
14. Derry and Williams, 322.
15. Paul Johnson, 191–92.
16. Chancellor, 123.

17. George R. Taylor, *The Transportation Revolution* (New York: Harper and Row, 1951), 33–36.
18. Ibid., 110–19.
19. Ibid., 113.
20. Paul Johnson, 191.
21. Thomas Sowell, *Conquest and Culture* (New York: Basic Books, 1998), 35.
22. John H. Clapham, *An Economic History of Modern Britain,* 3 vols. (Cambridge: Cambridge University Press, 1930), I: 390.
23. Tom Standage, *The Victorian Internet* (New York: Walker Publishing, 1998), 1–2.
24. Derry and Williams, 609–10.
25. Ibid., 40–51.
26. Ibid., 46–58.
27. John S. Gordon, *A Thread Across the Ocean* (New York: Walker and Co., 2002), 133.
28. Ibid, 139.
29. Maddison, *The World Economy: A Millennial Perspective,* 265.

CHAPTER SIX

1. Paul Johnson, 191–92.
2. Rosenberg and Birdzell, 262.
3. Goldstone, "Efflorescences and Economic Growth in World History."
4. Bethell, 1–3.
5. de Soto, 157–59.

SECTION II

1. Maddison, *The World Economy: A Millennial Perspective,* 264, 279, 327.

CHAPTER SEVEN

1. Adam Smith, I: 102.
2. Maddison, *The World Economy: A Millennial Perspective,* 264.
3. Tuchman, 248.
4. de Vries and van der Woude, 9–20.
5. Simon Schama, *The Embarrassment of Riches* (New York: Alfred A. Knopf, 1987), 587–93.
6. Johan Huizinga, *Dutch Civilization in the Seventeenth Century* (London: F. Ungar Publishing Co., 1968), 11.
7. de Vries and van der Woude, 21–23.
8. Ibid., 27–33.

9. Maddison, *The World Economy: A Millennial Perspective,* 248.
10. Ibid., 241, 261.
11. de Vries and van der Woude, 348, extracted from Figure 8–11.
12. Paul Kennedy, *The Rise and Fall of the Great Powers* (New York: Random House, 1987), 78.
13. Alexander Hamilton and James Madison, *Federalist Papers,* No. 20.
14. Professor Richard Sylla, personal communication.
15. Schama, 230.
16. Kenneth O. Morgan, *The Oxford Illustrated History of Britain* (Oxford: Oxford University Press, 1984), 330–37.
17. Douglass C. North and Barry R. Weingast, "Constitutions and Commitment: The Evolution of Institutional Governing Public Choice in Seventeenth-Century England," *Journal of Economic History* 49 (Dec. 1989): 803–32.
18. Erskine May, *Parliamentary Practice,* 1844, quoted in North and Weingast, 818.
19. T. S. Ashton, *An Economic History of England* (London: Methuen Publishing, 1955), 178.
20. See Chapter 2.
21. "The Economy—Capital: Precepts from Professor Summers," *Wall Street Journal,* 17 Oct. 2002.
22. Deane, 42–45.
23. Ibid., 45–46.
24. J. D. Chambers, "Enclosure and the Small Landowner," *Economic History Review* 10 (Nov. 1940): 118–27.
25. Adam Smith, I: 8–9.
26. Mokyr, ed., *The British Industrial Revolution,* 106–8.
27. 2001 Annual Report of Southwest Airlines.
28. Eric Hobsbawm, *Industry and Empire: The Birth of the Industrial Revolution,* rev. ed. (London: Penguin Group, 1990), 56.
29. Joel Mokyr, *The Lever of Riches* (Oxford, Oxford University Press, 1990), 96–98.
30. Ashton, *The Industrial Revolution, 1760–1830,* 53.
31. Derry and Williams, 557–58.
32. Deane, 90–97.
33. David Landes, "The Fable of the Dead Horse; or, The Industrial Revolution Revisited," in *The British Industrial Revolution,* ed. Joel Mokyr, 152.
34. Deane, 116.
35. Ashton, *The Industrial Revolution, 1760–1830,* 10.
36. Jan de Vries, "The Industrial Revolution and the Industrious Revolution," *Journal of Economic History* 54 (June 1994): 249–70.
37. Robert Uphaus, personal communication.
38. Friedrich Engels, *The Condition of the Working Class in England in 1844,* from http://www.marxists.org/archive/marx/works/1845/condition-working-class/ch02.htm.
39. Ibid., from http://www.marxists.org/archive/marx/works/1845/condition-working-class/ch04.htm.
40. Joyce Marlow, *The Peterloo Massacre* (London: Panther, 1971), 16.
41. E. J. Hobsbawm, "The British Standard of Living 1790–1850" *Economic History Review* 9 (Aug. 1957): 46–68.
42. Karl Marx and Frederick Engels, *Selected Works,* 3 vols. (Moscow: Progress Publishers, 1969), I: 163.
43. Deane, 286, 294.
44. Ashton, *The Industrial Revolution, 1760–1830,* 161.
45. Mokyr, ed., *The British Industrial Revolution,* 122.

46. Marlow, 93–103.
47. Ashton, *The Industrial Revolution, 1760–1830*, 5.
48. H. J. Habakkuk, "The Economic History of Modern Britain," *Journal of Economic History* 18 (Dec. 1958): 486–501.
49. Simon Kuznets "Economic Growth and Income Inequality," *American Economic Review* 45 (Mar. 1955): 1–28.
50. Mokyr, ed., *The British Industrial Revolution*, 6.
51. Deane, 1.
52. Rostow, xii, 7.
53. Ibid., 8.
54. David Halberstam, *The Best and the Brightest* (New York: Random House, 1972), 635–37.
55. de Vries and van der Woude, 712.
56. Robert J. Barro, *Determinants of Economic Growth* (Cambridge: MIT Press, 1999), 33.
57. Deane, 166.
58. Robert J. Irwin, *Free Trade Under Fire* (Princeton: Princeton University Press, 2002).
59. Adam Smith, I: 135.
60. Maddison, *Monitoring the World Economy, 1820–1992* (Paris: OECD, 1995), 106, 182, 196.

CHAPTER EIGHT

1. N. F. R. Crafts, "Industrial Revolution in England and France: Some Thoughts on the Question, 'Why was England First?'" *Economic History Review* 30 (Aug. 1977): 429–41.
2. H. Hauser, "The Characteristic Features of French Economic History from the Middle of the Sixteenth to the Middle of the Eighteenth Century," *Economic History Review* 4 (Oct. 1993): 271–72.
3. Jan de Vries, *Economy of Europe in an Age of Crisis, 1600–1750* (Cambridge: Cambridge University Press, 1976), 200–2.
4. Hauser, 262–63.
5. de Vries, *Economy of Europe in an Age of Crisis*, 216–17.
6. North and Thomas, 120–22.
7. Hilton L. Root, "The Redistributive Role of Government: Regulation in Old Regime France and England," *Comparative Studies in Society and History* 33 (Apr. 1991): 350–51.
8. de Vries, *Economy of Europe in an Age of Crisis*, 177.
9. Heckscher, 154.
10. North and Thomas, 126.
11. de Vries, *Economy of Europe in an Age of Crisis*, 89–90.
12. Heckscher, 160–61.
13. Abbott Payson Usher, "Colbert and Governmental Control of Industry in Seventeenth Century France," *Review of Economic Statistics* 16 (Nov. 1934): 238–40.
14. Mokyr, ed., *The British Industrial Revolution*, 81.
15. N. F. R. Crafts, "Macroinventions, Economic Growth, and 'Industrial Revolution' in Britain and France," *Economic History Review* 48 (Aug. 1995): 591–98.
16. Heckscher, 170–71.
17. Rondo E. Cameron, "Economic Growth and Stagnation in France, 1815–1914," *Journal of Modern History* 30 (Mar. 1958): 5–6.
18. Hauser, 263.

19. de Vries, *Economy of Europe in an Age of Crisis,* 170–71.
20. Hechscher, 80.
21. North and Thomas, 122–23.
22. Packard, *The Commercial Revolution,* 55–56.
23. Hauser, 268.
24. Heckscher, 85.
25. Ibid., 108.
26. Cameron, 9–12.
27. Alfred De Foville, "The Economic Movement in France," *Quarterly Journal of Economics* 4 (Jan. 1890): 227–29.
28. Laurence B. Packard, "International Rivalry and Free Trade Origins, 1660–78," *Quarterly Journal of Economics* 37 (May 1923): 412–35.
29. Peter Bernstein, *The Power of Gold* (New York: John Wiley & Sons, 2000), 121.
30. Buchan, 80.
31. Bernard Moses, "The Economic Condition of Spain in the Sixteenth Century," *Journal of Political Economy* 1 (1893): 515–16.
32. North and Thomas, 128.
33. de Vries, *Economy of Europe in an Age of Crisis,* 49.
34. Earl J. Hamilton, "Revisions in Economic History: VIII. The Decline of Spain," *Economic History Review* 8 (May 1938): 176.
35. Moses, 523.
36. Earl J. Hamilton, "Revisions in Economic History: VIII. The Decline of Spain," 175.
37. Ibid., 175.
38. John H. Elliott, "The Decline of Spain," *Past and Present* 20 (Nov. 1961): 65.
39. Ibid., 68.
40. From "Spain under Charles II," *Littell's Living Age,* vol. 100, 467; quoted in Earl J. Hamilton, "Revisions in Economic History: VIII. The Decline of Spain," 174.
41. Hauser, 261.
42. Elliott, 67.
43. Homer and Sylla, 128, 130.
44. Moses, 528.
45. de Vries, *Economy of Europe in an Age of Crisis,* 169–170.
46. Elliott, 67.
47. North and Thomas, 131.
48. Packard, *The Commercial Revolution,* 26–27.
49. Jaime Vicens Vives, *An Economic History of Spain* (Princeton, Princeton University Press, 1969), 521.
50. Ibid., 625–43.
51. Elliott, 65.
52. R. P. Dore, *Land Reform in Japan* (Oxford: Oxford University Press, 1959), 3.
53. Irene B. Taeuber, "Population: Population Growth and Economic Development in Japan," *Journal of Economic History* 11 (Autumn 1951): 419.
54. Dore, 8.
55. Ibid., 8–10.
56. Sir George Sansom, quoted in Dore, 12.
57. Mataji Miyamoto et al., "Economic Development in Preindustrial Japan, 1859–94," *Journal of Economic History* 25 (Dec. 1965): 541.
58. G. C. Allen, *A Short Economic History of Modern Japan* (London: Allen and Unwin, 1962), 14–19.

59. Edwin O. Reischauer, *The Japanese Today* (Cambridge: Belknap/Harvard, 1978), 82.
60. Maddison, *The World Economy: A Millennial Perspective,* 264.
61. Allen, 20.
62. Thomas C. Smith, "Pre-Modern Economic Growth: Japan and the West," *Past and Present* 60 (Aug. 1973): 144–59.
63. Thomas Smith, 145.
64. Miyamoto et al., 542.
65. Allen, 20–21, 23.
66. Ibid., 20–26.
67. Reischauer, 129–38.
68. Ibid., 126–29.
69. Miyamoto et al., 549–51.
70. Frank B. Tipton, "Government Policy and Economic Development in Germany and Japan: A Skeptical Reevaluation," *Journal of Economic History* 41 (Mar., 1981): 139–42.
71. Allen, 136.
72. John W. Dower, *Embracing Defeat: Japan in the Wake of World War II* (New York: W.W. Norton, 1999), 546.
73. Dore, 55–114.
74. Allen, 156.
75. Dower, 533.
76. Reischauer, 107.

CHAPTER NINE

1. Margolis, 133–36.
2. Jones, *The European Miracle,* 175.
3. Bernard Lewis, *What Went Wrong? The Clash Between Islam and Modernity in the Middle East* (New York: HarperCollins, 2002), 6–7.
4. Peter L. Bernstein, *Against the Gods* (New York: John Wiley & Sons, 1996), xxxii–xxxiii.
5. Jones, *The European Miracle,* 175.
6. Lewis, 11–12.
7. Ibid., 31.
8. Ibid., 22–23.
9. Ibid., 46–47.
10. Ibid., 36.
11. Bethell, 237.
12. Jones, *The European Miracle,* 181.
13. Lewis, 85–88.
14. Bethell, 226.
15. Lewis, 80.
16. Bethell, 228–29.
17. Rhoads Murphey, "The Decline of North Africa Since the Roman Occupation: Climatic or Human?" *Annals of the Association of American Geographers* 41 (June 1951): 116–132.
18. Lewis. 108–9.
19. Leonard Nakamura and Carlos E. J. M. Zarazaga, "Banking and Finance in Argentina in the Period 1900–35," Center for Latin American Economics, Working Paper No. 0501.

20. Paul Johnson, 627–51.
21. Janns J. Prem, "Spanish Colonization and Indian Property in Central Mexico, 1521–1620," *Annals of the Association of American Geographers* 82 (Sept. 1992): 444–59.
22. Lawrence E. Harrison, *Underdevelopment is a State of Mind: The Latin American Case* (Lanham, Maryland: Center for International Affairs, Harvard University and University Press of America, 1985), 48–54.
23. de Soto, 192–93.
24. Stephen H. Haber, "Industrial Concentration and the Capital Markets: A Comparative Study of Brazil, Mexico, and the United States, 1830–1930, *Journal of Economic History* 51 (Sept. 1991): 559–80.
25. Daron Acemoglu, Simon Johnson, and James A. Robinson, "Reversal of Fortune: Geography and Institutions in the Making of the Modern World Income Distribution," *Quarterly Journal of Economics* 117 (2002): 1231–94.
26. Sowell, 83–87.

CHAPTER TEN

1. Seymour M. Lipset, "Some Social Requisites of Democracy: Economic Development and Political Legitimacy," *American Political Science Review* 53 (Mar. 1959): 69–105.
2. Anders Gade et al., "'Chronic Painter's Syndrome': A Reanalysis of Psychological Test Data in a Group of Diagnosed Cases, Based on Comparisons with Matched Controls," *Acta Neurologica Scandinavica* 77 (Apr. 1988): 293–306.
3. Max Weber, *The Protestant Ethic and the Spirit of Capitalism* (New York: Charles Scribner's Sons, 1958).
4. Mark Valeri, "Religion, Discipline, and the Economy in Calvin's Geneva," *Sixteenth Century Journal* 28 (Spring 1997): 123–42.
5. Ronald Inglehart and Wayne E. Baker, "Modernization, Cultural Change, and the Persistence of Traditional Values," *American Sociological Review* 65 (Feb. 2000): 19–51.
6. Lewis, 155.
7. Maxine Rodinson, *Islam and Capitalism* (Austin, Texas: University of Texas, 1978).
8. Matthew 22:21.
9. Tuchman, 37.
10. Christian Welzel and Ronald Inglehart, "Human Development and the Explosion of Democracy: Analyzing Regime Change across 60 Societies," *European Journal of Political Research* 42 (May 2003): 341–79.
11. Reischauer, 156–68.
12. Fukuyama, 120.
13. "Why People Still Starve," *New York Times*, 13 July 2003.
14. Inglehart and Baker, 23–24.
15. Ibid., 33–34.
16. Sean Formato, "Fukuyama Discusses the Role of Social Capital," *Johns Hopkins Newsletter* (Apr. 19, 2001).
17. Bradford DeLong and Andrei Schleifer, "Princes and Merchants: European City Growth Before the Industrial Revolution," *Journal of Law and Economics* 36 (Oct. 1993): 671–702.
18. Robert J. Barro and Xavier Sala-I-Martin, *Economic Growth* (New York: McGraw-Hill, 1995), 433–34.

19. Robert J. Barro, *Determinants of Economic Growth*, 2d ed. (Cambridge: MIT Press, 1999), 52–61.
20. Ibid., 47.
21. Hadley Cantril, *The Pattern of Human Concerns* (New Brunswick, New Jersey: Rutgers University Press, 1965), 36.
22. Andrew J. Oswald, "Happiness and Economic Performance," *Economic Journal* 107 (Nov. 1997): 1815–31.
23. Robert H. Frank, "The Frame of Reference as a Public Good," *Economic Journal* 107 (Nov. 1997): 1833.
24. Ronald Inglehart, *Culture Shift in Advanced Industrial Society* (Princeton: Princeton University Press, 1990).
25. Richard A. Easterlin, "Does Economic Growth Improve the Human Lot? Some Empirical Evidence," in Paul A. David and Melvin W. Reder, eds., *Nations and Households in Economic Growth* (New York: Academic Press, 1974), 107–11.
26. Richard A. Easterlin, "Will Raising the Incomes of All Increase the Happiness of All?" *Journal of Economic Behavior and Organization* 27 (1995): 40.
27. Ronald Inglehart and Hans-Dieter Klingemann, "Genes, Culture, Democracy, and Happiness," in E. Diener and Mark Suh, eds., *Culture and Subjective Well-Being*, 165–84.
28. Karl Marx and Frederick Engels, *Selected Works,* 3 vols. (Moscow: Progress Publishers, 1969), I: 163.
29. Paul Krugman. See http://www.wws.princeton.edu/~pkrugman/incidents.html.
30. Robert J. Barro, June 2000 Fraser Institute Forum: Democracy and the Rule of Law. See http://oldfraser.lexi.net/publications/forum/2000/06/section_04_full.html.
31. See Cantril, footnote 27.
32. David Morawetz et al., "Income Distribution and Self-Rated Happiness: Some Empirical Evidence," *Economic Journal* 87 (Sept. 1997): 511–22.
33. Easterlin, "Will Raising the Incomes of All Increase the Happiness of All?" 35.
34. Philip Brickman and Donald T. Campbell, "Hedonic Relativism and Planning the Good Society," in M. H. Appley, ed., *Adaptation Level Theory: A Symposium* (New York: Academic Press 1971), 287–302.
35. Cantril, 205.

CHAPTER ELEVEN

1. Harold Demsetz, "Toward a Theory of Property Rights," *American Economic Review* 57 (May 1967): 347–59.
2. Mark Roe, *Political Determinants of Corporate Governance,* prepublication draft, used by permission of the author.
3. Thomas Piketty and Emmanuel Saez, "Income Inequality in the United States, 1913–98," NBER Working Paper No. 8467.
4. Marlow, 15–17.
5. Ibid., 13.
6. Deane, 208–37.
7. From Rexford G. Tugwell, "Roosevelt and the Bonus Marchers of 1932," *Political Science Quarterly* 87 (Sept. 1972): 364.
8. Ibid., 363–64.

9. Abstracted from John W. Killigrew, "The Army and the Bonus Incident," *Military Affairs* 26 (Summer 1962): 62.
10. Tugwell, 375–76.
11. Peter Flora et al., *State, Economy, and Society in Western Europe, 1815–1975,* 2 vols. (Chicago: Campus Verlag/Macmillan/St. James, 1983), I: 262.
12. Joel Slemrod and Jon Bakija, *Taxing Ourselves* (Cambridge: MIT Press, 1995), 266.
13. Peter H. Lindert, "Why the Welfare State Looks Like a Free Lunch," NBER Working Paper No. w9869, 1993.
14. Rafael Di Tella, "Preferences over Inflation and Unemployment: Evidence from Surveys of Happiness," *American Economic Review* 91 (Mar. 2001): 178–84.
15. "What I Learned in Bosnia," *New York Times,* 28 Oct. 2002.
16. See Luxembourg Income Study, http://www.lisproject.org/keyfigures/ineqtable.htm.

CHAPTER TWELVE

1. Tuchman, 87–91, 583–85, 593.
2. Kennedy, 153–54.
3. D. Syrett, *Shipping and the American War 1775–83* (London: University of London, Athlone Press, 1970), 243.
4. John Lukacs, *Five Days in London* (New Haven: Yale University Press, 2001).
5. R. H. Spector, *Eagle Against the Sun* (New York: Random House, 1985), 123.
6. B. H. Liddell Hart, *History of the Second World War* (New York: Perigee, 1982), 353.
7. Hanson, *Carnage and Culture,* 351.
8. Liddell Hart, 352.
9. Bernard Ireland, *War at Sea 1914–45* (London: Cassell, 2002), 172–89.
10. Herodotus, *History,* 1.53–56.
11. Richard H. Thaler, *The Winner's Curse* (Toronto: Free Press, 1991).
12. Kennedy, 723.
13. Quoted from Dugald Stewart, *Transactions of the Royal Society of Edinburgh,* Mar. 18, 1793.
14. Earl J. Hamilton, "Imports of American Gold and Silver Into Spain, 1503–1660," *Quarterly Journal of Economics* 43 (May 1929): 464.
15. Kennedy, 48.
16. Ibid., 47–48.
17. Packard, *The Commercial Revolution,* 68.
18. *The Oxford Dictionary of Quotations,* 3rd ed. (Oxford: Oxford University Press, 1979), 531.
19. Kennedy, 58–62.
20. Maddison, *The World Economy: A Millennial Perspective,* 261; Kennedy, 77, 81–85, 121.
21. French interest rates are calculated from the prices of previously issued *rentes;* see Homer and Sylla, 171–72.
22. Quoted in Kennedy, 133.
23. Homer and Sylla, 250, 287, 308, 343, 351.
24. Maddison, *Monitoring the World Economy, 1820–1992,* 180.
25. W. H. McNeill, *The Pursuit of Power* (Chicago: University of Chicago Press, 1983), 340.
26. Obituary, *New York Times,* 22 Apr. 1946.
27. Maddison, *The World Economy: A Millennial Perspective,* 264.

28. Kennedy, 242–45.

29. Maddison, *The World Economy: A Millennial Perspective,* 263.

30. Paul Bairoch, "International Industrialization Levels from 1750 to 1980," *Journal of European Economic History* 11 (Fall 1982): 304.

31. Stephen G. Brooks and William C. Wohlforth, "American Primacy in Perspective," *Foreign Affairs* 81 (July/Aug. 2002): 22. This article can also be accessed at: http://www. foreignaffairs.org/20020701faessay8517/stephen-g-brooks-william-c-wohlforth/american-primacy-in-perspective.html.

32. Ibid., 30.

33. D. Holloway, *The Soviet Union and the Arms Race,* 2d ed. (New Haven: Yale University Press, 1984), 114.

34. Kennedy, 384.

35. See Maddison, *The World Economy: A Millennial Perspective,* 274–75.

36. Michael Dobbs, *Down with Big Brother: The Fall of the Soviet Empire* (New York: Alfred A. Knopf, 1997), 129–130.

37. L. Brown, *State of the World, 1986* (New York, Worldwatch Institute, 1986), 207.

CHAPTER THIRTEEN

1. de Vries and van der Woude, 711–22.

2. Donella H. Meadows, ed., *Limits to Growth: A Report for the Club of Rome's Project on the Predicament of Mankind* (New York: Universe Books, 1972).

3. Simon Kuznets, *Six Lectures on Economic Growth* (Glencoe, Illinois: Free Press, 1959), 13–41.

4. Niall Ferguson and Laurence J. Kotlikoff, "Going Critical," *The National Interest* 73 (Fall 2003): 22–32.

5. Jagadeesh Gokhale and Ken Smetters, "Fiscal and Generational Imbalances: New Budget Measures for New Budget Realities," American Enterprise Institute Monograph, Working Paper, June 2003.

6. Maddison, *The World Economy: A Millennial Perspective,* 264, 322–27.

CHAPTER FOURTEEN

1. Sowell, 101–6.

2. Friedman's hypothesis states, "When a country reaches a certain level of economic development, when it has a middle class big enough to support a McDonald's, it becomes a McDonald's country. And people in McDonald's countries don't like to fight wars. They like to wait in line for burgers." For those wondering about the Falklands conflict, Argentina did not open its first franchise until 1986, four years after the conflict. It is easy to quibble with Friedman's hypothesis. One can argue, for example, that it was violated by the late 1990s bombings of Beirut and Belgrade (both of which have McDonalds franchises) by the Israelis and NATO, respectively. See Thomas L. Friedman, *The Lexus and the Olive Tree* (New York: Farrar, Straus and Giroux, 1999).

Index